LITTLE ANGELS

To my wonderful parents
William & Virgilia
And
To my little angels
Bill & Jill
My pride and joy.

Little Angels
An International Legal Perspective
on Child Discrimination

ANNE-MARIE MOONEY COTTER
The Social Security Disability Law Firm, USA

ASHGATE

Published by
Ashgate Publishing Limited
Wey Court East
Union Road
Farnham
Surrey, GU9 7PT
England

Ashgate Publishing Company
Suite 420
101 Cherry Street
Burlington
VT 05401–4405
USA

www.ashgate.com

British Library Cataloguing in Publication Data
Cotter, Anne-Marie Mooney.
    Little angels : an international legal perspective on child discrimination.
    1. Children – Legal status, laws, etc. 2. Age discrimination – Law and legislation.
    I. Title
    341.4'8572–dc23

Library of Congress Cataloging-in-Publication Data
Cotter, Anne-Marie Mooney.
    Little angels : an international legal perspective on child discrimination / by Anne-Marie Mooney Cotter.
        p. cm.
    Includes bibliographical references and index.
    ISBN 978–1–4094–2980–7 (hardback : alk. paper) – ISBN 978–1–4094–2981–4 (ebook) 1. Children (International law) 2. Children's rights. 3. Age discrimination – Law and legislation.
    I. Title.
    K639.C682 2012
    342.08'772–dc23   2012002355

ISBN 9781409429807
ISBN 9781409429814

Printed and bound in Great Britain by the
MPG Books Group, UK.

Contents

List of Tables

Biography

Dr Anne-Marie Mooney Cotter, Esq. is a Montrealer, fluent in both English and French. She earned her Bachelor's degree from McGill University at age 18, her Juris Doctor law degree from one of the leading civil rights institutions, Howard University School of Law, and her Doctorate degree (Ph.D.) from Concordia University, where she specialized in Political Economy International Law, particularly on the issue of equality. Her work experience has been extensive, Chief Advisor and later Administrative Law Judge appointed by the Prime Minister to the Veterans Review and Appeals Tribunal in Canada; Supervising Attorney and later Executive Director for the Legal Services Corporation in the United States; National Director for an environmental network in Canada; Faculty for Business Law at the Law School, Law Society of Ireland; Associate at the law firm of Blake, Cassels and Graydon LLP with a secondment as in-house counsel with Agrium Inc. in Canada; Attorney with the Disability Law Center of Alaska; and solo practitioner of the Social Security Disability Law Firm. She is also a gold medallist in figure skating. Dr Cotter is the wife of Mark Badger and the proud mother of Bill and Jill.

Chapter 1

Introduction to *Little Angels*

> So we come here today to dramatize a shameful condition. In a sense we've come to our nation's capital to cash a check. When the architects of our republic wrote the magnificent words of the Constitution and the Declaration of Independence, they were signing a promissory note to which every (human) was to fall heir. This note was the promise that all … would be guaranteed the unalienable rights of life, liberty, and the pursuit of happiness … A check which has come back marked insufficient funds. We refuse to believe that there are insufficient funds in the great vaults of opportunity of this nation. And so we've come to cash this check, a check that will give us upon demand the riches of freedom and the security of justice.[1]

In our universal quest for justice in general and for respect for our children and their rights in particular, and in the fight against child discrimination in *Little Angels*, we may learn from the immortal words of one of the greatest civil rights leaders and human rights activists, Dr Martin Luther King Jr. This book, *Little Angels*, focuses on the goal of child equality, and the importance of the law and legislation to combat child discrimination in these troubling times. This book examines child discrimination, specifically looking at the issue of child labor and the laws enacted to prevent underage labor for the protection of the most vulnerable of society, the children, the 'Little Angels'. Its overall aim is to better understand the issue of inequality and to improve the likelihood of achieving child equality in the future and ending child inequality. *Little Angels* examines the primary role of legislation, which has an impact on the court process, as well as the primary role of the judicial system, which has an impact on the fight for child rights. This is the tenth book in a series of books on discrimination law. Other titles in the series are *Gender Injustice*, dealing with gender discrimination, *Race Matters*, dealing with race discrimination, *This Ability*, dealing with disability discrimination, *Just A Number*, dealing with age discrimination, *Heaven Forbid*, dealing with religious discrimination, *Ask No Questions*, dealing with sexual orientation discrimination, *Pregnant Pause*, dealing with maternity discrimination, *Culture Clash*, dealing with ethnic discrimination, and *Class Act*, dealing with class discrimination. A similar approach and structure is used throughout the series to illustrate comparisons and contradictions in discrimination law.

Fundamental rights are rights which either are inherent in a person by natural law or are instituted in the citizen by the State. The ascending view of the natural law of divine origin over human law involves moral expectations in human beings

---

1   King Jr, Dr Martin Luther, *March on Washington*, 1963.

through a social contract, which includes minimum moral rights of which one may not be deprived by government or society. The competing view is that courts operating under the Constitution can enforce only those guarantees which are expressed. Thus, legislation has an impact on the court system and on society as a whole. Internationally and nationally, attempts have been made to improve the situation of all groups and outlaw discrimination.

In looking at the relationship between children and the law, the book deals comprehensively with the issue of child discrimination throughout its chapters by outlining important national legislation in the area affecting the overall country examined, with no particular position argued necessarily but with the intent to give the reader the knowledge to make up their own mind; also, for the most part, the countries examined were chosen because of their predominant common law background, because of their predominant use of the English language in legislation and case law, and because of their predominant role in the fight against discrimination: Chapter 1 introduces the reader to the core area of child inequality; Chapter 2 covers child inequality and rights around the world; Chapter 3 looks at the United Nations; Chapters 4 and 5 examine child inequality in Australia and New Zealand, and Africa and South Africa, respectively; Chapters 6 and 7 examine child inequality in Canada, Mexico and the United States, and the North American situation with the North American Free Trade Agreement as to its impact on child inequality, respectively; Chapters 8 and 9 examine child inequality in the United Kingdom and Ireland, and the European situation with the European Union Treaty as to its impact on child inequality, respectively; and Chapter 10 concludes this overview of child inequality. Statistics will be included in each chapter to show the extent of child labor.

In terms of the global estimate of 12.3 million victims of forced labor, 40–50 percent are estimated to be children and youths under 18 years.[2] The globalization process and the various economic agreements have a direct impact on people's lives as key players in the labor market today. This study seeks to comparatively analyze legislation impacting child equality in various countries internationally. It also examines the two most important trade agreements of our day, namely the North American Free Trade Agreement and the European Union Treaty in a historical and compelling analysis of equality. Although an important trade agreement with implications for labor, the North American Free Trade Agreement has a different system from the European system in that it has no overseeing court with jurisdiction over the respective countries. Further, the provisions for non-discrimination in the labor process are contained in a separate document, the North American Agreement on Labor Cooperation. On the other hand, the European Union Treaty takes a different approach, by directly providing for non-discrimination, as well as an overseeing court, the European Court of Justice, and the treaty is made part of the domestic law of every Member State, weakening past

---

2   International Labour Organization.

discriminatory laws and judgments. The European process actively implements child equality by way of European Union legislation.

North America, as the new world with its image of freedom and equality, is considered to have made great strides in civil rights. However, the American philosophy of survival of the fittest and the pursuit of materialism have slowed down the process. With the advent of the European Union, the coming together of nations has had a very positive influence on the enforcement of human rights, much more so than that of North America, because of the unique European approach. All parties must cooperate, and governments need to work with businesses, trade unions and society as a whole, and together, they can create an environment where people of all groups can participate at all levels of political life and decision-making. Indeed, combating child inequality and achieving child equality requires a strong 'child matters' focus in constitutional, legal, judicial and electoral frameworks for people of all groups to be actively involved at the national and international levels.

According to liberal democracy, the rule of law is the foundation stone for the conduct of institutions. *Little Angels* offers a defense of the notion that social reform is possible through key institutions, which include the legal system and its use of the law. For liberal democracy, the legislative system is the core for the governance of society in the way it functions toward social equality of opportunity. The law is of central importance in the debate for change from inequality to equality. Actionable and enforceable rights are legal norms, which represent social facts demarcating areas of action linked with universalized freedom.[3] Law is a powerful tool, which can and must be used to better society. Law is a rule of conduct enforced by sanctions, and administered by a determinate locus of power concentrated in a sovereign or a surrogate, the court. Therefore, the justice system and the courts play a vital role in enforcing the law.

Legitimacy has subjective guarantees of internalization with the acceptance and belief in authority, and objective guarantees of enforcement with the expectation of reactions to the behaviour.[4] Therefore, law must recognize equally all members of society, including minority women, in order for it to be effective. Further, in order for a law to be seen as legitimate from society's point of view and accepted by the people in general to be followed, a process of inclusive interaction by all affected must first be realized. When creating laws, this means that input from diverse groups is critical. Thus, laws have two components, namely, facts, which stabilize expectations and sustain the order of freedom, and norms, which provide a claim of approval by everyone. Law makes possible highly artificial communities whose integration is based simultaneously on the threat of internal sanctions and the supposition of a rationally motivated agreement.[5] Discrimination and injustice can be undercut through the effective use of both the law and the courts.

---

3   Habermas, Jurgen, *Between Facts and Norms*, 1998, p. xii.
4   Fried, Morton, *The Evolution of Political Society*, 1967, p. 23.
5   Habermas, Jurgen, *Between Facts and Norms*, 1998, p. 8.

Laws can go a long way in forbidding inequality and providing for equality; where one ends the other begins. There are two ranks of law, namely ordinary law of legislation, administration and adjudication, and higher constitutional law affecting rights and liberties, which encompasses the constitutions of the various nations as interpreted by the supreme courts. Law holds its legitimacy and validity by virtue of its coercive potential, its rational claim of acceptance as right. The legitimate legal order is found in its reflexive process; therefore, we must all believe that equality is a good and necessary thing, which is essential to the very growth of society.

Thus, conflict resolution is a process of reasoned agreement where, firstly, members assume the same meanings by the same words; secondly, members are rationally accountable for their actions; and thirdly, mutually acceptable resolutions can be reached so that supporting arguments justify the confidence in the notion that the truth in justice will not be proven false.[6] Disenchantment with the law and the legal process only serves to undermine the stabilization of communities. By legitimizing the legal process and holding up the ideals of equality in the fight against child discrimination, the law and the courts can bring about change.

People of all backgrounds have had to fight in the formulation of laws and in the enforcement of equality in the courts. Class rests on economic determination and historical change, and inequality in the distribution of private property among different classes of people has been a characteristic of society; the ruling class loathes that which it is not, that which is foreign to it, and this has traditionally been youth and minorities. The patriarchal system has freely fashioned laws and adjusted society to suit those in power, and this has traditionally been white Anglo-Saxon Protestant men; they are context- and time-specific but changeable. There are important criteria for analysis, including child and age, ethnicity and race, gender, poverty and class, disability, religion, and sexual orientation, and hence all these can, alone or combined, amount to discrimination.

The concept of equality is the ignoring of difference between individuals for a particular purpose in a particular context, or the deliberate indifference to specified differences in the acknowledgement of the existence of difference. The notion of rights and of equality should be bound to the notion of justice and fairness. While injustice involves a constraint of freedom and a violation of human dignity through a process of oppression and domination, justice involves the institutional conditions necessary for the development and exercise of individual capacities for collective communication and cooperation.[7] Discrimination is the withholding from the oppressed and subordinated what enables them to exercise private and public autonomy. The struggle must be continued to bring about psychological, sociological and institutional changes to allow all members of the human race to feel equal and to recognize one another as being so.

---

6   Ibid., at p. xv.
7   Habermas, Jurgen, *Between Facts and Norms*, 1998, p. 419.

Though humans are mortal and civilizations come and go, from Biblical times to our days, there has been a fixed pivot for the thoughts of all generations and for men of all continents, namely the equal dignity inherent in the human personality.[8] Even Pope John XXIII described the United Nations Declaration of Human Rights, in his 1963 Encyclical *Pacem in Terris*, as 'one of the most important acts of the United Nations' and as 'a step towards the politico-judicial organization of the world community'; 'In social life, every right conferred on man by nature creates in others (individuals and collectivities) a duty, that of recognizing and respecting that right.'[9] Further, Pope John Paul II described the importance of work and of just remuneration in his 1981 Encyclical *Laborem Exercens*:

> Work bears a particular mark of ... humanity, the mark of a person operating within a community of persons ... While work, in all its many senses, is an obligation, that is to say a duty, it is also a source of rights on the part of the worker. These rights must be examined in the broad context of human rights as a whole, which are connatural with man, and many of which are proclaimed by various international organisations and increasingly guaranteed by the individual States for their citizens. Respect for this broad range of human rights constitutes the fundamental condition for peace in the modern world: peace both within individual countries and societies and in international relations ... The human rights that flow from work are part of the broader context of those fundamental rights of the person ... The key problem of social ethic ... is that of just remuneration for work done ... Hence, in every case, a just wage is the concrete means of verifying the justice of the whole socio-economic system and, in any case, of checking that it is functioning justly.[10]

An improvement in equality of opportunity is sought rather than a utopian state of equality. No one should misunderstand this. Clearly, oppression exists. Rather, this book, *Little Angels*, seeks to add to the list of inequalities to be considered, and does not rule out other forms of injustices besides child inequality. Generalities are not presumed nor are they made here, for this would detract from the very purpose of this book, to bring to the forefront of discussion the reality of injustice, not to create further injustice.

---

8 Cassin, René, *From the Ten Commandments to the Rights of Man*, France, 1969.
9 Pope John XXIII, *Pacem in Terris*, Rome, 1963.
10 Pope John Paul II, *Laborem Exercens*, Rome, 1981.

Chapter 2
Little Angels in Child Discrimination

Introduction

In the quest for respect for our children and in the fight against child discrimination in *Little Angels*, this chapter will examine discrimination, looking at the United Nations Millennium Declaration; the World Conference on Human Rights; the Equal Remuneration Convention (No. 100); the Discrimination (Employment and Occupation) Convention (No. 111); the Employment Policy Convention (No. 122); Minimum Age (Industry) Convention (No. 5); Night Work of Young Persons (Industry) Convention (No. 6); Forced Labour Convention (No. 29); Abolition of Forced Labour Convention (No. 105); Minimum Age Convention (No. 138); the Worst Forms of Child Labour Convention (No. 182); and the Hague Global Child Labour Conference, Towards a World Without Child Labour. Governments and others must not only refrain from violating human rights, but must work actively to promote and protect these rights.

This book examines child discrimination, specifically looking at the issue of child labor and the laws enacted to prevent underage labor for the protection of the most vulnerable of society, the children, the 'Little Angels'. In general, the word discrimination comes from the Latin 'discriminare', which means to 'distinguish between'; discrimination is action based on prejudice resulting in unfair treatment of people. Unlawful discrimination can be characterized as direct or indirect: direct discrimination involves treating someone less favorably, because of the possession of a prohibited attribute such as class, than they would treat someone without the prohibited attribute who was in the same circumstances; and indirect discrimination involves setting a condition or requirement that a smaller proportion of those with the prohibited attribute can comply with than those who do not have the prohibited attribute without reasonable justification. Forms of invidious discrimination include distinctions based on age, class, gender, race, ethnicity, disability, religion, and sexual orientation. If the justification is rational, then the discrimination is not invidious. Many governments have attempted to control discrimination through civil rights legislation, equal opportunity laws and institutionalized policies of affirmative action. Within the equal opportunities / individual merit approach can be found a spectrum of tests for discrimination: at one end of the spectrum, there is the 'equality as mere rationality', where arbitrary and unreasonable behaviour is deemed discriminatory, but justifications for discrimination are accepted at face value; at the other end of the spectrum, there is the 'equality as fairness', where justifications are examined critically, the possibility of indirect discrimination is recognized, and burdens of proof may be shifted; and a third concept of equality is the 'equality of opportunity', which argues for institutional and structural changes to remove the barriers to equal participation of people belonging to different groups.

Further, prejudice is the process of pre-judging something, and refers to existing biases toward the members of certain groups, based on social stereotypes. Many prejudicial behaviors are picked up at a young age by children emulating their elders' way of thinking and speaking. Overall, equal opportunity refers to the idea that all people should start out in life from the same platform, in that all should have equal opportunities in life, regardless of where they were born or who their parents were. Egalitarianism is the moral doctrine that equality ought to prevail throughout society, and according to legal egalitarianism, everyone ought to be considered equal under the law. Tokenism occurs when a small group is chosen to participate in an initiative to demonstrate that a program is progressive or to show someone has consulted the constituency, but in fact has ignored their views, which is discriminatory in itself.

Standards or rules of behavior are norms, which help us to predict the behavior of others and, in turn, allow others to know what to expect of us, with our culture defining what is proper and improper behavior, what is right and wrong, and what we are expected to do and not to do.[1] The concept of the minority group has provided a valuable frame of reference for understanding the experiences of groups of people in society who are singled out, based on some cultural or physical characteristic, such as age, for discriminatory treatment; in terms of class and culture, they are a cross-cutting determinant, since cultural values and traditions determine to a large extent how a given society views class.[2] Specifically , Section 4 of the Mission Statement enunciates that there must be immediate and concerted action by all to create a peaceful, just and humane world based on human rights and fundamental freedoms ...

The implementation of principles of equality, including through national laws, strategies, policies, programs and development priorities, is the sovereign responsibility of each State, in conformity with human rights and fundamental freedoms.[3] While the Beijing Platform for Action came out of the World Conference on Women, many of its core values can be extended to include the rights of children. There must be immediate and concerted action by all to create a peaceful, just and humane world based on human rights and fundamental freedoms, including the principle of equality for people and from all walks of life, and to this end, broad-based and sustained economic growth in the context of sustainable development is necessary to sustain social development and social justice. Success will require a strong commitment on the part of governments, international organizations and institutions at all levels, and will also require

---

1   Harris, Diana K., *Age Norms*, in Erdman B. Palmore, Laurence Branch, Diana K. Harris, *Encyclopedia of Ageism*, The Haworth Press, Inc., New York, 2005.

2   Wirth, L., *The Problem of Minority Groups*, in R. Linton (ed.), *The Science of Man in the World Crisis* (pp. 347–72), Columbia University Press, New York, 1945.

3   United Nations, Beijing Platform for Action.

adequate mobilization of resources from multilateral, bilateral and private sources for the advancement of all humans for strengthening the capacity of national, sub-regional, regional and international institutions; a commitment to equal rights, equal responsibilities and equal opportunities for the equal participation of all regardless of class issues in all national, regional and international bodies in the policy-making processes; and the establishing or strengthening of mechanisms at all levels for accountability to the world's population. As globalization continues to influence economic opportunities worldwide, its effects remain uneven, creating both risks and opportunities for different groups. For many, globalization has intensified existing inequalities and insecurities, often translating into the loss of livelihoods, labor rights and social benefits.

Only a new era of international cooperation among peoples based on a spirit of partnership within an equitable international social and economic environment, along with a radical transformation of the relationship to one of full and equal partnership will enable the world to meet the challenges of the twenty-first century. Actions to be taken at the national and international levels by all governments, the United Nations' system, international and regional organizations, including international financial institutions, the private sector, non-governmental organizations (NGOs) and other actors of civil society, include the creation and maintenance of a non-discriminatory as well as youth-sensitive legal environment through review of legislation with a view to striving to remove discriminatory provisions. It will be critical for the international community to demonstrate a new commitment for the future to inspire a new generation to work together for a more just society.[4]

Therefore, governments and corporations should develop leadership training and opportunities to encourage all to take leadership roles both as students and as adults in civil society; develop appropriate education and information programs, particularly in conjunction with the mass media, that make the public, particularly parents, aware of the importance of non-discriminatory education for children and the equal sharing of family responsibilities by girls and boys; promote lifelong education and training to ensure the availability of a broad range of educational and training programs that lead to ongoing acquisition by women and girls of the knowledge and skills required for living in, contributing to and benefiting from their communities and nations; and finally, create flexible education, training and retraining programs for lifelong learning that facilitate transitions between women's activities at all stages of their lives. Overall, the promotion and protection of all human rights and fundamental freedoms is essential for the creation of an inclusive society for all. Obstacles affecting peoples and countries must be overcome in order to realize the full potential of opportunities presented for the benefit of all. The advancement of all children and the achievement of child equality are a matter of human rights and a condition for social justice.[5]

---

4   Ibid.
5   Ibid.

Millennium Declaration

At the beginning of the Millennium, heads of state and leaders of governments gathered at the United Nations Headquarters in New York to reaffirm faith in the Organisation and its Charter as indispensable foundations of a more peaceful, prosperous and just world, which produced the United Nations Millennium Declaration of 8 September 2000.[6] In terms of values and principles, the following is affirmed:

> 2. We recognize that, in addition to our separate responsibilities to our individual societies, we have a collective responsibility to uphold the principles of human dignity, equality and equity at the global level. As leaders we have a duty therefore to all the world's people, especially the most vulnerable and, in particular, the children of the world, to whom the future belongs.[7]

> 3. We reaffirm our commitment to the purposes and principles of the Charter of the United Nations, which have proved timeless and universal. Indeed, their relevance and capacity to inspire have increased, as nations and peoples have become increasingly interconnected and interdependent.[8]

In addition, the desire for globalization to have a positive rather than a negative contribution to human rights is stressed:

> 5. We believe that the central challenge we face today is to ensure that globalization becomes a positive force for all the world's people. For while globalization offers great opportunities, at present its benefits are very unevenly shared, while its costs are unevenly distributed. We recognize that developing countries and countries with economies in transition face special difficulties in responding to this central challenge. Thus, only through broad and sustained efforts to create a shared future, based upon our common humanity in all its diversity, can globalization be made fully inclusive and equitable. These efforts must include policies and measures, at the global level, which correspond to the needs of developing countries and economies in transition and are formulated and implemented with their effective participation.[9]

Further, under Article 6, certain fundamental values are considered as essential to international relations in the twenty-first century:

---

6   Millennium Declaration, 2000.
7   Ibid., at Article 2.
8   Ibid., at Article 3.
9   Ibid., at Article 5.

Freedom. Men and women have the right to live their lives and raise their children in dignity, free from hunger and from the fear of violence, oppression or injustice. Democratic and participatory governance based on the will of the people best assures these rights.

Equality. No individual and no nation must be denied the opportunity to benefit from development. The equal rights and opportunities of women and men must be assured.

Solidarity. Global challenges must be managed in a way that distributes the costs and burdens fairly in accordance with basic principles of equity and social justice. Those who suffer or who benefit least deserve help from those who benefit most.

Tolerance. Human beings must respect one other, in all their diversity of belief, culture and language. Differences within and between societies should be neither feared nor repressed, but cherished as a precious asset of humanity. A culture of peace and dialogue among all civilizations should be actively promoted.

Respect for nature. Prudence must be shown in the management of all living species and natural resources, in accordance with the precepts of sustainable development. Only in this way can the immeasurable riches provided to us by nature be preserved and passed on to our descendants. The current unsustainable patterns of production and consumption must be changed in the interest of our future welfare and that of our descendants.

Shared responsibility. Responsibility for managing worldwide economic and social development, as well as threats to international peace and security, must be shared among the nations of the world and should be exercised multilaterally. As the most universal and most representative organization in the world, the United Nations must play the central role.[10]

Finally, in order to translate these shared values into actions, a number of key objectives have been identified:

Development and poverty eradication:
11. We will spare no effort to free our fellow men, women and children from the abject and dehumanizing conditions of extreme poverty, to which more than a billion of them are currently subjected. We are committed to making the right to development a reality for everyone and to freeing the entire human race from want.[11]

---

10 Ibid., at Article 6.
11 Ibid., at Article 11.

Protecting our common environment:

21. We must spare no effort to free all of humanity, and above all our children and grandchildren, from the threat of living on a planet irredeemably spoilt by human activities, and whose resources would no longer be sufficient for their needs.[12]

Protecting the vulnerable:

26. We will spare no effort to ensure that children and all civilian populations that suffer disproportionately the consequences of natural disasters, genocide, armed conflicts and other humanitarian emergencies are given every assistance and protection so that they can resume normal life as soon as possible.[13]

World Conference on Human Rights

The World Conference on Human Rights brought together various nations in Vienna, Austria in 1993, forging 'a new vision for global action for human rights into the next century'.[14] The Preamble of the Vienna Declaration and Program of Action states:

> The World Conference on Human Rights,
> Considering that the promotion and protection of human rights is a matter of priority for the international community, and that the Conference affords a unique opportunity to carry out a comprehensive analysis of the international human rights system and of the machinery for the protection of human rights, in order to enhance and thus promote a fuller observance of those rights, in a just and balanced manner,
>
> Recognizing and affirming that all human rights derive from the dignity and worth inherent in the human person, and that the human person is the central subject of human rights and fundamental freedoms, and consequently should be the principal beneficiary and should participate actively in the realization of these rights and freedoms,
>
> Reaffirming their commitment to the purposes and principles contained in the Charter of the United Nations and the Universal Declaration of Human Rights,
>
> Reaffirming the commitment contained in … the Charter of the United Nations to take joint and separate action, placing proper emphasis on developing effective international cooperation for the realization of the purposes set out in Article 55, including universal respect for, and observance of, human rights and fundamental freedoms for all,

12   Ibid., at Article 21.
13   Ibid., at Article 26.
14   United Nations, World Conference on Human Rights.

Emphasizing the responsibilities of all States, in conformity with the Charter of the United Nations, to develop and encourage respect for human rights and fundamental freedoms for all, without distinction as to race, sex, language or religion,

Recalling the Preamble to the Charter of the United Nations, in particular the determination to reaffirm faith in fundamental human rights, in the dignity and worth of the human person, and in the equal rights of men and women and of nations large and small,

Recalling also the determination expressed in the Preamble of the Charter of the United Nations to save succeeding generations from the scourge of war, to establish conditions under which justice and respect for obligations arising from treaties and other sources of international law can be maintained, to promote social progress and better standards of life in larger freedom, to practice tolerance and good neighbourliness, and to employ international machinery for the promotion of the economic and social advancement of all peoples,

Emphasizing that the Universal Declaration of Human Rights, which constitutes a common standard of achievement for all peoples and all nations, is the source of inspiration and has been the basis for the United Nations in making advances in standard setting as contained in the existing international human rights instruments, in particular the International Covenant on Civil and Political Rights and the International Covenant on Economic, Social and Cultural Rights,

Considering the major changes taking place on the international scene and the aspirations of all the peoples for an international order based on the principles enshrined in the Charter of the United Nations, including promoting and encouraging respect for human rights and fundamental freedoms for all and respect for the principle of equal rights and self-determination of peoples, peace, democracy, justice, equality, rule of law, pluralism, development, better standards of living and solidarity,

Deeply concerned by various forms of discrimination and violence, to which women continue to be exposed all over the world,

Recognizing that the activities of the United Nations in the field of human rights should be rationalized and enhanced in order to strengthen the United Nations machinery in this field and to further the objectives of universal respect for observance of international human rights standards,

Having taken into account the Declarations adopted by the three regional meetings at Tunis, San José and Bangkok and the contributions made by Governments, and bearing in mind the suggestions made by intergovernmental and non-governmental organizations, as well as the studies prepared by independent experts during the preparatory process leading to the World Conference on Human Rights,

Welcoming the International Year of the World's Indigenous People 1993 as a reaffirmation of the commitment of the international community to ensure their enjoyment of all human rights and fundamental freedoms and to respect the value and diversity of their cultures and identities,

Recognizing also that the international community should devise ways and means to remove the current obstacles and meet challenges to the full realization of all human rights and to prevent the continuation of human rights violations resulting thereof throughout the world,

Invoking the spirit of our age and the realities of our time which call upon the peoples of the world and all States Members of the United Nations to rededicate themselves to the global task of promoting and protecting all human rights and fundamental freedoms so as to secure full and universal enjoyment of these rights,

Determined to take new steps forward in the commitment of the international community with a view to achieving substantial progress in human rights endeavors by an increased and sustained effort of international cooperation and solidarity,

Solemnly adopts the Vienna Declaration and Program of Action.[15]

Under Part I, emphasizing human rights as a birthright, Article 1 underlines international obligations and cooperation:

1. The World Conference on Human Rights reaffirms the solemn commitment of all States to fulfil their obligations to promote universal respect for, and observance and protection of, all human rights and fundamental freedoms for all in accordance with the Charter of the United Nations, other instruments relating to human rights, and international law. The universal nature of these rights and freedoms is beyond question.

In this framework, enhancement of international cooperation in the field of human rights is essential for the full achievement of the purposes of the United Nations.

---

15   World Conference on Human Rights, Vienna Declaration and Program of Action, at the Preamble.

Human rights and fundamental freedoms are the birthright of all human beings; their protection and promotion is the first responsibility of Governments.[16]

The important principle of self-determination is reinforced in Article 2:

2. All peoples have the right of self-determination. By virtue of that right they freely determine their political status, and freely pursue their economic, social and cultural development.[17]

Article 4 recognizes the promotion and protection of all human rights and fundamental freedoms as a priority objective:

4. The promotion and protection of all human rights and fundamental freedoms must be considered as a priority objective of the United Nations in accordance with its purposes and principles, in particular the purpose of international cooperation. In the framework of these purposes and principles, the promotion and protection of all human rights is a legitimate concern of the international community. The organs and specialized agencies related to human rights should therefore further enhance the coordination of their activities based on the consistent and objective application of international human rights instruments.[18]

Article 5 reinforces the ideal that human rights are to be enforced globally in a fair and equal manner:

5. All human rights are universal, indivisible and interdependent and interrelated. The international community must treat human rights globally in a fair and equal manner, on the same footing, and with the same emphasis. While the significance of national and regional particularities and various historical, cultural and religious backgrounds must be borne in mind, it is the duty of States, regardless of their political, economic and cultural systems, to promote and protect all human rights and fundamental freedoms.[19]

Further, the importance of fundamental freedoms is underlined in Article 15:

15. Respect for human rights and for fundamental freedoms without distinction of any kind is a fundamental rule of international human rights law. The speedy and comprehensive elimination of all forms of racism and racial discrimination, xenophobia and related intolerance is a priority task for the international community. Governments should take effective measures to prevent and

---

16   Ibid., at Part I, Article 1.
17   Ibid., at Part I, Article 2.
18   Ibid., at Part I, Article 4.
19   Ibid., at Part I, Article 5.

combat them. Groups, institutions, intergovernmental and non-governmental organizations and individuals are urged to intensify their efforts in cooperating and coordinating their activities against these evils.[20]

The vulnerability of certain groups of people is identified within Article 24, in order to create measures of protection:

> 24. Great importance must be given to the promotion and protection of the human rights of persons belonging to groups which have been rendered vulnerable, including migrant workers, the elimination of all forms of discrimination against them, and the strengthening and more effective implementation of existing human rights instruments. States have an obligation to create and maintain adequate measures at the national level, in particular in the fields of education, health and social support, for the promotion and protection of the rights of persons in vulnerable sectors of their populations and to ensure the participation of those among them who are interested in finding a solution to their own problems.[21]

Article 25 affirms the need to overcome poverty, which too often impacts disproportionately upon children and reinforces child discrimination:

> 25. The World Conference on Human Rights affirms that extreme poverty and social exclusion constitute a violation of human dignity and that urgent steps are necessary to achieve better knowledge of extreme poverty and its causes, including those related to the problem of development, in order to promote the human rights of the poorest, and to put an end to extreme poverty and social exclusion and to promote the enjoyment of the fruits of social progress. It is essential for States to foster participation by the poorest people in the decision-making process by the community in which they live, the promotion of human rights and efforts to combat extreme poverty.[22]

Further, the importance of education for understanding, tolerance and peace in combating child discrimination is emphasized under Article 33:

> 33. The World Conference on Human Rights reaffirms that States are duty-bound, as stipulated in the Universal Declaration of Human Rights and the International Covenant on Economic, Social and Cultural Rights and in other international human rights instruments, to ensure that education is aimed at strengthening the respect of human rights and fundamental freedoms. The World Conference on Human Rights emphasizes the importance of incorporating the subject of

---

20   Ibid., at Part I, Article 15.
21   World Conference on Human Rights, Vienna Declaration and Program of Action, at Part I, Article 24.
22   Ibid., at Part I, Article 25.

human rights education programs and calls upon States to do so. Education should promote understanding, tolerance, peace and friendly relations between the nations and all racial or religious groups and encourage the development of United Nations activities in pursuance of these objectives. Therefore, education on human rights and the dissemination of proper information, both theoretical and practical, play an important role in the promotion and respect of human rights with regard to all individuals without distinction of any kind such as race, sex, language or religion, and this should be integrated in the education policies at the national as well as international levels. The World Conference on Human Rights notes that resource constraints and institutional inadequacies may impede the immediate realization of these objectives.[23]

Finally, an effective framework of remedies to redress human rights grievances is underlined in Article 27, emphasizing the critical role of justice and the law:

27. Every State should provide an effective framework of remedies to redress human rights grievances or violations. The administration of justice, including law enforcement and prosecutorial agencies and, especially, an independent judiciary and legal profession in full conformity with applicable standards contained in international human rights instruments, are essential to the full and non-discriminatory realization of human rights and indispensable to the processes of democracy and sustainable development. In this context, institutions concerned with the administration of justice should be properly funded, and an increased level of both technical and financial assistance should be provided by the international community. It is incumbent upon the United Nations to make use of special programs of advisory services on a priority basis for the achievement of a strong and independent administration of justice.[24]

Under Part II of the Vienna Declaration and Program of Action, and in keeping with the rubric of equality, dignity and tolerance, as regards racism, racial discrimination, xenophobia and other forms of intolerance, Article 19 recognizes the elimination of discrimination as the primary objective of the world community:

19. The World Conference on Human Rights considers the elimination of racism and racial discrimination, in particular in their institutionalized forms such as apartheid or resulting from doctrines of racial superiority or exclusivity or contemporary forms and manifestations of racism, as a primary objective for the international community and a worldwide promotion program in the field of human rights. United Nations organs and agencies should strengthen their efforts to implement such a program of action related to the third decade to combat racism and racial discrimination as well as subsequent mandates to the same end.

23   Ibid., at Part I, Article 33.
24   Ibid., at Part I, Article 27.

The World Conference on Human Rights strongly appeals to the international community to contribute generously to the Trust Fund for the Program for the Decade for Action to Combat Racism and Racial Discrimination.[25]

Further, Article 20 emphasizes the need for development of policies of prevention of discrimination through legislation:

> 20. The World Conference on Human Rights urges all Governments to take immediate measures and to develop strong policies to prevent and combat all forms and manifestations of racism, xenophobia or related intolerance, where necessary by enactment of appropriate legislation, including penal measures, and by the establishment of national institutions to combat such phenomena.[26]

Finally, Article 25 recognizes the role of the Commission on Human Rights on combating discrimination:

> 25. The World Conference on Human Rights calls on the Commission on Human Rights to examine ways and means to promote and protect effectively the rights of persons belonging to minorities as set out in the Declaration on the Rights of Persons belonging to National or Ethnic, Religious and Linguistic Minorities. In this context, the World Conference on Human Rights calls upon the Centre for Human Rights to provide, at the request of Governments concerned and as part of its program of advisory services and technical assistance, qualified expertise on minority issues and human rights, as well as on the prevention and resolution of disputes, to assist in existing or potential situations involving minorities.[27]

Equal Remuneration Convention (No. 100)

Generally, the General Conference of the International Labour Organization, convened at Geneva, adopted the Equal Remuneration Convention (ILO No. 100) of 9 June 1951, the Preamble of which states:

> The General Conference of the International Labour Organisation,

> Having been convened at Geneva by the Governing Body of the International Labour Office, and having met in its thirty-fourth session on 6 June 1951, and

> Having decided upon the adoption of certain proposals with regard to the principle of equal remuneration for men and women workers for work of equal value, which is the seventh item on the agenda of the session, and

---

25   Ibid., at Part II, Article 19.
26   Ibid., at Part II, Article 20.
27   Ibid., at Part II, Article 25.

Having determined that these proposals shall take the form of an international Convention, Adopts this twenty-ninth day of June of the year one thousand nine hundred and fifty-one the following Convention, which may be cited as the Equal Remuneration Convention, 1951.[28]

The term remuneration is defined in Article 1:

1. For the purpose of this Convention:
(a) The term 'remuneration' includes the ordinary, basic or minimum wage or salary and any additional emoluments whatsoever payable directly or indirectly, whether in cash or in kind, by the employer to the worker and arising out of the worker's employment;
(b) The term 'equal remuneration for men and women workers for work of equal value' refers to rates of remuneration established without discrimination based on sex.[29]

Different methods for equality are envisioned in Article 2:

2(1) Each Member shall, by means appropriate to the methods in operation for determining rates of remuneration, promote and, in so far as is consistent with such methods, ensure the application to all workers of the principle of equal remuneration for ... workers for work of equal value.
(2) This principle may be applied by means of:
    (a) National laws or regulations;
    (b) Legally established or recognised machinery for wage determination;
    (c) Collective agreements between employers and workers; or
    (d) A combination of these various means.[30]

Further, objective methods of appraisal are ensured in Article 3:

3(1) Where such action will assist in giving effect to the provisions of this Convention, measures shall be taken to promote objective appraisal of jobs on the basis of the work to be performed.
(2) The methods to be followed in this appraisal may be decided upon by the authorities responsible for the determination of rates of remuneration, or, where such rates are determined by collective agreements, by the parties thereto.[31]

---

28   Equal Remuneration Convention, at the Preamble.
29   Ibid., at Article 1.
30   Ibid., at Article 2.
31   Ibid., at Article 3.

Discrimination (Employment and Occupation) Convention (No. 111)

The General Conference of the International Labour Organization, convened at Geneva, adopted on 5 July 1958 the Discrimination (Employment and Occupation) Convention (No. 111), which entered into force on 15 June 1960, the Preamble of which states:

> Having decided upon the adoption of certain proposals with regard to discrimination in the field of employment and occupation, and
>
> Having determined that these proposals shall take the form of an international Convention, and Considering that the Declaration of Philadelphia affirms that all human beings, irrespective of race, creed or sex, have the right to pursue both their material well-being and their spiritual development in conditions of freedom and dignity, of economic security and equal opportunity, and
>
> Considering further that discrimination constitutes a violation of rights enunciated by the Universal Declaration of Human Rights.[32]

Important in the fight against underage labor, the word discrimination is defined in Article 1 to include national extraction under Article 1(1)(a):

> 1(1) For the purpose of this Convention the term 'discrimination' includes:
> (a) any distinction, exclusion or preference made on the basis of race, color, sex, religion, political opinion, national extraction or social origin, which has the effect of nullifying or impairing equality of opportunity or treatment in employment or occupation;
> (b) such other distinction, exclusion or preference which has the effect of nullifying or impairing equality of opportunity or treatment in employment or occupation as may be determined by the Member concerned after consultation with representative employer's and worker's organizations, where such exist, and with other appropriate bodies.
> (2) Any distinction, exclusion or preference in respect of a particular job based on the inherent requirements thereof shall not be deemed to be discrimination.
>
> (3) For the purpose of this Convention the terms 'employment' and 'occupation' include access to vocational training, access to employment and to particular occupations, and terms and conditions of employment.[33]

Member commitment to equality of opportunity and treatment is contained in Article 2:

---

32 Discrimination (Employment and Occupation) Convention, at the Preamble.
33 Ibid., at Article 1.

2. Each Member for which this Convention is in force undertakes to declare and pursue a national policy designed to promote, by methods appropriate to national conditions and practice, equality of opportunity and treatment in respect of employment and occupation, with a view to eliminating any discrimination in respect thereof.[34]

Further, Article 3 specifically enunciates Member responsibilities:

3. Each Member for which this Convention is in force undertakes, by methods appropriate to national conditions and practice:
(a) To seek the co-operation of employers' and workers' organizations and other appropriate bodies in promoting the acceptance and observance of this policy;
(b) To enact such legislation and to promote such educational programs as may be calculated to secure the acceptance and observance of the policy;
(c) To repeal any statutory provisions and modify any administrative instructions or practices which are inconsistent with the policy;
(d) To pursue the policy in respect of employment under the direct control of a national authority;
(e) To ensure observance of the policy in activities of vocational guidance, vocational training and placement services under the direction of a national authority;
(f) To indicate in its annual reports on the application of the Convention the action taken in pursuance of the policy and the results secured by such action.[35]

Finally, special measures are provided for in Article 5:

5(1) Special measures of protection or assistance provided in other Conventions or Recommendations adopted by the International Labor Conference shall not be deemed to be discrimination.
(2) Any Member may, after consultation with representative employers' and workers' organizations, where such exist, determine that other special measures designed to meet the particular requirements of persons who, for reasons such as sex, age, disablement, family responsibilities or social or cultural status, are generally recognized to require special protection or assistance, shall not be deemed to be discrimination.[36]

---

34   Ibid., at Article 2.
35   Ibid., at Article 3.
36   Ibid., at Article 5.

Employment Policy Convention (No. 122)

The General Conference of the International Labour Organization, convened in Geneva, adopted on 9 July 1964 the Employment Policy Convention (No. 122), which entered into force on 9 July 1965, the Preamble of which states:

> Considering that the Declaration of Philadelphia recognizes the solemn obligation of the International Labour Organization to further among the nations of the world programs which will achieve full employment and the raising of standards of living, and that the Preamble to the Constitution of the International Labour Organization provides for the prevention of unemployment and the provision of an adequate living wage, and
>
> Considering further that under the terms of the Declaration of Philadelphia it is the responsibility of the International Labour Organization to examine and consider the bearing of economic and financial policies upon employment policy in the light of the fundamental objective that 'all human beings, irrespective of race, creed or sex, have the right to pursue both their material well-being and their spiritual development in conditions of freedom and dignity, of economic security and equal opportunity', and
>
> Considering that the Universal Declaration of Human Rights provides that 'everyone has the right to work, to free choice of employment, to just and favorable conditions of work and to protection against unemployment'.[37]

In the fight against underage labor, a commitment to full, productive and freely chosen employment is envisioned in Article 1:

> 1(1) With a view to stimulating economic growth and development, raising levels of living, meeting manpower requirements and overcoming unemployment and under-employment, each Member shall declare and pursue, as a major goal, an active policy designed to promote full, productive and freely chosen employment.
>
> (2) The said policy shall aim at ensuring that:
>
> (a) There is work for all who are available for and seeking work;
>
> (b) Such work is as productive as possible;
>
> (c) There is freedom of choice of employment and the fullest possible opportunity for each worker to qualify for, and to use his skills and endowments in, a job for which he is well suited, irrespective of race, color, sex, religion, political opinion, national extraction or social origin.
>
> (3) The said policy shall take due account of the stage and level of economic development and the mutual relationships between employment objectives and

---

37   Employment Policy Convention, at the Preamble.

other economic and social objectives, and shall be pursued by methods that are appropriate to national conditions and practices.[38]

Respectfully, national conditions are taken into account in the carrying out of the policy:

2. Each Member shall, by such methods and to such extent as may be appropriate under national conditions:
(a) Decide on and keep under review, within the framework of a coordinated economic and social policy, the measures to be adopted for attaining the objectives specified in article l;
(b) Take such steps as may be needed, including when appropriate the establishment of programs, for the application of these measures.[39]

Finally, a consultation process is envisioned in Article 3 for the implementation of the Employment Policy Convention:

3. In the application of this Convention, representatives of the persons affected by the measures to be taken, and in particular representatives of employers and workers, shall be consulted concerning employment policies, with a view to taking fully into account their experience and views and securing their full co-operation in formulating and enlisting support for such policies.[40]

Minimum Age (Industry) Convention (No. 5)

Specifically with regard to children, the Preamble of the Minimum Age (Industry) Convention, 1919 (No. 5) states:

The General Conference of the International Labour Organisation,
Having been convened at Washington by the Government of the United States of America on the 29th day of October 1919, and
Having decided upon the adoption of certain proposals with regard to the 'employment of children: minimum age of employment', which is part of the fourth item in the agenda for the Washington meeting of the Conference, and
Having determined that these proposals shall take the form of an international Convention,

adopts the following Convention, which may be cited as the Minimum Age (Industry) Convention, 1919, for ratification by the Members of the International

---

38   Ibid., at Article 1.
39   Ibid., at Article 2.
40   Ibid., at Article 3.

Labour Organisation in accordance with the provisions of the Constitution of the International Labour Organisation.[41]

Importantly, Article 2 calls for a minimum age:

> 2. Children under the age of fourteen years shall not be employed or work in any public or private industrial undertaking, or in any branch thereof, other than an undertaking in which only members of the same family are employed.[42]

However, Article 3 allows for an exception:

> 3. The provisions of Article 2 shall not apply to work done by children in technical schools, provided that such work is approved and supervised by public authority.[43]

Night Work of Young Persons (Industry) Convention (No. 6)

The Preamble of the Night Work of Young Persons (Industry) Convention, 1919 (No. 6) states:

> The General Conference of the International Labour Organisation,
> Having been convened by the Government of the United States of America at Washington, on the 29 October 1919, and
> Having decided upon the adoption of certain proposals with regard to the 'employment of children: during the night', which is part of the fourth item in the agenda for the Washington meeting of the Conference, and
> Having determined that these proposals shall take the form of an international Convention,
> adopts the following Convention, which may be cited as the Night Work of Young Persons (Industry) Convention, 1919, for ratification by the Members of the International Labour Organisation in accordance with the provisions of the Constitution of the International Labour Organisation.[44]

Article 3 defines 'night':

> 3.1. For the purpose of this Convention, the term night signifies a period of at least eleven consecutive hours, including the interval between ten o'clock in the evening and five o'clock in the morning.

---

41   Minimum Age (Industry) Convention, at the Preamble.
42   Ibid., at Article 2.
43   Ibid., at Article 3.
44   Night Work of Young Persons (Industry) Convention, at the Preamble

4. In those tropical countries in which work is suspended during the middle of the day, the night period may be shorter than eleven hours if compensatory rest is accorded during the day.[45]

Importantly, Article 2 constrains night work by age:

2.1. Young persons under eighteen years of age shall not be employed during the night in any public or private industrial undertaking, or in any branch thereof, other than an undertaking in which only members of the same family are employed, except as hereinafter provided for.[46]

However, Article 4 allows for an exception:

4. The provisions of Articles 2 and 3 shall not apply to the night work of young persons between the ages of sixteen and eighteen years in case of emergencies which could not have been controlled or foreseen, which are not of a periodical character, and which interfere with the normal working of the industrial undertaking.[47]

Finally, Article 7 allows for emergency situations:

7. The prohibition of night work may be suspended by the Government, for young persons between the ages of sixteen and eighteen years, when in case of serious emergency the public interest demands it.[48]

Forced Labour Convention (No. 29)

The Preamble of the Forced Labour Convention, 1930 (No. 29) states:

The General Conference of the International Labour Organisation,
Having been convened at Geneva by the Governing Body of the International Labour Office, and having met in its Fourteenth Session on 10 June 1930, and
Having decided upon the adoption of certain proposals with regard to forced or compulsory labour, which is included in the first item on the agenda of the Session, and
Having determined that these proposals shall take the form of an international Convention,
adopts this twenty-eighth day of June of the year one thousand nine hundred and thirty the following Convention, which may be cited as the Forced Labour

---

45   Ibid., at Article 3.
46   Ibid., at Article 2.
47   Ibid., at Article 4.
48   Ibid., at Article 7.

Convention, 1930, for ratification by the Members of the International Labour Organisation in accordance with the provisions of the Constitution of the International Labour Organisation.[49]

Article 2 defines forced or compulsory labor:

2.1. For the purposes of this Convention the term forced or compulsory labour shall mean all work or service which is exacted from any person under the menace of any penalty and for which the said person has not offered himself voluntarily.

2. Nevertheless, for the purposes of this Convention, the term forced or compulsory labour shall not include

(a) any work or service exacted in virtue of compulsory military service laws for work of a purely military character;

(b) any work or service which forms part of the normal civic obligations of the citizens of a fully self-governing country;

(c) any work or service exacted from any person as a consequence of a conviction in a court of law, provided that the said work or service is carried out under the supervision and control of a public authority and that the said person is not hired to or placed at the disposal of private individuals, companies or associations;

(d) any work or service exacted in cases of emergency, that is to say, in the event of war or of a calamity or threatened calamity, such as fire, flood, famine, earthquake, violent epidemic or epizootic diseases, invasion by animal, insect or vegetable pests, and in general any circumstance that would endanger the existence or the well-being of the whole or part of the population;

(e) minor communal services of a kind which, being performed by the members of the community in the direct interest of the said community, can therefore be considered as normal civic obligations incumbent upon the members of the community, provided that the members of the community or their direct representatives shall have the right to be consulted in regard to the need for such services.[50]

Duties are imposed under Article 1:

1.1. Each Member of the International Labour Organisation which ratifies this Convention undertakes to suppress the use of forced or compulsory labour in all its forms within the shortest possible period.

2. With a view to this complete suppression, recourse to forced or compulsory labour may be had, during the transitional period, for public purposes only and

---

49   C29 Forced Labour Convention, at the Preamble.

50   Ibid., at Article 2.

as an exceptional measure, subject to the conditions and guarantees hereinafter provided.[51]

Further, Article 9 holds:

> 9. Except as otherwise provided for in Article 10 of this Convention, any authority competent to exact forced or compulsory labour shall, before deciding to have recourse to such labour, satisfy itself
> (a) that the work to be done or the service to be rendered is of important direct interest for the community called upon to do work or render the service;
> (b) that the work or service is of present or imminent necessity;
> (c) that it has been impossible to obtain voluntary labour for carrying out the work or rendering the service by the offer of rates of wages and conditions of labour not less favourable than those prevailing in the area concerned for similar work or service; and
> (d) that the work or service will not lay too heavy a burden upon the present population, having regard to the labour available and its capacity to undertake the work.[52]

In addition, Article 4 prohibits forced or compulsory labor for private means:

> 4.1. The competent authority shall not impose or permit the imposition of forced or compulsory labour for the benefit of private individuals, companies or associations.
> 2. Where such forced or compulsory labour for the benefit of private individuals, companies or associations exists at the date on which a Member's ratification of this Convention is registered by the Director-General of the International Labour Office, the Member shall completely suppress such forced or compulsory labour from the date on which this Convention comes into force for that Member.[53]

Article 11 constrains forced or compulsory labor by age:

> 11.1. Only adult able-bodied males who are of an apparent age of not less than 18 and not more than 45 years may be called upon for forced or compulsory labour. Except in respect of the kinds of labour provided for in Article 10 of this Convention, the following limitations and conditions shall apply:
>
> (a) whenever possible prior determination by a medical officer appointed by the administration that the persons concerned are not suffering from any infectious

---

51   Ibid., at Article 1.
52   Ibid., at Article 9.
53   Ibid., at Article 4.

or contagious disease and that they are physically fit for the work required and for the conditions under which it is to be carried out;

(b) exemption of school teachers and pupils and officials of the administration in general;

(c) the maintenance in each community of the number of adult able-bodied men indispensable for family and social life;

(d) respect for conjugal and family ties.[54]

Time limits are covered under Article 12:

12.1. The maximum period for which any person may be taken for forced or compulsory labour of all kinds in any one period of twelve months shall not exceed sixty days, including the time spent in going to and from the place of work.

2. Every person from whom forced or compulsory labour is exacted shall be furnished with a certificate indicating the periods of such labour which he has completed.[55]

Working hours are outlined in Article 13:

13.1. The normal working hours of any person from whom forced or compulsory labour is exacted shall be the same as those prevailing in the case of voluntary labour, and the hours worked in excess of the normal working hours shall be remunerated at the rates prevailing in the case of overtime for voluntary labour.

2. A weekly day of rest shall be granted to all persons from whom forced or compulsory labour of any kind is exacted and this day shall coincide as far as possible with the day fixed by tradition or custom in the territories or regions concerned.[56]

Finally, punishment for illegal forced or compulsory labor is provided for under Article 25:

25. The illegal exaction of forced or compulsory labour shall be punishable as a penal offence, and it shall be an obligation on any Member ratifying this Convention to ensure that the penalties imposed by law are really adequate and are strictly enforced.[57]

---

54   Ibid., at Article 11.
55   Ibid., at Article 12.
56   Ibid., at Article 13.
57   Ibid., at Article 25.

Abolition of Forced Labour Convention (No. 105)

The Preamble of the Abolition of Forced Labour Convention, 1957 (No. 105) states:

> The General Conference of the International Labour Organisation,
>
> Having been convened at Geneva by the Governing Body of the International Labour Office, and having met in its Fortieth Session on 5 June 1957, and
>
> Having considered the question of forced labour, which is the fourth item on the agenda of the session, and
>
> Having noted the provisions of the Forced Labour Convention, 1930, and
>
> Having noted that the Slavery Convention, 1926, provides that all necessary measures shall be taken to prevent compulsory or forced labour from developing into conditions analogous to slavery and that the Supplementary Convention on the Abolition of Slavery, the Slave Trade and Institutions and Practices Similar to Slavery, 1956, provides for the complete abolition of debt bondage and serfdom, and
>
> Having noted that the Protection of Wages Convention, 1949, provides that wages shall be paid regularly and prohibits methods of payment which deprive the worker of a genuine possibility of terminating his employment, and
>
> Having decided upon the adoption of further proposals with regard to the abolition of certain forms of forced or compulsory labour constituting a violation of the rights of man referred to in the Charter of the United Nations and enunciated by the Universal Declaration of Human Rights, and
>
> Having determined that these proposals shall take the form of an international Convention,
>
> adopts this twenty-fifth day of June of the year one thousand nine hundred and fifty-seven the following Convention, which may be cited as the Abolition of Forced Labour Convention, 1957.[58]

Duties are imposed under Article 1:

> 1. Each Member of the International Labour Organisation which ratifies this Convention undertakes to suppress and not to make use of any form of forced or compulsory labour
>
> (a) as a means of political coercion or education or as a punishment for holding or expressing political views or views ideologically opposed to the established political, social or economic system;
>
> (b) as a method of mobilising and using labour for purposes of economic development;
>
> (c) as a means of labour discipline;
>
> (d) as a punishment for having participated in strikes;

---

58   Abolition of Forced Labour Convention, at the Preamble.

(e) as a means of racial, social, national or religious discrimination.[59]

Finally, Article 2 holds:

> 2. Each Member of the International Labour Organisation which ratifies this Convention undertakes to take effective measures to secure the immediate and complete abolition of forced or compulsory labour as specified in Article 1 of this Convention.[60]

The International Labour Organization (ILO) has sponsored the two key instruments of international law on child labor: firstly, the 1973 Minimum Age Convention No. 138, which establishes the obligation for countries to work towards a minimum age of 15 for legal employment; and secondly, the 1999 Convention No. 182 for the Elimination of the Worst Forms of Child Labour, which calls on governments to identify and quantify the incidence of such child labor, backed by national plans for its elimination by 2016.

Minimum Age Convention (No. 138)

The Minimum Age Convention, 1973 (No. 138), entitled the Convention concerning Minimum Age for Admission to Employment, entered into force on 19 June 1976. The Preamble states:

> The General Conference of the International Labour Organisation,
> Having been convened at Geneva by the Governing Body of the International Labour Office, and having met in its Fifty-eighth Session on 6 June 1973, and
> Having decided upon the adoption of certain proposals with regard to minimum age for admission to employment, which is the fourth item on the agenda of the session, and
> Noting the terms of the Minimum Age (Industry) Convention, 1919, the Minimum Age (Sea) Convention, 1920, the Minimum Age (Agriculture) Convention, 1921, the Minimum Age (Trimmers and Stokers) Convention, 1921, the Minimum Age (Non-Industrial Employment) Convention, 1932, the Minimum Age (Sea) Convention (Revised), 1936, the Minimum Age (Industry) Convention (Revised), 1937, the Minimum Age (Non-Industrial Employment) Convention (Revised), 1937, the Minimum Age (Fishermen) Convention, 1959, and the Minimum Age (Underground Work) Convention, 1965, and
> Considering that the time has come to establish a general instrument on the subject, which would gradually replace the existing ones applicable to limited economic sectors, with a view to achieving the total abolition of child labour, and

---

59   Ibid., at Article 1.
60   Ibid., at Article 2.

Having determined that these proposals shall take the form of an international Convention,

adopts this twenty-sixth day of June of the year one thousand nine hundred and seventy-three the following Convention, which may be cited as the Minimum Age Convention, 1973.[61]

A national policy for all Member States to combat child labor is envisioned under Article 1:

1. Each Member for which this Convention is in force undertakes to pursue a national policy designed to ensure the effective abolition of child labour and to raise progressively the minimum age for admission to employment or work to a level consistent with the fullest physical and mental development of young persons.[62]

Further, under Article 2, a minimum age is to be specified by all Member States:

2.1. Each Member which ratifies this Convention shall specify, in a declaration appended to its ratification, a minimum age for admission to employment or work within its territory and on means of transport registered in its territory; subject to Articles 4 to 8 of this Convention, no one under that age shall be admitted to employment or work in any occupation.

2. Each Member which has ratified this Convention may subsequently notify the Director-General of the International Labour Office, by further declarations, that it specifies a minimum age higher than that previously specified.

3. The minimum age specified in pursuance of paragraph 1 of this Article shall not be less than the age of completion of compulsory schooling and, in any case, shall not be less than 15 years.

4. Notwithstanding the provisions of paragraph 3 of this Article, a Member whose economy and educational facilities are insufficiently developed may, after consultation with the organisations of employers and workers concerned, where such exist, initially specify a minimum age of 14 years.

5. Each Member which has specified a minimum age of 14 years in pursuance of the provisions of the preceding paragraph shall include in its reports on the application of this Convention submitted under article 22 of the Constitution of the International Labour Organisation a statement

(a) that its reason for doing so subsists; or

(b) that it renounces its right to avail itself of the provisions in question as from a stated date.[63]

---

61   Minimum Age Convention, at the Preamble.
62   Ibid., at Article 1.
63   Ibid., at Article 2.

However, under Article 3, the minimum for any dangerous work shall not be less than 18 years:

> 3.1. The minimum age for admission to any type of employment or work which by its nature or the circumstances in which it is carried out is likely to jeopardise the health, safety or morals of young persons shall not be less than 18 years.
>
> 2. The types of employment or work to which paragraph 1 of this Article applies shall be determined by national laws or regulations or by the competent authority, after consultation with the organisations of employers and workers concerned, where such exist.
>
> 3. Notwithstanding the provisions of paragraph 1 of this Article, national laws or regulations or the competent authority may, after consultation with the organisations of employers and workers concerned, where such exist, authorise employment or work as from the age of 16 years on condition that the health, safety and morals of the young persons concerned are fully protected and that the young persons have received adequate specific instruction or vocational training in the relevant branch of activity.[64]

Several exceptions exist under the Convention. Article 4 allows for some flexibility for limited categories of employment:

> 4.1. In so far as necessary, the competent authority, after consultation with the organisations of employers and workers concerned, where such exist, may exclude from the application of this Convention limited categories of employment or work in respect of which special and substantial problems of application arise.
>
> 2. Each Member which ratifies this Convention shall list in its first report on the application of the Convention submitted under article 22 of the Constitution of the International Labour Organisation any categories which may have been excluded in pursuance of paragraph 1 of this Article, giving the reasons for such exclusion, and shall state in subsequent reports the position of its law and practice in respect of the categories excluded and the extent to which effect has been given or is proposed to be given to the Convention in respect of such categories.
>
> 3. Employment or work covered by Article 3 of this Convention shall not be excluded from the application of the Convention in pursuance of this Article.[65]

An exception exists for insufficiently developed Member States under Article 5:

> 5.1. A Member whose economy and administrative facilities are insufficiently developed may, after consultation with the organisations of employers and

---

64   Ibid., at Article 3.
65   Ibid., at Article 4.

workers concerned, where such exist, initially limit the scope of application of this Convention.

2. Each Member which avails itself of the provisions of paragraph 1 of this Article shall specify, in a declaration appended to its ratification, the branches of economic activity or types of undertakings to which it will apply the provisions of the Convention.

3. The provisions of the Convention shall be applicable as a minimum to the following: mining and quarrying; manufacturing; construction; electricity, gas and water; sanitary services; transport, storage and communication; and plantations and other agricultural undertakings mainly producing for commercial purposes, but excluding family and small-scale holdings producing for local consumption and not regularly employing hired workers.

4. Any Member which has limited the scope of application of this Convention in pursuance of this Article

(a) shall indicate in its reports under Article 22 of the Constitution of the International Labour Organisation the general position as regards the employment or work of young persons and children in the branches of activity which are excluded from the scope of application of this Convention and any progress which may have been made towards wider application of the provisions of the Convention;

(b) may at any time formally extend the scope of application by a declaration addressed to the Director-General of the International Labour Office.[66]

An exception exists for educational reasons under Article 6:

6. This Convention does not apply to work done by children and young persons in schools for general, vocational or technical education or in other training institutions, or to work done by persons at least 14 years of age in undertakings, where such work is carried out in accordance with conditions prescribed by the competent authority, after consultation with the organisations of employers and workers concerned, where such exist, and is an integral part of

(a) a course of education or training for which a school or training institution is primarily responsible;

(b) a programme of training mainly or entirely in an undertaking, which programme has been approved by the competent authority; or

(c) a programme of guidance or orientation designed to facilitate the choice of an occupation or of a line of training.[67]

An exception is provided for those between the ages of 13 and 17 under certain conditions under Article 7:

---

66   Ibid., at Article 5.
67   Ibid., at Article 6.

7.1. National laws or regulations may permit the employment or work of persons 13 to 15 years of age on light work which is

(a) not likely to be harmful to their health or development; and

(b) not such as to prejudice their attendance at school, their participation in vocational orientation or training programmes approved by the competent authority or their capacity to benefit from the instruction received.

2. National laws or regulations may also permit the employment or work of persons who are at least 15 years of age but have not yet completed their compulsory schooling on work which meets the requirements set forth in sub-paragraphs (a) and (b) of paragraph 1 of this Article.

3. The competent authority shall determine the activities in which employment or work may be permitted under paragraphs 1 and 2 of this Article and shall prescribe the number of hours during which and the conditions in which such employment or work may be undertaken.

4. Notwithstanding the provisions of paragraphs 1 and 2 of this Article, a Member which has availed itself of the provisions of paragraph 4 of Article 2 may, for as long as it continues to do so, substitute the ages 12 and 14 for the ages 13 and 15 in paragraph 1 and the age 14 for the age 15 in paragraph 2 of this Article.[68]

Further, an exception is permitted for children in artistic performances under Article 8:

8.1. After consultation with the organisations of employers and workers concerned, where such exist, the competent authority may, by permits granted in individual cases, allow exceptions to the prohibition of employment or work provided for in Article 2 of this Convention, for such purposes as participation in artistic performances.

2. Permits so granted shall limit the number of hours during which and prescribe the conditions in which employment or work is allowed.[69]

Finally, Article 9 calls for all necessary measures for enforcement:

9.1. All necessary measures, including the provision of appropriate penalties, shall be taken by the competent authority to ensure the effective enforcement of the provisions of this Convention.

2. National laws or regulations or the competent authority shall define the persons responsible for compliance with the provisions giving effect to the Convention.

3. National laws or regulations or the competent authority shall prescribe the registers or other documents which shall be kept and made available by the employer; such registers or documents shall contain the names and ages or dates

---

68   Ibid., at Article 7.
69   Ibid., at Article 8.

of birth, duly certified wherever possible, of persons whom he employs or who work for him and who are less than 18 years of age.[70]

Worst Forms of Child Labour Convention (No. 182)

The Worst Forms of Child Labour Convention, 1999 (No. 182), entitled the Convention concerning the Prohibition and Immediate Action for the Elimination of the Worst Forms of Child Labour, entered into force on 19 November 2000. The Preamble states:

> The General Conference of the International Labour Organization,
>
> Having been convened at Geneva by the Governing Body of the International Labour Office, and having met in its 87th Session on 1 June 1999, and
>
> Considering the need to adopt new instruments for the prohibition and elimination of the worst forms of child labour, as the main priority for national and international action, including international cooperation and assistance, to complement the Convention and the Recommendation concerning Minimum Age for Admission to Employment, 1973, which remain fundamental instruments on child labour, and
>
> Considering that the effective elimination of the worst forms of child labour requires immediate and comprehensive action, taking into account the importance of free basic education and the need to remove the children concerned from all such work and to provide for their rehabilitation and social integration while addressing the needs of their families, and
>
> Recalling the resolution concerning the elimination of child labour adopted by the International Labour Conference at its 83rd Session in 1996, and
>
> Recognizing that child labour is to a great extent caused by poverty and that the long-term solution lies in sustained economic growth leading to social progress, in particular poverty alleviation and universal education, and
>
> Recalling the Convention on the Rights of the Child adopted by the United Nations General Assembly on 20 November 1989, and
>
> Recalling the ILO Declaration on Fundamental Principles and Rights at Work and its Follow-up, adopted by the International Labour Conference at its 86th Session in 1998, and
>
> Recalling that some of the worst forms of child labour are covered by other international instruments, in particular the Forced Labour Convention, 1930, and the United Nations Supplementary Convention on the Abolition of Slavery, the Slave Trade, and Institutions and Practices Similar to Slavery, 1956, and
>
> Having decided upon the adoption of certain proposals with regard to child labour, which is the fourth item on the agenda of the session, and
>
> Having determined that these proposals shall take the form of an international Convention;

---

70   Ibid., at Article 9.

adopts this seventeenth day of June of the year one thousand nine hundred and ninety-nine the following Convention, which may be cited as the Worst Forms of Child Labour Convention, 1999.[71]

The role of Member States is outlined under Article 1:

1. Each Member which ratifies this Convention shall take immediate and effective measures to secure the prohibition and elimination of the worst forms of child labour as a matter of urgency.[72]

Child is defined under Article 2:

2. For the purposes of this Convention, the term child shall apply to all persons under the age of 18.[73]

The worst forms of child labor are defined under Article 3:

3. For the purposes of this Convention, the term the worst forms of child labour comprises:
(a) all forms of slavery or practices similar to slavery, such as the sale and trafficking of children, debt bondage and serfdom and forced or compulsory labour, including forced or compulsory recruitment of children for use in armed conflict;
(b) the use, procuring or offering of a child for prostitution, for the production of pornography or for pornographic performances;
(c) the use, procuring or offering of a child for illicit activities, in particular for the production and trafficking of drugs as defined in the relevant international treaties;
(d) work which, by its nature or the circumstances in which it is carried out, is likely to harm the health, safety or morals of children.[74]

Types of work are to be determined by national laws or by the competent authority under Article 4:

4.1. The types of work referred to under Article 3(d) shall be determined by national laws or regulations or by the competent authority, after consultation with the organizations of employers and workers concerned, taking into consideration relevant international standards, in particular Paragraphs 3 and 4 of the Worst Forms of Child Labour Recommendation, 1999.

---

71   Worst Forms of Child Labour Convention, at the Preamble.
72   Ibid., at Article 1.
73   Ibid., at Article 2.
74   Ibid., at Article 3.

2. The competent authority, after consultation with the organizations of employers and workers concerned, shall identify where the types of work so determined exist.

3. The list of the types of work determined under paragraph 1 of this Article shall be periodically examined and revised as necessary, in consultation with the organizations of employers and workers concerned.[75]

Monitoring mechanisms are stressed under Article 5:

5. Each Member shall, after consultation with employers' and workers' organizations, establish or designate appropriate mechanisms to monitor the implementation of the provisions giving effect to this Convention.[76]

In addition, programs of action are called for under Article 6:

6.1. Each Member shall design and implement programmes of action to eliminate as a priority the worst forms of child labour.

2. Such programmes of action shall be designed and implemented in consultation with relevant government institutions and employers' and workers' organizations, taking into consideration the views of other concerned groups as appropriate.[77]

Article 7 calls for all necessary measures for enforcement:

7.1. Each Member shall take all necessary measures to ensure the effective implementation and enforcement of the provisions giving effect to this Convention including the provision and application of penal sanctions or, as appropriate, other sanctions.

2. Each Member shall, taking into account the importance of education in eliminating child labour, take effective and time-bound measures to:

(a) prevent the engagement of children in the worst forms of child labour;

(b) provide the necessary and appropriate direct assistance for the removal of children from the worst forms of child labour and for their rehabilitation and social integration;

(c) ensure access to free basic education, and, wherever possible and appropriate, vocational training, for all children removed from the worst forms of child labour;

(d) identify and reach out to children at special risk; and

(e) take account of the special situation of girls.

---

75   Ibid., at Article 4.
76   Ibid., at Article 5.
77   Ibid., at Article 6.

3. Each Member shall designate the competent authority responsible for the implementation of the provisions giving effect to this Convention.[78]

Finally, Members are called to assist one another under Article 8:

8. Members shall take appropriate steps to assist one another in giving effect to the provisions of this Convention through enhanced international cooperation and/or assistance including support for social and economic development, poverty eradication programmes and universal education.[79]

The International Labour Organization estimates that the global number of child laborers stands at 306 million.[80] Roughly 70 percent of all 'children in employment', are classified as child laborers, because they are either under the minimum age for work or above that age and engaged in work that poses a threat to their health, safety or morals, or are subject to conditions of forced labor. Further, the number of children in hazardous work stands at 115 million. Children are more seriously affected by all the dangers that are faced by adult co-workers, because they differ in their anatomical, physiological and psychological characteristics.

One of the most important steps forward in recent years has been the overwhelming global consensus in support of 'Education for All': first, to ensure that youth can enter the workforce with the basic skills required to pursue a decent working life; and second, because if the minimum school leaving age is lower than the national general minimum age for entry into employment, child labor will be an inevitable result. Education is central to the worldwide movement against child labor. In terms of international trade measures, there is a linkage between trade policy and child labor. Addressing the problem of child labor in value chains, all the way from raw materials to retailing, including transportation, and not simply in supply chains, would entail supporting importing companies to monitor working conditions throughout the value chain, including at the beginning, where raw materials are produced, to the retailing of the finished product.[81]

Hague Global Child Labour Conference, Towards a World Without Child Labour

The Hague Global Child Labour Conference, Towards a World without Child Labour, was held in 2010. The Preamble of Mapping the Road to 2016, Roadmap for Achieving the Elimination of the Worst Forms of Child Labour by 2016, states:

---

78   Ibid., at Article 7.

79   Ibid., at Article 8.

80   International Labour Office, Accelerating Action against Child Labour, Global Report under the follow-up to the ILO Declaration on Fundamental Principles and Rights at Work 2010.

81   Ibid.

A new momentum is necessary if the world is to attain the goal of eliminating the worst forms of child labour by 2016 as agreed upon by the ILO tripartite constituents in the Global Action Plan. Around the world, 215 million boys and girls are engaged in child labour. One hundred and fifteen million of these children are exposed to its worst forms. Removing these children from the worst forms and offering them a future without child labour is an urgent priority.

We, participants at the *Global Child Labour Conference 2010. Towards a world without child labour, Mapping the road to 2016*, representatives from governments, employers' and workers' organizations, non-governmental and other civil society organizations, regional and international organizations, have gathered in the Hague, the Netherlands, on 10 and 11 May 2010, to take stock of progress made since the adoption of the ILO Worst Forms of Child Labour Convention, 1999 (No. 182), to assess remaining obstacles and to agree on measures to accelerate progress towards the elimination of the worst forms of child labour by 2016, while affirming the overarching goal of the effective abolition of child labour, which is reflected in the ILO Declaration on Fundamental Principles and Rights at Work (1998) and ILO Convention, 1973 (No. 138) to which ILO Convention, 1999 (No. 182) is complementary, and

Considering that action to eliminate the worst forms of child labour is most effective and sustainable when it is situated within action to eliminate all child labour, including through area-based and sector-based programmes, and

Acknowledging that the effective abolition of child labour is a moral necessity and that all ILO members have an obligation to respect, promote and realize that principle; that it can yield high social and economic returns, and that eradicating child labour – and providing the alternative of education and training, and decent work for adults and children of working age – contributes to households breaking out of the cycle of poverty, and helps countries advance human development, and

Recognizing that the international community has identified child labour as a significant impediment to the realization of children's rights, national development and the attainment of the Millennium Development Goals, particularly those related to poverty alleviation, education, gender equality and HIV/AIDS, and recognizing furthermore that the ILO Worst Forms of Child Labour Convention, 1999 (No. 182) and its accompanying Recommendation (No. 190) reflect a global consensus that immediate and effective measures are required to secure the prohibition and elimination of the worst forms of child labour as a matter of urgency, and

Noting that over the past decade action against the worst forms of child labour has been implemented in all parts of the world and that this has led to significant progress; that this demonstrates that the fight against child labour can be won with sound policy choices and substantial national and international resource commitments, and when capitalizing on new opportunities, such as the G-20 summits and the Global Jobs Pact, and

Acknowledging the available data concerning the incidence of child labour, by sector, with the highest incidence of child labour in agriculture (60%), and 26%

in services, while recognizing the need for more data collection covering hard-to-reach children including in domestic work, slavery, sexual exploitation and illicit activities, and

Agreeing that with six years remaining until the target date of 2016 for the elimination of the worst forms of child labour, it is imperative to substantially upscale and accelerate action, given the overall pace of progress and that the global economic crisis puts recent progress at risk, and

Recognizing further that now, more than ever, political leadership is needed to achieve the elimination of the worst forms of child labour, and that governments in partnership with all other relevant actors need to act swiftly and with determination in this endeavour, particularly in the informal economy where most child labour occurs, and

Acknowledging that international cooperation and/or assistance among Members for the prohibition and effective elimination of the worst forms of child labour should complement national efforts and may, as appropriate, be developed and implemented in consultation with employers' and workers' organizations,

Declare that we will substantially increase efforts to ensure that we achieve the goal of eliminating the worst forms of child labour by 2016 and we agree to this Roadmap, and we urge the international community to substantially increase its efforts in this regard.[82]

The guiding principles are:

Governments have the primary responsibility for enforcing the right to education for all children, and the elimination of the worst forms of child labour. The social partners and other civil society organisations, and international organisations have important roles in promoting and supporting such action.

Government responsibility should be assumed at the highest level and with the best interests of children in mind, taking into consideration the views of children and their families, and should include due attention to the most vulnerable children and the conditions that create their vulnerability. In doing so governments should assess the impact of relevant policies on the worst forms of child labour, taking into account gender and age, put in place preventive and time-bound measures and make adequate financial resources available to fight the worst forms of child labour, including through international cooperation.

In a globalized economy, government responsibility includes developing and strengthening policies and programmes, in consultation with social partners, that

---

82 The Hague Global Child Labour Conference, Towards a World without Child Labour, Mapping the Road to 2016, Roadmap for Achieving the Elimination of the Worst Forms of Child Labour by 2016, at the Preamble.

address child labour issues, in particular the worst forms, in international supply chains.

Government actions to combat child trafficking, prostitution, production of pornography and the trafficking of drugs should where necessary include international cooperation.

Governments should consider ways to address the potential vulnerability of children to, in particular, the worst forms of child labour, in the context of migratory flows.

All actors should work towards strengthening the world wide movement against child labour, including by using traditional and new media. They should, according to their expertise, raise awareness and sensitize the public on the rights of children to be free from child labour, the value of education and training, and the longer term costs of child labour, in terms of health, employment opportunities, persistent inequalities and intergenerational poverty.

There is no single policy that by itself will end the worst forms of child labour. However, evidence has shown that targeted action that simultaneously addresses the implementation and enforcement of legislation, the provision and accessibility of public services (including free, quality compulsory education, training and non-discriminatory social protection services), and the functioning of labour markets, yields high returns in the fight against child labour, including its worst forms. The elimination of child labour should therefore be integrated in broader policy frameworks at national and sub-national levels, and policy coordination should be strengthened through appropriate inter-ministerial mechanisms.[83]

Conclusion

In terms of child rights, the elimination of child labor is the goal. In order to protect human rights, it is necessary for States to avoid resorting to reservations of international agreements. The full enjoyment of equal rights by children is undermined by the discrepancies between some national legislation, and international law and international instruments on human rights. We must eliminate the perpetuation of de facto and de jure inequality to allow for the full enjoyment of human rights and fundamental freedoms in *Little Angels*.

---

83   Ibid.

Chapter 3
Little Angels in the United Nations

Introduction

In the quest for respect for our children and in the fight against child discrimination in *Little Angels*, this chapter will examine children's issues in the United Nations. It will look at important United Nations legislation, including vital United Nations legislation dealing with child discrimination in the fight for child equality, namely the Universal Declaration of Human Rights; the Charter of the United Nations; the Statute of the International Court of Justice; the International Covenant on Civil and Political Rights; the Optional Protocol to the International Covenant on Civil and Political Rights; the International Covenant on Economic, Social and Cultural Rights; for minority children, the International Convention on the Elimination of All Forms of Racial Discrimination; and for female children, the Convention on the Elimination of All Forms of Discrimination against Women and the Optional Protocol to the Convention on the Elimination of All Forms of Discrimination against Women; of paramount importance to children, the Convention on the Rights of the Child; the Optional Protocol to the Convention on the Rights of the Child on the involvement of children in armed conflict; the Optional Protocol to the Convention on the Rights of the Child on the sale of children, child prostitution and child pornography; and the Protocol to prevent, suppress and punish trafficking in persons, especially women and children, supplementing the United Nations Convention against Transnational Organized Crime. Through the work of the United Nations, international laws have been developed which require countries to work towards the elimination of all forms of discrimination, including child discrimination.

Universal Declaration of Human Rights

The Universal Declaration of Human Rights was adopted by the United Nations on 10 December 1948. The Preamble of the Universal Declaration of Human Rights states:

> Whereas recognition of the inherent dignity and of the equal and inalienable rights of all members of the human family is the foundation of freedom, justice and peace in the world,

Whereas disregard and contempt for human rights have resulted in barbarous acts which have outraged the conscience of mankind, and the advent of a world in which human beings shall enjoy freedom of speech and belief and freedom from fear and want has been proclaimed as the highest aspiration of the common people,

Whereas it is essential, if man is not to be compelled to have recourse, as a last resort, to rebellion against tyranny and oppression, that human rights should be protected by the rule of law,

Whereas it is essential to promote the development of friendly relations between nations,

Whereas the peoples of the United Nations have in the Charter reaffirmed their faith in fundamental human rights, in the dignity and worth of the human person and in the equal rights of men and women and have determined to promote social progress and better standards of life in larger freedom,

Whereas Member States have pledged themselves to achieve, in co-operation with the United Nations, the promotion of universal respect for and observance of human rights and fundamental freedoms,

Whereas a common understanding of these rights and freedoms is of the greatest importance for the full realization of this pledge.

The General Assembly of the United Nations proclaims:

This Universal Declaration of Human Rights as a common standard of achievement for all peoples and all nations, to the end that every individual and every organ of society, keeping this Declaration constantly in mind, shall strive by teaching and education to promote respect for these rights and freedoms and by progressive measures, national and international, to secure their universal and effective recognition and observance, both among the peoples of Member States themselves and among the peoples of territories under their jurisdiction.[1]

Internationally, the fundamental concept of human rights is one which human beings have striven both to suppress and promote. Article 1 recognizes human beings as free and equal:

---

1   United Nations, Universal Declaration of Human Rights, at the Preamble.

1. All human beings are born free and equal in dignity and rights. They are endowed with reason and conscience and should act towards one another in a spirit of brotherhood.[2]

In the fight for child equality, Article 2 is a helpful tool, since it holds that:

2. Everyone is entitled to all the rights and freedoms set forth in this Declaration, without distinction of any kind, such as race, color, sex, language, religion, political or other opinion, national or social origin, property, birth or other status.[3]

Importantly, equality before the law without discrimination is guaranteed in Article 7:

7. All are equal before the law and are entitled without any discrimination to equal protection of the law. All are entitled to equal protection against any discrimination in violation of this Declaration and against any incitement to such discrimination.[4]

In the effort to redress discriminatory action, Article 8 establishes that everyone has the right to an effective remedy by the competent national tribunals for acts violating the fundamental rights granted him by the constitution or by law.[5]

Article 16 guarantees equality between men and women, boys and girls without limitation:

16(1) Men and women of full age, without any limitation due to race, nationality or religion, have the right to marry and to found a family. They are entitled to equal rights as to marriage, during marriage and at its dissolution.
(2) Marriage shall be entered into only with the free and full consent of the intending spouses.
(3) The family is the natural and fundamental group unit of society and is entitled to protection by society and the State.[6]

Employment rights, including equal pay for equal work, are protected under Article 23:

23. (1) Everyone has the right to work, to free choice of employment, to just and favorable conditions of work and to protection against unemployment.

---

2   Ibid., at Article 1.
3   Ibid., at Article 2.
4   Ibid., at Article 7.
5   Ibid., at Article 8.
6   Ibid., at Article 16.

(2) Everyone, without any discrimination, has the right to equal pay for equal work.

(3) Everyone who works has the right to just and favorable remuneration ensuring for himself and his family an existence worthy of human dignity, and supplemented, if necessary, by other means of social protection.

(4) Everyone has the right to form and to join trade unions for the protection of his interests.[7]

The right to education as a means of enhancement and advancement is established in Article 26:

26(1) Everyone has the right to education, in that education shall be free, at least in the elementary and fundamental stages, and elementary education shall be compulsory. Technical and professional education shall be made generally available and higher education shall be equally accessible to all on the basis of merit.

(2) Education shall be directed to the full development of the human personality and to the strengthening of respect for human rights and fundamental freedoms; it shall promote understanding, tolerance and friendship among all nations, racial or religious groups, and shall further the activities of the United Nations for the maintenance of peace.

(3) Parents have a prior right to choose the kind of education that shall be given to their children.[8]

Charter of the United Nations

The Preamble of the Charter of the United Nations, signed on 26 June 1945, states:

We the Peoples of the United Nations determined
to save succeeding generations from the scourge of war, which twice in our lifetime has brought untold sorrow to mankind, and
to reaffirm faith in fundamental human rights, in the dignity and worth of the human person, in the equal rights of men and women and of nations large and small, and
to establish conditions under which justice and respect for the obligations arising from treaties and other sources of international law can be maintained, and
to promote social progress and better standards of life in larger freedom,

And for these ends

---

7   Ibid., at Article 23.
8   Ibid., at Article 26.

to practice tolerance and live together in peace with one another as good neighbours, and

to unite our strength to maintain international peace and security, and

to ensure, by the acceptance of principles and the institution of methods, that armed force shall not be used, save in the common interest, and

to employ international machinery for the promotion of the economic and social advancement of all peoples,

Have resolved to combine our efforts to accomplish these aims

Accordingly, our respective Governments, through representatives assembled in the city of San Francisco, who have exhibited their full powers found to be in good and due form, have agreed to the present Charter of the United Nations and do hereby establish an international organization to be known as the United Nations.[9]

The purposes of the United Nations as outlined in Article 1:

1(1) To maintain international peace and security, and to that end: to take effective collective measures for the prevention and removal of threats to the peace, and for the suppression of acts of aggression or other breaches of the peace, and to bring about by peaceful means, and in conformity with the principles of justice and international law, adjustment or settlement of international disputes or situations which might lead to a breach of the peace;

(2) To develop friendly relations among nations based on respect for the principle of equal rights and self-determination of peoples, and to take other appropriate measures to strengthen universal peace;

(3) To achieve international cooperation in solving international problems of an economic, social, cultural, or humanitarian character, and in promoting and encouraging respect for human rights and for fundamental freedoms for all without distinction as to race, sex, language, or religion; and

(4) To be a centre for harmonizing the actions of nations in the attainment of these common ends.[10]

In terms of international economic and social cooperation, Article 55 guarantees equal rights in employment:

55. With a view to the creation of conditions of stability and well-being which are necessary for peaceful and friendly relations among nations based on respect for the principle of equal rights and self-determination of peoples, the United Nations shall promote:

---

9   United Nations, Charter of the United Nations, at the Preamble.

10   Ibid., at Article 1.

a. higher standards of living, full employment, and conditions of economic and social progress and development;

b. solutions of international economic, social, health, and related problems; and international cultural and educational cooperation; and

c. universal respect for, and observance of, human rights and fundamental freedoms for all without distinction as to race, sex, language, or religion.[11]

Importantly, the International Court of Justice (ICJ) is established under Article 92 as the principal judicial organ of the United Nations:

92. The International Court of Justice shall be the principal judicial organ of the United Nations. It shall function in accordance with the annexed Statute, which is based upon the Statute of the Permanent Court of International Justice and forms an integral part of the present Charter.[12]

Further, Article 94 binds Member States in their compliance with the decisions of the ICJ:

94.1. Each Member of the United Nations undertakes to comply with the decision of the International Court of Justice in any case to which it is a party.
2. If any party to a case fails to perform the obligations incumbent upon it under a judgment rendered by the Court, the other party may have recourse to the Security Council, which may, if it deems necessary, make recommendations or decide upon measures to be taken to give effect to the judgment.[13]

Finally, according to Article 95, Member States may go further in finding solutions:

95. Nothing in the present Charter shall prevent Members of the United Nations from entrusting the solution of their differences to other tribunals by virtue of agreements already in existence or which may be concluded in the future.[14]

Statute of the International Court of Justice

The Statute of the International Court of Justice was signed on 26 June 1945. Article 1 holds:

---

11   Ibid., at Article 55.
12   Ibid., at Article 92.
13   Ibid., at Article 94.
14   Ibid., at Article 95.

1. The International Court of Justice established by the Charter of the United Nations as the principal judicial organ of the United Nations shall be constituted and shall function in accordance with the provisions of the present Statute.[15]

As to competence of the Court, Article 34 states:

34.1. Only states may be parties in cases before the Court.

2. The Court, subject to and in conformity with its Rules, may request of public international organizations information relevant to cases before it, and shall receive such information presented by such organizations on their own initiative.[16]

Further, jurisdiction of the Court is established under Article 36:

36.1. The jurisdiction of the Court comprises all cases which the parties refer to it and all matters specially provided for in the Charter of the United Nations or in treaties and conventions in force.

2. The states parties to the present Statute may at any time declare that they recognize as compulsory ipso facto and without special agreement, in relation to any other state accepting the same obligation, the jurisdiction of the Court in all legal disputes concerning:

a. the interpretation of a treaty;

b. any question of international law;

c. the existence of any fact which, if established, would constitute a breach of an international obligation;

d. the nature or extent of the reparation to be made for the breach of an international obligation.

3. The declarations referred to above may be made unconditionally or on condition of reciprocity on the part of several or certain states, or for a certain time.

…

5. Declarations made under Article 36 of the Statute of the Permanent Court of International Justice and which are still in force shall be deemed, as between the parties to the present Statute, to be acceptances of the compulsory jurisdiction of the International Court of Justice for the period which they still have to run and in accordance with their terms.

6. In the event of a dispute as to whether the Court has jurisdiction, the matter shall be settled by the decision of the Court.[17]

Finally, as to the application of choice of law, Article 38 maintains:

---

15 United Nations, Statute of the International Court of Justice, at Article 1.

16 Ibid., at Article 34.

17 Ibid., at Article 36.

38.1. The Court, whose function is to decide in accordance with international law such disputes as are submitted to it, shall apply:

a. international conventions, whether general or particular, establishing rules expressly recognized by the contesting states;

b. international custom, as evidence of a general practice accepted as law;

c. the general principles of law recognized by civilized nations;

d. subject to the provisions of Article 59, judicial decisions and the teachings of the most highly qualified publicists of the various nations, as subsidiary means for the determination of rules of law.

2. This provision shall not prejudice the power of the Court to decide a case *ex aequo et bono*, if the parties agree thereto.[18]

International Covenant on Civil and Political Rights (ICCPR)

The International Covenant on Civil and Political Rights was adopted and opened for signature, ratification and accession by the United Nations General Assembly in resolution 2200A (XXI) of 16 December 1966, and entered into force on 23 March 1976. The Covenant is divided into six parts: Part I reaffirms the right of self-determination; Part II formulates general obligations by States Parties, notably to implement the Covenant through legislative and other measures, to provide effective remedies to victims and to ensure equality, and it restricts the possibility of derogation; Part III outlines the general civil and political rights, including the right to life, the prohibition of torture, the right to liberty and security of person, the right to freedom of movement, the right to a fair hearing, the right to privacy, the right to freedom of religion, freedom of expression, freedom of peaceful assembly, the right to family life, the rights of children to special protection, the right to participate in the conduct of public affairs, the overarching right to equal treatment, and the special rights of persons belonging to ethnic, religious and linguistic minorities; Part IV regulates the election of members of the Human Rights Committee, the State reporting procedure and the interstate complaints mechanism; Part V stipulates that nothing in the Covenant shall be interpreted as impairing the inherent right of all peoples to fully enjoy and to utilize their natural resources; and Part VI provides that the Covenant shall extend to all parts of federal States and sets out the amendment procedure. The Covenant is not subject to denunciation.

In the Preamble of the Covenant on Civil and Political Rights, which includes the enjoyment of cultural rights, the States Parties to the present Covenant undertake the agreement:

Considering that, in accordance with the principles proclaimed in the Charter of the United Nations, recognition of the inherent dignity and of the equal and

---

18   Ibid., at Article 38.

inalienable rights of all members of the human family is the foundation of freedom, justice and peace in the world,

Recognizing that these rights derive from the inherent dignity of the human person,

Recognizing that, in accordance with the Universal Declaration of Human Rights, the ideal of free human beings enjoying civil and political freedom and freedom from fear and want can only be achieved if conditions are created whereby everyone may enjoy his civil and political rights, as well as his economic, social and cultural rights,

Considering the obligation of States under the Charter of the United Nations to promote universal respect for, and observance of, human rights and freedoms,

Realizing that the individual, having duties to other individuals and to the community to which he belongs, is under a responsibility to strive for the promotion and observance of the rights recognized in the present Covenant.[19]

Article 1 protects the right of self-determination and cultural development:

1(1) All peoples have the right of self-determination. By virtue of that right they freely determine their political status and freely pursue their economic, social and cultural development.
(2) All peoples may, for their own ends, freely dispose of their natural wealth and resources without prejudice to any obligations arising out of international economic co-operation, based upon the principle of mutual benefit, and international law. In no case may a people be deprived of its own means of subsistence.
(3) The States Parties to the present Covenant, including those having responsibility for the administration of Non-Self-Governing and Trust Territories, shall promote the realization of the right of self-determination, and shall respect that right, in conformity with the provisions of the Charter of the United Nations.[20]

Further, the obligations of Member States are established in Article 2 without regard to national origin, in that:

2(1) Each State Party to the present Covenant undertakes to respect and to ensure to all individuals within its territory and subject to its jurisdiction the

---

19   United Nations, International Covenant on Civil and Political Rights, at the Preamble.
20   Ibid., at Article 1.

rights recognized in the present Covenant, without distinction of any kind, such as race, colour, sex, language, religion, political or other opinion, national or social origin, property, birth or other status.

(2) Where not already provided for by existing legislative or other measures, each State Party to the present Covenant undertakes to take the necessary steps, in accordance with its constitutional processes and with the provisions of the present Covenant, to adopt such laws or other measures as may be necessary to give effect to the rights recognized in the present Covenant.

(3) Each State Party to the present Covenant undertakes:

(a) To ensure that any person whose rights or freedoms as herein recognized are violated shall have an effective remedy, notwithstanding that the violation has been committed by persons acting in an official capacity;

(b) To ensure that any person claiming such a remedy shall have his right thereto determined by competent judicial, administrative or legislative authorities, or by any other competent authority provided for by the legal system of the State, and to develop the possibilities of judicial remedy;

(c) To ensure that the competent authorities shall enforce such remedies when granted.[21]

Equality before the law regardless of national origin is guaranteed under Article 26:

26. All persons are equal before the law and are entitled without any discrimination to the equal protection of the law. In this respect, the law shall prohibit any discrimination and guarantee to all persons equal and effective protection against discrimination on any ground such as race, color, sex, language, religion, political or other opinion, national or social origin, property, birth or other status.[22]

Importantly, Article 24 guarantees the right of all including children to be free from discrimination:

24(1) Every child shall have, without any discrimination as to race, colour, sex, language, religion, national or social origin, property or birth, the right to such measures of protection as are required by his status as a minor, on the part of his family, society and the State.[23]

The Human Rights Committee is established under Article 28:

---

21   Ibid., at Article 2.
22   Ibid., at Article 26.
23   Ibid., at Article 24.

28.1. There shall be established a Human Rights Committee (hereafter referred to in the present Covenant as the Committee). It shall consist of eighteen members and shall carry out the functions hereinafter provided.

2. The Committee shall be composed of nationals of the States Parties to the present Covenant who shall be persons of high moral character and recognized competence in the field of human rights, consideration being given to the usefulness of the participation of some persons having legal experience.

3. The members of the Committee shall be elected and shall serve in their personal capacity.[24]

Finally, various procedures of recourse are permitted under Article 44:

44. The provisions for the implementation of the present Covenant shall apply without prejudice to the procedures prescribed in the field of human rights by or under the constituent instruments and the conventions of the United Nations and of the specialized agencies and shall not prevent the States Parties to the present Covenant from having recourse to other procedures for settling a dispute in accordance with general or special international agreements in force between them.[25]

Optional Protocol to the International Covenant on Civil and Political Rights

The Optional Protocol to the International Covenant on Civil and Political Rights (ICCPR) of 16 December 1966 allows individuals, whose countries are party to the ICCPR and the protocol, who claim their rights under the ICCPR have been violated, and who have exhausted all domestic remedies, to submit written communications to the UN Human Rights Committee. States Parties to the ICCPR undertake to ensure that all, including children, enjoy all the civil and political rights in the Covenant on a basis of equality.[26]

International Covenant on Economic, Social and Cultural Rights (ICESCR)

The International Covenant on Economic, Social and Cultural Rights was adopted and opened for signature, ratification and accession by General Assembly resolution 2200A (XXI) of 16 December 1966, and entered into force 3 January 1976.[27] In a

---

24   Ibid., at Article 28.
25   Ibid., at Article 44.
26   United Nations, Optional Protocol to the International Covenant on Civil and Political Rights.
27   United Nations, International Covenant on Economic, Social and Cultural Rights.

world where, according to the United Nations Development Programme (UNDP), 'a fifth of the developing world's population goes hungry every night, a quarter lacks access to even a basic necessity like safe drinking water, and a third lives in a state of abject poverty at such a margin of human existence that words simply fail to describe it',[28] the importance of renewed attention and commitment to the full realization of economic, social and cultural rights is self-evident with such marginalization.

In the Preamble of the International Covenant on Economic, Social and Cultural Rights, the States Parties to the present Covenant undertake the agreement:

> Considering that, in accordance with the principles proclaimed in the Charter of the United Nations, recognition of the inherent dignity and of the equal and inalienable rights of all the members of the human family is the foundation of freedom, justice and peace in world,
>
> Recognizing that these rights derive from the inherent dignity of the human person,
>
> Recognizing that, in accordance with the Universal Declaration of Human Rights, the ideal of free human beings enjoying freedom from fear and want can only be achieved if conditions are created whereby everyone may enjoy his economic, social and cultural rights, as well as his civil and political rights and freedom,
>
> Realizing that the individual, having duties to other individuals and to the community to which he belongs, is under a responsibility to strive for the promotion and observance of the rights recognized in the present Covenant.[29]

Article 1 covers self-determination:

> 1(1) All peoples have the right of self-determination. By virtue of that right they freely determine their political status and freely pursue their economic, social and cultural development.
>
> (2) All peoples may, for their own ends, freely dispose of their natural wealth and resources without prejudice to any obligations arising out of international economic co-operation, based upon the principle of mutual benefit, and international law. In no case may a people be deprived of its own means of subsistence.

---

28   United Nations Development Programme, *Human Development Report*, Oxford University Press, Oxford, 1994, p. 2.

29   United Nations, International Covenant on Economic, Social and Cultural Rights, at the Preamble.

(3) The States Parties to the present Covenant, including those having responsibility for the administration of Non-Self-Governing and Trust Territories, shall promote the realization of the right of self-determination, and shall respect that right, in conformity with the provisions of the Charter of the United Nations.[30]

Importantly, Article 2 promotes human rights:

2(1) Each State Party to the present Covenant undertakes to take steps, individually and through international assistance and co-operation, especially economic and technical, to the maximum of its available resources, with a view to achieving progressively the full realization of the rights recognized in the present Covenant by all appropriate means, including particularly the adoption of legislative measures.
(2) The States Parties to the present Covenant undertake to guarantee that the rights enunciated in the present Covenant will be exercised without discrimination of any kind as to race, colour, sex, language, religion, political or other opinion, national or social origin, property, birth or other status.
(3) Developing countries, with due regard to human rights and their national economy, may determine to what extent they would guarantee the economic rights recognized in the present Covenant to non-nationals.[31]

Additionally, mindful of child labor issues, Article 6 includes the important right to work:

6(1) The States Parties to the present Covenant recognize the right to work, which includes the right of everyone to the opportunity to gain his living by work which he freely chooses or accepts, and will take appropriate steps to safeguard this right.
(2) The steps to be taken by a State Party to the present Covenant to achieve the full realization of this right shall include technical and vocational guidance and training programmes, policies and techniques to achieve steady economic, social and cultural development and full and productive employment under conditions safeguarding fundamental political and economic freedoms to the individual.[32]

Article 7 is an important guarantee for equal rights in terms of equal pay and access to employment:

7. The States to the present Covenant recognize the right of everyone to the enjoyment of just and favorable conditions of work which ensure, in particular:

---

30   Ibid., at Article 1.
31   Ibid., at Article 2.
32   Ibid., at Article 6.

(a) Remuneration which provides all workers, as a minimum, with:

(i) Fair wages and equal remuneration for work of equal value without distinction of any kind, … with equal pay for equal work;

(ii) A decent living for themselves and their families in accordance with the provisions of the present Covenant;

(b) Safe and healthy working conditions;

(c) Equal opportunity for everyone to be promoted in his employment to an appropriate higher level, subject to no considerations other than those of seniority and competence;

(d) Rest, leisure and reasonable limitation of working hours and periodic holidays with pay, as well as remuneration for public holidays.[33]

Article 13 guarantees the right to education for enhancement of the person, vital to children:

13(1) The States Parties to the present Covenant recognize the right of everyone to education. They agree that education shall be directed to the full development of the human personality and the sense of its dignity, and shall strengthen the respect for human rights and fundamental freedoms. They further agree that education shall enable all persons to participate effectively in a free society, promote understanding, tolerance and friendship among all nations and all racial, ethnic or religious groups, and further the activities of the United Nations for the maintenance of peace.

(2) The States Parties to the present Covenant recognize that, with a view to achieving the full realization of this right:

(a) Primary education shall be compulsory and available free to all;

(b) Secondary education in its different forms, including technical and vocational secondary education, shall be made generally available and accessible to all by every appropriate means, and in particular by the progressive introduction of free education;

(c) Higher education shall be made equally accessible to all, on the basis of capacity, by every appropriate means, and in particular by the progressive introduction of free education;

(d) Fundamental education shall be encouraged or intensified as far as possible for those persons who have not received or completed the whole period of their primary education;

(e) The development of a system of schools at all levels shall be actively pursued, an adequate fellowship system shall be established, and the material conditions of teaching staff shall be continuously improved.

(3) The States Parties to the present Covenant undertake to have respect for the liberty of parents and, when applicable, legal guardians to choose for their children schools, other than those established by the public authorities, which

---

33 Ibid., at Article 7.

conform to such minimum educational standards as may be laid down or approved by the State and to ensure the religious and moral education of their children in conformity with their own convictions.

(4) No part of this article shall be construed so as to interfere with the liberty of individuals and bodies to establish and direct educational institutions, subject always to the observance of the principles set forth in paragraph I of this article and to the requirement that the education given in such institutions shall conform to such minimum standards as may be laid down by the State.[34]

International Convention on the Elimination of All Forms of Racial Discrimination (ICEAFRD)

Important for minority children who suffer double discrimination based on age and race/ethnicity, the International Convention on the Elimination of All Forms of Racial Discrimination was adopted on 21 December 1965.[35] It was the first human rights instrument to establish an international monitoring system and was also revolutionary in its provision of national measures toward the advancement of specific groups. The Preamble of the International Convention on the Elimination of All Forms of Racial Discrimination guarantees freedom from discrimination:

The States Parties to this Convention,

Considering that the Charter of the United Nations is based on the principles of the dignity and equality inherent in all human beings, and that all Member States have pledged themselves to take joint and separate action, in co-operation with the Organization, for the achievement of one of the purposes of the United Nations which is to promote and encourage universal respect for and observance of human rights and fundamental freedoms for all, without distinction as to race, sex, language or religion,

Considering that the Universal Declaration of Human Rights proclaims that all human beings are born free and equal in dignity and rights and that everyone is entitled to all the rights and freedoms set out therein, without distinction of any kind, in particular as to race, color or national origin,

Considering that all human beings are equal before the law and are entitled to equal protection of the law against any discrimination and against any incitement to discrimination,

---

34   Ibid., at Article 13.
35   United Nations, International Convention on the Elimination of All Forms of Racial Discrimination.

Considering that the United Nations has condemned colonialism and all practices of segregation and discrimination associated therewith, in whatever form and wherever they exist, and that the Declaration on the Granting of Independence to Colonial Countries and Peoples of 14 December 1960 (General Assembly resolution 1514 (XV)) has affirmed and solemnly proclaimed the necessity of bringing them to a speedy and unconditional end,

Considering that the United Nations Declaration on the Elimination of All Forms of Racial Discrimination of 20 November 1963 (General Assembly resolution 1904 (XVIII)) solemnly affirms the necessity of speedily eliminating racial discrimination throughout the world in all its forms and manifestations and of securing understanding of and respect for the dignity of the human person,

Convinced that any doctrine of superiority based on racial differentiation is scientifically false, morally condemnable, socially unjust and dangerous, and that there is no justification for racial discrimination, in theory or in practice, anywhere,

Reaffirming that discrimination between human beings on the grounds of race, color or ethnic origin is an obstacle to friendly and peaceful relations among nations and is capable of disturbing peace and security among peoples and the harmony of persons living side by side even within one and the same State,

Convinced that the existence of racial barriers is repugnant to the ideals of any human society,

Alarmed by manifestations of racial discrimination still in evidence in some areas of the world and by governmental policies based on racial superiority or hatred, such as policies of apartheid, segregation or separation,

Resolved to adopt all necessary measures for speedily eliminating racial discrimination in all its forms and manifestations, and to prevent and combat racist doctrines and practices in order to promote understanding between races and to build an international community free from all forms of racial segregation and racial discrimination,

Bearing in mind the Convention concerning Discrimination in respect of Employment and Occupation adopted by the International Labour Organization in 1958, and the Convention against Discrimination in Education adopted by the United Nations Educational, Scientific and Cultural Organization in 1960,

Desiring to implement the principles embodied in the United Nations Declaration on the Elimination of All Forms of Racial Discrimination and to secure the earliest adoption of practical measures to that end ...[36]

Article 1(1) defines racial discrimination:

1(1) In this Convention, the term 'racial discrimination' shall mean any distinction, exclusion, restriction or preference based on race, color, descent, or national or ethnic origin which has the purpose or effect of nullifying or impairing the recognition, enjoyment or exercise, on an equal footing, of human rights and fundamental freedoms in the political, economic, social, cultural or any other field of public life.
(2) This Convention shall not apply to distinctions, exclusions, restrictions or preferences made by a State Party to this Convention between citizens and non-citizens.
(3) Nothing in this Convention may be interpreted as affecting in any way the legal provisions of States Parties concerning nationality, citizenship or naturalization, provided that such provisions do not discriminate against any particular nationality.[37]

Further, affirmative action programs by way of special measures are covered under Article 1(4):

1(4) Special measures taken for the sole purpose of securing adequate advancement of certain racial or ethnic groups or individuals requiring such protection as may be necessary in order to ensure such groups or individuals equal enjoyment or exercise of human rights and fundamental freedoms shall not be deemed racial discrimination, provided, however, that such measures do not, as a consequence, lead to the maintenance of separate rights for different racial groups and that they shall not be continued after the objectives for which they were taken have been achieved.[38]

Article 2(1) outlines State commitments to equality, which include effective measures to end discriminatory laws:

2(1) States Parties condemn racial discrimination and undertake to pursue by all appropriate means and without delay a policy of eliminating racial discrimination in all its forms and promoting understanding among all races, and, to this end:
(a) Each State Party undertakes to engage in no act or practice of racial discrimination against persons, groups of persons or institutions and to ensure

36 Ibid., at the Preamble.
37 Ibid., at Article 1(1).
38 Ibid., at Article 1(4).

that all public authorities and public institutions, national and local, shall act in conformity with this obligation;

(b) Each State Party undertakes not to sponsor, defend or support racial discrimination by any persons or organizations;

(c) Each State Party shall take effective measures to review governmental, national and local policies, and to amend, rescind or nullify any laws and regulations which have the effect of creating or perpetuating racial discrimination wherever it exists;

(d) Each State Party shall prohibit and bring to an end, by all appropriate means, including legislation as required by circumstances, racial discrimination by any persons, group or organization;

(e) Each State Party undertakes to encourage, where appropriate, integrationist multi-racial organizations and movements and other means of eliminating barriers between races, and to discourage anything which tends to strengthen racial division.[39]

Parties are further bound to additional protection of groups under Article 2(2):

2(2) States Parties shall, when the circumstances so warrant, take, in the social, economic, cultural and other fields, special and concrete measures to ensure the adequate development and protection of certain racial groups or individuals belonging to them, for the purpose of guaranteeing them the full and equal enjoyment of human rights and fundamental freedoms. These measures shall in no case entail as a consequence the maintenance of unequal or separate rights for different racial groups after the objectives for which they were taken have been achieved.[40]

As well as the specific prohibition and elimination of discrimination, Article 5 guarantees the equal protection of the law through various rights:

5. In compliance with the fundamental obligations laid down in article 2 of this Convention, States Parties undertake to prohibit and to eliminate racial discrimination in all its forms and to guarantee the right of everyone, without distinction as to race, color, or national or ethnic origin, to equality before the law, notably in the enjoyment of the following rights:

(a) The right to equal treatment before the tribunals and all other organs administering justice;

(b) The right to security of person and protection by the State against violence or bodily harm, whether inflicted by government officials or by any individual, group or institution;

---

39   Ibid., at Article 2(1).
40   Ibid., at Article 2(2).

(c) Political rights, in particular the rights to participate in elections, to vote and to stand for election, on the basis of universal and equal suffrage, to take part in the Government as well as in the conduct of public affairs at any level and to have equal access to public service;

(d) Other civil rights, in particular:

(i) The right to freedom of movement and residence within the border of the State;

(ii) The right to leave any country, including one's own, and to return to one's country;

(iii) The right to nationality;

(iv) The right to marriage and choice of spouse;

(v) The right to own property alone as well as in association with others;

(vi) The right to inherit;

(vii) The right to freedom of thought, conscience and religion;

(viii) The right to freedom of opinion and expression;

(ix) The right to freedom of peaceful assembly and association;

(e) Economic, social and cultural rights, in particular:

(i) The rights to work, to free choice of employment, to just and favorable conditions of work, to protection against unemployment, to equal pay for equal work, to just and favorable remuneration;

(ii) The right to form and join trade unions;

(iii) The right to housing;

(iv) The right to public health, medical care, social security and social services;

(v) The right to education and training;

(vi) The right to equal participation in cultural activities;

(f) The right of access to any place or service intended for use by the general public, such as transport, hotels, restaurants, cafes, theatres and parks.[41]

Protection to people, including children, suffering from discrimination is guaranteed under Article 6 through the court system and its tribunals:

6. States Parties shall assure to everyone within their jurisdiction effective protection and remedies, through the competent national tribunals and other State institutions, against any acts of racial discrimination which violate his human rights and fundamental freedoms contrary to this Convention, as well as the right to seek from such tribunals just and adequate reparation or satisfaction for any damage suffered as a result of such discrimination.[42]

Importantly, in order to combat prejudices created by discrimination, certain measures are outlined in Article 7:

---

41 Ibid., at Article 5.
42 Ibid., at Article 6.

7. States Parties undertake to adopt immediate and effective measures, particularly in the fields of teaching, education, culture and information, with a view to combating prejudices which lead to racial discrimination and to promoting understanding, tolerance and friendship among nations and racial or ethnical groups, as well as to propagating the purposes and principles of the Charter of the United Nations, the Universal Declaration of Human Rights, the United Nations Declaration on the Elimination of All Forms of Racial Discrimination, and this Convention.[43]

A Committee is established especially to enforce this Covenant in order to better combat discrimination, as indicated in Article 8:

8(1) There shall be established a Committee on the Elimination of Racial Discrimination (hereinafter referred to as the Committee) consisting of eighteen experts of high moral standing and acknowledged impartiality elected by States Parties from among their nationals, who shall serve in their personal capacity, consideration being given to equitable geographical distribution and to the representation of the different forms of civilization as well as of the principal legal systems.[44]

Positive measures to enforce State commitments are detailed in Article 9:

9(1) States Parties undertake to submit to the Secretary-General of the United Nations, for consideration by the Committee, a report on the legislative, judicial, administrative or other measures which they have adopted and which give effect to the provisions of this Convention ...
(2) The Committee shall report annually, through the Secretary-General, to the General Assembly of the United Nations on its activities and may make suggestions and general recommendations based on the examination of the reports and information received from the States Parties.[45]

Finally, in case of unresolved disputes, jurisdiction is granted to the International Court of Justice under Article 22:

22. Any dispute between two or more States Parties with respect to the interpretation or application of this Convention, which is not settled by negotiation or by the procedures expressly provided for in this Convention, shall, at the request of any of the parties to the dispute, be referred to the International

---

43   Ibid., at Article 7.
44   Ibid., at Article 8.
45   Ibid., at Article 9.

Court of Justice for decision, unless the disputants agree to another mode of settlement.[46]

Convention on the Elimination of All Forms of Discrimination against Women (CEDAW)

Important for female children who suffer double discrimination based on age and gender, the Convention on the Elimination of All Forms of Discrimination against Women (CEDAW) was adopted on 18 December 1979.[47] It is the most comprehensive treaty specifically on the human rights of females, establishing legally binding obligations to end discrimination; described as the 'International Bill of Rights for Women', the Convention provides for equality between women and men, girls and boys in the enjoyment of civil, political, economic, social and cultural rights. In the Preamble of the Convention on the Elimination of All Forms of Discrimination against Women, the States Parties undertake the agreement:

Noting that the Charter of the United Nations reaffirms faith in fundamental human rights, in the dignity and worth of the human person and in the equal rights of men and women,

Noting that the Universal Declaration of Human Rights affirms the principle of the inadmissibility of discrimination and proclaims that all human beings are born free and equal in dignity and rights and that everyone is entitled to all the rights and freedoms set forth therein, without distinction of any kind, including distinction based on sex,

Noting that the States Parties to the International Covenants on Human Rights have the obligation to ensure the equal rights of men and women to enjoy all economic, social, cultural, civil and political rights,

Considering the international conventions concluded under the auspices of the United Nations and the specialized agencies promoting equality of rights of men and women,

Noting also the resolutions, declarations and recommendations adopted by the United Nations and the specialized agencies promoting equality of rights of men and women,

---

46   Ibid., at Article 22.
47   United Nations, Convention on the Elimination of All Forms of Discrimination against Women.

Concerned, however, that despite these various instruments extensive discrimination against women continues to exist,

Recalling that discrimination against women violates the principles of equality of rights and respect for human dignity, is an obstacle to the participation of women, on equal terms with men, in the political, social, economic and cultural life of their countries, hampers the growth of the prosperity of society and the family and makes more difficult the full development of the potentialities of women in the service of their countries and of humanity,

Concerned that in situations of poverty women have the least access to food, health, education, training and opportunities for employment and other needs,

Convinced that the establishment of the new international economic order based on equity and justice will contribute significantly towards the promotion of equality between men and women,

Emphasizing that the eradication of apartheid, all forms of racism, racial discrimination, colonialism, neo-colonialism, aggression, foreign occupation and domination and interference in the internal affairs of States is essential to the full enjoyment of the rights of men and women,

Affirming that the strengthening of international peace and security, the relaxation of international tension, mutual co-operation among all States irrespective of their social and economic systems, general and complete disarmament, in particular nuclear disarmament under strict and effective international control, the affirmation of the principles of justice, equality and mutual benefit in relations among countries and the realization of the right of peoples under alien and colonial domination and foreign occupation to self-determination and independence, as well as respect for national sovereignty and territorial integrity, will promote social progress and development and as a consequence will contribute to the attainment of full equality between men and women,

Convinced that the full and complete development of a country, the welfare of the world and the cause of peace require the maximum participation of women on equal terms with men in all fields,

Bearing in mind the great contribution of women to the welfare of the family and to the development of society, so far not fully recognized, the social significance of maternity and the role of both parents in the family and in the upbringing of children, and aware that the role of women in procreation should not be a basis for discrimination but that the upbringing of children requires a sharing of responsibility between men and women and society as a whole,

Aware that a change in the traditional role of men as well as the role of women in society and in the family is needed to achieve full equality between men and women,

Determined to implement the principles set forth in the Declaration on the Elimination of Discrimination against Women and, for that purpose, to adopt the measures required for the elimination of such discrimination in all its forms and manifestations.[48]

Article 1 defines 'discrimination against women':

1. For the purposes of the present Convention, the term 'discrimination against women' shall mean any distinction, exclusion or restriction made on the basis of sex which has the effect or purpose of impairing or nullifying the recognition, enjoyment or exercise by women, irrespective of their marital status, on a basis of equality of men and women, of human rights and fundamental freedoms in the political, economic, social, cultural, civil or any other field.[49]

Article 2 outlines the condemnation of discrimination against females:

2. States Parties condemn discrimination against women in all its forms, agree to pursue by all appropriate means and without delay a policy of eliminating discrimination against women and, to this end, undertake:
(a) To embody the principle of the equality of men and women in their national constitutions or other appropriate legislation if not yet incorporated therein and to ensure, through law and other appropriate means, the practical realization of this principle;
(b) To adopt appropriate legislative and other measures, including sanctions where appropriate, prohibiting all discrimination against women;
(c) To establish legal protection of the rights of women on an equal basis with men and to ensure through competent national tribunals and other public institutions the effective protection of women against any act of discrimination;
(d) To refrain from engaging in any act or practice of discrimination against women and to ensure that public authorities and institutions shall act in conformity with this obligation;
(e) To take all appropriate measures to eliminate discrimination against women by any person, organization or enterprise;
(f) To take all appropriate measures, including legislation, to modify or abolish existing laws, regulations, customs and practices which constitute discrimination against women;

---

48 Ibid., at the Preamble.
49 Ibid., at Article 1.

(g) To repeal all national penal provisions which constitute discrimination against women.[50]

Further, Article 4 contains an affirmative action strategy:

> 4(1) Adoption by States Parties of temporary special measures aimed at accelerating de facto equality between men and women shall not be considered discrimination as defined in the present Convention, but shall in no way entail as a consequence the maintenance of unequal or separate standards; these measures shall be discontinued when the objectives of equality of opportunity and treatment have been achieved.
>
> (2) Adoption by States Parties of special measures, including those measures contained in the present Convention, aimed at protecting maternity shall not be considered discriminatory.[51]

Crucially, Article 11(1) guarantees employment rights for females in terms of access to employment and equal pay:

> 11(1). States Parties shall take all appropriate measures to eliminate discrimination against women in the field of employment in order to ensure, on a basis of equality of men and women, the same rights, in particular:
> (a) The right to work as an inalienable right of all human beings;
> (b) The right to the same employment opportunities, including the application of the same criteria for selection in matters of employment;
> (c) The right to free choice of profession and employment, the right to promotion, job security and all benefits and conditions of service and the right to receive vocational training and retraining, including apprenticeships, advanced vocational training and recurrent training;
> (d) The right to equal remuneration, including benefits, and to equal treatment in respect of work of equal value, as well as equality of treatment in the evaluation of the quality of work;
> (e) The right to social security, particularly in cases of retirement, unemployment, sickness, invalidity and old age and other incapacity to work, as well as the right to paid leave;
> (f) The right to protection of health and to safety in working conditions, including the safeguarding of the function of reproduction.[52]

Finally, the important concept of equality before the law is guaranteed in Article 15:

---

50   Ibid., at Article 2.
51   Ibid., at Article 4.
52   Ibid., at Article 11(1).

15(1). States Parties shall accord to women equality with men before the law.

(2). States Parties shall accord to women, in civil matters, a legal capacity identical to that of men and the same opportunities to exercise that capacity. In particular, they shall give women equal rights to conclude contracts and to administer property and shall treat them equally in all stages of procedure in courts and tribunals.

(3). States Parties agree that all contracts and all other private instruments of any kind with a legal effect which is directed at restricting the legal capacity of women shall be deemed null and void.[53]

Optional Protocol to the Convention on the Elimination of All Forms of Discrimination against Women

The Optional Protocol to the Convention on the Elimination of All Forms of Discrimination against Women (CEDAW) was adopted by the United Nations Commission on the Status of Women on 10 December 1999.[54] In the Preamble of the Optional Protocol to the Convention on the Elimination of All Forms of Discrimination against Women, the States Parties undertake the agreement:

Noting that the Charter of the United Nations reaffirms faith in fundamental human rights, in the dignity and worth of the human person and in the equal rights of men and women,

Also noting that the Universal Declaration of Human Rights proclaims that all human beings are born free and equal in dignity and rights and that everyone is entitled to all the rights and freedoms set forth therein, without distinction of any kind, including distinction based on sex,

Recalling that the International Covenants on Human Rights and other international human rights instruments prohibit discrimination on the basis of sex,

Also recalling the Convention on the Elimination of All Forms of Discrimination against Women ('the Convention'), in which the States Parties thereto condemn discrimination against women in all its forms and agree to pursue by all appropriate means and without delay a policy of eliminating discrimination against women,

---

53   Ibid., at Article 15.

54   United Nations, Optional Protocol to the Convention on the Elimination of All Forms of Discrimination against Women.

Reaffirming their determination to ensure the full and equal enjoyment by women of all human rights and fundamental freedoms and to take effective action to prevent violations of these rights and freedoms.[55]

Convention on the Rights of the Child

The Convention on the Rights of the Child (CRC) was adopted and opened for signature, ratification and accession by General Assembly resolution 44/25 of 20 November 1989, and entered into force 2 September 1990. The Preamble of the Convention on the Rights of the Child states:

The States Parties to the present Convention,

Considering that, in accordance with the principles proclaimed in the Charter of the United Nations, recognition of the inherent dignity and of the equal and inalienable rights of all members of the human family is the foundation of freedom, justice and peace in the world,

Bearing in mind that the peoples of the United Nations have, in the Charter, reaffirmed their faith in fundamental human rights and in the dignity and worth of the human person and have determined to promote social progress and better standards of life in larger freedom,

Recognizing that the United Nations has, in the Universal Declaration of Human Rights and in the International Covenants on Human Rights, proclaimed and agreed that everyone is entitled to all the rights and freedoms set forth therein, without distinction of any kind, such as race, colour, sex, language, religion, political or other opinion, national or social origin, property, birth or other status,

Recalling that, in the Universal Declaration of Human Rights, the United Nations has proclaimed that childhood is entitled to special care and assistance,

Convinced that the family, as the fundamental group of society and the natural environment for the growth and well-being of all its members and particularly children, should be afforded the necessary protection and assistance so that it can fully assume its responsibilities within the community,

Recognizing that the child, for the full and harmonious development of his or her personality, should grow up in a family environment, in an atmosphere of happiness, love and understanding,

---

55   Ibid., at the Preamble.

Considering that the child should be fully prepared to live an individual life in society and brought up in the spirit of the ideals proclaimed in the Charter of the United Nations and in particular in the spirit of peace, dignity, tolerance, freedom, equality and solidarity,

Bearing in mind that the need to extend particular care to the child has been stated in the Geneva Declaration of the Rights of the Child of 1924 and in the Declaration of the Rights of the Child adopted by the General Assembly on 20 November 1959 and recognized in the Universal Declaration of Human Rights, in the International Covenant on Civil and Political Rights (in particular in articles 23 and 24), in the International Covenant on Economic, Social and Cultural Rights (in particular in article 10) and in the statutes and relevant instruments of specialized agencies and international organizations concerned with the welfare of children,

Bearing in mind that, as indicated in the Declaration of the Rights of the Child, 'the child, by reason of his physical and mental immaturity, needs special safeguards and care, including appropriate legal protection, before as well as after birth',

Recalling the provisions of the Declaration on Social and Legal Principles relating to the Protection and Welfare of Children, with Special Reference to Foster Placement and Adoption Nationally and Internationally; the United Nations Standard Minimum Rules for the Administration of Juvenile Justice (The Beijing Rules); and the Declaration on the Protection of Women and Children in Emergency and Armed Conflict,

Recognizing that, in all countries in the world, there are children living in exceptionally difficult conditions and that such children need special consideration,

Taking due account of the importance of the traditions and cultural values of each people for the protection and harmonious development of the child,

Recognizing the importance of international co-operation for improving the living conditions of children in every country, in particular in the developing countries,

Have agreed as follows.[56]

A child is defined in Article 1:

---

56   Convention on the Rights of the Child, at the Preamble.

1. For the purposes of the present Convention, a child means every human being below the age of eighteen years unless under the law applicable to the child, majority is attained earlier.[57]

Article 6 protects the right to life:

6.1. States Parties recognize that every child has the inherent right to life.
2. States Parties shall ensure to the maximum extent possible the survival and development of the child.[58]

Article 2 contains an anti-discrimination provision:

2.1. States Parties shall respect and ensure the rights set forth in the present Convention to each child within their jurisdiction without discrimination of any kind, irrespective of the child's or his or her parent's or legal guardian's race, colour, sex, language, religion, political or other opinion, national, ethnic or social origin, property, disability, birth or other status.
2. States Parties shall take all appropriate measures to ensure that the child is protected against all forms of discrimination or punishment on the basis of the status, activities, expressed opinions, or beliefs of the child's parents, legal guardians, or family members.[59]

Importantly, the best interests of the child are paramount under Article 3:

3.1. In all actions concerning children, whether undertaken by public or private social welfare institutions, courts of law, administrative authorities or legislative bodies, the best interests of the child shall be a primary consideration.
2. States Parties undertake to ensure the child such protection and care as is necessary for his or her well-being, taking into account the rights and duties of his or her parents, legal guardians, or other individuals legally responsible for him or her, and, to this end, shall take all appropriate legislative and administrative measures.
3. States Parties shall ensure that the institutions, services and facilities responsible for the care or protection of children shall conform with the standards established by competent authorities, particularly in the areas of safety, health, in the number and suitability of their staff, as well as competent supervision.[60]

Further, all appropriate means of protection are called for under Article 4:

---

57   Ibid., at Article 1.
58   Ibid., at Article 6.
59   Ibid., at Article 2.
60   Ibid., at Article 3.

4. States Parties shall undertake all appropriate legislative, administrative and other measures for the implementation of the rights recognized in the present Convention. With regard to economic, social and cultural rights, States Parties shall undertake such measures to the maximum extent of their available resources and, where needed, within the framework of international co-operation.[61]

In addition, the protection of the law is afforded the child under Article 16:

16.1. No child shall be subjected to arbitrary or unlawful interference with his or her privacy, family, home or correspondence, nor to unlawful attacks on his or her honour and reputation.
2. The child has the right to the protection of the law against such interference or attacks.[62]

Finally, protective measures are provided for under Article 19:

19.1. States Parties shall take all appropriate legislative, administrative, social and educational measures to protect the child from all forms of physical or mental violence, injury or abuse, neglect or negligent treatment, maltreatment or exploitation, including sexual abuse, while in the care of parent(s), legal guardian(s) or any other person who has the care of the child.
2. Such protective measures should, as appropriate, include effective procedures for the establishment of social programmes to provide necessary support for the child and for those who have the care of the child, as well as for other forms of prevention and for identification, reporting, referral, investigation, treatment and follow-up of instances of child maltreatment described heretofore, and, as appropriate, for judicial involvement.[63]

Parental rights are contained in Article 5:

5. States Parties shall respect the responsibilities, rights and duties of parents or, where applicable, the members of the extended family or community as provided for by local custom, legal guardians or other persons legally responsible for the child, to provide, in a manner consistent with the evolving capacities of the child, appropriate direction and guidance in the exercise by the child of the rights recognized in the present Convention.[64]

Further, Article 9 protects against parent–child separation:

61　Ibid., at Article 4.
62　Ibid., at Article 16.
63　Ibid., at Article 19.
64　Ibid., at Article 5.

9.1. States Parties shall ensure that a child shall not be separated from his or her parents against their will, except when competent authorities subject to judicial review determine, in accordance with applicable law and procedures, that such separation is necessary for the best interests of the child. Such determination may be necessary in a particular case such as one involving abuse or neglect of the child by the parents, or one where the parents are living separately and a decision must be made as to the child's place of residence.

2. In any proceedings pursuant to paragraph 1 of the present article, all interested parties shall be given an opportunity to participate in the proceedings and make their views known.

3. States Parties shall respect the right of the child who is separated from one or both parents to maintain personal relations and direct contact with both parents on a regular basis, except if it is contrary to the child's best interests.

4. Where such separation results from any action initiated by a State Party, such as the detention, imprisonment, exile, deportation or death (including death arising from any cause while the person is in the custody of the State) of one or both parents or of the child, that State Party shall, upon request, provide the parents, the child or, if appropriate, another member of the family with the essential information concerning the whereabouts of the absent member(s) of the family unless the provision of the information would be detrimental to the well-being of the child. States Parties shall further ensure that the submission of such a request shall of itself entail no adverse consequences for the person(s) concerned.[65]

Finally, parental responsibilities toward the child are recognized under Article 18:

18.1. States Parties shall use their best efforts to ensure recognition of the principle that both parents have common responsibilities for the upbringing and development of the child. Parents or, as the case may be, legal guardians, have the primary responsibility for the upbringing and development of the child. The best interests of the child will be their basic concern.

2. For the purpose of guaranteeing and promoting the rights set forth in the present Convention, States Parties shall render appropriate assistance to parents and legal guardians in the performance of their child-rearing responsibilities and shall ensure the development of institutions, facilities and services for the care of children.

3. States Parties shall take all appropriate measures to ensure that children of working parents have the right to benefit from child-care services and facilities for which they are eligible.[66]

The freedom of views is guaranteed under Article 12:

---

65   Ibid., at Article 9.
66   Ibid., at Article 18.

12.1. States Parties shall assure to the child who is capable of forming his or her own views the right to express those views freely in all matters affecting the child, the views of the child being given due weight in accordance with the age and maturity of the child.

2. For this purpose, the child shall in particular be provided the opportunity to be heard in any judicial and administrative proceedings affecting the child, either directly, or through a representative or an appropriate body, in a manner consistent with the procedural rules of national law.[67]

Further, freedom of expression is protected under Article 13:

13.1. The child shall have the right to freedom of expression; this right shall include freedom to seek, receive and impart information and ideas of all kinds, regardless of frontiers, either orally, in writing or in print, in the form of art, or through any other media of the child's choice.

2. The exercise of this right may be subject to certain restrictions, but these shall only be such as are provided by law and are necessary:

(a) For respect of the rights or reputations of others; or

(b) For the protection of national security or of public order (ordre public), or of public health or morals.[68]

In addition, the freedom of thought, conscience and religion is guaranteed under Article 14:

14.1. States Parties shall respect the right of the child to freedom of thought, conscience and religion.

2. States Parties shall respect the rights and duties of the parents and, when applicable, legal guardians, to provide direction to the child in the exercise of his or her right in a manner consistent with the evolving capacities of the child.

3. Freedom to manifest one's religion or beliefs may be subject only to such limitations as are prescribed by law and are necessary to protect public safety, order, health or morals, or the fundamental rights and freedoms of others.[69]

Finally, the freedom of association is protected under Article 15:

15.1. States Parties recognize the rights of the child to freedom of association and to freedom of peaceful assembly.

2. No restrictions may be placed on the exercise of these rights other than those imposed in conformity with the law and which are necessary in a democratic society in the interests of national security or public safety, public order (ordre

---

67 Ibid., at Article 12.
68 Ibid., at Article 13.
69 Ibid., at Article 14.

public), the protection of public health or morals or the protection of the rights and freedoms of others.[70]

The role of the media toward the child is outlined under Article 17:

17. States Parties recognize the important function performed by the mass media and shall ensure that the child has access to information and material from a diversity of national and international sources, especially those aimed at the promotion of his or her social, spiritual and moral well-being and physical and mental health. To this end, States Parties shall:

(a) Encourage the mass media to disseminate information and material of social and cultural benefit to the child and in accordance with the spirit of article 29;

(b) Encourage international co-operation in the production, exchange and dissemination of such information and material from a diversity of cultural, national and international sources;

(c) Encourage the production and dissemination of children's books;

(d) Encourage the mass media to have particular regard to the linguistic needs of the child who belongs to a minority group or who is indigenous;

(e) Encourage the development of appropriate guidelines for the protection of the child from information and material injurious to his or her well-being, bearing in mind the provisions of articles 13 and 18.[71]

Refugee status is covered under Article 22:

22.1. States Parties shall take appropriate measures to ensure that a child who is seeking refugee status or who is considered a refugee in accordance with applicable international or domestic law and procedures shall, whether unaccompanied or accompanied by his or her parents or by any other person, receive appropriate protection and humanitarian assistance in the enjoyment of applicable rights set forth in the present Convention and in other international human rights or humanitarian instruments to which the said States are Parties.

2. For this purpose, States Parties shall provide, as they consider appropriate, co-operation in any efforts by the United Nations and other competent intergovernmental organizations or non-governmental organizations co-operating with the United Nations to protect and assist such a child and to trace the parents or other members of the family of any refugee child in order to obtain information necessary for reunification with his or her family. In cases where no parents or other members of the family can be found, the child shall be accorded the same protection as any other child permanently or temporarily

---

70   Ibid., at Article 15.
71   Ibid., at Article 17.

deprived of his or her family environment for any reason, as set forth in the present Convention.[72]

Rights of the disabled child are recognized under Article 23:

23.1. States Parties recognize that a mentally or physically disabled child should enjoy a full and decent life, in conditions which ensure dignity, promote self-reliance and facilitate the child's active participation in the community.
2. States Parties recognize the right of the disabled child to special care and shall encourage and ensure the extension, subject to available resources, to the eligible child and those responsible for his or her care, of assistance for which application is made and which is appropriate to the child's condition and to the circumstances of the parents or others caring for the child.
3. Recognizing the special needs of a disabled child, assistance extended in accordance with paragraph 2 of the present article shall be provided free of charge, whenever possible, taking into account the financial resources of the parents or others caring for the child and shall be designed to ensure that the disabled child has effective access to and receives education, training, health care services, rehabilitation services, preparation for employment and recreation opportunities in a manner conducive to the child's achieving the fullest possible social integration and individual development, including his or her cultural and spiritual development
4. States Parties shall promote, in the spirit of international co-operation, the exchange of appropriate information in the field of preventive health care and of medical, psychological and functional treatment of disabled children, including dissemination of and access to information concerning methods of rehabilitation, education and vocational services, with the aim of enabling States Parties to improve their capabilities and skills and to widen their experience in these areas. In this regard, particular account shall be taken of the needs of developing countries.[73]

The importance of health care for children is recognized under Article 24:

24.1. States Parties recognize the right of the child to the enjoyment of the highest attainable standard of health and to facilities for the treatment of illness and rehabilitation of health. States Parties shall strive to ensure that no child is deprived of his or her right of access to such health care services.
2. States Parties shall pursue full implementation of this right and, in particular, shall take appropriate measures:
 (a) To diminish infant and child mortality;

---

72 Ibid., at Article 22.
73 Ibid., at Article 23.

(b) To ensure the provision of necessary medical assistance and health care to all children with emphasis on the development of primary health care;

(c) To combat disease and malnutrition, including within the framework of primary health care, through, inter alia, the application of readily available technology and through the provision of adequate nutritious foods and clean drinking-water, taking into consideration the dangers and risks of environmental pollution;

(d) To ensure appropriate pre-natal and post-natal health care for mothers;

(e) To ensure that all segments of society, in particular parents and children, are informed, have access to education and are supported in the use of basic knowledge of child health and nutrition, the advantages of breastfeeding, hygiene and environmental sanitation and the prevention of accidents;

(f) To develop preventive health care, guidance for parents and family planning education and services.

3. States Parties shall take all effective and appropriate measures with a view to abolishing traditional practices prejudicial to the health of children.

4. States Parties undertake to promote and encourage international co-operation with a view to achieving progressively the full realization of the right recognized in the present article. In this regard, particular account shall be taken of the needs of developing countries.[74]

As well, a child's adequate standard of living is protected under Article 27:

27.1. States Parties recognize the right of every child to a standard of living adequate for the child's physical, mental, spiritual, moral and social development.

2. The parent(s) or others responsible for the child have the primary responsibility to secure, within their abilities and financial capacities, the conditions of living necessary for the child's development.

3. States Parties, in accordance with national conditions and within their means, shall take appropriate measures to assist parents and others responsible for the child to implement this right and shall in case of need provide material assistance and support programmes, particularly with regard to nutrition, clothing and housing.

4. States Parties shall take all appropriate measures to secure the recovery of maintenance for the child from the parents or other persons having financial responsibility for the child, both within the State Party and from abroad. In particular, where the person having financial responsibility for the child lives in a State different from that of the child, States Parties shall promote the accession to international agreements or the conclusion of such agreements, as well as the making of other appropriate arrangements.[75]

---

74 Ibid., at Article 24.
75 Ibid., at Article 27.

The paramount right to education for children is guaranteed under Article 28:

28.1. States Parties recognize the right of the child to education and with a view to achieving this right progressively and on the basis of equal opportunity, they shall, in particular:

(a) Make primary education compulsory and available free to all;

(b) Encourage the development of different forms of secondary education, including general and vocational education, make them available and accessible to every child and take appropriate measures such as the introduction of free education and offering financial assistance in case of need;

(c) Make higher education accessible to all on the basis of capacity by every appropriate means;

(d) Make educational and vocational information and guidance available and accessible to all children;

(e) Take measures to encourage regular attendance at schools and the reduction of drop-out rates.

2. States Parties shall take all appropriate measures to ensure that school discipline is administered in a manner consistent with the child's human dignity and in conformity with the present Convention.

3. States Parties shall promote and encourage international cooperation in matters relating to education, in particular with a view to contributing to the elimination of ignorance and illiteracy throughout the world and facilitating access to scientific and technical knowledge and modern teaching methods. In this regard, particular account shall be taken of the needs of developing countries.[76]

Further, in terms of education, Article 29 states:

29.1. States Parties agree that the education of the child shall be directed to:

(a) The development of the child's personality, talents and mental and physical abilities to their fullest potential;

(b) The development of respect for human rights and fundamental freedoms, and for the principles enshrined in the Charter of the United Nations;

(c) The development of respect for the child's parents, his or her own cultural identity, language and values, for the national values of the country in which the child is living, the country from which he or she may originate, and for civilizations different from his or her own;

(d) The preparation of the child for responsible life in a free society, in the spirit of understanding, peace, tolerance, equality of sexes, and friendship among all peoples, ethnic, national and religious groups and persons of indigenous origin;

(e) The development of respect for the natural environment.

---

76   Ibid., at Article 28.

2. No part of the present article or article 28 shall be construed so as to interfere with the liberty of individuals and bodies to establish and direct educational institutions, subject always to the observance of the principle set forth in paragraph 1 of the present article and to the requirements that the education given in such institutions shall conform to such minimum standards as may be laid down by the State.[77]

Cultural protection is afforded under Article 30:

30. In those States in which ethnic, religious or linguistic minorities or persons of indigenous origin exist, a child belonging to such a minority or who is indigenous shall not be denied the right, in community with other members of his or her group, to enjoy his or her own culture, to profess and practise his or her own religion, or to use his or her own language.[78]

Article 31 guarantees leisure time for the child:

31.1. States Parties recognize the right of the child to rest and leisure, to engage in play and recreational activities appropriate to the age of the child and to participate freely in cultural life and the arts.
2. States Parties shall respect and promote the right of the child to participate fully in cultural and artistic life and shall encourage the provision of appropriate and equal opportunities for cultural, artistic, recreational and leisure activity.[79]

Importantly, child labor protection is covered under Article 32:

32.1. States Parties recognize the right of the child to be protected from economic exploitation and from performing any work that is likely to be hazardous or to interfere with the child's education, or to be harmful to the child's health or physical, mental, spiritual, moral or social development.
2. States Parties shall take legislative, administrative, social and educational measures to ensure the implementation of the present article. To this end and having regard to the relevant provisions of other international instruments, States Parties shall in particular:
    (a) Provide for a minimum age or minimum ages for admission to employment;
    (b) Provide for appropriate regulation of the hours and conditions of employment;

---

77   Ibid., at Article 29.
78   Ibid., at Article 30.
79   Ibid., at Article 31.

(c) Provide for appropriate penalties or other sanctions to ensure the effective enforcement of the present article.[80]

Protection from sexual exploitation is included under Article 34:

34. States Parties undertake to protect the child from all forms of sexual exploitation and sexual abuse. For these purposes, States Parties shall in particular take all appropriate national, bilateral and multilateral measures to prevent:

(a) The inducement or coercion of a child to engage in any unlawful sexual activity;

(b) The exploitative use of children in prostitution or other unlawful sexual practices;

(c) The exploitative use of children in pornographic performances and materials.[81]

Further, the trafficking of children is covered under Article 35:

35. States Parties shall take all appropriate national, bilateral and multilateral measures to prevent the abduction of, the sale of or traffic in children for any purpose or in any form.[82]

Finally, Article 36 takes under consideration all other forms of exploitation:

36. States Parties shall protect the child against all other forms of exploitation prejudicial to any aspects of the child's welfare.[83]

Protection against cruel punishment is outlined under Article 37:

37. States Parties shall ensure that:

(a) No child shall be subjected to torture or other cruel, inhuman or degrading treatment or punishment. Neither capital punishment nor life imprisonment without possibility of release shall be imposed for offences committed by persons below eighteen years of age;

(b) No child shall be deprived of his or her liberty unlawfully or arbitrarily. The arrest, detention or imprisonment of a child shall be in conformity with the law and shall be used only as a measure of last resort and for the shortest appropriate period of time;

---

80 Ibid., at Article 32.
81 Ibid., at Article 34.
82 Ibid., at Article 35.
83 Ibid., at Article 36.

(c) Every child deprived of liberty shall be treated with humanity and respect for the inherent dignity of the human person and in a manner which takes into account the needs of persons of his or her age. In particular, every child deprived of liberty shall be separated from adults unless it is considered in the child's best interest not to do so and shall have the right to maintain contact with his or her family through correspondence and visits, save in exceptional circumstances;

(d) Every child deprived of his or her liberty shall have the right to prompt access to legal and other appropriate assistance, as well as the right to challenge the legality of the deprivation of his or her liberty before a court or other competent, independent and impartial authority and to a prompt decision on any such action.[84]

Special protection in times of armed conflict is covered under Article 38:

38.1. States Parties undertake to respect and to ensure respect for rules of international humanitarian law applicable to them in armed conflicts which are relevant to the child.

2. States Parties shall take all feasible measures to ensure that persons who have not attained the age of fifteen years do not take a direct part in hostilities.

3. States Parties shall refrain from recruiting any person who has not attained the age of fifteen years into their armed forces. In recruiting among those persons who have attained the age of fifteen years but who have not attained the age of eighteen years, States Parties shall endeavour to give priority to those who are oldest.

4. In accordance with their obligations under international humanitarian law to protect the civilian population in armed conflicts, States Parties shall take all feasible measures to ensure protection and care of children who are affected by an armed conflict.[85]

Recovery and social reintegration if needed are provided for under Article 39:

39. States Parties shall take all appropriate measures to promote physical and psychological recovery and social reintegration of a child victim of: any form of neglect, exploitation, or abuse; torture or any other form of cruel, inhuman or degrading treatment or punishment; or armed conflicts. Such recovery and reintegration shall take place in an environment which fosters the health, self-respect and dignity of the child.[86]

The rights of the child in criminal cases are afforded under Article 40:

---

84   Ibid., at Article 37.
85   Ibid., at Article 38.
86   Ibid., at Article 39.

40.1. States Parties recognize the right of every child alleged as, accused of, or recognized as having infringed the penal law to be treated in a manner consistent with the promotion of the child's sense of dignity and worth, which reinforces the child's respect for the human rights and fundamental freedoms of others and which takes into account the child's age and the desirability of promoting the child's reintegration and the child's assuming a constructive role in society.
2. To this end and having regard to the relevant provisions of international instruments, States Parties shall, in particular, ensure that:

(a) No child shall be alleged as, be accused of, or recognized as having infringed the penal law by reason of acts or omissions that were not prohibited by national or international law at the time they were committed;

(b) Every child alleged as or accused of having infringed the penal law has at least the following guarantees:

(i) To be presumed innocent until proven guilty according to law;

(ii) To be informed promptly and directly of the charges against him or her, and, if appropriate, through his or her parents or legal guardians and to have legal or other appropriate assistance in the preparation and presentation of his or her defence;

(iii) To have the matter determined without delay by a competent, independent and impartial authority or judicial body in a fair hearing according to law, in the presence of legal or other appropriate assistance and, unless it is considered not to be in the best interest of the child, in particular, taking into account his or her age or situation, his or her parents or legal guardians;

(iv) Not to be compelled to give testimony or to confess guilt; to examine or have examined adverse witnesses and to obtain the participation and examination of witnesses on his or her behalf under conditions of equality;

(v) If considered to have infringed the penal law, to have this decision and any measures imposed in consequence thereof reviewed by a higher competent, independent and impartial authority or judicial body according to law;

(vi) To have the free assistance of an interpreter if the child cannot understand or speak the language used;

(vii) To have his or her privacy fully respected at all stages of the proceedings.
3. States Parties shall seek to promote the establishment of laws, procedures, authorities and institutions specifically applicable to children alleged as, accused of, or recognized as having infringed the penal law, and, in particular:

(a) The establishment of a minimum age below which children shall be presumed not to have the capacity to infringe the penal law;

(b) Whenever appropriate and desirable, measures for dealing with such children without resorting to judicial proceedings, providing that human rights and legal safeguards are fully respected.

4. A variety of dispositions, such as care, guidance and supervision orders; counselling; probation; foster care; education and vocational training programmes and other alternatives to institutional care shall be available to ensure that children are dealt with in a manner appropriate to their well-being and proportionate both to their circumstances and the offence.[87]

Importantly, Article 41 provides that more protection can be afforded under national law:

41. Nothing in the present Convention shall affect any provisions which are more conducive to the realization of the rights of the child and which may be contained in:
   (a) The law of a State party; or
   (b) International law in force for that State.[88]

Finally, Article 43 establishes a Committee on the Rights of the Child:

43.1. For the purpose of examining the progress made by States Parties in achieving the realization of the obligations undertaken in the present Convention, there shall be established a Committee on the Rights of the Child, which shall carry out the functions hereinafter provided.
2. The Committee shall consist of ten experts of high moral standing and recognized competence in the field covered by this Convention. The members of the Committee shall be elected by States Parties from among their nationals and shall serve in their personal capacity, consideration being given to equitable geographical distribution, as well as to the principal legal systems.
3. The members of the Committee shall be elected by secret ballot from a list of persons nominated by States Parties. Each State Party may nominate one person from among its own nationals.
4. The initial election to the Committee shall be held no later than six months after the date of the entry into force of the present Convention and thereafter every second year. At least four months before the date of each election, the Secretary-General of the United Nations shall address a letter to States Parties inviting them to submit their nominations within two months. The Secretary-General shall subsequently prepare a list in alphabetical order of all persons thus nominated, indicating States Parties which have nominated them and shall submit it to the States Parties to the present Convention.
5. The elections shall be held at meetings of States Parties convened by the Secretary-General at United Nations Headquarters. At those meetings, for which two thirds of States Parties shall constitute a quorum, the persons elected to the

87   Ibid., at Article 40.
88   Ibid., at Article 41.

Committee shall be those who obtain the largest number of votes and an absolute majority of the votes of the representatives of States Parties present and voting.

6. The members of the Committee shall be elected for a term of four years. They shall be eligible for re-election if renominated. The term of five of the members elected at the first election shall expire at the end of two years; immediately after the first election, the names of these five members shall be chosen by lot by the Chairman of the meeting.

7. If a member of the Committee dies or resigns or declares that for any other cause he or she can no longer perform the duties of the Committee, the State Party which nominated the member shall appoint another expert from among its nationals to serve for the remainder of the term, subject to the approval of the Committee.

8. The Committee shall establish its own rules of procedure.

9. The Committee shall elect its officers for a period of two years.

10. The meetings of the Committee shall normally be held at United Nations Headquarters or at any other convenient place as determined by the Committee. The Committee shall normally meet annually. The duration of the meetings of the Committee shall be determined and reviewed, if necessary, by a meeting of the States Parties to the present Convention, subject to the approval of the General Assembly.

11. The Secretary-General of the United Nations shall provide the necessary staff and facilities for the effective performance of the functions of the Committee under the present Convention.

12. With the approval of the General Assembly, the members of the Committee established under the present Convention shall receive emoluments from United Nations resources on such terms and conditions as the Assembly may decide.[89]

Optional Protocol to the Convention on the Rights of the Child on the involvement of children in armed conflict

Worldwide, an estimated 300,000 children are engaged in armed conflicts, and are often forcibly recruited or abducted to join armies, some under the age of ten.[90] The Optional Protocol to the Convention on the Rights of the Child on the involvement of children in armed conflict is an effort to strengthen implementation of the Convention and increase the protection of children during armed conflicts. When ratifying the Protocol, States must make a declaration regarding the age at which national armed forces will permit voluntary recruitment, as well as the steps that States will take to ensure that such recruitment is never forced or coerced; this is important, because the Optional Protocol does not establish age 18 as a minimum

---

89   Ibid., at Article 43.
90   United Nations.

for voluntary recruitment into the armed forces, only for direct participation in armed conflict.

The Optional Protocol to the Convention on the Rights of the Child on the involvement of children in armed conflict entered into force on 12 February 2002. The Preamble states:

The States Parties to the present Protocol,

Encouraged by the overwhelming support for the Convention on the Rights of the Child, demonstrating the widespread commitment that exists to strive for the promotion and protection of the rights of the child,

Reaffirming that the rights of children require special protection, and calling for continuous improvement of the situation of children without distinction, as well as for their development and education in conditions of peace and security,

Disturbed by the harmful and widespread impact of armed conflict on children and the long-term consequences it has for durable peace, security and development,

Condemning the targeting of children in situations of armed conflict and direct attacks on objects protected under international law, including places that generally have a significant presence of children, such as schools and hospitals,

Noting the adoption of the Rome Statute of the International Criminal Court, in particular, the inclusion therein as a war crime, of conscripting or enlisting children under the age of 15 years or using them to participate actively in hostilities in both international and non-international armed conflict,

Considering therefore that to strengthen further the implementation of rights recognized in the Convention on the Rights of the Child there is a need to increase the protection of children from involvement in armed conflict,

Noting that article 1 of the Convention on the Rights of the Child specifies that, for the purposes of that Convention, a child means every human being below the age of 18 years unless, under the law applicable to the child, majority is attained earlier,

Convinced that an optional protocol to the Convention that raises the age of possible recruitment of persons into armed forces and their participation in hostilities will contribute effectively to the implementation of the principle that the best interests of the child are to be a primary consideration in all actions concerning children,

Noting that the twenty-sixth International Conference of the Red Cross and Red Crescent in December 1995 recommended, inter alia, that parties to conflict take every feasible step to ensure that children below the age of 18 years do not take part in hostilities,

Welcoming the unanimous adoption, in June 1999, of International Labour Organization Convention No. 182 on the Prohibition and Immediate Action for the Elimination of the Worst Forms of Child Labour, which prohibits, inter alia, forced or compulsory recruitment of children for use in armed conflict,

Condemning with the gravest concern the recruitment, training and use within and across national borders of children in hostilities by armed groups distinct from the armed forces of a State, and recognizing the responsibility of those who recruit, train and use children in this regard,

Recalling the obligation of each party to an armed conflict to abide by the provisions of international humanitarian law,

Stressing that the present Protocol is without prejudice to the purposes and principles contained in the Charter of the United Nations, including Article 51, and relevant norms of humanitarian law,

Bearing in mind that conditions of peace and security based on full respect of the purposes and principles contained in the Charter and observance of applicable human rights instruments are indispensable for the full protection of children, in particular during armed conflict and foreign occupation,

Recognizing the special needs of those children who are particularly vulnerable to recruitment or use in hostilities contrary to the present Protocol owing to their economic or social status or gender,

Mindful of the necessity of taking into consideration the economic, social and political root causes of the involvement of children in armed conflict,

Convinced of the need to strengthen international cooperation in the implementation of the present Protocol, as well as the physical and psychosocial rehabilitation and social reintegration of children who are victims of armed conflict,

Encouraging the participation of the community and, in particular, children and child victims in the dissemination of informational and educational programmes concerning the implementation of the Protocol,

Have agreed as follows.[91]

Article 1 calls for all feasible measures of protection:

1. States Parties shall take all feasible measures to ensure that members of their armed forces who have not attained the age of 18 years do not take a direct part in hostilities.[92]

Article 2 protects those under the age of 18 as regards compulsory service:

2. States Parties shall ensure that persons who have not attained the age of 18 years are not compulsorily recruited into their armed forces.[93]

Article 3 provides for measures regarding voluntary recruitment:

3.1. States Parties shall raise the minimum age for the voluntary recruitment of persons into their national armed forces from that set out in article 38, paragraph 3, of the Convention on the Rights of the Child, taking account of the principles contained in that article and recognizing that under the Convention persons under the age of 18 years are entitled to special protection.

2. Each State Party shall deposit a binding declaration upon ratification of or accession to the present Protocol that sets forth the minimum age at which it will permit voluntary recruitment into its national armed forces and a description of the safeguards it has adopted to ensure that such recruitment is not forced or coerced.

3. States Parties that permit voluntary recruitment into their national armed forces under the age of 18 years shall maintain safeguards to ensure, as a minimum, that:

(a) Such recruitment is genuinely voluntary;

(b) Such recruitment is carried out with the informed consent of the person's parents or legal guardians;

(c) Such persons are fully informed of the duties involved in such military service;

(d) Such persons provide reliable proof of age prior to acceptance into national military service.

---

91   Optional Protocol to the Convention on the Rights of the Child on the involvement of children in armed conflict, at the Preamble.

92   Ibid., at Article 1.

93   Ibid., at Article 2.

4. Each State Party may strengthen its declaration at any time by notification to that effect addressed to the Secretary-General of the United Nations, who shall inform all States Parties. Such notification shall take effect on the date on which it is received by the Secretary-General.

5. The requirement to raise the age in paragraph 1 of the present article does not apply to schools operated by or under the control of the armed forces of the States Parties, in keeping with articles 28 and 29 of the Convention on the Rights of the Child.[94]

Article 4 regards armed groups distinct from armed forces and the protection of those under the age of 18:

4.1. Armed groups that are distinct from the armed forces of a State should not, under any circumstances, recruit or use in hostilities persons under the age of 18 years.

2. States Parties shall take all feasible measures to prevent such recruitment and use, including the adoption of legal measures necessary to prohibit and criminalize such practices.

3. The application of the present article shall not affect the legal status of any party to an armed conflict.[95]

Importantly, Article 5 states that additional protections may be provided under national and international law:

5. Nothing in the present Protocol shall be construed as precluding provisions in the law of a State Party or in international instruments and international humanitarian law that are more conducive to the realization of the rights of the child.[96]

Article 6 provides that all necessary legal and administrative measures should be used to enforce the Protocol:

6.1. Each State Party shall take all necessary legal, administrative and other measures to ensure the effective implementation and enforcement of the provisions of the present Protocol within its jurisdiction.

2. States Parties undertake to make the principles and provisions of the present Protocol widely known and promoted by appropriate means, to adults and children alike.

3. States Parties shall take all feasible measures to ensure that persons within their jurisdiction recruited or used in hostilities contrary to the present Protocol

---

94   Ibid., at Article 3.
95   Ibid., at Article 4.
96   Ibid., at Article 5.

are demobilized or otherwise released from service. States Parties shall, when necessary, accord to such persons all appropriate assistance for their physical and psychological recovery and their social reintegration.[97]

Finally, Article 7 calls on the full cooperation and assistance by Member States to the implementation of the Protocol:

7.1. States Parties shall cooperate in the implementation of the present Protocol, including in the prevention of any activity contrary thereto and in the rehabilitation and social reintegration of persons who are victims of acts contrary thereto, including through technical cooperation and financial assistance. Such assistance and cooperation will be undertaken in consultation with the States Parties concerned and the relevant international organizations.

2. States Parties in a position to do so shall provide such assistance through existing multilateral, bilateral or other programmes or, inter alia, through a voluntary fund established in accordance with the rules of the General Assembly.[98]

Optional Protocol to the Convention on the Rights of the Child on the sale of children, child prostitution and child pornography

Worldwide, an estimated one million children enter the multi-billion dollar commercial sex trade every year.[99] The Optional Protocol to the Convention on the Rights of the Child on the sale of children, child prostitution and child pornography supplements the Convention by providing States with detailed requirements to end the sexual exploitation and abuse of children; it protects children from being sold for non-sexual purposes, such as other forms of forced labor, illegal adoption and organ donation, and creates obligations on governments to criminalize and punish the activities related to these offences by requiring punishment not only for those offering or delivering children for the purposes of sexual exploitation, transfer of organs or children for profit or forced labor, but also for anyone accepting the child for these activities.

The Optional Protocol on the sale of children, child prostitution and child pornography entered into force on 18 January 2002. The Preamble states:

The States Parties to the present Protocol,

Considering that, in order further to achieve the purposes of the Convention on the Rights of the Child and the implementation of its provisions, especially

---

97   Ibid., at Article 6.
98   Ibid., at Article 7.
99   United Nations.

articles 1, 11, 21, 32, 33, 34, 35 and 36, it would be appropriate to extend the measures that States Parties should undertake in order to guarantee the protection of the child from the sale of children, child prostitution and child pornography,

Considering also that the Convention on the Rights of the Child recognizes the right of the child to be protected from economic exploitation and from performing any work that is likely to be hazardous or to interfere with the child's education, or to be harmful to the child's health or physical, mental, spiritual, moral or social development,

Gravely concerned at the significant and increasing international traffic in children for the purpose of the sale of children, child prostitution and child pornography,

Deeply concerned at the widespread and continuing practice of sex tourism, to which children are especially vulnerable, as it directly promotes the sale of children, child prostitution and child pornography,

Recognizing that a number of particularly vulnerable groups, including girl children, are at greater risk of sexual exploitation and that girl children are disproportionately represented among the sexually exploited,

Concerned about the growing availability of child pornography on the Internet and other evolving technologies, and recalling the International Conference on Combating Child Pornography on the Internet, held in Vienna in 1999, in particular its conclusion calling for the worldwide criminalization of the production, distribution, exportation, transmission, importation, intentional possession and advertising of child pornography, and stressing the importance of closer cooperation and partnership between Governments and the Internet industry,

Believing that the elimination of the sale of children, child prostitution and child pornography will be facilitated by adopting a holistic approach, addressing the contributing factors, including underdevelopment, poverty, economic disparities, inequitable socio-economic structure, dysfunctioning families, lack of education, urban–rural migration, gender discrimination, irresponsible adult sexual behaviour, harmful traditional practices, armed conflicts and trafficking in children,

Believing also that efforts to raise public awareness are needed to reduce consumer demand for the sale of children, child prostitution and child pornography, and believing further in the importance of strengthening global partnership among all actors and of improving law enforcement at the national level,

Noting the provisions of international legal instruments relevant to the protection of children, including the Hague Convention on Protection of Children and Cooperation in Respect of Intercountry Adoption, the Hague Convention on the Civil Aspects of International Child Abduction, the Hague Convention on Jurisdiction, Applicable Law, Recognition, Enforcement and Cooperation in Respect of Parental Responsibility and Measures for the Protection of Children, and International Labour Organization Convention No. 182 on the Prohibition and Immediate Action for the Elimination of the Worst Forms of Child Labour,

Encouraged by the overwhelming support for the Convention on the Rights of the Child, demonstrating the widespread commitment that exists for the promotion and protection of the rights of the child,

Recognizing the importance of the implementation of the provisions of the Programme of Action for the Prevention of the Sale of Children, Child Prostitution and Child Pornography and the Declaration and Agenda for Action adopted at the World Congress against Commercial Sexual Exploitation of Children, held in Stockholm from 27 to 31 August 1996, and the other relevant decisions and recommendations of pertinent international bodies,

Taking due account of the importance of the traditions and cultural values of each people for the protection and harmonious development of the child, Have agreed as follows.[100]

Article 1 strictly calls for the prohibition of the sale of children, their prostitution and pornography:

1. States Parties shall prohibit the sale of children, child prostitution and child pornography as provided for by the present Protocol.[101]

Article 2 defines sale, prostitution and pornography:

2. For the purposes of the present Protocol:
(a) Sale of children means any act or transaction whereby a child is transferred by any person or group of persons to another for remuneration or any other consideration;
(b) Child prostitution means the use of a child in sexual activities for remuneration or any other form of consideration;

---

100   Optional Protocol on the sale of children, child prostitution and child pornography, at the Preamble.
101   Ibid., at Article 1.

(c) Child pornography means any representation, by whatever means, of a child engaged in real or simulated explicit sexual activities or any representation of the sexual parts of a child for primarily sexual purposes.[102]

Further, Article 3 ensures that certain acts will be considered criminal:

3.1. Each State Party shall ensure that, as a minimum, the following acts and activities are fully covered under its criminal or penal law, whether such offences are committed domestically or transnationally or on an individual or organized basis:

(a) In the context of sale of children as defined in article 2:

(i) Offering, delivering or accepting, by whatever means, a child for the purpose of:

a. Sexual exploitation of the child;

b. Transfer of organs of the child for profit;

c. Engagement of the child in forced labour;

(ii) Improperly inducing consent, as an intermediary, for the adoption of a child in violation of applicable international legal instruments on adoption;

(b) Offering, obtaining, procuring or providing a child for child prostitution, as defined in article 2;

(c) Producing, distributing, disseminating, importing, exporting, offering, selling or possessing for the above purposes child pornography as defined in article 2.

2. Subject to the provisions of the national law of a State Party, the same shall apply to an attempt to commit any of the said acts and to complicity or participation in any of the said acts.

3. Each State Party shall make such offences punishable by appropriate penalties that take into account their grave nature.

4. Subject to the provisions of its national law, each State Party shall take measures, where appropriate, to establish the liability of legal persons for offences established in paragraph 1 of the present article. Subject to the legal principles of the State Party, such liability of legal persons may be criminal, civil or administrative.

5. States Parties shall take all appropriate legal and administrative measures to ensure that all persons involved in the adoption of a child act in conformity with applicable international legal instruments.[103]

Article 4 provides for jurisdiction over the acts:

4.1. Each State Party shall take such measures as may be necessary to establish its jurisdiction over the offences referred to in article 3, paragraph 1, when the

---

102   Ibid., at Article 2.
103   Ibid., at Article 3.

offences are committed in its territory or on board a ship or aircraft registered in that State.

2. Each State Party may take such measures as may be necessary to establish its jurisdiction over the offences referred to in article 3, paragraph 1, in the following cases:

(a) When the alleged offender is a national of that State or a person who has his habitual residence in its territory;

(b) When the victim is a national of that State.

3. Each State Party shall also take such measures as may be necessary to establish its jurisdiction over the aforementioned offences when the alleged offender is present in its territory and it does not extradite him or her to another State Party on the ground that the offence has been committed by one of its nationals.

4. The present Protocol does not exclude any criminal jurisdiction exercised in accordance with internal law.[104]

Article 5 deems the acts as extraditable offences:

5.1. The offences referred to in article 3, paragraph 1, shall be deemed to be included as extraditable offences in any extradition treaty existing between States Parties and shall be included as extraditable offences in every extradition treaty subsequently concluded between them, in accordance with the conditions set forth in such treaties.

2. If a State Party that makes extradition conditional on the existence of a treaty receives a request for extradition from another State Party with which it has no extradition treaty, it may consider the present Protocol to be a legal basis for extradition in respect of such offences. Extradition shall be subject to the conditions provided by the law of the requested State.

3. States Parties that do not make extradition conditional on the existence of a treaty shall recognize such offences as extraditable offences between themselves subject to the conditions provided by the law of the requested State.

4. Such offences shall be treated, for the purpose of extradition between States Parties, as if they had been committed not only in the place in which they occurred but also in the territories of the States required to establish their jurisdiction in accordance with article 4.

5. If an extradition request is made with respect to an offence described in article 3, paragraph 1, and the requested State Party does not or will not extradite on the basis of the nationality of the offender, that State shall take suitable measures to submit the case to its competent authorities for the purpose of prosecution.[105]

Article 6 calls for assistance by Member States for the pursuit of crimes:

---

104   Ibid., at Article 4.
105   Ibid., at Article 5.

6.1. States Parties shall afford one another the greatest measure of assistance in connection with investigations or criminal or extradition proceedings brought in respect of the offences set forth in article 3, paragraph 1, including assistance in obtaining evidence at their disposal necessary for the proceedings.

2. States Parties shall carry out their obligations under paragraph 1 of the present article in conformity with any treaties or other arrangements on mutual legal assistance that may exist between them. In the absence of such treaties or arrangements, States Parties shall afford one another assistance in accordance with their domestic law.[106]

Further, Article 10 calls on the full cooperation and assistance by Member States to the implementation of the Protocol:

10.1. States Parties shall take all necessary steps to strengthen international cooperation by multilateral, regional and bilateral arrangements for the prevention, detection, investigation, prosecution and punishment of those responsible for acts involving the sale of children, child prostitution, child pornography and child sex tourism. States Parties shall also promote international cooperation and coordination between their authorities, national and international non-governmental organizations and international organizations.

2. States Parties shall promote international cooperation to assist child victims in their physical and psychological recovery, social reintegration and repatriation.

3. States Parties shall promote the strengthening of international cooperation in order to address the root causes, such as poverty and underdevelopment, contributing to the vulnerability of children to the sale of children, child prostitution, child pornography and child sex tourism.

4. States Parties in a position to do so shall provide financial, technical or other assistance through existing multilateral, regional, bilateral or other programmes.[107]

Article 7 provides for seizure and confiscation of goods and proceeds:

7. States Parties shall, subject to the provisions of their national law:

(a) Take measures to provide for the seizure and confiscation, as appropriate, of:

(i) Goods, such as materials, assets and other instrumentalities used to commit or facilitate offences under the present protocol;

(ii) Proceeds derived from such offences;

(b) Execute requests from another State Party for seizure or confiscation of goods or proceeds referred to in subparagraph (a);

---

106   Ibid., at Article 6.
107   Ibid., at Article 10.

(c) Take measures aimed at closing, on a temporary or definitive basis, premises used to commit such offences.[108]

Article 8 ensures the protection of children throughout the various stages of the criminal process:

8.1. States Parties shall adopt appropriate measures to protect the rights and interests of child victims of the practices prohibited under the present Protocol at all stages of the criminal justice process, in particular by:

(a) Recognizing the vulnerability of child victims and adapting procedures to recognize their special needs, including their special needs as witnesses;

(b) Informing child victims of their rights, their role and the scope, timing and progress of the proceedings and of the disposition of their cases;

(c) Allowing the views, needs and concerns of child victims to be presented and considered in proceedings where their personal interests are affected, in a manner consistent with the procedural rules of national law;

(d) Providing appropriate support services to child victims throughout the legal process;

(e) Protecting, as appropriate, the privacy and identity of child victims and taking measures in accordance with national law to avoid the inappropriate dissemination of information that could lead to the identification of child victims;

(f) Providing, in appropriate cases, for the safety of child victims, as well as that of their families and witnesses on their behalf, from intimidation and retaliation;

(g) Avoiding unnecessary delay in the disposition of cases and the execution of orders or decrees granting compensation to child victims.

2. States Parties shall ensure that uncertainty as to the actual age of the victim shall not prevent the initiation of criminal investigations, including investigations aimed at establishing the age of the victim.

3. States Parties shall ensure that, in the treatment by the criminal justice system of children who are victims of the offences described in the present Protocol, the best interest of the child shall be a primary consideration.

4. States Parties shall take measures to ensure appropriate training, in particular legal and psychological training, for the persons who work with victims of the offences prohibited under the present Protocol.

5. States Parties shall, in appropriate cases, adopt measures in order to protect the safety and integrity of those persons and/or organizations involved in the prevention and/or protection and rehabilitation of victims of such offences.

6. Nothing in the present article shall be construed to be prejudicial to or inconsistent with the rights of the accused to a fair and impartial trial.[109]

---

108   Ibid., at Article 7.
109   Ibid., at Article 8.

Article 9 calls on Member States to adopt laws, administrative measures, social policies and programs to prevent offences against children:

> 9.1. States Parties shall adopt or strengthen, implement and disseminate laws, administrative measures, social policies and programmes to prevent the offences referred to in the present Protocol. Particular attention shall be given to protect children who are especially vulnerable to such practices.
> 2. States Parties shall promote awareness in the public at large, including children, through information by all appropriate means, education and training, about the preventive measures and harmful effects of the offences referred to in the present Protocol. In fulfilling their obligations under this article, States Parties shall encourage the participation of the community and, in particular, children and child victims, in such information and education and training programmes, including at the international level.
> 3. States Parties shall take all feasible measures with the aim of ensuring all appropriate assistance to victims of such offences, including their full social reintegration and their full physical and psychological recovery.
> 4. States Parties shall ensure that all child victims of the offences described in the present Protocol have access to adequate procedures to seek, without discrimination, compensation for damages from those legally responsible.
> 5. States Parties shall take appropriate measures aimed at effectively prohibiting the production and dissemination of material advertising the offences described in the present Protocol.[110]

Finally, Article 11 states that additional protections may be provided under national and international law:

> 11. Nothing in the present Protocol shall affect any provisions that are more conducive to the realization of the rights of the child and that may be contained in:
> (a) The law of a State Party;
> (b) International law in force for that State.[111]

Protocol to prevent, suppress and punish trafficking in persons, especially women and children, supplementing the United Nations Convention against Transnational Organized Crime

As an added protection to children, the Protocol to prevent, suppress and punish trafficking in persons, especially women and children, supplementing the United

---

110   Ibid., at Article 9.
111   Ibid., at Article 11.

Nations Convention against Transnational Organized Crime entered into force on 9 September 2003. The Preamble states:

The States Parties to this Protocol,

Declaring that effective action to prevent and combat trafficking in persons, especially women and children, requires a comprehensive international approach in the countries of origin, transit and destination that includes measures to prevent such trafficking, to punish the traffickers and to protect the victims of such trafficking, including by protecting their internationally recognized human rights,

Taking into account the fact that, despite the existence of a variety of international instruments containing rules and practical measures to combat the exploitation of persons, especially women and children, there is no universal instrument that addresses all aspects of trafficking in persons,

Concerned that, in the absence of such an instrument, persons who are vulnerable to trafficking will not be sufficiently protected,

Recalling General Assembly resolution 53/111 of 9 December 1998, in which the Assembly decided to establish an open-ended intergovernmental ad hoc committee for the purpose of elaborating a comprehensive international convention against transnational organized crime and of discussing the elaboration of, inter alia, an international instrument addressing trafficking in women and children,

Convinced that supplementing the United Nations Convention against Transnational Organized Crime with an international instrument for the prevention, suppression and punishment of trafficking in persons, especially women and children, will be useful in preventing and combating that crime,

Have agreed as follows.[112]

Article 2 outlines the purpose of the Protocol:

2. The purposes of this Protocol are:
(a) To prevent and combat trafficking in persons, paying particular attention to women and children;

---

112 Protocol to prevent, suppress and punish trafficking in persons, especially women and children, supplementing the United Nations Convention against Transnational Organized Crime, at the Preamble.

(b) To protect and assist the victims of such trafficking, with full respect for their human rights; and

(c) To promote cooperation among States Parties in order to meet those objectives.[113]

Article 3 defines terms:

3. For the purposes of this Protocol:

(a) 'Trafficking in persons' shall mean the recruitment, transportation, transfer, harbouring or receipt of persons, by means of the threat or use of force or other forms of coercion, of abduction, of fraud, of deception, of the abuse of power or of a position of vulnerability or of the giving or receiving of payments or benefits to achieve the consent of a person having control over another person, for the purpose of exploitation. Exploitation shall include, at a minimum, the exploitation of the prostitution of others or other forms of sexual exploitation, forced labour or services, slavery or practices similar to slavery, servitude or the removal of organs;

(b) The consent of a victim of trafficking in persons to the intended exploitation set forth in subparagraph (a) of this article shall be irrelevant where any of the means set forth in subparagraph (a) have been used;

(c) The recruitment, transportation, transfer, harbouring or receipt of a child for the purpose of exploitation shall be considered 'trafficking in persons' even if this does not involve any of the means set forth in subparagraph (a) of this article;

(d) 'Child' shall mean any person under eighteen years of age.[114]

Article 4 covers the scope of application of the Protocol:

4. This Protocol shall apply, except as otherwise stated herein, to the prevention, investigation and prosecution of the offences established in accordance with article 5 of this Protocol, where those offences are transnational in nature and involve an organized criminal group, as well as to the protection of victims of such offences.[115]

Article 5 calls for the criminalization of trafficking:

5.1. Each State Party shall adopt such legislative and other measures as may be necessary to establish as criminal offences the conduct set forth in article 3 of this Protocol, when committed intentionally.

---

113 Ibid., at Article 2.
114 Ibid., at Article 3.
115 Ibid., at Article 4.

2. Each State Party shall also adopt such legislative and other measures as may be necessary to establish as criminal offences:

(a) Subject to the basic concepts of its legal system, attempting to commit an offence established in accordance with paragraph 1 of this article;

(b) Participating as an accomplice in an offence established in accordance with paragraph 1 of this article; and

(c) Organizing or directing other persons to commit an offence established in accordance with paragraph 1 of this article.[116]

Article 6 provides for assistance to and protection of victims of trafficking in persons:

6.1. In appropriate cases and to the extent possible under its domestic law, each State Party shall protect the privacy and identity of victims of trafficking in persons, including, inter alia, by making legal proceedings relating to such trafficking confidential.

2. Each State Party shall ensure that its domestic legal or administrative system contains measures that provide to victims of trafficking in persons, in appropriate cases:

(a) Information on relevant court and administrative proceedings;

(b) Assistance to enable their views and concerns to be presented and considered at appropriate stages of criminal proceedings against offenders, in a manner not prejudicial to the rights of the defence.

3. Each State Party shall consider implementing measures to provide for the physical, psychological and social recovery of victims of trafficking in persons, including, in appropriate cases, in cooperation with non-governmental organizations, other relevant organizations and other elements of civil society, and, in particular, the provision of:

(a) Appropriate housing;

(b) Counselling and information, in particular as regards their legal rights, in a language that the victims of trafficking in persons can understand;

(c) Medical, psychological and material assistance; and

(d) Employment, educational and training opportunities.

4. Each State Party shall take into account, in applying the provisions of this article, the age, gender and special needs of victims of trafficking in persons, in particular the special needs of children, including appropriate housing, education and care.

5. Each State Party shall endeavour to provide for the physical safety of victims of trafficking in persons while they are within its territory.

---

116   Ibid., at Article 5.

6. Each State Party shall ensure that its domestic legal system contains measures that offer victims of trafficking in persons the possibility of obtaining compensation for damage suffered.[117]

Further, Article 7 covers the status of victims of trafficking in persons in receiving States:

7.1. In addition to taking measures pursuant to article 6 of this Protocol, each State Party shall consider adopting legislative or other appropriate measures that permit victims of trafficking in persons to remain in its territory, temporarily or permanently, in appropriate cases.

2. In implementing the provision contained in paragraph 1 of this article, each State Party shall give appropriate consideration to humanitarian and compassionate factors.[118]

In addition, Article 8 deals with the repatriation of victims of trafficking in persons:

8.1. The State Party of which a victim of trafficking in persons is a national or in which the person had the right of permanent residence at the time of entry into the territory of the receiving State Party shall facilitate and accept, with due regard for the safety of that person, the return of that person without undue or unreasonable delay.

2. When a State Party returns a victim of trafficking in persons to a State Party of which that person is a national or in which he or she had, at the time of entry into the territory of the receiving State Party, the right of permanent residence, such return shall be with due regard for the safety of that person and for the status of any legal proceedings related to the fact that the person is a victim of trafficking and shall preferably be voluntary.

3. At the request of a receiving State Party, a requested State Party shall, without undue or unreasonable delay, verify whether a person who is a victim of trafficking in persons is its national or had the right of permanent residence in its territory at the time of entry into the territory of the receiving State Party.

4. In order to facilitate the return of a victim of trafficking in persons who is without proper documentation, the State Party of which that person is a national or in which he or she had the right of permanent residence at the time of entry into the territory of the receiving State Party shall agree to issue, at the request of the receiving State Party, such travel documents or other authorization as may be necessary to enable the person to travel to and re-enter its territory.

5. This article shall be without prejudice to any right afforded to victims of trafficking in persons by any domestic law of the receiving State Party.

---

117   Ibid., at Article 6.
118   Ibid., at Article 7.

6. This article shall be without prejudice to any applicable bilateral or multilateral agreement or arrangement that governs, in whole or in part, the return of victims of trafficking in persons.[119]

Article 9 requires the prevention of trafficking in persons:

9.1. States Parties shall establish comprehensive policies, programmes and other measures:
(a) To prevent and combat trafficking in persons; and
(b) To protect victims of trafficking in persons, especially women and children, from revictimization.
2. States Parties shall endeavour to undertake measures such as research, information and mass media campaigns and social and economic initiatives to prevent and combat trafficking in persons.
3. Policies, programmes and other measures established in accordance with this article shall, as appropriate, include cooperation with non-governmental organizations, other relevant organizations and other elements of civil society.
4. States Parties shall take or strengthen measures, including through bilateral or multilateral cooperation, to alleviate the factors that make persons, especially women and children, vulnerable to trafficking, such as poverty, underdevelopment and lack of equal opportunity.
5. States Parties shall adopt or strengthen legislative or other measures, such as educational, social or cultural measures, including through bilateral and multilateral cooperation, to discourage the demand that fosters all forms of exploitation of persons, especially women and children, that leads to trafficking.[120]

Article 10 calls for the cooperation among law enforcement and immigration authorities in information exchange and training:

10.1. Law enforcement, immigration or other relevant authorities of States Parties shall, as appropriate, cooperate with one another by exchanging information, in accordance with their domestic law, to enable them to determine:
(a) Whether individuals crossing or attempting to cross an international border with travel documents belonging to other persons or without travel documents are perpetrators or victims of trafficking in persons;
(b) The types of travel document that individuals have used or attempted to use to cross an international border for the purpose of trafficking in persons; and
(c) The means and methods used by organized criminal groups for the purpose of trafficking in persons, including the recruitment and transportation of victims,

---

119   Ibid., at Article 8.
120   Ibid., at Article 9.

routes and links between and among individuals and groups engaged in such trafficking, and possible measures for detecting them.

2. States Parties shall provide or strengthen training for law enforcement, immigration and other relevant officials in the prevention of trafficking in persons. The training should focus on methods used in preventing such trafficking, prosecuting the traffickers and protecting the rights of the victims, including protecting the victims from the traffickers. The training should also take into account the need to consider human rights and child- and gender-sensitive issues and it should encourage cooperation with non-governmental organizations, other relevant organizations and other elements of civil society.

3. A State Party that receives information shall comply with any request by the State Party that transmitted the information that places restrictions on its use.[121]

Importantly, Article 11 deals with border measures:

11.1. Without prejudice to international commitments in relation to the free movement of people, States Parties shall strengthen, to the extent possible, such border controls as may be necessary to prevent and detect trafficking in persons.

2. Each State Party shall adopt legislative or other appropriate measures to prevent, to the extent possible, means of transport operated by commercial carriers from being used in the commission of offences established in accordance with article 5 of this Protocol.

3. Where appropriate, and without prejudice to applicable international conventions, such measures shall include establishing the obligation of commercial carriers, including any transportation company or the owner or operator of any means of transport, to ascertain that all passengers are in possession of the travel documents required for entry into the receiving State.

4. Each State Party shall take the necessary measures, in accordance with its domestic law, to provide for sanctions in cases of violation of the obligation set forth in paragraph 3 of this article.

5. Each State Party shall consider taking measures that permit, in accordance with its domestic law, the denial of entry or revocation of visas of persons implicated in the commission of offences established in accordance with this Protocol.

6. Without prejudice to article 27 of the Convention, States Parties shall consider strengthening cooperation among border control agencies by, inter alia, establishing and maintaining direct channels of communication.[122]

Article 12 provides for the security and control of documents:

---

121   Ibid., at Article 10.
122   Ibid., at Article 11.

12. Each State Party shall take such measures as may be necessary, within available means:

(a) To ensure that travel or identity documents issued by it are of such quality that they cannot easily be misused and cannot readily be falsified or unlawfully altered, replicated or issued; and

(b) To ensure the integrity and security of travel or identity documents issued by or on behalf of the State Party and to prevent their unlawful creation, issuance and use.[123]

Further, Article 13 deals with the legitimacy and validity of documents:

13. At the request of another State Party, a State Party shall, in accordance with its domestic law, verify within a reasonable time the legitimacy and validity of travel or identity documents issued or purported to have been issued in its name and suspected of being used for trafficking in persons.[124]

Finally, Article 14 is a saving clause for the Protocol:

14.1. Nothing in this Protocol shall affect the rights, obligations and responsibilities of States and individuals under international law, including international humanitarian law and international human rights law and, in particular, where applicable, the 1951 Convention and the 1967 Protocol relating to the Status of Refugees and the principle of non-refoulement as contained therein.

2. The measures set forth in this Protocol shall be interpreted and applied in a way that is not discriminatory to persons on the ground that they are victims of trafficking in persons. The interpretation and application of those measures shall be consistent with internationally recognized principles of non-discrimination.[125]

Conclusion

On the international level, attempts have been made to provide legislatively for equality to end child discrimination. Historically, children have had no input in the Constitution and the laws of the land. In recycling discrimination, 'the stream always tries to return to its habitual course'.[126] However, international law has made great strides to overcome prejudice against children, as shown in *Little Angels*.

---

123 Ibid., at Article 12.

124 Ibid., at Article 13.

125 Ibid., at Article 14.

126 Canadian Advisory Council on the Status of Women, *Feminist Guide to the Canadian Constitution*, Ottawa, 1992, at p. 57.

Chapter 4
Little Angels in Australia and New Zealand

Introduction

In the quest for respect for our children and in the fight against child discrimination in *Little Angels*, this chapter will examine child issues in Australia and New Zealand. It will initially look at the situation in Australia, examining such legislation as the Racial Discrimination Act, the Racial Hatred Act, the Sex Discrimination Act, the Human Rights Act, the Human Rights and Equal Opportunity Commission Act, and the Workplace Relations Act; and in New Zealand, the Treaty of Waitangi, the Race Relations Act, the Bill of Rights, the Human Rights Act and the Education Act.

Australia

Australia has a federal constitutional system in which legislative, executive and judicial powers are distributed between the federal government, and those of the six States, namely New South Wales (NSW), Victoria (Vic), Queensland (Qld), South Australia (SA), Tasmania (Tas), and Western Australia (WA), and two internal self-governing Territories, namely the Australian Capital Territory (ACT) and the Northern Territory (NT). Overall, in terms of education and training, important for children, the critical area of concern is inequalities and inadequacies in and unequal access to education and training, with corrective action to ensure equal access to education; eradicate illiteracy; improve access to vocational training, science and technology, and continuing education; develop non-discriminatory education and training; allocate sufficient resources for and monitor the implementation of educational reforms; and promote lifelong education and training. Access to education and training is vital for equality.[1] Education remains the key to improving economic status in a changing economy and equipping individuals to achieve their goals and widen their life choices. A well-functioning economy needs a workforce that fully utilizes all its human capital, and promotes skills development and education without discrimination. In terms of human rights, the critical area of concern is the lack of respect for and adequate promotion and protection of human rights, with corrective action, through the full implementation of all human rights instruments. Human rights are an inalienable, integral and indivisible aspect of ife,

---

1   Government of Australia, *Australia's Beijing Plus Five Action Plan 2001–2005*.

Table 4.1 Employment statistics for Australia by age, showing underage employment.

Age group	Total			Men			Women		
	Total population	Active population	Activity rate	Total population	Active population	Activity rate	Total population	Active population	Activity rate
Total	21343.9	11211.4	52.5	10595.4	6116.1	57.7	10748.5	5095.2	47.4
Total (15+)	17207.7	11211.4	65.2	8473.2	6116.1	72.2	8734.5	5095.2	58.3
0–9	2733.4	–	–	1402.1	–	–	1331.2	–	–
10–14	1402.9	–	–	720.0	–	–	682.8	–	–
15–19	1462.0	842.2	57.6	749.4	426.3	56.9	712.5	416.0	58.4
20–24	1502.8	1219.5	81.1	760.4	640.0	84.2	742.4	579.4	78.0
25–29	1489.0	1247.9	83.8	749.7	684.9	91.4	739.3	563.1	76.2
30–34	1456.6	1202.1	82.5	725.7	674.4	92.9	731.0	527.6	72.2
35–39	1583.1	1294.7	81.8	784.2	723.7	92.3	798.9	571.0	71.5
40–44	1509.4	1276.9	84.6	749.2	682.0	91.0	760.2	594.9	78.2
45–49	1544.7	1309.6	84.8	764.3	687.2	89.9	780.5	622.4	79.7
50–54	1409.0	1138.2	80.8	698.1	607.1	87.0	710.9	531.1	74.7
55–59	1285.2	878.7	68.4	638.7	484.5	75.9	646.5	394.1	61.0
60–64	1126.7	540.7	48.0	563.8	326.9	58.0	562.9	213.8	38.0
65–69	834.7	176.2	21.1	413.5	116.8	28.3	421.2	59.4	14.1
70+	2004.3	84.7	4.2	876.1	62.2	7.1	1128.2	22.5	2.0

Source: International Labour Organization, Laborsta, 2008.

in the legislative protections and the existence of agencies to enable citizens to exercise their rights and responsibilities.[2]

Enforcement of legislation concerning education and employment rests mainly with individual States and Territories. Under Australian law, the age of majority is 18; however, the minimum age of employment and regulation of children in employment varies across each State and Territory. Further, there is no federal legislation in Australia setting a minimum age for employment, but States and Territories regulate the employment of children through laws setting a minimum age for leaving compulsory education, claiming unemployment benefits, and engaging in certain occupations.[3] Specific laws regulating the employment of children under the age of 15 years include the Workplace Relations Act 1996 (Cth) § 16(2); Child Employment Act 2006 (Qld); Child Employment Regulation 2006 (Qld); Fair Work Act 1994 (SA) § 98A; Child Labour Award 2006 (SA); Children and Young Persons (Care and Protection) Act 1988 (NSW); Children and Young Persons (Care and Protection – Child Employment) Regulation 2005 (NSW); and Child Employment Act 2003 (Vic). In terms of New South Wales, the Children and Young Persons (Care and Protection – Child Employment) Regulation 2010 provides under Clause 14 that a child cannot be employed for more than five consecutive days; an employer must not employ a child for more than four hours on any day on which the child receives schooling; an employer must not employ a child later than 8p.m. on three consecutive days if the day following each day on which the child is employed is a day on which the child is to receive schooling; and the total period of time for which a child is employed during any week, when added to the time that the child receives schooling during that week, must not exceed 50 hours.[4] In terms of Victoria, the Child Employment Act 2003 introduced maximum daily hours of work, mandated rest breaks, minimum ages for certain occupations, a prohibition against certain types of employment, a provision restricting children to 'light work' and a system of checks for employers and other persons directly supervising children.[5] In terms of Queensland, the Child Employment Act 2006 provides for a general minimum working age tied to compulsory schooling requirements, while allowing children below this age to work only in certain circumstances and with various restrictions imposed; it strives to ensure that work does not interfere with children's schooling and that children are prevented from performing work that may be harmful to their health or safety or their physical, mental, moral or social development.[6] In terms of Western Australia, the Children and Community Services Act 2004 prohibits

---

2   Ibid.

3   US Department of Labor, Bureau of International Labor Affairs, Laws Governing Exploitative Child Labor Report Australia, 2004.

4   Children and Young Persons (Care and Protection – Child Employment) Regulation, NSW Australia, 2010.

5   Child Employment Act, Victoria Australia, 2003.

6   Child Employment Act, Queensland Australia, 2006.

the employment of children under the age of 15 except under strict conditions.[7] However, many children continue to work on an unpaid basis in family businesses, and are not protected by employment legislation; appropriate child labor laws are necessary as they help set community standards to combat child discrimination.[8]

Australia has ratified the Worst Forms of Child Labour Convention, 1999 (No. 182) (C. 182) in 2006; however, it has not yet ratified the Minimum Age Convention, 1973 (No. 138) (C. 138).

Racial Discrimination Act (RDA)

For minority children who suffer age and race/ethnic discrimination, the Racial Discrimination Act 1975 (RDA), also known as An Act relating to the Elimination of Racial and other Discrimination, prohibits discrimination on the grounds of race, colour, descent and national or ethnic origin.[9] The Preamble of the Racial Discrimination Act states:

> Whereas a Convention entitled the 'International Convention on the Elimination of all Forms of Racial Discrimination' was opened for signature on 21 December 1965:
> And whereas the Convention entered into force on 2 January 1969:
> And whereas it is desirable, in pursuance of all relevant powers of the Parliament, including, but not limited to, its power to make laws with respect to external affairs, with respect to the people of any race for whom it is deemed necessary to make special laws and with respect to immigration, to make the provisions contained in this Act for the prohibition of racial discrimination and certain other forms of discrimination and, in particular, to make provision for giving effect to the Convention:
> Be it therefore enacted by the Queen, the Senate and the House of Representatives of Australia.[10]

Importantly, Section 9 prohibits discrimination:

> 9(1) It is unlawful for a person to do any act involving a distinction, exclusion, restriction or preference based on race, colour, descent or national or ethnic origin which has the purpose or effect of nullifying or impairing the recognition, enjoyment or exercise, on an equal footing, of any human right or fundamental freedom in the political, economic, social, cultural or any other field of public life.
> (1A) Where:

---

7   Children and Community Services Act, Western Australia Australia, 2004.
8   Patrick Parkinson, *The Child Labour Problem in Australia*.
9   Racial Discrimination Act, Australia.
10   Ibid., at the Preamble.

(a) a person requires another person to comply with a term, condition or requirement which is not reasonable having regard to the circumstances of the case; and

(b) the other person does not or cannot comply with the term, condition or requirement; and

(c) the requirement to comply has the purpose or effect of nullifying or impairing the recognition, enjoyment or exercise, on an equal footing, by persons of the same race, colour, descent or national or ethnic origin as the other person, of any human right or fundamental freedom in the political, economic, social, cultural or any other field of public life;

the act of requiring such compliance is to be treated, for the purposes of this Part, as an act involving a distinction based on, or an act done by reason of, the other person's race, colour, descent or national or ethnic origin.

(2) A reference in this section to a human right or fundamental freedom in the political, economic, social, cultural or any other field of public life includes any right of a kind referred to in Article 5 of the Convention.

(3) This section does not apply in respect of the employment, or an application for the employment, of a person on a ship or aircraft (not being an Australian ship or aircraft) if that person was engaged, or applied, for that employment outside Australia.[11]

In addition, Section 10 guarantees equality before the law:

10(1) If, by reason of, or of a provision of, a law of the Commonwealth or of a State or Territory, persons of a particular race, colour or national or ethnic origin do not enjoy a right that is enjoyed by persons of another race, colour or national or ethnic origin, or enjoy a right to a more limited extent than persons of another race, colour or national or ethnic origin, then, notwithstanding anything in that law, persons of the first-mentioned race, colour or national or ethnic origin shall, by force of this section, enjoy that right to the same extent as persons of that other race, colour or national or ethnic origin.[12]

Importantly, Section 15 guards against discrimination in employment:

15(1) It is unlawful for an employer or a person acting or purporting to act on behalf of an employer:

(a) to refuse or fail to employ a second person on work of any description which is available and for which that second person is qualified;

(b) to refuse or fail to offer or afford a second person the same terms of employment, conditions of work and opportunities for training and promotion

---

11   Ibid., at Section 9.
12   Ibid., at Section 10.

as are made available for other persons having the same qualifications and employed in the same circumstances on work of the same description; or

(c) to dismiss a second person from his or her employment;

by reason of the race, colour or national or ethnic origin of that second person or of any relative or associate of that second person.

(2) It is unlawful for a person concerned with procuring employment for other persons or procuring employees for any employer to treat any person seeking employment less favorably than other persons in the same circumstances by reason of the race, colour or national or ethnic origin of the person so seeking employment or of any relative or associate of that person.

(3) It is unlawful for an organization of employers or employees, or a person acting or purporting to act on behalf of such an organization, to prevent, or to seek to prevent, another person from offering for employment or from continuing in employment by reason of the race, colour or national or ethnic origin of that other person or of any relative or associate of that other person.[13]

Interestingly, Section 18 prohibits certain offensive behavior based on hatred:

18. Where:

(a) an act is done for 2 or more reasons; and

(b) one of the reasons is the race, colour, descent or national or ethnic origin of a person (whether or not it is the dominant reason or a substantial reason for doing the act);

then, for the purposes of this Part, the act is taken to be done for that reason.

18B If:

(a) an act is done for 2 or more reasons; and

(b) one of the reasons is the race, colour or national or ethnic origin of a person (whether or not it is the dominant reason or a substantial reason for doing the act);

then, for the purposes of this Part, the act is taken to be done because of the person's race, colour or national or ethnic origin.

18C(1) It is unlawful for a person to do an act, otherwise than in private, if:

(a) the act is reasonably likely, in all the circumstances, to offend, insult, humiliate or intimidate another person or a group of people; and

(b) the act is done because of the race, colour or national or ethnic origin of the other person or of some or all of the people in the group.[14]

Offences are listed under Section 27:

27(2) A person shall not:

(a) refuse to employ another person;

---

13   Ibid., at Section 15.
14   Ibid., at Section 18.

(b) dismiss, or threaten to dismiss, another person from the other person's employment;

(c) prejudice, or threaten to prejudice, another person in the other person's employment; or

(d) intimidate or coerce, or impose any pecuniary or other penalty upon, another person;

by reason that the other person:

(e) has made, or proposes to make, a complaint under this Act or the Human Rights and Equal Opportunity Commission Act 1986;

(f) has furnished, or proposes to furnish, any information or documents to a person exercising or performing any powers or functions under this Act or the Human Rights and Equal Opportunity Commission Act 1986; or

(g) has attended, or proposes to attend, a conference held under this Act or the Human Rights and Equal Opportunity Commission Act 1986.[15]

Section 19 establishes the office of the Race Discrimination Commissioner:

19. For the purposes of this Act there shall be a Race Discrimination Commissioner.[16]

Finally, the functions of the Race Commission are outlined in Section 20.

20(1) The following functions are hereby conferred on the Commission:

(b) to promote an understanding and acceptance of, and compliance with, this Act;

(c) to develop, conduct and foster research and educational programs and other programs for the purpose of:

(i) combating racial discrimination and prejudices that lead to racial discrimination;

(ii) promoting understanding, tolerance and friendship among racial and ethnic groups; and

(iii) propagating the purposes and principles of the Convention;

(d) to prepare, and to publish in such manner as the Commission considers appropriate, guidelines for the avoidance of infringements ...

(e) where the Commission considers it appropriate to do so, with the leave of the court hearing the proceedings and subject to any conditions imposed by the court, to intervene in proceedings that involve racial discrimination issues;

(f) to inquire into, and make determinations on, matters referred to it by the Minister or the Commissioner.[17]

---

15   Ibid., at Section 27.
16   Ibid., at Section 19.
17   Ibid., at Section 20.

Racial Hatred Act (RHA)

In addition, for minority children who suffer age and race/ethnic discrimination, the Racial Hatred Act 1995 (RHA) is entitled 'An Act to prohibit certain conduct involving the hatred of other people on the ground of race, colour or national or ethnic origin, and for related purposes'.[18] It extends the coverage of the Racial Discrimination Act (RDA) to allow people to complain about racially and ethnically offensive or abusive behavior, including racial and ethnic vilification. It covers public acts, which are done, in whole or in part, because of the race, color, or national or ethnic origin of a person or group and reasonably likely in all circumstances to offend, insult, humiliate or intimidate that person or group. In order to protect freedom of speech, under the Act, the following things are not unlawful if 'done reasonably and in good faith': an artistic work or performance; an academic or scientific publication, discussion or debate; a fair and accurate report on a matter of public interest; and a fair comment if the comment is an expression of a person's genuine belief. In bringing a complaint under the RHA, the complainant is responsible for proving that the act was done in public, that it was done because of his ethnicity and that it was reasonably likely to offend, insult, humiliate or intimidate a reasonable person of that ethnicity. In claiming an exception, the respondent is responsible for establishing that the act was a genuine exception and that it was done reasonably and in good faith.

The case of *Bryant* v. *Queensland Newspapers Pty Ltd*, [1997] HREOC 15/05/97 (unreported), covered the interpretation of the Racial Hatred Act. The complainant sued the respondent newspaper for publishing articles and letters in its weekly publication, which referred to English people as Poms or Pommies, alleging that the use of these terms is insulting and offensive to English people. However, for the act to be unlawful, it had to be reasonably likely, in all the circumstances, to offend, insult, humiliate or intimidate the person or group of people referred to. The president of the Human Rights and Equal Opportunity Commission accepted that the complainant was offended by the use of the words but found that the relevant provisions of the Act allow a fair degree of journalistic licence, including the use of flamboyant or colloquial language.[19]

Sex Discrimination Act

For female children who suffer age and gender discrimination, the Sex Discrimination Act 1984 prohibits discrimination on the grounds of gender, marital status, pregnancy, and potential pregnancy and family responsibilities. Section 3 outlines the objects of the Act:

---

18   Racial Hatred Act, Australia.
19   *Bryant* v. *Queensland Newspapers Pty Ltd*, [1997] HREOC 15/05/97 (unreported).

3(a) to give effect to certain provisions of the Convention on the Elimination of All Forms of Discrimination against Women; and

(b) to eliminate, so far as is possible, discrimination against persons on the ground of sex, marital status, pregnancy or potential pregnancy in the areas of work, accommodation, education, the provision of goods, facilities and services, the disposal of land, the activities of clubs and the administration of Commonwealth laws and programs; and

(ba) to eliminate, so far as possible, discrimination involving dismissal of employees on the ground of family responsibilities; and

(c) to eliminate, so far as is possible, discrimination involving sexual harassment in the workplace, in educational institutions and in other areas of public activity; and

(d) to promote recognition and acceptance within the community of the principle of the equality of men and women.[20]

Importantly, Section 5 deals directly with the definition of gender discrimination:

5(1) For the purposes of this Act, a person (in this subsection referred to as the discriminator) discriminates against another person (in this subsection referred to as the aggrieved person) on the ground of the sex of the aggrieved person if, by reason of:

(a) the sex of the aggrieved person;

(b) a characteristic that appertains generally to persons of the sex of the aggrieved person; or

(c) a characteristic that is generally imputed to persons of the sex of the aggrieved person; the discriminator treats the aggrieved person less favourably than, in circumstances that are the same or are not materially different, the discriminator treats or would treat a person of the opposite sex.

(2) For the purposes of this Act, a person (the discriminator) discriminates against another person (the aggrieved person) on the ground of the sex of the aggrieved person if the discriminator imposes, or proposes to impose, a condition, requirement or practice that has, or is likely to have, the effect of disadvantaging persons of the same sex as the aggrieved person.[21]

Indirect discrimination and the reasonableness test are dealt with under Section 7B:

7B(1) A person does not discriminate against another person by imposing, or proposing to impose, a condition, requirement or practice that has, or is likely to have, the disadvantaging effect mentioned in subsection 5(2), 6(2) or 7(2) if the condition, requirement or practice is reasonable in the circumstances.

20　Sex Discrimination Act, Australia, at Section 3.

21　Ibid., at Section 5.

(2) The matters to be taken into account in deciding whether a condition, requirement or practice is reasonable in the circumstances include:
(a) the nature and extent of the disadvantage resulting from the imposition, or proposed imposition, of the condition, requirement or practice; and
(b) the feasibility of overcoming or mitigating the disadvantage; and
(c) whether the disadvantage is proportionate to the result sought by the person who imposes, or proposes to impose, the condition, requirement or practice.[22]

Further, the burden of proof is contained in Section 7C:

7C In a proceeding under this Act, the burden of proving that an act does not constitute discrimination because of section 7B lies on the person who did the act.[23]

In terms of affirmative action, Section 7D stipulates:

7D(1) A person may take special measures for the purpose of achieving substantive equality between:
(a) men and women; or
(b) people of different marital status; or
(c) women who are pregnant and people who are not pregnant; or
(d) women who are potentially pregnant and people who are not potentially pregnant; or
(e) women who are breastfeeding and people who are not breastfeeding; or
(f) people with family responsibilities and people without family responsibilities.[24]

The Act provides an important role for the HREOC in addressing the issue of gender discrimination, and its functions are defined under Section 48:

48(1) The following functions are hereby conferred on the Commission:
...
(d) to promote an understanding and acceptance of, and compliance with, this Act;
(e) to undertake research and educational programs, and other programs, on behalf of the Commonwealth for the purpose of promoting the objects of this Act;
(f) to examine enactments, and ... proposed enactments, for the purpose of ascertaining whether they are or would be inconsistent with or contrary to the objects of this Act, and to report to the Minister the results of any such

---

22 Ibid., at Section 7B.
23 Ibid., at Section 7C.
24 Ibid., at Section 7D.

examination. The HREOC is to report to the Minister as to the laws that should be made by the Parliament, or action that should be taken by the Commonwealth; (ga) to prepare, and to publish in such manner as the Commission considers appropriate, guidelines for the avoidance of discrimination; and

(gb) where the Commission considers it appropriate to do so, with the leave of the court and subject to any conditions imposed by the court, to intervene in proceedings …[25]

Human Rights Act

Important in the fight against child discrimination, the Human Rights Act 2004, also known as An Act to Respect, Protect and Promote Human Rights, is the first Bill of Rights in Australia, specifically in the Australian Capital Territory (ACT). The Preamble of the Human Rights Act states:

1. Human rights are necessary for individuals to live lives of dignity and value.

2. Respecting, protecting and promoting the rights of individuals improves the welfare of the whole community.

3. Human rights are set out in this Act so that individuals know what their rights are.

4. Setting out these human rights also makes it easier for them to be taken into consideration in the development and interpretation of legislation.

5. This Act encourages individuals to see themselves, and each other, as the holders of rights, and as responsible for upholding the human rights of others.

6. Few rights are absolute. Human rights may be subject only to the reasonable limits in law that can be demonstrably justified in a free and democratic society. One individual's rights may also need to be weighed against another individual's rights.

7. Although human rights belong to all individuals, they have special significance for Indigenous people – the first owners of this land, members of its most enduring cultures, and individuals for whom the issue of rights protection has great and continuing importance. The Legislative Assembly for the Australian Capital Territory therefore enacts as follows:[26]

Section 5 defines human rights and Section 6 defines who possesses human rights:

5. In this Act:
human rights means the civil and political rights.[27]

---

25 Ibid., at Section 48.
26 Human Rights Act, Australia, at the Preamble.
27 Ibid., at Section 5.

6. Only individuals have human rights.[28]

Importantly, Section 7 notes that the Act is not exhaustive:

> 7. This Act is not exhaustive of the rights an individual may have under domestic or international law.[29]

Equality before the law is recognized in Section 8:

> 8. Recognition and equality before the law
> (1) Everyone has the right to recognition as a person before the law.
> (2) Everyone has the right to enjoy his or her human rights without distinction or discrimination of any kind.
> (3) Everyone is equal before the law and is entitled to the equal protection of the law without discrimination. In particular, everyone has the right to equal and effective protection against discrimination on any ground.[30]

However, Section 28 is a limiting clause:

> 28(1) Human rights may be subject only to reasonable limits set by Territory laws that can be demonstrably justified in a free and democratic society.
> (2) In deciding whether a limit is reasonable, all relevant factors must be considered, including the following:
>> (a) the nature of the right affected;
>> (b) the importance of the purpose of the limitation;
>> (c) the nature and extent of the limitation;
>> (d) the relationship between the limitation and its purpose;
>> (e) any less restrictive means reasonably available to achieve the purpose
> the limitation seeks to achieve.[31]

Section 31 deals with interpretation of human rights:

> 31(1) International law, and the judgments of foreign and international courts and tribunals, relevant to a human right may be considered in interpreting the human right.
> (2) In deciding whether material mentioned in subsection (1) or any other material should be considered, and the weight to be given to the material, the following matters must be taken into account:

---

28   Ibid., at Section 6.
29   Ibid., at Section 7.
30   Ibid., at Section 8.
31   Ibid., at Section 28.

(a) the desirability of being able to rely on the ordinary meaning of this Act, having regard to its purpose and its provisions read in the context of the Act as a whole;

(b) the undesirability of prolonging proceedings without compensating advantage;

(c) the accessibility of the material to the public.[32]

Further, Section 32 covers a declaration of incompatibility with the Act:

32(1) This section applies if

(a) a proceeding is being heard by the Supreme Court; and

(b) an issue arises in the proceeding about whether a Territory law is consistent with a human right.

(2) If the Supreme Court is satisfied that the Territory law is not consistent with the human right, the court may declare that the law is not consistent with the human right (the *declaration of incompatibility*).

(3) The declaration of incompatibility does not affect

(a) the validity, operation or enforcement of the law; or

(b) the rights or obligations of anyone.

(4) The registrar of the Supreme Court must promptly give a copy of the declaration of incompatibility to the Attorney-General.[33]

The Human Rights Commissioner's special role is noted in Section 36:

36(1) The human rights commissioner may intervene in a proceeding before a court that involves the application of this Act with the leave of the court.

(2) The court may give leave subject to conditions.[34]

Finally, it is stressed in Section 40B that Public Authorities are held to a higher standard in terms of respect for the Act:

40B Public authorities must act consistently with human rights

(1) It is unlawful for a public authority

(a) to act in a way that is incompatible with a human right; or

(b) in making a decision, to fail to give proper consideration to a relevant human right.

(2) Subsection (1) does not apply if the act is done or decision made under a law in force in the Territory and

(a) the law expressly requires the act to be done or decision made in a particular way and that way is inconsistent with a human right; or

---

32   Ibid., at Section 31.
33   Ibid., at Section 32.
34   Ibid., at Section 36.

(b) the law cannot be interpreted in a way that is consistent with a human right.[35]

Human Rights and Equal Opportunity Commission Act (HREOCA)

The Human Rights and Equal Opportunity Commission Act 1986 (HREOCA) gives effect to relevant international conventions and declarations.[36] Importantly, the Human Rights and Equal Opportunity Commission (HREOC) inquires into complaints under federal anti-discrimination law and educates the community about obligations under domestic legislation. It is charged with increasing the understanding, acceptance and observance of human rights in Australia, and has a mandate to carry out related research and education activities; it liaises internationally with governments and agencies in respect of international treaties, and ensures that Australia meets its obligations under international instruments. The HREOCA enables the HREOC to investigate complaints of breaches of conventions by Commonwealth government agencies and may also investigate complaints of discrimination in employment by any employer. According to Section 46PO(4), the Federal Magistrates Court can act in a number of ways:

> 46PO(4) If the court concerned is satisfied that there has been unlawful discrimination by any respondent, the court may make such orders (including a declaration of right) as it thinks fit, including any of the following orders or any order to a similar effect:
> (a) an order declaring that the respondent has committed unlawful discrimination and directing the respondent not to repeat or continue such unlawful discrimination;
> (b) an order requiring a respondent to perform any reasonable act or course of conduct to redress any loss or damage suffered by an applicant;
> (c) an order requiring a respondent to employ or re-employ an applicant;
> (d) an order requiring a respondent to pay to an applicant damages by way of compensation for any loss or damage suffered because of the conduct of the respondent;
> (e) an order requiring a respondent to vary the termination of a contract or agreement to redress any loss or damage suffered by an applicant;
> (f) an order declaring that it would be inappropriate for any further action to be taken in the matter.[37]

35　Ibid., at Section 40B.
36　Human Rights and Equal Opportunity Commission Act, Australia.
37　Ibid., at Section 46PO(4).

Workplace Relations Act

In the fight against child discrimination, the Workplace Relations Act 1996 has provisions to safeguard groups of workers, and provides for equal remuneration for work of equal value without discrimination. Section 3 enunciates the principal objectives:

> 3. The principal object of this Act is to provide a framework for cooperative workplace relations which promotes the economic prosperity and welfare of the people of Australia by:
>
> …
>
> (m) respecting and valuing the diversity of the work force by helping to prevent and eliminate discrimination on the basis of race, colour, sex, sexual preference, age, physical or mental disability, marital status, family responsibilities, pregnancy, religion, political opinion, national extraction or social origin.[38]

Employment is not to be terminated on certain grounds:

> 659(2) Except as provided by subsection (3) or (4), an employer must not terminate an employee's employment for any one or more of the following reasons, or for reasons including any one or more of the following reasons:
>
> …
>
> (f) race, colour, sex, sexual preference, age, physical or mental disability, marital status, family responsibilities, pregnancy, religion, political opinion, national extraction or social origin.[39]

The Commission is to take into account discrimination issues under Section 104:

> 104. In the performance of its functions, the Commission must take into account the following:
> (a) the need to apply the principle of equal pay for work of equal value;
> (b) the need to prevent and eliminate discrimination because of, or for reasons including, race, colour, sex, sexual preference, age, physical or mental disability, marital status, family responsibilities, pregnancy, religion, political opinion, national extraction or social origin.[40]

Finally, the functions of the Workplace Authority Director are enumerated under Section 150B, which specifically mentions the need to prevent and eliminate discrimination:

---

38   Workplace Relations Act, Australia, at Section 3.
39   Ibid., at Section 659(2).
40   Ibid., at Section 104.

150B(2) In performing his or her functions relating to workplace agreements, the Workplace Authority Director must have particular regard to:

...

(d) the need to prevent and eliminate discrimination because of, or for reasons including, race, colour, sex, sexual preference, age, physical or mental disability, marital status, family responsibilities, pregnancy, religion, political opinion, national extraction or social origin.[41]

New Zealand

In New Zealand, there are restrictions on the employment of young persons through education and occupational safety and health legislation. The Health and Safety in Employment Act 1992 sets out duties to provide safe workplaces, and it applies to all workers regardless of age; the Health and Safety Employment Regulations 1995 restrict young people under age 15 from working in dangerous workplaces, and they restrict people under 16 from night work; and the Health and Safety in Employment Regulations 1995 as amended in 2008 protect young people from hazardous work and extend age restrictions on hazardous work and night work.[42] New Zealand believes that practical programs of action tailored to the different circumstances of child laborers are necessary to provide solutions to the exploitation of our young, since by undertaking work appropriate to their age and level of maturity, children learn essential skills and add to their families and their own well-being.[43] New Zealand has ratified the Worst Forms of Child Labour Convention, 1999 (No. 182) (C. 182) in 2001; however, it has not ratified the Minimum Age Convention, 1973 (No. 138) (C. 138).

Treaty of Waitangi

In the late 1830s, there were approximately 125,000 Māori in New Zealand and about 2000 settlers. More immigrants were arriving all the time though, and Captain William Hobson was sent to act for the British Crown in the negotiation of a treaty between the Crown and the Māori. The Colonial Secretary, Lord Normanby, instructed Hobson:

All dealings with the Aborigines for their Lands must be conducted on the same principles of sincerity, justice, and good faith as must govern your transactions with them for the recognition of Her Majesty's Sovereignty in the Islands. Nor

---

41   Ibid., at Section 150B.

42   Health and Safety in Employment Act 1992; Health and Safety in Employment Regulations 1995, New Zealand.

43   New Zealand Government, Speech on the Global Report a Future without Child Labour, John Chetwin, Secretary of Labour, 2002.

Table 4.2 **Employment statistics for New Zealand by age, showing underage employment.**

Age group	Total			Men			Women		
	Total population	Active population	Activity rate	Total population	Active population	Activity rate	Total population	Active population	Activity rate
Total	4271.1	2283.2	53.5	2093.3	1214.8	58.0	2177.8	1068.4	49.1
Total (15+)	3381.5	2283.2	67.5	1637.5	1214.8	74.2	1743.9	1068.3	61.3
0–9	587.9	–	–	301.1	–	–	286.9	–	–
10–14	301.5	–	–	154.6	–	–	146.9	–	–
15–19	322.5	172.9	53.6	164.7	89.7	54.5	157.8	83.1	52.7
20–24	297.3	216.1	72.7	150.2	115.5	76.9	147.1	100.6	68.4
25–29	273.6	223.9	81.8	134.4	120.6	89.7	139.2	103.3	74.2
30–34	271.4	222.1	81.8	129.7	119.4	92.1	141.6	102.7	72.5
35–39	312.5	256.7	82.1	148.7	136.2	91.6	163.9	120.6	73.6
40–44	314.2	267.5	85.1	151.5	137.6	90.8	162.7	129.9	79.8
45–49	319.5	276.1	86.4	155.1	142.3	91.7	164.3	133.9	81.5
50–54	276.7	237.4	85.8	135.8	122.7	90.4	140.9	114.7	81.4
55–59	244.3	196.7	80.5	120.5	105.3	87.4	123.8	91.3	73.7
60–64	211.2	135.4	64.1	103.9	77.3	74.4	107.3	58.0	54.1
65–69	166.4	54.0	32.5	81.0	32.2	39.8	85.4	21.9	25.6
70–74	126.1	17.3	13.7	60.4	11.3	18.7	65.7	6.0	9.1
75+	245.8	7.1	2.9	101.6	4.7	4.6	144.2	2.3	1.6

Source: International Labour Organization, Laborsta, 2008.

is this all. They must not be permitted to enter into any Contracts in which they might be the ignorant and unintentional authors of injuries to themselves. You will not, for example, purchase from them any Territory the retention of which by them would be essential, or highly conducive, to their own comfort, safety or subsistence. The acquisition of Land by the Crown for the future Settlement of British Subjects must be confined to such Districts as the Natives can alienate without distress or serious inconvenience to themselves. To secure the observance of this rule will be one of the first duties of their official protector.[44]

The Preamble of the English version of the Treaty of Waitangi, which came into effect on 6 February 1840, states:

HER MAJESTY VICTORIA Queen of the United Kingdom of Great Britain and Ireland regarding with Her Royal favour the Native Chiefs and Tribes of New Zealand and anxious to protect their just Rights and Property and to secure to them the enjoyment of Peace and Good Order has deemed it necessary in consequence of the great number of Her Majesty's Subjects who have already settled in New Zealand and the rapid extension of Emigration both from Europe and Australia which is still in progress to constitute and appoint a functionary properly authorized to treat with the Aborigines of New Zealand for the recognition of Her Majesty's Sovereign authority over the whole or any part of those islands, Her Majesty therefore being desirous to establish a settled form of Civil Government with a view to avert the evil consequences which must result from the absence of the necessary Laws and Institutions alike to the native population and to Her subjects has been graciously pleased to empower and to authorize me William Hobson a Captain in Her Majesty's Royal Navy Consul and Lieutenant Governor of such parts of New Zealand as may be or hereafter shall be ceded to Her Majesty to invite the confederated and independent Chiefs of New Zealand to concur in the following Articles and Conditions.[45]

Article 1 states:

The Chiefs of the Confederation of the United Tribes of New Zealand and the separate and independent Chiefs who have not become members of the Confederation cede to Her Majesty the Queen of England absolutely and without reservation all the rights and powers of Sovereignty which the said Confederation or Individual Chiefs respectively exercise or possess, or may be supposed to exercise or to possess over their respective Territories as the sole Sovereigns thereof.[46]

---

44   Colonial Secretary, Lord Normanby.
45   Treaty of Waitangi, New Zealand, at the Preamble.
46   Ibid., at Article 1.

Article 2 states:

> Her Majesty the Queen of England confirms and guarantees to the Chiefs and
> Tribes of New Zealand and to the respective families and individuals thereof
> the full exclusive and undisturbed possession of their Lands and Estates Forests
> Fisheries and other properties which they may collectively or individually possess
> so long as it is their wish and desire to retain the same in their possession; but the
> Chiefs of the United Tribes and the individual Chiefs yield to Her Majesty the
> exclusive right of Preemption over such lands as the proprietors thereof may be
> disposed to alienate at such prices as may be agreed upon between the respective
> Proprietors and persons appointed by Her Majesty to treat with them in that
> behalf.[47]

Article 3 states:

> In consideration thereof Her Majesty the Queen of England extends to the
> Natives of New Zealand Her Royal protection and imparts to them all the Rights
> and Privileges of British Subjects.
> W HOBSON Lieutenant Governor.
> Now therefore We the Chiefs of the Confederation of the United Tribes of
> New Zealand being assembled in Congress at Victoria in Waitangi and We the
> Separate and Independent Chiefs of New Zealand claiming authority over the
> Tribes and Territories which are specified after our respective names, having
> been made fully to understand the Provisions of the foregoing Treaty, accept and
> enter into the same in the full spirit and meaning thereof: in witness of which we
> have attached our signatures or marks at the places and the dates respectively
> specified.[48]

Race Relations Act

For minority children who suffer age and race/ethnic discrimination, the Race
Relations Act 1971 guards against discrimination in a number of areas. In terms of
employment, Section 5 states:

> 5(1) It shall be unlawful for any [person who is an] employer, or any person
> acting or purporting to act on behalf of any [person who is an] employer
> (a) To refuse or omit to employ any person on work of any description which is
> available and for which that person is qualified; or
> (b) To refuse or omit to offer or afford any person the same terms of employment,
> conditions of work, fringe benefits, and opportunities for training, promotion,
> and transfer as are made available for persons of the same or substantially similar

---

47   Ibid., at Article 2.
48   Ibid., at Article 3.

qualifications employed in the same or substantially similar circumstances on work of that description; or

(c) To dismiss any person, or subject any person to any detriment, in circumstances in which other persons employed by that employer on work of that description are not or would not be dismissed or are not or would not be subjected to such detriment

by reason of the colour, race, or ethnic or national origins of that person ...

(3) Nothing in this section shall apply in respect of the employment of any person for any purpose for which persons of a particular ethnic or national origin have or are commonly found to have a particular qualification or aptitude.[49]

Importantly, in terms of measures to ensure equality, Section 9 states:

9. Anything done or omitted which would otherwise constitute a breach of any of the provisions of sections 4 to 7 of this Act shall not constitute such a breach if

(a) It is done or omitted in good faith for the purpose of assisting or advancing persons or groups of persons, being in each case persons of a particular colour, race, or ethnic or national origin; and

(b) Those groups or persons need or may reasonably be supposed to need assistance or advancement in order to achieve an equal place with other members of the community.[50]

Interestingly, in terms of disharmony, Section 9A states:

9A(1) It shall be unlawful for any person

(a) To publish or distribute written matter which is threatening, abusive, or insulting, or to broadcast by means of radio or television words which are threatening, abusive, or insulting; or

(b) To use in any public place ... or within the hearing of persons in any such public place, or at any meeting to which the public are invited or have access, words which are threatening, abusive, or insulting,

being matter or words likely to excite hostility or ill-will against, or bring into contempt or ridicule, any group of persons in New Zealand on the ground of the colour, race, or ethnic or national origins of that group of persons.[51]

Bill of Rights Act

According to the Preamble of the Bill of Rights Act 1990, as amended by the Human Rights Act, the Bill of Rights aims to affirm, protect, and promote human rights and fundamental freedoms in New Zealand; and to affirm New Zealand's

---

49   Ibid., at Section 5.
50   Ibid., at Section 9.
51   Ibid., at Section 9A.

commitment to the International Covenant on Civil and Political Rights.[52] It applies to acts done by the legislative, executive and judicial branches of the government, or by any person or body in the performance of any public function, power or duty conferred or imposed on that person or body by or pursuant to law.

Freedom from discrimination is guaranteed under Section 19:

> 19(1) Everyone has the right to freedom from discrimination on the grounds of discrimination in the Human Rights Act 1993.
>
> (2) Measures taken in good faith for the purpose of assisting or advancing persons or groups of persons disadvantaged because of discrimination that is unlawful by virtue of Part II of the Human Rights Act 1993 do not constitute discrimination.[53]

Further, remedies are contained in Section 27:

> 27(1) Every person has the right to the observance of the principles of natural justice by any tribunal or other public authority which has the power to make a determination in respect of that person's right, obligations, or interests protected or recognized by law.
>
> (2) Every person whose rights, obligations, or interests protected or recognized by law have been affected by a determination of any tribunal or other public authority has the right to apply, in accordance with law, for judicial review of that determination.
>
> (3) Every person has the right to bring civil proceedings against, and to defend civil proceedings brought by, the Crown, and to have those proceedings heard, according to law, in the same way as civil proceedings between individuals.[54]

Importantly, Section 28 provides for other rights and freedoms not specifically mentioned:

> 28. An existing right or freedom shall not be held to be abrogated or restricted by reason only that the right or freedom is not included in this Bill of Rights or is included only in part.[55]

Human Rights Act (HRA)

The Human Rights Act 1993 (HRA) protects New Zealanders from unlawful discrimination in a number of areas of life. The functions and powers of the Human Rights Commission (HRC) are enumerated in Section 5:

---

52 Bill of Rights Act, New Zealand, at the Preamble.
53 Ibid., at Section 19.
54 Ibid., at Section 27.
55 Ibid., at Article 28.

5(1) The primary functions of the Commission are

(a) to advocate and promote respect for, and an understanding and appreciation of, human rights in New Zealand society; and

(b) to encourage the maintenance and development of harmonious relations between individuals and among the diverse groups in New Zealand society.

(2) The Commission has, in order to carry out its primary functions under subsection (1), the following functions:

(a) to be an advocate for human rights and to promote and protect, by education and publicity, respect for, and observance of, human rights:

(b) to encourage and co-ordinate programmes and activities in the field of human rights:

(c) to make public statements in relation to any matter affecting human rights, including statements promoting an understanding of, and compliance with, this Act or the New Zealand Bill of Rights Act 1990 (for example, statements promoting understanding of measures to ensure equality, of indirect discrimination, or of institutions and procedures under this Act for dealing with complaints of unlawful discrimination):

(d) to promote by research, education, and discussion a better understanding of the human rights dimensions of the Treaty of Waitangi and their relationship with domestic and international human rights law:

(e) to prepare and publish, as the Commission considers appropriate, guidelines and voluntary codes of practice for the avoidance of acts or practices that may be inconsistent with, or contrary to, this Act:

(f) to receive and invite representations from members of the public on any matter affecting human rights:

(g) to consult and co-operate with other persons and bodies concerned with the protection of human rights:

(h) to inquire generally into any matter, including any enactment or law, or any practice, or any procedure, whether governmental or non-governmental, if it appears to the Commission that the matter involves, or may involve, the infringement of human rights:

...

(j) to apply to a court or tribunal, under rules of court or regulations specifying the tribunal's procedure, to be appointed as intervener or as counsel assisting the court or tribunal, or to take part in proceedings before the court or tribunal in another way permitted by those rules or regulations, if, in the Commission's opinion, taking part in the proceedings in that way will facilitate the performance of its functions stated in paragraph (a):

(k) to report to the Prime Minister on

(i) any matter affecting human rights, including the desirability of legislative, administrative, or other action to give better protection to human rights and to ensure better compliance with standards laid down in international instruments on human rights:

(ii) the desirability of New Zealand becoming bound by any international instrument on human rights:

(iii) the implications of any proposed legislation (including subordinate legislation) or proposed policy of the Government that the Commission considers may affect human rights:

(l) to make public statements in relation to any group of persons in, or who may be coming to, New Zealand who are or may be subject to hostility, or who have been or may be brought into contempt, on the basis that that group consists of persons against whom discrimination is unlawful under this Act:

(m) to develop a national plan of action, in consultation with interested parties, for the promotion and protection of human rights in New Zealand:

…

(o) to exercise or perform any other functions, powers, and duties conferred or imposed on it by or under this Act or any other enactment.[56]

Importantly, prohibited grounds of discrimination are listed under Section 21:

Section 21(1) For the purposes of this Act, the prohibited grounds of discrimination are:

(a) sex, which includes pregnancy and childbirth:

(b) marital status, which means being—

(i) single; or

(ii) married, in a civil union, or in a de facto relationship; or

(iii) the surviving spouse of a marriage or the surviving partner of a civil union or de facto relationship; or

(iv) separated from a spouse or civil union partner; or

(v) a party to a marriage or civil union that is now dissolved, or to a de facto relationship that is now ended:

(c) religious belief:

(d) ethical belief, which means the lack of a religious belief, whether in respect of a particular religion or religions or all religions:

(e) colour:

(f) race:

(g) ethnic or national origins, which includes nationality or citizenship:

(h) disability, which means:

(i) physical disability or impairment:

(ii) physical illness:

(iii) psychiatric illness:

(iv) intellectual or psychological disability or impairment:

(v) any other loss or abnormality of psychological, physiological, or anatomical structure or function:

(vi) reliance on a guide dog, wheelchair, or other remedial means:

---

56   Human Rights Act, New Zealand, at Section 5(1).

(vii) the presence in the body of organisms capable of causing illness:

(i) age, which means:

(i) for the purposes of sections 22 to 41 and section 70 of this Act and in relation to any different treatment based on age that occurs in the period beginning with 1 February 1994 and ending with the close of 31 January 1999, any age commencing with the age of 16 years and ending with the date on which persons of the age of the person whose age is in issue qualify for national superannuation under section 3 of the Social Welfare (Transitional Provisions) Act 1990 (irrespective of whether or not the particular person qualifies for national superannuation at that age or any other age):

(ii) for the purposes of sections 22 to 41 and section 70 of this Act and in relation to any different treatment based on age that occurs on or after 1 February 1999, any age commencing with the age of 16 years:

(iii) for the purposes of any other provision of Part II of this Act, any age commencing with the age of 16 years:

(j) political opinion, which includes the lack of a particular political opinion or any political opinion:

(k) employment status, which means:

(i) being unemployed; or

(ii) being a recipient of a benefit or compensation under the Social Security Act 1964 or an entitlement under the Accident Compensation Act 2001:

(l) family status, which means:

(i) having the responsibility for part-time care or full-time care of children or other dependants; or

(ii) having no responsibility for the care of children or other dependants; or

(iii) being married to, or being in a civil union or de facto relationship with, a particular person; or

(iv) being a relative of a particular person;

(m) sexual orientation, which means a heterosexual, homosexual, lesbian, or bisexual orientation.

(2) Each of the grounds specified in subsection (1) of this section is a prohibited ground of discrimination, for the purposes of this Act, if:

(a) it pertains to a person or to a relative or associate of a person; and

(b) it either:

(i) currently exists or has in the past existed; or

(ii) is suspected or assumed or believed to exist or to have existed by the person alleged to have discriminated.[57]

Indirect discrimination is defined in Section 65:

65. Where any conduct, practice, requirement, or condition that is not apparently in contravention of any provision of this Part of this Act has the effect of treating

---

57   Ibid., at Section 21(1).

a person or group of persons differently on one of the prohibited grounds of discrimination in a situation where such treatment would be unlawful under any provision of this Part of this Act other than this section, that conduct, practice, condition, or requirement shall be unlawful under that provision unless the person whose conduct or practice is in issue, or who imposes the condition or requirement, establishes good reason for it.[58]

Further, as regards discrimination in employment, Section 22(1) states:

22(1) Where an applicant for employment or an employee is qualified for work of any description, it shall be unlawful for an employer, or any person acting or purporting to act on behalf of an employer:

(a) to refuse or omit to employ the applicant on work of that description which is available; or

(b) to offer or afford the applicant or the employee less favourable terms of employment, conditions of work, superannuation or other fringe benefits, and opportunities for training, promotion, and transfer than are made available to applicants or employees of the same or substantially similar capabilities employed in the same or substantially similar circumstances on work of that description; or

(c) to terminate the employment of the employee, or subject the employee to any detriment, in circumstances in which the employment of other employees employed on work of that description would not be terminated, or in which other employees employed on work of that description would not be subjected to such detriment; or

(d) to retire the employee, or to require or cause the employee to retire or resign (applies to all (a), (b), (c) and (d)) by reason of any of the prohibited grounds of discrimination.[59]

However, Section 59 includes an exception in relation to courses and counselling:

59. Nothing ... shall prevent the holding or provision, at any educational establishment, of courses or counselling restricted to persons of a particular sex, race, ethnic, or national origin, or sexual orientation, where highly personal matters, such as sexual matters or the prevention of violence, are involved.[60]

Further, Section 27 includes exceptions in relation to authenticity and privacy:

58   Ibid., at Section 65.
59   Ibid., at Section 22(1).
60   Ibid., at Section 59.

27(4) Nothing ... shall prevent different treatment based on sex, race, ethnic or
national origins, or sexual orientation where the position is that of a counsellor
on highly personal matters such as sexual matters or the prevention of violence.
(5) Where, as a term or condition of employment, a position ordinarily obliges or
qualifies the holder of that position to live in premises provided by the employer,
the employer does not commit a breach ... by omitting to apply that term or
condition in respect of employees of a particular sex or marital status if in all the
circumstances it is not reasonably practicable for the employer to do so.[61]

Section 35 outlines the general qualification on exceptions:

35. No employer shall be entitled ... to accord to any person in respect of any
position different treatment based on a prohibited ground of discrimination
even though some of the duties of that position would fall within any of those
exceptions if, with some adjustment of the activities of the employer (not
being an adjustment involving unreasonable disruption of the activities of the
employer), some other employee could carry out those particular duties.[62]

Importantly, Section 66 guards against victimization:

66(1) It shall be unlawful for any person to treat or to threaten to treat any other
person less favourably than he or she would treat other persons in the same or
substantially similar circumstances
(a) on the ground that that person, or any relative or associate of that person,
(i) intends to make use of his or her rights under this Act or to make a disclosure
under the Protected Disclosures Act 2000; or
(ii) has made use of his or her rights, or promoted the rights of some other
person, under this Act, or has made a disclosure, or has encouraged disclosure
by some other person, under the Protected Disclosures Act 2000; or
(iii) has given information or evidence in relation to any complaint, investigation,
or proceeding under this Act or arising out of a disclosure under the Protected
Disclosures Act 2000; or
(iv) has declined to do an act that would contravene this Act; or
(v) has otherwise done anything under or by reference to this Act; or
(b) on the ground that he or she knows that that person, or any relative or associate
of that person, intends to do any of the things mentioned in subparagraphs (i) to
(v) of paragraph (a) or that he or she suspects that that person, or any relative or
associate of that person, has done, or intends to do, any of those things.

---

61   Ibid., at Section 27.
62   Ibid., at Section 35.

(2) Subsection (1) shall not apply where a person is treated less favourably because he or she has knowingly made a false allegation or otherwise acted in bad faith.[63]

Measures to ensure equality are established under Section 73:

73(1) Anything done or omitted which would otherwise constitute a breach of any of the provisions of this Part of this Act shall not constitute such a breach if:

(a) it is done or omitted in good faith for the purpose of assisting or advancing persons or groups of persons, being in each case persons against whom discrimination is unlawful by virtue of this Part of this Act; and

(b) those persons or groups need or may reasonably be supposed to need assistance or advancement in order to achieve an equal place with other members of the community.[64]

The Act makes government, government agencies, and anyone who performs a public function, accountable for unlawful discrimination under the HRA. An act or omission by the government or anyone else performing a public function that is inconsistent with the right to freedom from discrimination must be shown to be a reasonable limit on the right to be free from discrimination, prescribed by law, which is demonstrably justified in a free and democratic society; if the government cannot show this, then the act or omission is unlawful discrimination. Complaints can be made about policies, practices and even legislation.

Education Act

The Education Act 1989 came into force on 1 October 1989. According to Section 20, New Zealand citizens and residents between 6 and 16 must go to school:

20(1) Except as provided in this Act, every person who is not a foreign student is required to be enrolled at a registered school at all times during the period beginning on the person's sixth birthday and ending on the person's 16th birthday.

(2) Before a child's seventh birthday, the child is not required to be enrolled at any school more than 3 kilometres walking distance from the child's residence.[65]

Further, according to Section 25, students required to enrol must attend school:

---

63   Ibid., at Section 66.
64   Ibid., at Section 73.
65   Education Act, Section 20.

25(1) Except as provided in this Act, every student of a registered school (other than a correspondence school) who is required by section 20 to be enrolled at a registered school shall attend the school whenever it is open.

(2) Every board shall take all reasonable steps to ensure that students who are required by subsection (1) to attend the school whenever it is open do so.[66]

Finally, Section 30 protects against employment of school-age children:

30(1) No person shall employ any person who has not turned 16 at any time

(a) within school hours; or

(ab) in the case of a person who is a student participating in a secondary-tertiary programme, when the employment interferes with the person's ability to undertake the secondary-tertiary programme; or

(b) in the case of a person enrolled at a correspondence school, when the employment interferes with the person's ability to do the work of the course in which the student is enrolled; or

(c) in the case of a person who has been granted a certificate of exemption under section 21, when the employment interferes with the person's ability to be taught as well and regularly as in a registered school; or

(d) if the employment then

(i) prevents or interferes with the person's attendance at school; or

(ia) in the case of a person who is a participating student, interferes with the person's ability to undertake his or her secondary-tertiary programme; or

(ii) in the case of a person enrolled at a correspondence school, interferes with the person's ability to do the work of the course in which the person is enrolled, unless there has been produced to the employer a certificate of exemption, or other satisfactory evidence that the person is exempted (otherwise than under section 21(1)) from enrolment at any school.

(2) Every person who

(a) being a parent of any other person, permits the other person to be employed contrary to subsection (1); or

(b) employs any other person in contravention of the subsection,

commits an offence, and is liable on summary conviction to a fine not exceeding $1,000.[67]

Conclusion

Despite strong legislative provisions both in Australia and New Zealand, there is still progress to be made to achieve equal outcomes and opportunities for all. Child equality and the rights contained within legislation rely on the overall legal system,

---

66   Ibid., at Section 25.

67   Ibid., at Section 30.

as well as cultural attitudes, for implementation and enforcement. However, as we have seen in this chapter, gaps do exist in the coverage of legislation, and in the manner by which it is enforced. Taking concrete action to advance human rights and support opportunity and choice require a concerted effort across the whole of government, in addition to the important ongoing role of specialist human rights monitoring and complaints mechanisms, as shown in *Little Angels*.

Chapter 5
Little Angels in Africa and South Africa

Introduction

In the quest for respect for our children and in the fight against child discrimination in *Little Angels*, this chapter will examine child issues in the continent of Africa, and in South Africa. It will initially look at the situation in Africa, examining such legislation as the Charter of the Organization of African Unity, the African Charter on Human and Peoples' Rights and the Protocol of the African Charter on Human and Peoples' Rights, and the Protocol on Rights of Women in Africa; and then in South Africa, the Interim Constitution Schedule 4 and the Constitution, the Employment Equity Act, the Promotion of Equality and Prevention of Unfair Discrimination Act, and the Children's Act.

Africa

Africa is not a single uniform entity; within Africa there is much diversity, in terms of culture, gender relations, geography, society, family, economy, and natural resources. As well, Africa is not static; it is a continent in flux and is rapidly undergoing fundamental changes, namely the growth of urban populations, deterioration of the environment and increasing desertification, deterioration of living standards, growing dependency on world markets, increasing numbers of young people and children, and civil strife and conflict. In sub-Saharan Africa 65 million children, or one in four, are child laborers.[1] Africa is home to the highest proportion of working children and the region where the least progress is being made, especially that of free, compulsory and universal primary education, as an estimated one in three children are not in school. Although it has 19 percent of the world's population of primary school age, sub-Saharan Africa accounts for 47 percent of the world's out-of-school children. Conflict has also been endemic in some countries, leading to the abuse and exploitation of millions of children. Overall, there have been significant changes in the political landscape in Africa, with more than half of countries in the region now holding democratic elections. However, the general picture remains a challenging one, with the region having half of the world's poor. A major constraint to progress in Africa has been persistent

---

1   International Labour Office, Accelerating Action against Child Labour, Global Report under the follow-up to the ILO Declaration on Fundamental Principles and Rights at Work, 2010.

conflict in a significant number of countries, including some of the largest States such as Sudan and the Democratic Republic of the Congo. The International Labour Organization estimates the present value of the cost of eliminating child labor in sub-Saharan Africa at around US$140 billion, of which US$107 billion would be education supply costs for teachers, new schools and materials. The total benefits, however, amount to US$734 billion, or 5.2 times the cost, making it a major investment in Africa's future.[2]

Charter of the Organization of African Unity

The heads of African States and governments assembled in the city of Addis Ababa, Ethiopia, and on 25 May 1963 signed the Charter of the Organization of African Unity, which entered into force on 13 September 1963. The Preamble of the Charter of the Organization of African Unity states:

Convinced that it is the inalienable right of all people to control their own destiny,

Conscious of the fact that freedom, equality, justice and dignity are essential objectives for the achievement of the legitimate aspirations of the African peoples,

Conscious of our responsibility to harness the natural and human resources of our continent for the total advancement of our peoples in all spheres of human endeavour,

Inspired by a common determination to promote understanding among our peoples and cooperation among our states in response to the aspirations of our peoples for brother-hood and solidarity, in a larger unity transcending ethnic and national differences,

Convinced that, in order to translate this determination into a dynamic force in the cause of human progress, conditions for peace and security must be established and maintained,

Determined to safeguard and consolidate the hard-won independence as well as the sovereignty and territorial integrity of our states, and to fight against neo-colonialism in all its forms,

Dedicated to the general progress of Africa,

---

2   Ibid.

Persuaded that the Charter of the United Nations and the Universal Declaration of Human Rights, to the Principles of which we reaffirm our adherence, provide a solid foundation for peaceful and positive cooperation among States,

Desirous that all African States should henceforth unite so that the welfare and well-being of their peoples can be assured,

Resolved to reinforce the links between our states by establishing and strengthening common institutions.[3]

Article I establishes the Organization of African Unity:

I.1. The High Contracting Parties do by the present Charter establish an organization to be known as the ORGANIZATION OF AFRICAN UNITY.

2. The Organization shall include the Continental African States, Madagascar and other Islands surrounding Africa.[4]

Its purposes are outlined in Article II, which includes cultural cooperation under II.2(c):

II. 1. The Organization shall have the following purposes:
    (a) To promote the unity and solidarity of the African States;
    (b) To coordinate and intensify their cooperation and efforts to achieve a better life for the peoples of Africa;
    (c) To defend their sovereignty, their territorial integrity and independence;
    (d) To eradicate all forms of colonialism from Africa; and
    (e) To promote international cooperation, having due regard to the Charter of the United Nations and the Universal Declaration of Human Rights.
2. To these ends, the Member States shall coordinate and harmonize their general policies, especially in the following fields:
    (a) Political and diplomatic cooperation;
    (b) Economic cooperation, including transport and communications;
    (c) Educational and cultural cooperation;
    (d) Health, sanitation and nutritional cooperation;
    (e) Scientific and technical cooperation; and
    (f) Cooperation for defense and security.[5]

The various institutions are outlined in Article VII:

---

3   Charter of the Organization of African Unity, at the Preamble.
4   Ibid., at Article I.
5   Ibid., at Article II.

VII. The Organization shall accomplish its purposes through the following principal institutions:
1. The Assembly of Heads of State and Government.
2. The Council of Ministers.
3. The General Secretariat.
4. The Commission of Mediation, Conciliation and Arbitration.[6]

The Assembly of Heads of State and Government is provided for in Article VIII:

VIII. The Assembly of Heads of State and Government shall be the supreme organ of the Organization. It shall, subject to the provisions of this Charter, discuss matters of common concern to Africa with a view to coordinating and harmonizing the general policy of the Organization. It may in addition review the structure, functions and acts of all the organs and any specialized agencies which may be created in accordance with the present Charter.[7]

The Council of Ministers is provided for in Article XII:

XII. 1. The Council of Ministers shall consist of Foreign Ministers or other Ministers as are designated by the Governments of Member States.
2. The Council of Ministers shall meet at least twice a year. When requested by any Member State and approved by two-thirds of all Member States, it shall meet in extraordinary session.[8]

The General Secretariat is provided for in Article XVI:

XVI. There shall be a Secretary-General of the Organization, who shall be appointed by the Assembly of Heads of State and Government. The Secretary-General shall direct the affairs of the Secretariat.[9]

The Commission of Mediation, Conciliation and Arbitration is provided for in Article XIX:

XIX. Member States pledge to settle all disputes among themselves by peaceful means and, to this end decide to establish a Commission of Mediation, Conciliation and Arbitration, the composition of which and condition of service shall be defined by a separate Protocol to be approved by the Assembly of Heads

---

6   Ibid., at Article VII.
7   Ibid., at Article VIII.
8   Ibid., at Article XII.
9   Ibid., at Article XVI.

of State and Government. Said Protocol shall be regarded as forming an integral part of the present Charter.[10]

The Specialized Commission is provided for in Article XX:

XX. The Assembly shall establish such Specialized Commissions as it may deem necessary, including the following:
1. Economic and Social Commission.
2. Educational, Scientific, Cultural and Health Commission.
3. Defense Commission.[11]

African Charter on Human and Peoples' Rights

The African Charter on Human and Peoples' Rights was adopted by the eighteenth Assembly of Heads of State and Government on 27 June 1981 in Nairobi, Kenya. The Preamble of the African Charter on Human and Peoples' Rights states:

The African States members of the Organization of African Unity, parties to the present Convention entitled African Charter on Human and Peoples' Rights

Considering the Charter of the Organization of African Unity, which stipulates that 'freedom, equality, justice and dignity are essential objectives for the achievement of the legitimate aspirations of the African peoples';

Reaffirming the pledge they solemnly made in Article 2 of the said Charter to eradicate all forms of colonialism from Africa, to coordinate and intensify their cooperation and efforts to achieve a better life for the peoples of Africa and to promote international cooperation having due regard to the Charter of the United Nations and the Universal Declaration of Human Rights;

Taking into consideration the virtues of their historical tradition and the values of African civilization which should inspire and characterize their reflection on the concept of human and peoples' rights;

Recognizing on the one hand, that fundamental human rights stem from the attitudes of human beings, which justifies their international protection, and on the other hand that the reality and respect of peoples' rights should necessarily guarantee human rights;

Considering that the enjoyment of rights and freedoms also implies the performance of duties on the part of everyone;

10   Ibid., at Article XIX.
11   Ibid., at Article XX.

Convinced that it is henceforth essential to pay particular attention to the right to development and that civil and political rights cannot be dissociated from economic, social and cultural rights in their conception as well as universality and that the satisfaction of economic, social and cultural rights is a guarantee for the enjoyment of civil and political rights;

Conscious of their duty to achieve the total liberation of Africa, the peoples of which are still struggling for their dignity and genuine independence, and undertaking to eliminate colonialism, neo-colonialism, apartheid, zionism and to dismantle aggressive foreign military bases and all forms of discrimination, particularly those based on race, ethnic group, colour, sex, language, religion or political opinion;

Reaffirming their adherence to the principles of human and peoples' rights and freedoms contained in the declarations, conventions and other instruments adopted by the Organization of African Unity, the Movement of Non-Aligned Countries and the United Nations;

Firmly convinced of their duty to promote and protect human and peoples' rights and freedoms and taking into account the importance traditionally attached to these rights and freedoms in Africa.[12]

In terms of rights and duties and specifically human and peoples' rights, Article 1 states:

1. The Member States of the Organization of African Unity, parties to the present Charter shall recognize the rights, duties and freedoms enshrined in the Charter and shall undertake to adopt legislative or other measures to give effect to them.[13]

Article 2 specifically protects against discrimination:

2. Every individual shall be entitled to the enjoyment of the rights and freedoms recognized and guaranteed in the present Charter without distinction of any kind such as race, ethnic group, colour, sex, language, religion, political or any other opinion, national and social origin, fortune, birth or any status.[14]

Importantly, Article 3 guarantees equal protection of the law:

3.1. Every individual shall be equal before the law.

---

12 African Charter on Human and Peoples' Rights, at the Preamble.
13 Ibid., at Article 1.
14 Ibid., at Article 2.

2. Every individual shall be entitled to equal protection of the law.[15]

The important concept of equality is guaranteed in Article 19:

19. All peoples shall be equal; they shall enjoy the same respect and shall have the same rights. Nothing shall justify the domination of a people by another.[16]

Article 5 upholds the dignity of the human person:

5. Every individual shall have the right to the respect of the dignity inherent in a human being and to the recognition of his legal status. All forms of exploitation and degradation of man, particularly slavery, slave trade, torture, cruel, inhuman or degrading punishment and treatment shall be prohibited.[17]

In looking at the importance of the courts in safeguarding rights, Article 7 establishes that:

7.1. Every individual shall have the right to have his cause heard. This comprises: (a) the right to an appeal to competent national organs against acts of violating his fundamental rights as recognized and guaranteed by conventions, laws, regulations and customs in force; (b) the right to be presumed innocent until proved guilty by a competent court or tribunal; (c) the right to defence, including the right to be defended by counsel of his choice; (d) the right to be tried within a reasonable time by an impartial court or tribunal. 2. No one may be condemned for an act or omission which did not constitute a legally punishable offence at the time it was committed. No penalty may be inflicted for an offence for which no provision was made at the time it was committed. Punishment is personal and can be imposed only on the offender.[18]

Employment rights and equal pay for equal work are guaranteed in Article 15:

15. Every individual shall have the right to work under equitable and satisfactory conditions, and shall receive equal pay for equal work.[19]

The right to education and the importance of community are recognized in Article 17:

17.1. Every individual shall have the right to education.

---

15 Ibid., at Article 3.
16 Ibid., at Article 19.
17 Ibid., at Article 5.
18 Ibid., at Article 7.
19 Ibid., at Article 15.

2. Every individual may freely take part in the cultural life of his community.

3. The promotion and protection of morals and traditional values recognized by the community shall be the duty of the State.[20]

Important in the fight against discrimination, Article 20 upholds the self-determination of people:

20.1. All peoples shall have the right to existence. They shall have the unquestionable and inalienable right to self-determination. They shall freely determine their political status and shall pursue their economic and social development according to the policy they have freely chosen.

2. Colonized or oppressed peoples shall have the right to free themselves from the bonds of domination by resorting to any means recognized by the international community.

3. All peoples shall have the right to the assistance of the State Parties to the present Charter in their liberation struggle against foreign domination, be it political, economic or cultural.[21]

The paramount role of the Courts is guaranteed in Article 26:

26. State Parties to the present Charter shall have the duty to guarantee the independence of the Courts and shall allow the establishment and improvement of appropriate national institutions entrusted with the promotion and protection of the rights and freedoms guaranteed by the present Charter.[22]

Duties of individuals towards one another are established in Article 27:

27.1. Every individual shall have duties towards his family and society, the State and other legally recognized communities and the international community.

2. The rights and freedoms of each individual shall be exercised with due regard to the rights of others, collective security, morality and common interest.[23]

Respect and tolerance without discrimination are espoused in Article 28:

28. Every individual shall have the duty to respect and consider his fellow beings without discrimination, and to maintain relations aimed at promoting, safeguarding and reinforcing mutual respect and tolerance.[24]

---

20   Ibid., at Article 17.
21   Ibid., at Article 20.
22   Ibid., at Article 26.
23   Ibid., at Article 27.
24   Ibid., at Article 28.

Important for equality, in Article 29, the individual shall also have the duty to preserve and strengthen positive cultural values:

> 29.2. To serve his national community by placing his physical and intellectual abilities at its service;
>
> ...
>
> 7. To preserve and strengthen positive African cultural values in his relations with other members of the society, in the spirit of tolerance, dialogue and consultation and, in general, to contribute to the promotion of the moral well-being of society.[25]

The African Commission on Human and Peoples' Right is established under Article 30:

> 30. An African Commission on Human and Peoples' Rights, hereinafter called 'the Commission', shall be established within the Organization of African Unity to promote human and peoples' rights and ensure their protection in Africa.[26]

The mandate of the Commission is contained in Article 45:

> 45. The functions of the Commission shall be:
> 1. To promote human and peoples' rights and in particular:
> (a) to collect documents, undertake studies and researches on African problems in the field of human and peoples' rights, organize seminars, symposia and conferences, disseminate information, encourage national and local institutions concerned with human and peoples' rights and, should the case arise, give its views or make recommendations to Governments.
> (b) to formulate and lay down principles and rules aimed at solving legal problems relating to human and peoples' rights and fundamental freedoms upon which African Governments may base their legislation.
> (c) cooperate with other African and international institutions concerned with the promotion and protection of human and peoples' rights.
> 2. Ensure the protection of human and peoples' rights under conditions laid down by the present Charter.
> 3. Interpret all the provisions of the present Charter at the request of a State Party, an institution of the OAU or an African Organization recognized by the OAU.
> 4. Perform any other tasks which may be entrusted to it by the Assembly of Heads of State and Government.[27]

---

25 Ibid., at Article 29.
26 Ibid., at Article 30.
27 Ibid., at Article 45.

The procedure of the Commission is contained in Article 46:

> 46. The Commission may resort to any appropriate method of investigation; it may hear from the Secretary General of the Organization of African Unity or any other person capable of enlightening it.[28]

Finally, exhaustion of remedies is recognized under Article 50:

> 50. The Commission can only deal with a matter submitted to it after making sure that all local remedies, if they exist, have been exhausted, unless it is obvious to the Commission that the procedure of achieving these remedies would be unduly prolonged.[29]

Protocol to the African Charter on Human and Peoples' Rights on the Establishment of an African Court on Human and Peoples' Rights

The Preamble of the Protocol to the African Charter on Human and Peoples' Rights on the Establishment of an African Court on Human and Peoples' Rights 2003 states:

> The Member States of the Organization of African Unity hereinafter referred to as the OAU, States Parties to the African Charter on Human and Peoples' Rights,
>
> Considering that the Charter of the Organization of African Unity recognizes that freedom, equality, justice, peace and dignity are essential objectives for the achievement of the legitimate aspirations of the African Peoples;
>
> Noting that the African Charter on Human and Peoples' Rights reaffirms adherence to the principles of Human and Peoples' Rights, freedoms and duties contained in the declarations, conventions and other instruments adopted by the Organization of African Unity, and other international organizations;
>
> Recognizing that the twofold objective of the African Commission on Human and Peoples' Rights is to ensure on the one hand promotion and on the other protection of Human and Peoples' Rights, freedom and duties;
>
> Recognizing further, the efforts of the African Charter on Human and Peoples' Rights in the promotion and protection of Human and Peoples' Rights since its inception in 1987;

---

28   Ibid., at Article 46.
29   Ibid., at Article 50.

Firmly convinced that the attainment of the objectives of the African Charter on Human and Peoples' Rights requires the establishment of an African Court on Human and Peoples' Rights to complement and reinforce the functions of the African Commission on Human and Peoples' Rights.[30]

An African Court of Human and Peoples' Rights is established under Article 1:

1. There shall be established within the Organization of African Unity an African Court of Human and Peoples' Rights hereinafter referred to as 'the Court', the organization, jurisdiction and functioning of which shall be governed by the present Protocol.[31]

The relationship between the Court and the Commission is enunciated under Article 2:

2. The Court shall, bearing in mind the provisions of this Protocol, complement the protective mandate of the African Commission on Human and Peoples' Rights hereinafter referred to as 'the Commission', conferred upon it by the African Charter on Human and Peoples' Rights, hereinafter referred to as 'the Charter'.[32]

The jurisdiction of the Court is established under Article 3:

3.1. The jurisdiction of the Court shall extend to all cases and disputes submitted to it concerning the interpretation and application of the Charter, this Protocol and any other relevant Human Rights instrument ratified by the States concerned.
2. In the event of a dispute as to whether the Court has jurisdiction, the Court shall decide.[33]

The Court may issue advisory opinions as outlined under Article 4:

4.1. At the request of a Member State of the OAU, the OAU, any of its organs, or any African organization recognized by the OAU, the Court may provide an opinion on any legal matter relating to the Charter or any other relevant human rights instruments, provided that the subject matter of the opinion is not related to a matter being examined by the Commission.

---

30   Protocol to the African Charter on Human and Peoples' Rights on the Establishment of an African Court on Human and Peoples' Rights, at the Preamble.
31   Ibid., at Article 1.
32   Ibid., at Article 2.
33   Ibid., at Article 3.

2. The Court shall give reasons for its advisory opinions provided that every judge shall be entitled to deliver a separate [or] dissenting decision.[34]

Access to the Court is established under Article 5:

5.1. The following are entitled to submit cases to the Court:
(a) The Commission
(b) The State Party, which had lodged a complaint to the Commission
(c) The State Party against which the complaint has been lodged at the Commission
(d) The State Party whose citizen is a victim of human rights violation
(e) African Intergovernmental Organizations
2. When a State Party has an interest in a case, it may submit a request to the Court to be permitted to join.
3. The Court may entitle relevant non-governmental organizations (NGOs) with observer status before the Commission, and individuals to institute cases directly before it …[35]

The issue of admissibility of cases is examined in Article 6:

6.1. The Court, when deciding on the admissibility of a case instituted under Article 5 … of this Protocol, may request the opinion of the Commission which shall give it as soon as possible.
2. The Court shall rule on the admissibility of cases taking into account the provisions of Article 56 of the Charter.
3. The Court may consider cases or transfer them to the Commission.[36]

Article 7 establishes the sources of law:

7. The Court shall apply the provision of the Charter and any other relevant human rights instruments ratified by the States concerned.[37]

The independence of the Court is underlined in Article 17:

17.1. The independence of the judges shall be fully ensured in accordance with international law.
2. No judge may hear any case in which the same judge has previously taken part as agent, counsel or advocate for one of the parties or as a member of a national

---

34   Ibid., at Article 4.
35   Ibid., at Article 5.
36   Ibid., at Article 6.
37   Ibid., at Article 7.

or international court or a commission of enquiry or in any other capacity. Any doubt on this point shall be settled by decision of the Court.[38]

Evidence is outlined under Article 26:

26.1. The Court shall hear submissions by all parties and if deemed necessary, hold an enquiry. The States concerned shall assist by providing relevant facilities for the efficient handling of the case.

2. The Court may receive written and oral evidence including expert testimony and shall make its decision on the basis of such evidence.[39]

Findings of the Court are provided for under Article 27:

27.1. If the Court finds that there has been violation of a human or peoples' rights, it shall make appropriate orders to remedy the violation, including the payment of fair compensation or reparation.

2. In cases of extreme gravity and urgency, and when necessary to avoid irreparable harm to persons, the Court shall adopt such provisional measures as it deems necessary.[40]

Importantly, the judgment of the Court is underlined under Article 28:

28.1. The Court shall render its judgment within ninety (90) days of having completed its deliberations.

2. The judgment of the Court decided by majority shall be final and not subject to appeal.

3. Without prejudice to sub-Article 2 ... the Court may review its decision in the light of new evidence under conditions to be set out in the Rules of Procedure.

4. The Court may interpret its own decision.

5. The judgment of the Court shall be read in open court, due notice having been given to the parties.

6. Reasons shall be given for the judgment of the Court.

7. If the judgment of the court does not represent, in whole or in part, the unanimous decision of the judges, any judge shall be entitled to deliver a separate or dissenting opinion.[41]

Finally, Article 30 provides for the execution of judgment:

---

38 Ibid., at Article 17.
39 Ibid., at Article 26.
40 Ibid., at Article 27.
41 Ibid., at Article 28.

30. The States Parties to the present Protocol undertake to comply with the judgment in any case to which they are parties within the time stipulated by the Court and to guarantee its execution.[42]

Protocol on the Rights of Women in Africa

In the Preamble to the Protocol on the Rights of Women in Africa 2003, important to female children specifically and to women in general, the State Parties to the Protocol on the Rights of Women in Africa undertake the agreement to eliminate discrimination:

Considering that Article 66 of the African Charter on Human and Peoples' Rights provides for special protocols or agreements, if necessary, to supplement the provisions of the African Charter, and that the OAU Assembly of Heads of State and Government meeting in its Thirty-first Ordinary Session in Addis Ababa, Ethiopia, in June 1995, endorsed by resolution AHG/Res.240 (XXXI) the recommendation of the African Commission on Human and Peoples' Rights to elaborate a Protocol on the Rights of Women in Africa;

Considering that Article 2 of the African Charter on Human and Peoples' Rights enshrines the principle of non-discrimination on the grounds of race, ethnic group, colour, sex, language, religion, political or any other opinion, national and social origin, fortune, birth or other status;

Further considering that Article 18 of the African Charter on Human and Peoples' Rights calls on all Member States to eliminate every discrimination against women and to ensure the protection of the rights of women as stipulated in international declarations and conventions;

Noting that Articles 60 and 61 of the African Charter on Human and Peoples' Rights recognize regional and international human rights instruments and African practices consistent with international norms on human and peoples' rights as being important reference points for the application and interpretation of the African Charter;

Recalling that women's rights have been recognized and guaranteed in all international human rights instruments, notably the Universal Declaration of Human Rights, the International Covenant on Civil and Political Rights, the International Covenant on Economic, Social and Cultural Rights, the Convention on the Elimination of All Forms of Discrimination against Women and all other international conventions and covenants relating to the rights of women as being inalienable, interdependent and indivisible human rights;

---

42   Ibid., at Article 30.

Noting that women's rights and women's essential role in development have been reaffirmed in the United Nations Plans of Action on the Environment and Development in 1992, on Human Rights in 1993, on Population and Development in 1994 and on Social Development in 1995;

Further noting that the Plans of Action adopted in Dakar and in Beijing call on all Member States of the United Nations, which have made a solemn commitment to implement them, to take concrete steps to give greater attention to the human rights of women in order to eliminate all forms of discrimination and of gender-based violence against women;

Bearing in mind related Resolutions, Declarations, Recommendations, Decisions and other Conventions aimed at eliminating all forms of discrimination and at promoting equality between men and women;

Concerned that despite the ratification of the African Charter on Human and Peoples' Rights and other international human rights instruments by the majority of Member States, and their solemn commitment to eliminate all forms of discrimination and harmful practices against women, women in Africa still continue to be victims of discrimination and harmful practices;

Firmly convinced that any practice that hinders or endangers the normal growth and affects the physical, emotional and psychological development of women and girls should be condemned and eliminated, and

Determined to ensure that the rights of women are protected in order to enable them to enjoy fully all their human rights.[43]

Article 1 defines 'Discrimination against women' to mean any distinction, exclusion or restriction based on sex, or any differential treatment whose objective or effects compromise or destroy the recognition, enjoyment or the exercise by women, regardless of their marital status, of human rights and fundamental freedoms in all spheres of life.[44] Further, 'Harmful Practices (HPs)' means all behavior, attitudes and practices which negatively affect the fundamental rights of women and girls, such as their right to life, health and bodily integrity.[45]

Importantly, Article 2 is paramount in the fight for the elimination of discrimination:

2(1) State Parties shall combat all forms of discrimination against women through appropriate legislative measures. In this regard they shall:

---

43 Protocol on the Rights of Women in Africa, at the Preamble.
44 Ibid., at Article 1.
45 Ibid., at Article 1.

(a) include in their national constitutions and other legislative instruments the principle of equality between men and women and ensure its effective application;

(b) enact and effectively implement appropriate national legislative measures to prohibit all forms of harmful practices which endanger the health and general well-being of women and girls;

(c) integrate a gender perspective in their policy decisions, legislation, development plans, activities and all other spheres of life;

(d) take positive action in those areas where discrimination against women in law and in fact continues to exist;

(e) support the local, national, regional and continental initiatives directed at eradicating all forms of discrimination against women.

2. States Parties shall commit themselves to modify the social and cultural patterns of conduct of women and men through public education, information, education and communication strategies, with a view to achieving the elimination of harmful cultural and traditional practices and all other practices which are based on the idea of the inferiority or the superiority of either of the sexes, or on stereotyped roles for women and men.[46]

In looking at the important concern of economic and social welfare rights, Article 13 is paramount for equal rights, including specifically under Article 13(g) which provides for a minimum age to prohibit underage work and the exploitation of children:

13. State Parties shall guarantee women equal opportunities to work. In this respect, they shall:

(a) promote equality in access to employment;

b) promote the right to equal remuneration for jobs of equal value for men and women;

c) ensure transparency in employment and dismissal relating to women in order to address issues of sexual harassment in the workplace;

d) allow women freedom to choose their occupation, and protect them from exploitation by their employers;

e) create conditions to promote and support the occupations and economic activities dominated by women, in particular, within the informal sector;

f) encourage the establishment of a system of protection and social insurance for women working in the informal sector;

g) introduce a minimum age of work and prohibit children below that age from working, and prohibit the exploitation of children, especially the girl-child;

h) take the necessary measures to recognise the economic value of the work of women in the home;

i) guarantee adequate pre and post-natal maternity leave;

---

46   Ibid., at Article 2(1).

j) ensure equality in taxation for men and women;

k) recognise the right of salaried women to the same allowances and entitlements as those granted to salaried men for their spouses and children;

l) recognise motherhood and the upbringing of children as a social function for which the State, the private sector and both parents must take responsibility.[47]

Finally, Article 17 guarantees the right to positive cultural context:

17(1) Women shall have the right to live in a positive cultural context and to participate at all levels in the determination of cultural policies.

(2) States Parties shall take all appropriate measures to enhance the participation of women in the formulation of cultural policies at all levels.[48]

South Africa

South Africa has a long and sad history of colonial conquest, racial domination, and gender discrimination; however, South Africa also has a long and proud history of struggle for the protection and promotion of human rights and social justice. The World Bank outlined the social and economic inequalities: poverty in South Africa has a strong racial dimension as nearly 95 percent of South Africa's poor are African, 5 percent are coloured, and less than 1 percent are Indian or white.[49] Further, Africans have nearly twice the unemployment (38 percent) of coloureds (21 percent), more than three times the unemployment rate of Indians (11 percent), and nearly ten times the unemployment rate of whites (4 percent). These imbalances have deprived, and continue to deprive, many South Africans, especially black South Africans, of the full and equal enjoyment of their fundamental human rights and freedoms.[50] South Africa has ratified the Worst Forms of Child Labour Convention, 1999 (No. 182) (C. 182) in 2000, and has ratified the Minimum Age Convention, 1973 (No. 138) (C. 138) in 2000.

Interim Constitution Schedule 4

The Constitutional Principles for the Republic of South Africa are contained in Schedule 4 of the Interim Constitution (Act 200 of 1993). Article I guarantees equality among all races:

---

47   Ibid., at Article 13.

48   Ibid., at Article 17.

49   Ministry in the Office of the President: Reconstruction and Development Programme, Key Indicators of Poverty in South Africa.

50   Ibid.

Table 5.1 **Employment statistics for South Africa by age, showing underage employment.**

Age group	Total			Men			Women		
	Total population	Active population	Activity rate	Total population	Active population	Activity rate	Total population	Active population	Activity rate
Total	48683.0	17788.0	36.5	23443.0	9589.0	40.9	25240.0	8199.0	32.5
Total (15+)	*33012.0*	*–*	*–*	*15516.8*	*–*	*–*	*17495.2*	*–*	*–*
0–9	10393.9	–	–	5260.8	–	–	5133.1	–	–
10–14	5277.1	–	–	2665.4	–	–	2611.7	–	–
15–19	5152.5	465.3	9.0	2596.4	255.5	9.8	2556.2	209.7	8.2
20–24	4784.8	2553.4	53.4	2369.8	1395.7	58.9	2415.1	1157.7	47.9
25–29	4366.4	3268.4	74.9	2121.4	1777.4	83.8	2245.0	1490.9	66.4
30–34	3913.5	3053.7	78.0	1893.4	1660.6	87.7	2020.1	1393.0	69.0
35–39	3144.0	2485.4	79.1	1456.7	1295.1	88.9	1687.2	1190.3	70.5
40–44	2392.8	1834.1	76.7	1083.7	952.2	87.9	1309.1	881.8	67.4
45–49	2239.3	1635.9	73.1	1008.6	855.9	84.9	1230.6	780.0	63.4
50–54	1941.7	1269.3	65.4	869.4	686.5	79.0	1072.3	582.8	54.4
55–59	1568.2	845.2	53.9	699.7	468.7	67.0	868.6	376.5	43.3
60–64	1248.6	377.5	30.2	548.2	241.2	44.0	700.5	136.3	19.5
65+	2260.2	–	–	869.6	–	–	1390.6	–	–

Source: International Labour Organization, Laborsta, 2008.

I. The Constitution of South Africa shall provide for the establishment of one sovereign state, a common South African citizenship and a democratic system of government committed to achieving equality between men and women and people of all races.[51]

Article II also guarantees fundamental rights, freedoms and civil liberties by holding that everyone shall enjoy all universally accepted fundamental rights, freedoms and civil liberties, which shall be provided for and protected by entrenched and justiciable provisions in the Constitution.[52] Further, Article IV is the Supremacy clause, which states that the Constitution shall be the supreme law of the land; it shall be binding on all organs of state at all levels of government.[53]

Importantly, the prohibition against discrimination, in terms of 'all forms of discrimination', and the promotion of equality are contained within Article III:

III. The Constitution shall prohibit racial, gender and all other forms of discrimination and shall promote racial and gender equality and national unity.[54]

The fundamental guarantee of equality of all before the law is contained in Article V:

V. The legal system shall ensure the equality of all before the law and an equitable legal process. Equality before the law includes laws, programmes or activities that have as their object the amelioration of the conditions of the disadvantaged, including those disadvantaged on the grounds of race, colour or gender.[55]

The separation of powers for objectivity and accountability is contained in Article VI, which establishes that there shall be a separation of powers between the legislature, executive and judiciary, with appropriate checks and balances to ensure accountability, responsiveness and openness.[56] Further, the important role of the judiciary is outlined in Article VII, by holding that the judiciary shall be appropriately qualified, independent and impartial, and shall have the power and jurisdiction to safeguard and enforce the Constitution and all fundamental rights.[57]

51   Interim Constitution of South Africa, Schedule 4, Article I.
52   Ibid., at Article II.
53   Ibid., at Article IV.
54   Ibid., at Article III.
55   Ibid., at Article V.
56   Ibid., at Article VI.
57   Ibid., at Article VII.

Constitution of South Africa

The Constitution of the Republic of South Africa 1996 was first adopted by the Constitutional Assembly on 8 May 1996 (Act 108 of 1996), and was signed into law on 10 December 1996. The Preamble of the Constitution reads:

> We, the people of South Africa,
> Recognize the injustices of our past;
> Honour those who suffered for justice and freedom in our land;
> Respect those who have worked to build and develop our country; and
> Believe that South Africa belongs to all who live in it, united in our diversity.
> We therefore, through our freely elected representatives, adopt this Constitution as the supreme law of the Republic so as to
> Heal the divisions of the past and establish a society based on democratic values, social justice and fundamental human rights;
> Lay the foundations for a democratic and open society in which government is based on the will of the people and every citizen is equally protected by law;
> Improve the quality of life of all citizens and free the potential of each person; and
> Build a united and democratic South Africa able to take its rightful place as a sovereign state in the family of nations.
> May God protect our people.
> Nkosi Sikelel' iAfrika. Morena boloka setjhaba sa heso.
> God seën Suid-Afrika. God bless South Africa.
> Mudzimu fhatutshedza Afurika. Hosi katekisa Afrika.[58]

The Founding Provisions of the Republic of South Africa are found in Section 1 of the Constitution which stresses equality and the advancement of human rights, by stating:

> 1. The Republic of South Africa is one, sovereign, democratic state founded on the following values:
> (a) Human dignity, the achievement of equality and the advancement of human rights and freedoms.
> (b) Non-racialism and non-sexism.
> (c) Supremacy of the constitution and the rule of law.
> (d) Universal adult suffrage, a national common voters roll, regular elections and a multi-party system of democratic government, to ensure accountability, responsiveness and openness.[59]

The Supremacy Clause is found in Section 2 of the Constitution, which holds:

---

58   Constitution of South Africa, at the Preamble.
59   Ibid., at Section 1.

2. This Constitution is the supreme law of the Republic; law or conduct inconsistent with it is invalid, and the obligations imposed by it must be fulfilled.[60]

Importantly, the right to equality is espoused in Section 3, which states:

3(1) There is a common South African citizenship.
(2) All citizens are
(a) equally entitled to the rights, privileges and benefits of citizenship; and
(b) equally subject to the duties and responsibilities of citizenship.
(3) National legislation must provide for the acquisition, loss and restoration of citizenship.[61]

Chapter 2 of the Constitution enumerates the Bill of Rights for South Africa. Section 7 states:

7(1) This Bill of Rights is a cornerstone of democracy in South Africa. It enshrines the rights of all people in our country and affirms the democratic values of human dignity, equality and freedom.
(2) The state must respect, protect, promote and fulfil the rights in the Bill of Rights.
(3) The rights in the Bill of Rights are subject to the limitations contained or referred to in Section 36, or elsewhere in the Bill.[62]

Application and jurisdiction of the Bill of Rights are outlined in Section 8:

8(1) The Bill of Rights applies to all law, and binds the legislature, the executive, the judiciary and all organs of state.
(2) A provision of the Bill of Rights binds a natural or a juristic person if, and to the extent that, it is applicable, taking into account the nature of the right and the nature of any duty imposed by the right.
(3) When applying a provision of the Bill of Rights to a natural or juristic person in terms of subsection (2), a court
(a) in order to give effect to a right in the Bill, must apply, or if necessary develop, the common law to the extent that legislation does not give effect to that right; and
(b) may develop rules of the common law to limit the right, provided that the limitation is in accordance with Section 36(1).

---

60 Ibid., at Section 2.
61 Ibid., at Section 3.
62 Ibid., at Section 7.

(4) A juristic person is entitled to the rights in the Bill of Rights to the extent required by the nature of the rights and the nature of that juristic person.[63]

In terms of equality and non-derogable rights, Section 9 goes on to outline and guarantee the important concept of equal protection:

> 9(1) Everyone is equal before the law and has the right to equal protection and benefit of the law.
> (2) Equality includes the full and equal enjoyment of all rights and freedoms. To promote the achievement of equality, legislative and other measures designed to protect or advance persons, or categories of persons, disadvantaged by unfair discrimination may be taken.
> (3) The state may not unfairly discriminate directly or indirectly against anyone on one or more grounds, including race, gender, sex, pregnancy, marital status, ethnic or social origin, colour, sexual orientation, age, disability, religion, conscience, belief, culture, language and birth.
> (4) No person may unfairly discriminate directly or indirectly against anyone on one or more grounds in terms of subsection (3). National legislation must be enacted to prevent or prohibit unfair discrimination.
> (5) Discrimination on one or more of the grounds listed in subsection (3) is unfair unless it is established that the discrimination is fair.[64]

Freedom of expression is contained in Section 16:

> 16(1) Everyone has the right to freedom of expression, which includes
> (a) freedom of the press and other media;
> (b) freedom to receive or impart information or ideas;
> (c) freedom of artistic creativity; and
> (d) academic freedom and freedom of scientific research.
> (2) The right in subsection (1) does not extend to
> …
> (c) advocacy of hatred that is based on race, ethnicity, gender or religion, and that constitutes incitement to cause harm.[65]

On human dignity, Section 10 states:

> 10. Everyone has inherent dignity and the right to have their dignity respected and protected.[66]

---

63   Ibid., at Section 8.
64   Ibid., at Section 9.
65   Ibid., at Section 16.
66   Ibid., at Section 10.

Further, in the interpretation of the Bill of Rights, Section 39 states the importance of human dignity and equality:

39(1) When interpreting the Bill of Rights, a court, tribunal or forum
(a) must promote the values that underlie an open and democratic society based on human dignity, equality and freedom;
(b) must consider international law; and
(c) may consider foreign law.
(2) When interpreting any legislation, and when developing the common law or customary law, every court, tribunal or forum must promote the spirit, purport and objects of the Bill of Rights.
(3) The Bill of Rights does not deny the existence of any other rights or freedoms that are recognized or conferred by common law, customary law or legislation, to the extent that they are consistent with the Bill.[67]

In safeguarding the right to employment under the principle of freedom of trade, occupation and profession, Section 22 states:

22. Every citizen has the right to choose their trade, occupation or profession freely. The practice of a trade, occupation or profession may be regulated by law.[68]

In terms of labor relations, Section 23 establishes:

23(1) Everyone has the right to fair labour practices.
(2) Every worker has the right
(a) to form and join a trade union;
(b) to participate in the activities and programmes of a trade union; and
(c) to strike.[69]

In looking at the important right to education for children, Section 29 states:

29(1) Everyone has the right
(a) to a basic education, including adult basic education; and
(b) to further education, which the state, through reasonable measures, must make progressively available and accessible.
(2) Everyone has the right to receive education in the official language or languages of their choice in public educational institutions where that education is reasonably practicable. In order to ensure the effective access to, and

---

67 Ibid., at Section 39.
68 Ibid., at Section 22.
69 Ibid., at Section 23.

implementation of, this right, the state must consider all reasonable educational alternatives, including single medium institutions, taking into account
(a) equity;
(b) practicability; and
(c) the need to redress the results of past racially discriminatory laws and practices.
(3) Everyone has the right to establish and maintain, at their own expense, independent educational institutions that
(a) do not discriminate on the basis of race;
(b) are registered with the state; and
(c) maintain standards that are not inferior to standards at comparable public educational institutions.
(4) Subsection (3) does not preclude state subsidies for independent educational institutions.[70]

In guaranteeing the right to administrative action, Section 33 states:

33(1) Everyone has the right to administrative action that is lawful, reasonable and procedurally fair.[71]

Further, the right to access to the courts is outlined in Section 34, which holds:

34. Everyone has the right to have any dispute that can be resolved by the application of law decided in a fair public hearing before a court or, where appropriate, another independent and impartial tribunal or forum.[72]

The Constitution also goes on to provide for a limitation of rights under Section 36(1), which states:

36(1) The rights in the Bill of Rights may be limited only in terms of law of general application to the extent that the limitation is reasonable and justifiable in an open and democratic society based on human dignity, equality and freedom, taking into account all relevant factors, including
(a) the nature of the right;
(b) the importance of the purpose of the limitation;
(c) the nature and extent of the limitation;
(d) the relation between the limitation and its purpose; and
(e) less restrictive means to achieve the purpose.[73]

---

70 Ibid., at Section 29.
71 Ibid., at Section 33.
72 Ibid., at Section 34.
73 Ibid., at Section 36(1).

In order to guarantee rights enumerated under the Constitution, Section 38 ensures the enforcement of such rights, by holding that:

> 38. Anyone listed in this Article has the right to approach a competent court, alleging that a right in the Bill of Rights has been infringed or threatened, and the court may grant appropriate relief, including a declaration of rights. The persons who may approach a court are
> (a) anyone acting in their own interest;
> (b) anyone acting on behalf of another person who cannot act in their own name;
> (c) anyone acting as a member of, or in the interest of, a group or class of persons;
> (d) anyone acting in the public interest; and
> (e) an association acting in the interest of its members.[74]

The powers of the courts in constitutional matters are outlined in Section 172(1), which holds:

> 172(1) When deciding a constitutional matter within its power, a court (a) must declare that any law or conduct that is inconsistent with the Constitution is invalid to the extent of its inconsistency; and
> (b) may make any order that is just and equitable, including
> (i) an order limiting the retrospective effect of the declaration of invalidity; and
> (ii) an order suspending the declaration of invalidity for any period and on any conditions, to allow the competent authority to correct the defect.[75]

Under the establishment and governing principles, Section 181 lists several important institutions mandated to strengthen constitutional democracy, namely the Public Protector; the Human Rights Commission; the Commission for the Promotion and Protection of the Rights of Cultural, Religious and Linguistic Communities; the Auditor-General; and the Electoral Commission.[76] Finally, the functions of the Human Rights Commission are listed under Section 184, which states:

> 184(1) The South African Human Rights Commission must
> (a) promote respect for human rights and a culture of human rights;
> (b) promote the protection, development and attainment of human rights; and (c) monitor and assess the observance of human rights in the Republic.
> (2) The South African Human Rights Commission has the powers, as regulated by national legislation, necessary
> (a) to perform its functions, including the power
> (b) to investigate and to report on the observance of human rights;

---

74 Ibid., at Section 38.
75 Ibid., at Section 172(1).
76 Ibid., at Section 181.

(c) to take steps to secure appropriate redress where human rights have been violated; and

(d) to carry out research; and to educate.[77]

Employment Equity Act

The Preamble of the Employment Equity Act 1998, an Act to provide for employment equity and to provide for matters incidental thereto, states:

> Recognizing
> that as a result of apartheid and other discriminatory laws and practices, there are disparities in employment, occupation and income within the national labour market; and that those disparities create such pronounced disadvantages for certain categories of people that they cannot be redressed simply by repealing discriminatory laws,
> Therefore, in order to
> promote the constitutional right of equality and the exercise of true democracy; eliminate unfair discrimination in employment; ensure the implementation of employment equity to redress the effects of discrimination; achieve a diverse workforce broadly representative of our people; promote economic development and efficiency in the workforce; and give effect to the obligations of the Republic as a member of the International Labour Organization.[78]

The purpose of the Act is defined in Section 2:

> 2. The purpose of this Act is to achieve equity in the workplace by
> (a) promoting equal opportunity and fair treatment in employment through the elimination of unfair discrimination; and
> (b) implementing affirmative action measures to redress the disadvantages in employment experienced by designated groups, in order to ensure their equitable representation in all occupational categories and levels in the workforce.[79]

Interpretation of the Act is outlined in Section 3:

> 3. This Act must be interpreted
> (a) in compliance with the Constitution
> (b) so as to give effect to its purpose;
> (c) taking into account any relevant code of good practice issued in terms of this Act or any other employment law; and

---

77   Ibid., at Section 184.
78   Employment Equity Act, at the Preamble.
79   Ibid., at Section 2.

(d) in compliance with the international law obligations of the Republic, in particular those contained in the Discrimination (Employment and Occupation) Convention (No. 111) 1958.[80]

The elimination and the prohibition of unfair discrimination are called for in Sections 5 and 6(1):

5. Every employer must take steps to promote equal opportunity in the workplace by eliminating unfair discrimination in any employment policy or practice.[81]

6(1) No person may unfairly discriminate, directly or indirectly, against an employee, in any employment policy or practice, on one or more grounds, including race, gender, sex, pregnancy, marital status, family responsibility, ethnic or social origin, colour, sexual orientation, age, disability, religion, HIV status, conscience, belief, political opinion, culture, language and birth.[82]

Article 6(2) allows for affirmative action programs and bona fide occupational qualifications:

6(2) It is not unfair discrimination to

(a) take affirmative action measures consistent with the purpose of this Act; or

(b) distinguish, exclude or prefer any person on the basis of an inherent requirement of a job.[83]

Further, Section 15 goes on to outline affirmative action measures which are permitted:

15(1) Affirmative action measures are measures designed to ensure that suitably qualified people from designated groups have equal employment opportunities and are equitably represented in all occupational categories and levels in the workforce of a designated employer.

(2) Affirmative action measures implemented by a designated employer must include

(a) measures to identify and eliminate employment barriers, including unfair discrimination, which adversely affect people from designated groups;

(b) measures designed to further diversity in the workplace based on equal dignity and respect of all people;

(c) making reasonable accommodation for people from designated groups in order to ensure that they enjoy equal opportunities and are equitably represented in the workforce of a designated employer;

---

80   Ibid., at Section 3.
81   Ibid., at Section 5.
82   Ibid., at Section 6(1).
83   Ibid., at Section 6(2).

(d) subject to subsection (3), measures to

(i) ensure the equitable representation of suitably qualified people from designated groups in all occupational categories and levels in the workforce; and

(ii) retain and develop people from designated groups and to implement appropriate training measures, including measures in terms of an Act of Parliament providing for skills development.

(3) The measures referred to in subsection (2)(d) include preferential treatment and numerical goals, but exclude quotas.[84]

According to the burden of proof outlined in Section 11:

11. Whenever unfair discrimination is alleged in terms of this Act, the employer against whom the allegation is made must establish that it is fair.[85]

To combat discrimination, Section 20 outlines the requirement of an employment equity plan:

20(1) A designated employer must prepare and implement an employment equity plan which will achieve reasonable progress towards employment equity in that employer's workforce.

(2) An employment equity plan prepared in terms of subsection (1) must state

(a) the objectives to be achieved for each year of the plan;

(b) the affirmative action measures to be implemented as required by subsection 15(2);

(c) where underrepresentation of people from designated groups has been identified by the analysis, the numerical goals to achieve the equitable representation of suitably qualified people from designated groups within each occupational category and level in the workforce, the timetable within which this is to be achieved, and the strategies intended to achieve those goals;

(d) the timetable for each year of the plan for the achievement of goals and objectives other than numerical goals;

(e) the duration of the plan, which may not be shorter than one year or longer than five years;

(f) the procedures that will be used to monitor and evaluate the implementation of the plan and whether reasonable progress is being made towards implementing employment equity;

(g) the internal procedures to resolve any dispute about the interpretation or implementation of the plan;

(h) the persons in the workforce, including senior managers, responsible for monitoring and implementing the plan; and

---

84   Ibid., at Section 15.
85   Ibid., at Section 11.

(i) any other prescribed matter.[86]

The functions of the Commission for Employment Equity are enumerated in Section 30:

30(1) The Commission advises the Minister on

(a) codes of good practice issued by the Minister;

(b) regulations made by the Minister; and

(c) policy and any other matter concerning this Act.

(2) In addition to the functions in subsection (1) the Commission may

(a) make awards recognizing achievements of employers in furthering the purpose of this Act;

(b) research and report to the Minister on any matter relating to the application of this Act, including appropriate and well-researched norms and benchmarks for the setting of numerical goals in various sectors; and

(c) perform any other prescribed function.[87]

In terms of a Code of Good Practice, according to the Employment Equity Act, the process of developing a plan has three sequential phases: planning, development, and implementation and monitoring.[88] The planning phase of the process should include assignment of responsibility and accountability to one or more senior managers; a communication, awareness and training program; consultation with relevant stakeholders; an analysis of existing employment policies, procedures, and practices; an analysis of the existing workforce profile; an analysis of relevant demographic information; and the development of meaningful benchmark comparisons. The development phase should include objectives set; corrective measures formulated; time frames established; the plan drawn up; resources identified and allocated for the implementation of the plan; and the plan communicated. The implementation and monitoring phase should include implementation; monitoring and evaluating progress; reviewing the plan; and reporting on progress.[89]

Promotion of Equality and Prevention of Unfair Discrimination Act

The Preamble of the Promotion of Equality and Prevention of Unfair Discrimination Act 2000 states:

---

86   Ibid., at Section 20.

87   Ibid., at Section 30.

88   Government of South Africa, Code of Good Practice: Preparation, Implementation and Monitoring of Employment Equity Plans.

89   Ibid.

The consolidation of democracy in our country requires the eradication of social and economic inequalities, especially those that are systematic in nature, which were generated in our history by colonialism, apartheid and patriarchy, and which brought pain and suffering to the great majority of our people …
The Constitution provides for the enactment of national legislation to prevent or prohibit unfair discrimination and to promote the achievement of equality;
This implies the advancement, special legal and other measures, of historically disadvantaged individuals, communities and social groups who were dispossessed of their land and resources, deprived of their human dignity and who continue to endure the consequences;
This Act endeavours to facilitate the transition to a democratic society, united in its diversity, marked by human relations that are caring and compassionate, and guided by the principles of equality, fairness, equity, social progress, justice, human dignity and freedom.[90]

The objects of the Act are outlined in Section 2:

2. The objects of the Act are
(a) to enact legislation required by Section 9 of the Constitution;
(b) to give effect to the letter and spirit of the Constitution, in particular
(i) the equal enjoyment of all rights and freedoms by every person,
(ii) the promotion of equality,
(iii) the values of non-racialism and non-sexism contained in Section 1 of the Constitution,
(iv) the prevention of unfair discrimination and protection of human dignity as contemplated in Sections 9 and 10 of the Constitution, and
(v) the prohibition of advocacy of hatred based on race, ethnicity, gender or religion, that constitutes incitement to cause harm;
(c) to provide for measures to facilitate the eradication of unfair discrimination, hate speech and harassment, particularly on the grounds of race, gender and disability; and
(d) to provide for procedures for the determination of circumstances under which discrimination in unfair …[91]

Further, 'prohibited grounds' are defined as:

(xxii)(a) race, gender, sex, pregnancy, marital status, ethnic or social origin, colour, sexual orientation, age, disability, religion, conscience, belief, culture, language and birth; or
(b) any other ground where discrimination based on that other ground

---

90   Promotion of Equality and Prevention of Unfair Discrimination Act, at the Preamble.
91   Ibid., at Section 2.

(i) causes or perpetuates systematic disadvantage;

(ii) undermines human dignity; or

(iii) adversely affects the equal enjoyment of a person's rights and freedoms in a serious manner that is comparable to discrimination on a ground in paragraph (a).[92]

Section 6 guarantees the prevention and general prohibition of unfair discrimination:

6. Neither the State nor any person may unfairly discriminate against any person.[93]

Further, Section 7 prohibits unfair discrimination:

7. Subject to section 6, no person may unfairly discriminate against any person on the ground of race, including

(a) the dissemination of any propaganda or idea, which propounds the racial superiority or inferiority of any person, including incitement to, or participation in, any form of racial violence;

(b) the engagement in any activity which is intended to promote, or has the effect of promoting, exclusivity, based on race;

(c) the exclusion of persons of a particular race group under any rule or practice that appears to be legitimate but which is actually aimed at maintaining exclusive control by a particular race group;

(d) the provision or continued provision of inferior services to any racial group, compared to those of another racial group;

(e) the denial of access to opportunities, including access to services or contractual opportunities for rendering services for consideration, or failing to take steps to reasonably accommodate the needs of such persons.[94]

In terms of the burden of proof in discrimination cases, Section 13 stipulates:

13(1) If the complainant makes out a prima facie case of discrimination

(a) the respondent must prove, in the facts before the court, that the discrimination did not take place as alleged; or

(b) the respondent must prove that the conduct is not based on one or more of the prohibited grounds.

(2) If the discrimination did take place

(a) on a ground in paragraph (a) of the definition of 'prohibited grounds'... then it is unfair, unless the respondent proves that the discrimination is fair;

---

92   Ibid.
93   Ibid., at Section 6.
94   Ibid., at Section 7.

(b) on a ground in paragraph (b) of the definition of 'prohibited grounds', then it is unfair

(i) if one or more of the conditions set out in paragraph (b) of the definition of 'prohibited grounds' is established; and

(ii) unless the respondent proves that the discrimination is fair.[95]

In terms of guiding principles, Section 4 states:

4(1) In the adjudication of any proceedings which are instituted in terms of or under this Act, the following principles should apply:

(a) the expeditious and informal processing of cases, which facilitate participation by the parties to the proceedings;

(b) access to justice to all persons in relevant judicial and other dispute resolution forums; the use of rules of procedure in terms of Section 19 and criteria to facilitate participation;

(c) the use of corrective or restorative measures in conjunction with measures of a deterrent nature; and

(d) the development of special skills and capacity for persons applying this Act in order to ensure effective implementation and administration thereof.

(2) In the application of this Act, the following should be recognized and taken into account:

(a) the existence of systematic discrimination and inequalities, particularly in respect of race, gender and disability in all spheres of life as a result of past and present unfair discrimination, brought about by colonialism, the apartheid system and patriarchy; and

(b) the need to take measures at all levels to eliminate such discrimination and inequalities.[96]

Section 14 establishes the determination of fairness or unfairness:

14(1) It is not unfair discrimination to take measures designed to protect or advance persons or categories of persons disadvantaged by unfair discrimination or the members of such groups or categories of persons.

(2) In determining whether the respondent has proved that the discrimination is fair, the following must be taken into account:

(a) The context;

(b) the factors referred to in subsection (3);

(c) whether the discrimination reasonably and justifiably differentiates between persons according to objectively determinable criteria, intrinsic to the activity concerned.

(3) The factors referred to in subsection (2)(b) include the following:

---

95   Ibid., at Section 13.
96   Ibid., at Section 4.

(a) Whether the discrimination impairs or is likely to impair human dignity;

(b) the impact or likely impact of the discrimination on the complainant;

(c) the position of the complainant in society and whether he or she suffers from patterns of disadvantage or belongs to a group that suffers from patterns of disadvantage;

(d) the nature and extent of the discrimination;

(e) whether the discrimination is systematic in nature;

(f) whether the discrimination has a legitimate purpose;

(g) whether and to what extent the discrimination achieves its purpose;

(h) whether there are less restrictive and less disadvantageous means to achieve the purpose;

(i) whether and to what extent the respondent has taken such steps as being reasonable in the circumstances to

(i) address the disadvantage which arises from or is related to one or more of the prohibited grounds; or

(ii) accommodate diversity.[97]

Finally, according to Section 25, the State has several duties:

25(1) The State must, where necessary with the assistance of the relevant constitutional institutions,

(a) develop awareness of fundamental rights in order to promote a climate of understanding, mutual respect and equality;

(b) take measures to develop and implement programmes in order to promote equality; and

(c) where necessary or appropriate

(i) develop action plans to address any unfair discrimination, hate speech or harassment;

(ii) enact further legislation that seeks to promote equality and to establish a legislative framework in line with the objectives of this Act;

(iii) develop codes of practice as contemplated in this Act in order to promote equality, and develop guidelines, including codes in respect of reasonable accommodation;

(iv) provide assistance, advice and training on issues of equality;

(v) develop appropriate internal mechanisms to deal with complaints of unfair discrimination, hate speech or harassment; and

(vi) conduct information campaigns to popularize this Act.[98]

---

97 Ibid., at Section 14.
98 Ibid., at Section 25.

Children's Act

The Children's Act 2005 was brought into force to give effect to certain rights of children as contained in the Constitution; to set out principles relating to the care and protection of children; to define parental responsibilities and rights; to make further provision regarding children's courts; to provide for the issuing of contribution orders; to make new provision for the adoption of children; to provide for inter-country adoption; to give effect to the Hague Convention on Intercountry Adoption; to prohibit child abduction and to give effect to the Hague Convention on International Child Abduction; to provide for surrogate motherhood; to create certain new offences relating to children; and to provide for matters connected therewith.[99] The Preamble states:

> Whereas the Constitution establishes a society based on democratic values, social justice and fundamental human rights and seeks to improve the quality of life of all citizens and to free the potential of each person;
>
> And whereas every child has the rights set out in section 28 of the Constitution;
>
> And whereas the State must respect, protect, promote and fulfill those rights;
>
> And whereas protection of children's rights leads to a corresponding improvement in the lives of other sections of the community because it is neither desirable nor possible to protect children's rights in isolation from their families and communities;
>
> And whereas the United Nations has in the Universal Declaration of Human Rights proclaimed that children are entitled to special care and assistance;
>
> And whereas the need to extend particular care to the child has been stated in the Geneva Declaration on the Rights of the Child, in the United Nations Declaration on the Rights of the Child, in the Convention on the Rights of the Child and in the African Charter on the Rights and Welfare of the Child and recognised in the Universal Declaration of Human Rights and in the statutes and relevant instruments of specialised agencies and international organisations concerned with the welfare of children;
>
> And whereas it is necessary to effect changes to existing laws relating to children in order to afford them the necessary protection and assistance so that they can fully assume their responsibilities within the community as well as that the child, for the full and harmonious development of his or her personality, should

---

99   Children's Act.

grow up in a family environment and in an atmosphere of happiness, love and understanding,

Be it therefore enacted by the Parliament of the Republic of South Africa, as follows.[100]

Section 1 provides definitions:

1(1) In this Act, unless the context indicates otherwise
'child' means a person under the age of 18 years;
'child labour' means work by a child which
(a) is exploitative, hazardous or otherwise inappropriate for a person of that age; and
(b) places at risk the child's well-being, education, physical or mental health, or spiritual, moral, emotional or social development.[101]

The objects of the Act are outlined under Section 2:

2. The objects of this Act are
(a) to promote the preservation and strengthening of families;
(b) to give effect to the following constitutional rights of children, namely
    (i) family care or parental care or appropriate alternative care when removed from the family environment;
    (ii) social services;
    (iii) protection from maltreatment, neglect, abuse or degradation; and
    (iv) that the best interests of a child are of paramount importance in every matter concerning the child;
(c) to give effect to the Republic's obligations concerning the well-being of children in terms of international instruments binding on the Republic;
(d) to make provision for structures, services and means for promoting and monitoring the sound physical, psychological, intellectual, emotional and social development of children;
(e) to strengthen and develop community structures which can assist in providing care and protection for children;
(f) to protect children from discrimination, exploitation and any other physical, emotional or moral harm or hazards;
(g) to provide care and protection to children who are in need of care and protection;
(h) to recognise the special needs that children with disabilities may have; and

---

100   Ibid., at the Preamble.
101   Ibid., at Section 1.

(i) generally, to promote the protection, development and well-being of children.[102]

The best interests of the child are paramount in Section 7:

7(1) Whenever a provision of this Act requires the best interests of the child standard to be applied, the following factors must be taken into consideration where relevant, namely

(a) the nature of the personal relationship between

(i) the child and the parents, or any specific parent; and

(ii) the child and any other care-giver or person relevant in those circumstances;

(b) the attitude of the parents, or any specific parent, towards

(i) the child; and

(ii) the exercise of parental responsibilities and rights in respect of the child;

(c) the capacity of the parents, or any specific parent, or of any other care-giver or person, to provide for the needs of the child, including emotional and intellectual needs;

(d) the likely effect on the child of any change in the child's circumstances, including the likely effect on the child of any separation from

(i) both or either of the parents; or

(ii) any brother or sister or other child, or any other care-giver or person, with whom the child has been living;

(e) the practical difficulty and expense of a child having contact with the parents, or any specific parent, and whether that difficulty or expense will substantially affect the child's right to maintain personal relations and direct contact with the parents, or any specific parent, on a regular basis;

(f) the need for the child

(i) to remain in the care of his or her parent, family and extended family; and

(ii) to maintain a connection with his or her family, extended family, culture or tradition;

(g) the child's

(i) age, maturity and stage of development;

(ii) gender;

(iii) background; and

(iv) any other relevant characteristics of the child;

(h) the child's physical and emotional security and his or her intellectual, emotional, social and cultural development;

(i) any disability that a child may have;

(j) any chronic illness from which a child may suffer;

---

102   Ibid., at Section 2.

(k) the need for a child to be brought up within a stable family environment and, where this is not possible, in an environment resembling as closely as possible a caring family environment;

(l) the need to protect the child from any physical or psychological harm that may be caused by

(i) subjecting the child to maltreatment, abuse, neglect, exploitation or degradation or exposing the child to violence or exploitation or other harmful behaviour; or

(ii) exposing the child to maltreatment, abuse, degradation, ill-treatment, violence or harmful behaviour towards another person;

(m) any family violence involving the child or a family member of the child; and

(n) which action or decision would avoid or minimise further legal or administrative proceedings in relation to the child.

(2) In this section 'parent' includes any person who has parental responsibilities and rights in respect of a child.[103]

Further, Section 9 states:

9. In all matters concerning the care, protection and well-being of a child the standard that the child's best interest is of paramount importance, must be applied.[104]

Section 17 sets the age of majority:

17. A child, whether male or female, becomes a major upon reaching the age of 18 years.[105]

The trafficking of children is strictly prohibited under Section 284:

284(1) No person, natural or juristic, or a partnership may traffic a child or allow a child to be trafficked.

(2) It is no defence to a charge of contravening subsection (1) that

(a) a child who is a victim of trafficking or a person having control over that child has consented to

(i) the intended exploitation; or

(ii) the adoption of the child facilitated or secured through illegal means; or

(b) the intended exploitation or adoption of a child referred to in paragraph (a) did not occur.

(3) In order to establish the liability, in terms of subsection (1), of an employer or principal, the conduct of an employee or agent of or any other person acting

103 Ibid., at Section 7.
104 Ibid., at Section 9.
105 Ibid., at Section 17.

on behalf of the employer or principal may be attributed to the employer or principal if that person is acting

(a) within the scope of his or her employment;

(b) within the scope of his or her actual or apparent authority; or

(c) with the express or implied consent of a director, member or partner of the employer or principal.

(4) A finding by a court that an employer or principal has contravened subsection (1) serves as a ground for revoking the licence or registration of the employer or principal to operate.[106]

Further, behaviour facilitating the trafficking in children is prohibited under Section 285:

285(1) No person, natural or juristic, or a partnership, may

(a) knowingly lease or sublease or allow any room, house, building or establishment to be used for the purpose of harbouring a child who is a victim of trafficking; and

(b) advertise, publish, print, broadcast, distribute or cause the advertisement, publication, printing, broadcast or distribution of information that suggests or alludes to trafficking by any means, including the use of the Internet or other information technology.

(2) Every Internet service provider operating in the Republic must report to the South African Police Service any site on its server that contains information in contravention of subsection (1).[107]

Assistance to a child who is a victim of trafficking is provided for under Section 286:

286(1) With due regard to the safety of a child and without delay

(a) the Director-General: Foreign Affairs must facilitate the return to the Republic of a child who is a citizen or permanent resident of the Republic and who is a victim of trafficking; and

(b) the Director-General: Home Affairs must

(i) facilitate and accept the return of a child contemplated in paragraph (a);

(ii) issue such travel documents or other authorisations as may be necessary to enable such a child to travel to and enter the Republic;

(iii) at the request of another state that is a party to the UN Protocol to Prevent Trafficking in Persons or to an agreement relating to trafficking in children, verify that the child who is a victim of trafficking is a citizen or permanent resident of the Republic; and

---

106   Ibid., at Section 284.
107   Ibid., at Section 285.

(iv) upon the child's entry into the Republic refer the child to a designated social worker for investigation in terms of section 155(2).

(2) (a) If it is essential in the best interests of a child who has been trafficked, the Director-General must authorise an adult at state expense to escort the child from the place where the child was found to the place from which the child was trafficked.

(b) The Director-General may not act in terms of paragraph (a) unless he or she is satisfied that the parent, guardian, care-giver or other person who has parental responsibilities and rights in respect of the child does not have the financial means to travel to the place where the child is in order to escort the child back.[108]

Finally, Section 287 cautions against parental involvement in trafficking:

287. If a court has reason to believe that the parent or guardian of a child or any other person who has parental responsibilities and rights in respect of a child, has trafficked the child or allowed the child to be trafficked, the court may
(a) suspend all parental responsibilities and rights of that parent, guardian, or other person; and
(b) place that child in temporary safe care, pending an inquiry by a children's court.[109]

Conclusion

In terms of child equality in Africa, African states should share experiences on best practices in order to complement each other so as to ensure effective child protection mainstreaming; continue to ensure that child issues are integrated in all development programs and plans; develop common indicators for monitoring child issues at regional levels; and encourage and support the initiation and coordination of periodical conferences/seminars on children's issues. Indeed, a renewal of commitment to our children is overdue in Africa, where there is a great disparity in the level of human rights protection available to its inhabitants. Almost all African countries have constitutions or civil codes that prohibit discrimination. However, the level of protection varies from nation to nation, and entrenched attitudes and practices, as well as limited resources, limit the practical effect on 'Little Angels'.

---

108   Ibid., at Section 286.
109   Ibid., at Section 287.

Chapter 6
Little Angels in Canada, Mexico and the United States

Introduction

In the quest for respect for our children and in the fight against child discrimination in *Little Angels*, this chapter will examine child issues in Canada, the United States and, minimally, Mexico. It will initially look at the situation in Canada, examining such legislation as the Canadian Constitution, the Canadian Bill of Rights, the Canadian Human Rights Act, the Canada Employment Equity Act and the Canada Labour Code; then minimally in Mexico, the Constitución Política de los Estados Unidos Mexicanos; and finally in the United States, the Declaration of Independence, the Federalist Papers, the American Constitution, the Equal Pay Act, the Civil Rights Act and the Fair Labor Standards Act. Although neighbors, Canada and the United States have had separate histories and thus have undergone very different paths, with some rights having more of an impact in one country than the other.

Canada

Most jurisdictions in Canada, federal and provincial, permit those under age to have relatively broad access to jobs and work experience.[1] Generally, children and youths under the age of 18 may work as long as it does not hurt their health, welfare, or safety or interfere with school attendance; most provinces do not allow children under the age of 14 to work except in special cases.[2] Most jurisdictions restrict the number of hours minors can work, and each province has laws that require minors to be in school at certain times of the day; in most provinces, workers under a certain age may not work after 10 or 11p.m, and may not work more than two or three hours a day on a school day, or more than eight hours on a non-school day.[3] The primacy of education is paramount.[4] The employment of children and young persons subject to compulsory school attendance is severely limited during school hours; this ensures their presence in school during the crucial years when they acquire basic skills. Further, several provisions are aimed at

---

1   Human Resources and Social Development Canada, Labour Law Analysis, 2006.
2   Commission for Labour Cooperation, Guide to Child Labour Laws in Canada.
3   Ibid.
4   Government of Canada, Minimum Age for Employment in Canada.

Table 6.1 Employment statistics for Canada by age, showing underage employment.

Age group	Total			Men			Women		
	Total population	Active population	Activity rate	Total population	Active population	Activity rate	Total population	Active population	Activity rate
Total	–	18245.1	0.0	–	9654.0	0.0	–	8591.2	0.0
Total (15+)	*26924.7*	*18245.0*	*67.8*	*13251.8*	*9654.0*	*72.9*	*13673.0*	*8591.0*	*62.8*
15–19	2157.1	1207.1	56.0	1103.8	601.4	54.5	1053.3	605.7	57.5
20–24	2218.8	1742.5	78.5	1128.6	912.1	80.8	1090.2	830.4	76.2
25–29	2255.2	1940.8	86.1	1133.2	1025.2	90.5	1121.9	915.6	81.6
30–34	2209.3	1921.0	87.0	1106.3	1026.9	92.8	1103.1	894.1	81.1
35–39	2257.7	1980.0	87.7	1112.1	1039.9	93.5	1145.6	940.1	82.1
40–44	2534.1	2234.7	88.2	1283.4	1188.9	92.6	1250.8	1045.8	83.6
45–49	2661.7	2332.2	87.6	1317.2	1201.7	91.2	1344.6	1130.5	84.1
50–54	2505.1	2096.7	83.7	1252.4	1104.9	88.2	1252.7	991.8	79.2
55–59	2115.4	1511.8	71.5	1040.9	802.7	77.1	1074.4	709.1	66.0
60–64	1767.2	849.6	48.1	866.6	479.6	55.3	900.6	370.0	41.1
65+	4243.1	428.6	10.1	1907.3	270.7	14.2	2335.8	157.9	6.8

Source: International Labour Organization, Laborsta, 2008.

preventing the exposure of young persons to occupations or situations which may be harmful to their growth or character. Finally, the physical safety of children, adolescents and other workers is vital, and provisions, particularly those found in occupational health and safety legislation, seek to protect young workers from hazardous environments, substances or occupations, and to protect other workers in the workplace. Overall, legislators in Canada have also recognized the fact that due to various factors, such as lack of experience, young workers are at greater risk in the workplace than other workers.[5] Canada has ratified the Worst Forms of Child Labour Convention, 1999 (No. 182) (C. 182) in 2000; however, it has not ratified the Minimum Age Convention, 1973 (No. 138) (C. 138).

Canadian Constitution

The Canadian Constitution is made up of the Constitution Act of 1867 (formerly the British North America Act) and its various amendments, and the Constitution Act of 1982, which includes the Canadian Charter of Rights and Freedoms, encompassing Articles 1 to 34. It was proclaimed in force and entrenched on 17 April 1982.

The Constitution Act of 1867 sets out the division of powers between the federal government and the provincial governments. The exclusive powers of the Parliament of Canada are found in Section 91:

> 91. It shall be lawful for the Queen, by and with the Advice and Consent of the Senate and House of Commons, to make laws for the Peace, Order, and good Government of Canada, in relation to all Matters not coming within the Classes of Subjects by this Act assigned exclusively to the Legislatures of the Provinces; and for greater Certainty, but not so as to restrict the Generality of the foregoing Terms of this Section, it is hereby declared that (notwithstanding anything in this Act) the exclusive Legislative Authority of the Parliament of Canada extends to all Matters coming within the Classes of Subjects next hereinafter enumerated; that is to say,
> 1A. The Public Debt and Property.
> 2. The Regulation of Trade and Commerce.
> 2A. Unemployment insurance.
> 3. The raising of Money by any Mode or System of Taxation.
> 4. The borrowing of Money on the Public Credit.
> 5. Postal Service.
> 6. The Census and Statistics.
> 7. Militia, Military and Naval Service, and Defence.
> 8. The fixing of and providing for the Salaries and Allowances of Civil and other Officers of the Government of Canada.
> 9. Beacons, Buoys, Lighthouses, and Sable Island.

---

5   Ibid.

10. Navigation and Shipping.

11. Quarantine and the Establishment and Maintenance of Marine Hospitals.

12. Sea Coast and Inland Fisheries.

13. Ferries between a Province and any British or Foreign Country or between Two Provinces.

14. Currency and Coinage.

15. Banking, Incorporation of Banks, and the Issue of Paper Money.

16. Savings Banks.

17. Weights and Measures.

18. Bills of Exchange and Promissory Notes.

19. Interest.

20. Legal Tender.

21. Bankruptcy and Insolvency.

22. Patents of Invention and Discovery.

23. Copyrights.

24. Indians, and Lands reserved for the Indians.

25. Naturalization and Aliens.

26. Marriage and Divorce.

27. The Criminal Law, except the Constitution of Courts of Criminal Jurisdiction, but including the Procedure in Criminal Matters.

28. The Establishment, Maintenance, and Management of Penitentiaries.

29. Such Classes of Subjects as are expressly excepted in the Enumeration of the Classes of Subjects by this Act assigned exclusively to the Legislatures of the Provinces.

And any Matter coming within any of the Classes of Subjects enumerated in this section shall not be deemed to come within the Class of Matters of a local or private Nature comprised in the Enumeration of the Classes of Subjects by this Act assigned exclusively to the Legislatures of the Provinces.[6]

The exclusive powers of provincial legislatures are found in Section 92:

92. In each Province the Legislature may exclusively make Laws in relation to Matters coming within the Classes of Subject next hereinafter enumerated; that is to say,

1. Repealed.

2. Direct Taxation within the Province in order to the raising of a Revenue for Provincial Purposes.

3. The borrowing of Money on the sole Credit of the Province.

4. The Establishment and Tenure of Provincial Offices and the Appointment and Payment of Provincial Officers.

5. The Management and Sale of the Public Lands belonging to the Province and of the Timber and Wood thereon.

---

6   Constitution Act of 1867, at Section 91.

6. The Establishment, Maintenance, and Management of Public and Reformatory Prisons in and for the Province.

7. The Establishment, Maintenance, and Management of Hospitals, Asylums, Charities, and Eleemosynary Institutions in and for the Province, other than Marine Hospitals.

8. Municipal Institutions in the Province.

9. Shop, Saloon, Tavern, Auctioneer, and other Licences in order to the raising of a Revenue for Provincial, Local, or Municipal Purposes.

10. Local Works and Undertakings other than such as are of the following Classes:

(*a*) Lines of Steam or other Ships, Railways, Canals, and other Works and Undertakings connecting the Province with any other or others of the Provinces, or extending beyond the Limits of the Province;

(*b*) Lines of Steam Ships between the Province and any British or Foreign Country;

(*c*) Such Works as, although wholly situate within the Province, are before or after the Execution declared by the Parliament of Canada to be for the general Advantage of Canada or for the Advantage of Two or more of the Provinces.

11. The Incorporation of Companies with Provincial Objects.

12. The Solemnization of Marriage in the Province.

13. Property and Civil Rights in the Province.

14. The Administration of Justice in the Province, including the Constitution, Maintenance, and Organization of Provincial Courts, both of Civil and of Criminal Jurisdiction, and including Procedure in Civil Matters in those Courts.

15. The Imposition of Punishment by Fine, Penalty, or Imprisonment for enforcing any Law of the Province made in relation to any Matter coming within any of the Classes of Subjects enumerated in this Section.

16. Generally all Matters of a merely local or private Nature in the Province.[7]

Further, the purpose of the Constitution Act of 1982 and the Charter of Rights and Freedoms is to protect and safeguard the rights and freedoms enumerated, and to contain governmental action within reasonable limits. The supremacy of the Constitution is contained in Section 52(1):

52(1) The Constitution of Canada is the supreme law of Canada and any law that is inconsistent with the provisions of the Constitution is, to the extent of the inconsistency, of no force or effect.[8]

Section 32 provides for its application to the Parliament and government of Canada, as well as to the legislature and government of each province.[9] The purpose of

---

7   Ibid., at Section 92.

8   Constitution Act of 1982, Canada, at Section 52(1).

9   Ibid., at Section 32.

the Canadian Constitution was to protect and safeguard the rights and freedoms enumerated, and to contain governmental action within reasonable limits.

Fundamental Freedoms   These are protected under Section 2 of the Charter, which states:

> 2. Everyone has the following fundamental freedoms:
> (a) freedom of conscience and religion;
> (b) freedom of thought, belief, opinion and expression, including freedom of the press and other means of communication;
> (c) freedom of peaceful assembly; and
> (d) freedom of association.[10]

Civil Rights   Important in the fight against discrimination, the Charter guarantees equality of rights, and also deals with affirmative action programs to help reverse the discrimination process. Section 15 came into effect on 17 April 1985 after a three-year implemented delay:

> 15(1) Every individual is equal before and under the law and has the right to the equal protection and equal benefit of the law without discrimination and, in particular, without discrimination based on race, national or ethnic origin, colour, religion, sex, age or mental or physical disability.
> (2) Subsection (1) does not preclude any law, program or activity that has as its object the amelioration of conditions of disadvantaged individuals or groups including those that are disadvantaged because of race, national or ethnic origin, colour, religion, sex, age or mental or physical disability.[11]

Further, the Charter implements equality through Section 28, which states:

> 28. Notwithstanding anything in this Charter, the rights and freedoms referred to in it are guaranteed equally to male and female persons.[12]

This provision cannot be overridden by legislation or Act of Parliament.

Multiculturalism and Aboriginal Rights   Section 27 provides for multiculturalism:

> 27. This Charter shall be interpreted in a manner consistent with the preservation and enhancement of the multicultural heritage of Canadians.[13]

---

10   Ibid., at Section 2.
11   Ibid., at Section 15.
12   Ibid., at Section 28.
13   Ibid., at Section 27.

Further, Section 35(1) and (2), entitled 'Rights of the Aboriginal Peoples of Canada', states:

> 35(1) The existing aboriginal and treaty rights of the aboriginal peoples of Canada are hereby recognized and affirmed.
> (2) In this Act, 'aboriginal peoples of Canada' includes the Indian, Inuit and Métis peoples of Canada.[14]

Official Languages   The Official Languages of Canada are recognized in Section 16:

> 16.1 (1) The English linguistic community and the French linguistic community in New Brunswick have equality of status and equal rights and privileges, including the right to distinct educational institutions and such distinct cultural institutions as are necessary for the preservation and promotion of those communities.
> (2) The role of the legislature and government of New Brunswick to preserve and promote the status, rights and privileges referred to in subsection (1) is affirmed.[15]

Enforcement of Guaranteed Rights and Freedoms   The enforcement of rights and freedoms is contained in Section 24:

> 24. (1) Anyone whose rights or freedoms, as guaranteed by this Charter, have been infringed or denied may apply to a court of competent jurisdiction to obtain such remedy as the court considers appropriate and just in the circumstances.
> (2) Where, in proceedings under subsection (1), a court concludes that evidence was obtained in a manner that infringed or denied any rights or freedoms guaranteed by this Charter, the evidence shall be excluded if it is established that, having regard to all the circumstances, the admission of it in the proceedings would bring the administration of justice into disrepute.[16]

Provisions in Denial of Rights   Section 33 of the Charter is the infamous 'notwithstanding' clause, allowing the Canadian provinces to opt out of the Constitution for successive and infinite five-year periods. It provides:

> 33. Parliament or the legislature of a province may expressly declare in an Act of Parliament or of the legislature ... that the Act or a provision thereof shall operate notwithstanding a provision included in ... Section ... 15 of this Charter.[17]

---

14   Ibid., at Section 35.
15   Ibid., at Section 16.
16   Ibid., at Section 24.
17   Ibid., at Section 33.

The Canadian Constitution extends power to judges to review legislative action on the basis of congruence with protected values in the Charter, and treats the judicial branch of government as a partner with the legislative and executive branches, in determining the rights of citizens. However, Section 33, the overriding clause, will ensure that legislatures rather than judges have the final say on important matters of public policy, so that laws offensive to certain provisions of the Charter may be upheld.

Section 1 of the Charter is also an overriding clause and states:

> 1. The Canadian Charter of Rights and Freedoms set out is subject only to such reasonable limits prescribed by law as can be demonstrably justified in a free and democratic society.[18]

Thus, fundamental freedoms, as well as legal and equality rights, can be subjected to this notwithstanding clause. Remarkably, the right against discrimination is not absolute. The Canadian Charter of Rights and Freedoms may be used to strengthen inequalities, by weighing in on the side of power, and undermine popular movements.

In terms of the burden of proof, Section 1 of the Charter has two functions: first, it guarantees the rights and freedoms set out in the provisions which follow it; and second, it states explicitly the exclusive justificatory criteria, outside Section 33 of the Charter, against which limitations on those rights and freedoms may be measured. The onus of proving that a limitation on any Charter right is reasonable and demonstrably justified in a free and democratic society rests upon the party seeking to uphold the limitation. Limits on constitutionally guaranteed rights are meant to be exceptions to the general guarantee. The presumption is that Charter rights are guaranteed unless the party invoking Section 1 can bring itself within the exceptional criteria justifying their being limited. The standard of proof under Section 1 is a preponderance of probabilities. Proof beyond a reasonable doubt would be unduly onerous on the party seeking to limit the right, because concepts such as 'reasonableness', 'justifiability' and 'free and democratic society' are not amenable to such a standard. Nevertheless, the preponderance of probability test must be applied rigorously.

The Supreme Court of Canada uses the purposive approach to interpret the Charter, whereby the underlying purpose of the legislative provision and the nature of the interest are identified. A two-step procedure is utilized to see whether the limit of the Charter contained in Section 1 can uphold an infringement of a right. Two questions are asked: (1) has the right been violated?; and (2) can the violation be justified under Section 1? The burden of proof is such that the onus of establishing a prima facie infringement of the Charter is on the person alleging it, while the onus of justifying a reasonable limit on the protected right is on the party invoking Section 1. Two criteria must be satisfied in order to come

---

18   Ibid., at Section 1.

within Section 1 of the Charter: (1) the objective of the limiting measure must be sufficiently important, and the concerns must be pressing and substantial to justify overriding a constitutionally protected right; and (2) the means must be reasonable and demonstrably justified according to a proportionality test, which balances the interests of society against those of individuals. There are three components to the test: (1) the measure must be carefully designed to achieve the stated objective, and must not be arbitrary, unfair or irrational; (2) the measure should impair the right as little as possible; and (3) proportionality must exist between the effect of the limiting measure and its objectives (*Regina* v. *Oakes*, [1986] 1 SCR 103).[19]

Canadian Bill of Rights

In addition to the Canadian Constitution, there is the Canadian Bill of Rights, enacted on 10 August 1960.

Fundamental Freedoms   The Bill of Rights in Section 1 outlines the human rights and fundamental freedoms guaranteed:

> 1. It is hereby recognized and declared that in Canada there have existed and shall continue to exist without discrimination by reason of race, national origin, colour, religion or sex, the following human rights and fundamental freedoms, namely,
> (a) the right of the individual to life, liberty, security of the person and enjoyment of property and the right not to be deprived thereof except by due process of law;
> (b) the right of the individual to equality before the law and the protection of the law;
> (c) freedom of religion;
> (d) freedom of speech;
> (e) freedom of assembly and of association; and
> (f) freedom of the press.[20]

Canadian Human Rights Act (CHRA)

The Canadian Human Rights Act (CHRA) came into force on 1 March 1978. The CHRA has been very influential for those seeking relief from human rights abuses and discrimination through a channel other than the traditional court system, namely the Canadian Human Rights Tribunal (CHRT); the Act implements a complaint process through a commission, which assumes that systemic discrimination does not exist but for a few cases, and differs from a proactive approach, which places an obligation on the employer to determine if systemic gendered wage discrimination exists and to remedy it within a time frame.

The purpose of the CHRA is outlined in Section 2:

---

19   *Regina* v. *Oakes*, [1986] 1 SCR 103.
20   Bill of Rights, Canada, at Section 1.

2. The purpose of this Act is to extend the laws in Canada to give effect, within the purview of matters coming within the legislative authority of Parliament, to the principle that all individuals should have an opportunity equal with other individuals to make for themselves the lives that they are able and wish to have and to have their needs accommodated, consistent with their duties and obligations as members of society, without being hindered in or prevented from doing so by discriminatory practices based on race, national or ethnic origin, colour, religion, age, sex, sexual orientation, marital status, family status, disability or conviction for an offence for which a pardon has been granted.[21]

Important in the fight against discrimination, Section 3(1) states:

3(1) For all purposes of this Act, the prohibited grounds of discrimination are race, national or ethnic origin, colour, religion, age, sex, sexual orientation, marital status, family status, disability and conviction for which a pardon has been granted.
(2) Where the ground of discrimination is pregnancy or child-birth, the discrimination shall be deemed to be on the ground of sex.
3.1. For greater certainty, a discriminatory practice includes a practice based on one or more prohibited grounds of discrimination or on the effect of a combination of prohibited grounds.[22]

Further, Sections 7 and 10 go on to enumerate what is considered to be discriminatory:

7. It is a discriminatory practice, directly or indirectly:
(a) to refuse to employ or continue to employ any individual, or
(b) in the course of employment, to differentiate adversely in relation to an employee, on a prohibited ground of discrimination. [1976~77, c.33, s.7.3][23]

10. It is a discriminatory practice for an employer, employee organization or organization of employers:
(a) to establish or pursue a policy or practice, or
(b) to enter into an agreement affecting recruitment, referral, hiring, promotion, training, apprenticeship, transfer or any other matter relating to employment or prospective employment, that deprives or tends to deprive an individual or class of individuals of any employment opportunities on a prohibited ground of discrimination. [1976~77, c.33, s.10; 1980~81~82~83, c.143, s.5.][24]

---

21   Ibid., at Section 2.
22   Canadian Human Rights Act, Canada, at Section 3.
23   Ibid., at Section 7.
24   Ibid., at Section 10.

Under Section 11, it is discriminatory directly or indirectly to refuse to employ or, in the course of employment, to differentiate adversely against an employee in recruitment, referral, hiring, promotion, training or transfer policies:

11(2) In assessing the value of work performed by employees employed in the same establishment, the criterion to be applied is the composite of the skill, effort and responsibility required in the performance of the work and the conditions under which the work is performed.[25]

Further, Section 15(1) allows for a bona fide occupational exception:

15(1) It is not a discriminatory practice if
(a) any refusal, exclusion, expulsion, suspension, limitation, specification or preference in relation to any employment is established by an employer to be based on a bona fide occupational requirement.[26]

However, important in the fight against discrimination, special programs are allowed under Section 16:

16. It is not a discriminatory practice for a person to adopt or carry out a special program, plan or arrangement designed to prevent disadvantages that are likely to be suffered by, or to eliminate or reduce disadvantages that are suffered by, any group of individuals when those disadvantages would be or are based on or related to the race, national or ethnic origin, colour, religion, age, sex, marital status, family status or disability of members of that group, by improving opportunities respecting goods, services, facilities, accommodation or employment in relation to that group.[27]

Finally, Section 48(1) establishes the Canadian Human Rights Tribunal.[28]

The CHRA looks at comparable worth, applying the same wages where respective work is shown to be equal in value through a combination of skill, effort, responsibility and working conditions, and makes comparisons between dissimilar jobs. It is a discriminatory practice to establish different wages, so that if people do work of equal value in the same establishment then they must be paid equally; discriminatory practices for wage inequities include segregated employment, exclusion of those categorically from the existing evaluation system, under-valuation of certain positions, fewer promotion opportunities, senior rules disadvantaging some minorities, and discriminatory transfers, promotion and

---

25   Ibid., at Section 11.
26   Ibid., at Section 15(1).
27   Ibid., at Section 16.
28   Ibid., at Section 48(1).

layoffs.[29] There are, however, some reasonable factors to permit a pay difference, such as periodic pay increases for length of service or working in remote locations. The CHRC only has jurisdiction over the federal public service and federally regulated employers in the quest for equal pay for work of equal value. One drawback to the federal law is that it is limited to comparisons within the same establishment. If discrimination is found and there is no agreement for adjustment, a conciliator is appointed or a tribunal is established, with its decision appealable to the courts. Discrimination includes practices or attitudes, whether by design or impact, which have the effect of limiting the individual's right to the opportunities generally available, because of attributes other than actual characteristics.

The Canadian Human Rights Tribunal found that there is not a prima facie case of discrimination when others are better-qualified (*Folch* v. *Canadian Airlines*, 1992 CHRT).[30] The rational connection test, the potential for a rational connection between the basic fact and the presumed fact to justify a reverse onus provision, does not specifically apply to the interpretation of the CHRA. A basic fact may rationally tend to prove a presumed fact, but still not prove its existence beyond a reasonable doubt, which is an important aspect of the presumption of innocence. The appropriate stage for invoking the rational connection test is therefore under Section 1 of the Charter (*Regina* v. *Oakes*, [1986] 1 SCR 103).[31] However, in terms of the onus of proof with respect to a complaint under the Act, the burden and order of proof in discrimination cases involving refusal of employment appears clear and constant through all Canadian jurisdictions: a complainant must first establish a prima facie case of discrimination; once that is done the burden shifts to the respondent to provide a reasonable explanation for the otherwise discriminatory behavior. Thereafter, assuming the employer has provided an explanation, the complainant has the eventual burden of showing that the explanation provided was merely 'pretext' and that the true motivation behind the employer's actions was in fact discriminatory (*Basi* v. *Canadian National Railway* (1984), 9 CHRR 4. D/5029, 5037 (CHR Tribunal)).[32]

In an employment complaint, the Commission usually establishes a prima facie case by proving: (1) that the complainant was qualified for the particular employment; (2) that the complainant was not hired; and (3) that someone no better qualified but lacking the distinguishing feature which is the gravamen of the human rights complaint subsequently obtained the position. If these elements are proved, there is an evidentiary onus on the respondent to provide an explanation of events equally consistent with the conclusion that discrimination on the basis prohibited by the Code is not the correct explanation of what occurred (*Shakes* v.

---

29 Labor Canada, *Equal Pay for Work of Equal Value*, Ottawa, 1986, p. 21.

30 *Folch* v. *Canadian Airlines*, 1992 CHRT.

31 *Regina* v. *Oakes*, [1986] 1 SCR 103.

32 *Basi* v. *Canadian National Railway* (1984), 9 CHRR 4. D/5029, 5037 (CHR Tribunal).

Rex Pak Ltd (1982), 3 CHRR D/1001, 1002).[33] Should the respondent lead evidence of a non-discriminatory reason for refusing to employ the complainant, then the Complainant and the Commission can still establish that the reason advanced for non-employment is in fact a pretext, and that discrimination on an unlawful ground was one of the operative reasons for the respondent's actions (*Blake* v. *Ministry of Correctional Services and Mimico Correctional Institute* (1984), 5 CHRR D/2417 (Ontario)).[34] The ultimate onus of proof to establish the complaint on a balance of probabilities lies with the complainant and the Commission. Discrimination can be established by direct evidence or by circumstantial evidence, which is evidence that is consistent with the fact that is sought to be proven and inconsistent with any other rational conclusion. It is not necessary to find that the respondent intended to discriminate against the complainant; it is sufficient to establish the complaint if it is found, on the balance of probabilities, that the respondent in fact discriminated against the complainant on one of the grounds alleged in their complaint (*Ontario Human Rights Commission* v. *Simpsons-Sears Ltd*, [1985] SCR 536, 547).[35]

Canada Employment Equity Act

The purpose of the Canada Employment Equity Act 1995 is outlined in Section 2:

> 2. The purpose of this Act is to achieve equality in the workplace so that no person shall be denied employment opportunities or benefits for reasons unrelated to ability and, in the fulfilment of that goal, to correct the conditions of disadvantage in employment experienced by women, aboriginal peoples, persons with disabilities and members of visible minorities by giving effect to the principle that employment equity means more than treating persons in the same way but also requires special measures and the accommodation of differences.[36]

Section 5 establishes a duty of employers:

> 5. Every employer shall implement employment equity by
> (*a*) identifying and eliminating employment barriers against persons in designated groups that result from the employer's employment systems, policies and practices that are not authorized by law; and
> (*b*) instituting such positive policies and practices and making such reasonable accommodations as will ensure that persons in designated groups achieve a degree of representation in each occupational group in the employer's workforce that reflects their representation in

---

33   *Shakes* v. *Rex Pak Ltd* (1982), 3 CHRR D/1001, 1002.

34   *Blake* v. *Ministry of Correctional Services and Mimico Correctional Institute* (1984), 5 CHRR D/2417 (Ontario).

35   *Ontario Human Rights Commission* v. *Simpsons-Sears Ltd*, [1985] SCR 536, 547.

36   Canada Employment Equity Act, 1995, Canada, at Section 2.

(i) the Canadian workforce, or

(ii) those segments of the Canadian workforce that are identifiable by qualification, eligibility or geography and from which the employer may reasonably be expected to draw employees.[37]

However, Section 6 provides:

6. The obligation to implement employment equity does not require an employer
(*a*) to take a particular measure to implement employment equity where the taking of that measure would cause undue hardship to the employer;
(*b*) to hire or promote persons who do not meet the essential qualifications for the work to be performed;
(*c*) with respect to the public sector, to hire or promote persons without basing the hiring or promotion on merit in cases where the *Public Service Employment Act* requires that hiring or promotion be based on merit; or
(*d*) to create new positions in its workforce.[38]

Further, Section 10 provides for the implementation of an employment equity plan:

10. (1) The employer shall prepare an employment equity plan that
(*a*) specifies the positive policies and practices that are to be instituted by the employer in the short term for the hiring, training, promotion and retention of persons in designated groups and for the making of reasonable accommodations for those persons, to correct the underrepresentation of those persons identified by the analysis ...
(*b*) specifies the measures to be taken by the employer in the short term for the elimination of any employment barriers identified by the review ...
(*c*) establishes a timetable for the implementation of the matters referred to in paragraphs (*a*) and (*b*);
(*d*) where underrepresentation has been identified by the analysis, establishes short term numerical goals for the hiring and promotion of persons in designated groups in order to increase their representation in each occupational group in the workforce in which underrepresentation has been identified and sets out measures to be taken in each year to meet those goals;
(*e*) sets out the employer's longer term goals for increasing the representation of persons in designated groups in the employer's workforce and the employer's strategy for achieving those goals; and
(*f*) provides for any other matter that may be prescribed.[39]

---

37   Ibid., at Section 5.
38   Ibid., at Section 6.
39   Ibid., at Section 10.

Finally, Article 29 provides for tribunal procedures:

> 29. (1) A Tribunal may
> (*a*) in the same manner and to the same extent as a superior court of record, summon and enforce the attendance of witnesses and compel them to give oral and written evidence on oath and to produce such documents and things as the Tribunal considers necessary for a full review;
> (*b*) administer oaths; and
> (*c*) receive and accept such evidence and other information, whether on oath or by affidavit or otherwise, as the Tribunal sees fit, whether or not that evidence or information would be admissible in a court of law.
>
> (2) A Tribunal shall conduct any matter that comes before it as informally and expeditiously as the circumstances and considerations of fairness and natural justice permit.
>
> (3) Subject to subsection (4), a hearing before a Tribunal shall be conducted in public.
>
> (4) A hearing before a Tribunal may, on the request of an employer, be held *in camera* if the employer establishes to the satisfaction of the Tribunal that the circumstances of the case so require.
>
> (5) A Tribunal shall provide the parties to a proceeding before the Tribunal with written reasons for its decision.
>
> (6) A Tribunal shall, on request by any person, provide the person with a copy of any decision of the Tribunal, including a decision under subsection (4) to hold a hearing *in camera*, together with the written reasons for the decision.[40]

Canada Labour Code

According to the Canada Labour Code 1985, Section 179 deals with employees under the age of 17:

> 179. An employer may employ a person under the age of seventeen years only
> (a) in an occupation specified by the regulations; and
> (b) subject to the conditions fixed by the regulations for employment in that occupation.[41]

---

40   Ibid., at Article 29.
41   Canada Labour Code, at Section 179.

Mexico

Constitución Política de los Estados Unidos Mexicanos

The equality of all persons before the law is guaranteed by the Constitución Política de los Estados Unidos Mexicanos, the Political Constitution of the United Mexican States. The supremacy of the Constitution with its rights is covered under Article 1:

> 1. Every person in the United Mexican States shall enjoy the guarantees granted by this Constitution, which cannot be restricted or suspended except in such cases and under such conditions as are herein provided.[42]

Important in the advancement of people, education is guaranteed under Article 3:

> 3. The education imparted by the Federal State shall be designed to develop harmoniously all the faculties of the human being and shall foster in him at the same time a love of country and a consciousness of international solidarity, in independence and justice.
>
> (1) Freedom of religious beliefs being guaranteed by Article 24, the standard which shall guide such education shall be maintained entirely apart from any religious doctrine and, based on the results of scientific progress, shall strive against ignorance and its effects, servitudes, fanaticism, and prejudices. Moreover:
>
> (a) It shall be democratic, considering democracy not only as a legal structure and a political regimen, but as a system of life founded on a constant economic, social, and cultural betterment of the people;
>
> (b) It shall be national insofar as, without hostility or exclusiveness, it shall achieve the understanding of our problems, the utilization of our resources, the defense of our political independence, the assurance of our economic independence, and the continuity and growth of our culture; and
>
> (c) It shall contribute to better human relationships, not only with the elements which it contributes toward strengthening and at the same time inculcating, together with respect for the dignity of the person and the integrity of the family, the conviction of the general interest of society, but also by the care which it devotes to the ideals of brotherhood and equality of rights of all men, avoiding privileges of race, creed, class, sex, or persons.
>
> (2) Private persons may engage in education of all kinds and grades. But as regards elementary, secondary, and normal education (and that of any kind or grade designed for laborers and farm workers) they must previously obtain, in every case, the express authorization of the public power. Such authorization

---

42   Constitución Política de los Estados Unidos Mexicanos, Mexico, at Article 1.

Table 6.2 Employment statistics for Mexico by age, showing underage employment.

Age group	Total			Men			Women		
	Total population	Active population	Activity rate	Total population	Active population	Activity rate	Total population	Active population	Activity rate
Total	106572.9	45460.0	42.7	51265.3	28329.1	55.3	55307.6	17130.9	31.0
Total (15+)	74658.3	45110.9	60.4	35014.0	28083.3	80.2	39644.3	17027.5	43.0
0–9	20664.4	–	–	10438.7	–	–	10225.7	–	–
10–14	11224.8	338.5	3.0	5803.4	238.3	4.1	5421.5	100.2	1.8
15–19	10851.2	3904.9	36.0	5387.0	2578.4	47.9	5464.2	1326.5	24.3
20–24	8895.4	5511.5	62.0	4202.7	3345.2	79.6	4692.6	2166.2	46.2
25–29	7802.6	5582.2	71.5	3622.7	3404.7	94.0	4180.0	2177.5	52.1
30–34	7744.9	5631.7	72.7	3592.7	3454.3	96.1	4152.2	2177.4	52.4
35–39	7678.7	5704.5	74.3	3544.4	3419.2	96.5	4134.3	2285.3	55.3
40–44	6892.3	5171.8	75.0	3193.1	3065.1	96.0	3699.3	2106.7	56.9
45–49	5919.8	4331.9	73.2	2739.8	2601.5	95.0	3180.0	1730.4	54.4
50–54	4915.6	3327.5	67.7	2328.2	2136.3	91.8	2587.5	1191.2	46.0
55–59	3857.4	2392.5	62.0	1826.3	1583.6	86.7	2031.0	808.9	39.8
60–64	3149.9	1515.5	48.1	1436.9	1027.9	71.5	1713.0	487.6	28.5
65–69	2333.8	952.6	40.8	1110.6	686.3	61.8	1223.2	266.2	21.8
70–74	1861.2	586.7	31.5	822.7	415.2	50.5	1038.5	171.6	16.5
75+	2755.4	497.5	18.1	1207.0	365.5	30.3	1548.4	131.9	8.5

Source: International Labour Organization, Laborsta, 2008.

may be refused or revoked by decisions against which there can be no judicial proceedings or recourse.

(3) Private institutions devoted to education of the kinds and grades specified in the preceding section must be without exception in conformity with the provisions of sections I and II of the first paragraph of this article and must also be in harmony with official plans and programs.

(4) Religious corporations, ministers of religion, stock companies which exclusively or predominantly engage in educational activities, and associations or companies devoted to propagation of any religious creed shall not in any way participate in institutions giving elementary, secondary and normal education and education for laborers or field workers.

(5) The State may in its discretion withdraw at any time the recognition of official validity of studies conducted in private institutions.

(6) Elementary education shall be compulsory.

(7) All education given by the State shall be free.

(8) The Congress of the Union, with a view to unifying and coordinating education throughout the Republic, shall issue the necessary laws for dividing the social function of education among the Federation, the States and the Municipalities, for fixing the appropriate financial allocations for this public service and for establishing the penalties applicable to officials who do not comply with or enforce the pertinent provisions, as well as the penalties applicable to all those who infringe such provisions.[43]

Further, Article 31 states:

> 31.I. To see that their children or wards, under fifteen years of age, attend public or private schools to obtain primary, elementary and military education during the time prescribed by the Law on Public Education in each State.[44]

Article 4 protects employment rights:

> 4. No person can be prevented from engaging in the profession, industrial or commercial pursuit, or occupation of his choice, provided it is lawful. The exercise of this liberty shall only be forbidden by judicial order when the rights of third parties are infringed, or by administrative order, issued in the manner provided by law, when the rights of society are violated. No one may be deprived of the fruits of his labor except by judicial decision.
>
> The law in each state shall determine the professions which may be practiced only with a degree, and set forth the requirements for obtaining it and the authorities empowered to issue it.[45]

---

43 Ibid., at Article 3.
44 Ibid., at Article 31.
45 Ibid., at Article 4.

Finally, the restriction of underage employment is covered under Article 123:

> 123. The Congress of the Union, without contravening the following basic principles, shall formulate labor laws which shall apply to:
>
> A. Workers, day laborers, domestic servants, artisans (obreros, jornaleros, empleados domésticos, artesanos) and in a general way to all labor contracts:
>
> I. The maximum duration of work for one day shall be eight hours.
>
> II. The maximum duration of nightwork shall be seven hours. The following are prohibited: unhealthful or dangerous work by women and by minors under sixteen years of age; industrial nightwork by either of these classes; work by women in commercial establishments after ten o'clock at night and work (of any kind) by persons under sixteen after ten o'clock at night.
>
> III. The use of labor of minors under fourteen years of age is prohibited. Persons above that age and less than sixteen shall have a maximum work day of six hours.[46]

Mexico has ratified the Worst Forms of Child Labour Convention, 1999 (No. 182) (C. 182) in 2000; however, it has not ratified the Minimum Age Convention, 1973 (No. 138) (C. 138).

United States of America

Declaration of Independence

The concepts of equality and good government, found in the US judicial system, were equally important principles to the Founding Fathers of the United States. The Declaration of Independence 1776, the bedrock of the United States' jurisprudence system, was enshrined on 4 July 1776. It fundamentally states:

> We hold these truths to be self-evident, that all men are created equal; that they are endowed by their Creator with certain unalienable rights; that among these are life, liberty and the pursuit of happiness. That, to secure these rights, governments are instituted among men, deriving their just powers from the consent of the governed; that whenever any form of government becomes destructive of these ends, it is the right of the people to alter or to abolish it, and to institute a new government, laying its foundation on such principles, and organize its powers in such form, as to them shall seem most likely to effect their safety and happiness.[47]

---

46 Ibid., at Article 123.
47 Declaration of Independence, United States.

Table 6.3 Employment statistics for the United States by age, showing underage employment.

Age group	Total			Men			Women		
	Total population	Active population	Activity rate	Total population	Active population	Activity rate	Total population	Active population	Activity rate
Total	–	154287	0.0	–	82520	0.0	–	71767	0.0
16–19	17075	6858	40.2	8660	3472	40.1	8415	3385	40.2
20–24	20409	15174	74.3	10249	8065	78.7	10160	7109	70.0
25–29	20815	17293	83.1	10451	9431	90.2	10363	7862	75.9
30–34	19179	16039	83.6	9548	8871	92.9	9631	7168	74.4
35–39	20537	17218	83.8	10142	9404	92.7	10395	7814	75.2
40–44	21162	17843	84.3	10425	9568	91.8	10737	8275	77.1
45–49	22644	18870	83.3	11108	9962	89.7	11536	8908	77.2
50–54	21316	17133	80.4	10404	8966	86.2	10912	8167	74.8
55–59	18444	13480	73.1	8929	7035	78.8	9515	6445	67.7
60–64	15047	8135	54.1	7194	4310	59.9	7852	3825	48.7
65–69	11242	3451	30.7	5246	1866	35.6	5995	1585	26.4
70–74	8639	1534	17.8	3912	858	21.9	4728	676	14.3
75+	17281	1258	7.3	6844	711	10.4	10437	547	5.2

Source: International Labour Organization, Laborsta, 2008.

Federalist Papers

Influential thinkers, such as Jefferson, Madison and Jay, believed in a national government and a Bill of Rights, which they outlined in the Federalist Papers 1787–88.[48] The Constitution is founded on the assent and ratification of the people. Among the three branches of government, the Judicial branch is considered the least dangerous to the political rights of the Constitution. The Executive branch dispenses the honors and holds the sword, the Legislative branch controls the purse and prescribes the rules to regulate duties and rights, and the Judiciary has no influence over the sword or the purse, needing the aid of the Executive for the efficacy of judgments. Oppression can proceed from the Courts, but liberty will not be endangered if the branches are separate. As a recognition of popular rights, the judgments of many unite into one, with the voluntary consent of a whole people. The Federalist Papers give us an important insight into the making of the Constitution, showing us early on the concept of equality of man and the formation of one government out of many people. The importance of the Judiciary must not be overlooked, as it is a major contributor of policy through its judgments, often itself influencing the sword, the Executive, and the purse, the Legislature.[49]

American constitutionalism is the product of the revolutionary movement in political thought of Hobbes, the parent of the modern American political process.[50] The chief purpose of political institutions is the management of social conflict. According to Hobbes, the only source of public authority is the private need of independently situated political actors, with a prior right to act based on self-defined standards of conscience and interest. If used wisely, the Constitution can serve to remedy past injustices of discrimination.[51]

United States Constitution

The Constitution is the fundamental law of the land, and its Preamble states:

> We, the people of the United States, to secure the blessings of liberty to ourselves and our prosperity, do ordain and establish this Constitution for the United States of America.[52]

Civil Rights   The Fifth and Fourteenth Amendments of the Constitution, enacted in 1791 and 1868 respectively, are of paramount importance in the fight for human rights. With the due process clause of the Fifth Amendment including an equal protection component, the Fifth and Fourteenth Amendments provide due process

48   Federalist Papers, United States.
49   Ibid.
50   Coleman, Frank, *Hobbes and America*, University of Toronto, Toronto, 1977, p. 3.
51   Ibid.
52   United States Constitution, at the Preamble.

of law and equal protection to citizens from federal and state actions, respectively. They thus prohibit government from invidious discrimination. The clauses state:

Amendment V
No person shall ... be deprived of life, liberty, or property, without due process of law ...[53]

Amendment XIV
1. No state shall make or enforce any law which shall abridge the privileges or immunities of citizens of the United States; nor shall any state deprive any person of life, liberty, or property, without due process of law; nor deny to any person within its jurisdiction the equal protection of the laws.[54]

The 39th Article of the Magna Carta of 1215 is a foundation for the Fifth and Fourteenth Amendments of the American Constitution regarding due process and the rights of life, liberty and property. The Magna Carta states:

No free man shall be taken or imprisoned or dispossessed, or outlawed or banished, or in any way destroyed, nor will we go upon him nor send upon him, except by the legal judgement of his peers or by the law of the land.[55]

Further, the Thirteenth Amendment, enacted in 1865, was the initial step in ending a great injustice in the United States, which had lasted for centuries, namely slavery. It states:

Amendment XIII
1. Neither slavery nor involuntary servitude, except as a punishment for crime whereof the party shall have been duly convicted, shall exist within the United States, or any place subject to their jurisdiction.[56]

Fundamental Freedoms   The First Amendment to the Constitution, enacted in 1791, guarantees the freedoms of religion and expression. It states:

Amendment I
Congress shall make no law respecting an establishment of religion, or prohibiting the free exercise thereof; or abridging the freedom of speech, or of the press; or the right of the people peaceably to assemble, and to petition the government for a redress of grievances.[57]

---

53   Ibid., at Amendment V.
54   Ibid., at Amendment XIV.
55   Magna Carta.
56   United States Constitution, at Amendment XIII.
57   Ibid., at Amendment I.

The American Founding Fathers designed the United States Constitution to be a set of broad guidelines for successive generations, and it has survived for over two hundred years due to the common sense of the American people, the prudence of their representatives, and the calculated wisdom of its judicial interpreters, the Supreme Court of the United States.[58] Chief Justice Marshall said of the Constitution, 'It was intended to endure for ages to come and consequentially to be adapted to the various crises of human affairs' (*McCullough* v. *Maryland*, 4 Wheaton 415 (1819)).[59] It was a common opinion that each branch of government in matters pertaining to itself be the final judge of its own powers; however, it was the function of the judiciary, and especially the Supreme Court, to construe in the last resort the meaning of the Constitution, with its opinion final and binding. Justice Hughes stated, 'We are under a Constitution but the Constitution is what the judges say it is.' The United States Constitution, through Article 6(2) known as the Supremacy Clause, is the supreme law of the land:

> 6(2) This Constitution, and the Laws of the United States which shall be made in Pursuance thereof; and all Treaties made, or which shall be made, under the Authority of the United States, shall be the supreme Law of the Land; and the Judges in every State shall be bound thereby, any Thing in the Constitution or Laws of any State to the Contrary notwithstanding.[60]

The seminal case of *Marbury* v. *Madison*, 1 Cranch 137 (1803), brought forth the important principles that (1) the Constitution is the supreme law of the land; (2) the powers granted to various branches of government are limited; and (3) the sole and essential function of the Court is to determine which law should prevail in conflict of laws.[61]

In discrimination cases, the United States Supreme Court examines the legislative purpose of the governmental action alleged to be contrary to existing legislation. The cause of action is examined to see whether a plaintiff is a member of a class, which as a matter of law can invoke the power of the court. The equal protection clause and the due process clause of the Constitutional Amendments confer a constitutional right to be free from discrimination, which does not serve an important government objective or is not substantially related to the achievement of the objective (*Davis* v. *Passman*, 442 U.S. 228 (1979)).[62] In the past, the Supreme Court has found that it was a mistake to resolve Fifth Amendment cases through the Civil Rights Act, since a law which has a disproportionate impact is

---

58   North, Arthur, *The Supreme Court, Judicial Process and Judicial Politics*, Appleton Century Crofts, New York, 1964, p. 2.

59   *McCullough* v. *Maryland*, 4 Wheaton 415 (1819).

60   United States Constitution, Article 6(2).

61   *Marbury* v. *Madison*, 1 Cranch 137 (1803).

62   *Davis* v. *Passman*, 442 US 228 (1979).

not necessarily unconstitutional, and therefore, the statutory standards of the Civil Rights Act are more prohibiting to judicial review.

Over the years, in examining court challenges, the United States Supreme Court has developed three different levels of review and accompanying burden of proof, depending upon the type of action brought in a legal proceeding. The Court will first examine the legislative purpose of the governmental action alleged to be contrary to the constitutional amendments, and the plaintiff's burden to prove his case will then come into play. The three levels of review are: (1) the minimum rationality level applied to see the rational basis for the means to the ends; (2) the heightened scrutiny level where the defendant government must show that the restriction has a substantial relationship to an important government interest, applied in quasi-suspect classifications, such as gender discrimination cases; and (3) most importantly, the strict scrutiny level where the defendant government must show a compelling interest for the restriction, a hard burden to meet, applied in suspect classifications affecting fundamental rights, such as race or ethnic discrimination cases. Thus, the concept of the burden of proof is an important element in court cases.

In a dynamic society, the creativity of judges is important for the development of law and the adaptability of the Constitution to the needs of modern society, according to the Realist Theory; the courts are the best means for recognizing social change, in order to focus social attitudes on unachieved goals and assist in their attainment through a decision-making process of judgments and thus policy-making, according to the Free Legal Decision Sociological Jurisprudence Theory.[63] History has a record of the past and provides the Court with a reservoir of social wisdom and political insight; it points out the evils against which the great constitutional clauses were designed as remedies. The adjudicative process depends on a delicate symbiotic relationship, whereby the Court must know us better than we know ourselves, acting as a voice of the spirit to remind us of our better selves.[64] Law is the fabric of a free society, organized with a minimum of force and a maximum of reason, in an ideal sense of right and justice. The power of constitutional decisions rests upon the accuracy of the Court's perceptions of this kind of common will and upon its ability ultimately to command a consensus; the rule of law, the capacity to command free assent, is the substitute for power.[65]

Equal Pay Act

The Equal Pay Act's declaration of purpose is:

---

63   North, Arthur, *The Supreme Court, Judicial Process and Judicial Politics*, Appleton Century Crofts, New York, 1964, p. 8.

64   Cox, Archibald, *The Role of the Supreme Court in American Government*, Oxford University Press, New York, 1976, p. 117.

65   Cox, Archibald, *Civil Rights, The Constitution and the Court*, Harvard University Press, Cambridge, 1967, p. 21.

The Congress hereby finds that the existence ... of wage differentials based on sex

(1) depresses wages and living standards for employees necessary for their health and efficiency;

(2) prevents the maximum utilization of the available labor resources;

(3) tends to cause labor disputes, thereby burdening, affecting, and obstructing commerce;

(4) burdens commerce and the free flow of goods in commerce; and

(5) constitutes an unfair method of competition.[66]

Important for women and girls, the Equal Pay Act 1963 establishes that it is unlawful for an employer to pay unequal wages for equal work based on a discriminatory distinction. An exception is made where there is a system of (1) seniority; (2) merit; (3) earnings based on quantity or quality of production; or (4) something other than gender. The Equal Pay Act states:

206(d)(1) No employer having employees ... shall discriminate, within any establishment ... between employees on the basis of sex by paying wages to employees in such establishment at a rate less than the rate at which he pays wages to employees of the opposite sex in such establishment for equal work on jobs the performance of which requires equal skill, effort and responsibility, and which are performed under similar working conditions except where such payment is made pursuant to (1) a seniority system, (2) a merit system, (3) a system which measures earnings by quantity or quality of product or (4) a differential based on any other factor other than sex.[67]

The Equal Pay Act only includes jobs that are very much alike or closely related, considered virtually or substantially identical (*Brennan* v. *City Stores*, 479 F.2d. 235 (1973)).[68] Jobs, though not identical, can be considered equal for Equal Pay Act standards, if there is only an insubstantial difference in skill, effort and responsibility (*Murphy* v. *Miller Brewer Co.*, 307 F.Supp. 829 (1969)).[69] For the Equal Pay Act, there is discrimination when there is a different wage rate for equal work, that is work which requires equal skill, effort and responsibility under similar working conditions (*Corning Glass* v. *Brennan*, 417 US 188 (1974)).[70] Equal protection is violated only by intentional discrimination, and a different impact standing alone is not enough. Further, there is no legal duty to undo the effects of previous discrimination (*American Nurses' Association* v. *State of Illinois*, 783

---

66   Equal Pay Act, United States.

67   Ibid., at Section 206(d)(1).

68   *Brennan* v. *City Stores*, 479 F.2d. 235 (1973).

69   *Murphy* v. *Miller Brewer Co.*, 307 F.Supp. 829 (1969).

70   *Corning Glass Works* v. *Brennan*, 417 US 188 (1974).

F.2d. 716 (1986)).[71] Therefore, the plaintiff has the burden of establishing that equal pay for equal work was not received. Then, the defendant must show the different wages were based on seniority, merit, a quantitative or qualitative system, or reasons other than sex (*Spaulding* v. *University of Washington*, 740 F.2d. 686 (1984)).[72] The court, however, is concerned with the actual job performance and content, not job description, titles or classifications, and the scrutiny is done on a case by case basis. If skill is irrelevant to job requirements, it is not considered; therefore, a non-job related pretext can act as a shield for invidious discrimination.

Civil Rights Act

Important in the fight against discrimination, Title VII, the Civil Rights Act 1964, incorporating some of the provisions of the earlier Equal Pay Act with the Bennett Act Amendment, was implemented to safeguard important civil liberties, and serves to strengthen legislation, thereby helping the courts rule against discrimination. Section 703(a) guards against discrimination in employment:

> 703(a) It shall be an unlawful employment practice for an employer,
> (1) to fail or refuse to hire or to discharge any individual, or otherwise to discriminate against any individual with respect to his compensation, terms, conditions, or privilege of employment, because of such individual's race, color, religion, sex, or national origin, or
> (2) to limit, segregate, or classify his employees or applicants for employment in any way which would deprive or tend to deprive any individual of employment opportunities or otherwise adversely affect his status as an employee, because of such individual's race, color, religion, sex, or national origin.[73]

Further, training programs are covered under Section 703(d):

> 703(d) It shall be an unlawful employment practice for any employer, labor organization, or joint labor management committee controlling apprenticeship or other training or retraining, including on the job training programs to discriminate against any individual because of his race, color, religion, sex, or national origin in admission to, or employment in, any program established to provide apprenticeship or other training.[74]

A bona fide occupational qualification exception is outlined in Section 703(e):

> 703(e) Notwithstanding any other provision of this subchapter,

---

71   *American Nurses' Association* v. *State of Illinois*, 783 F.2d. 716 (1986).
72   *Spaulding* v. *University of Washington*, 740 F.2d. 686 (1984).
73   Civil Rights Act, United States, at Section 703(a).
74   Ibid., at Section 703(d).

(1) it shall not be an unlawful employment practice for an employer to hire and employ employees, for an employment agency to classify, or refer for employment any individual, for a labor organization to classify its membership or to classify or refer for employment any individual, or for an employer, labor organization, or joint labor management committee controlling apprenticeship or other training or retraining programs to admit or employ any individual in any such program, on the basis of his religion, sex, or national origin in those certain instances where religion, sex, or national origin is a bona fide occupational qualification reasonably necessary to the normal operation of that particular business or enterprise, and

(2) it shall not be an unlawful employment practice for a school, college, university, or other educational institution or institution of learning to hire and employ employees of a particular religion if such school, college, university, or other educational institution or institution of learning is, in whole or in substantial part, owned, supported, controlled, or managed by a particular religion or by a particular religious corporation, association, or society, or if the curriculum of such school, college, university, or other educational institution or institution of learning is directed toward the propagation of a particular religion.[75]

Section 703(h) covers unequal pay:

703(h) Notwithstanding any other provision of this title, it shall be a lawful employment practice for an employer to apply different standards of compensation, or different terms, conditions, or privileges of employment pursuant to a bona fide seniority or merit system, or a system which measures earnings by quantity or quality of production or to employees who work in different locations, provided that such are not the result of an intention to discriminate because of race, color, religion, sex, or national origin. It shall not be an unlawful employment practice under this title for any employer to differentiate upon the basis of sex in determining the amount of wages or compensation paid to employees of such employer if such differentiation is authorized by the provisions of Section 6(d) of the Fair Standards Act.[76]

Section 703(j) guards against preferential treatment:

703(j) Nothing contained in this subchapter shall be interpreted to require any employer, employment agency, labor organization, or joint labor management committee subject to this subchapter to grant preferential treatment to any individual or to any group because of the race, color, religion, sex, or national origin of such individual or group on account of an imbalance which may exist with respect to the total number or percentage of persons of any race, color,

75 Ibid., at Section 703(e).
76 Ibid., at Section 703(h).

religion, sex, or national origin employed by any employer, referred or classified for employment by any employment agency or labor organization, admitted to membership or classified by any labor organization, or admitted to, or employed in, any apprenticeship or other training program, in comparison with the total number or percentage of persons of such race, color, religion, sex, or national origin in any community, State, section, or other area, or in the available work force in any community, State, section, or other area.[77]

The establishment of a discriminatory employment practice based on disparate impact is noted in Section 703(k):

703(k)(1)(A) An unlawful employment practice based on disparate impact is established under this title only if

(i) a complaining party demonstrates that a respondent uses a particular employment practice that causes a disparate impact on the basis of race, color, religion, sex, or national origin and the respondent fails to demonstrate that the challenged practice is job related for the position in question and consistent with business necessity.[78]

Further, the duty of a complainant party in a discrimination case is outlined in Section 703(m):

703(m) Except as otherwise provided in this title, an unlawful employment practice is established when the complaining party demonstrates that race, color, religion, sex, or national origin was a motivating factor for any employment practice, even though other factors also motivated the practice.[79]

Section 706(g) provides for adjudicative relief on account of discrimination:

706(g) If the court finds that the respondent has intentionally engaged in or is intentionally engaging in an unlawful employment practice charged in the complaint, the court may enjoin the respondent from engaging in such unlawful employment practice, and order such affirmative action as may be appropriate, which may include, but is not limited to, reinstatement or hiring of employees, with or without back pay ... or any other equitable relief as the court deems appropriate ... No order of the court shall require the admission or reinstatement of an individual as a member of a union, or the hiring, reinstatement, or promotion of an individual as an employee, or the payment to him of any back pay, if such individual was refused admission, suspended, or expelled, or was refused employment or advancement or was suspended or discharged for any

---

77   Ibid., at Section 703(j).
78   Ibid., at Section 703(k).
79   Ibid., at Section 703(m).

reason other than discrimination on account of race, color, religion, sex, or national origin or in violation of section 704(a).[80]

Finally, opposition to a discriminatory practice is protected under Section 704(a):

> 704(a) It shall be an unlawful employment practice for an employer to discriminate against any of his employees or applicants for employment, for an employment agency, or joint labor management committee controlling apprenticeship or other training or retraining, including on the job training programs, to discriminate against any individual, or for a labor organization to discriminate against any member thereof or applicant for membership, because he has opposed any practice made an unlawful employment practice by this subchapter, or because he has made a charge, testified, assisted, or participated in any manner in an investigation, proceeding, or hearing under this subchapter.[81]

The Civil Rights Act eliminates artificial, arbitrary and unnecessary barriers to employment in the form of invidious discrimination, unless there is a demonstrably reasonable measure of job performance (*Griggs* v. *Duke Power Co.*, 401 US 424 (1971)).[82] Title VII prohibits discrimination allowing for compensation, thus recognizing equal pay as a legal right (*American Federation of State, County and Municipal Employees* v. *Washington*, 770 F.2d. 1401 (1985)).[83]

For discrimination cases brought under the Civil Rights Act, the plaintiff has the burden of showing he belongs to a minority, has applied for a job, was qualified for the job that the employer tried to fill but was rejected, and the employer continued to seek applicants (*McDonnell Douglas Corp.* v. *Green*, 411 U.S. 792 (1973)).[84] Then, in rebutting a prima facie case, the defendant is required to show the absence of a discriminatory motive for his actions. However, this was later revised by the court, so that the defendant is not required to show the absence, but must merely articulate a legitimate non-discriminatory reason for the employee's rejection (*Board of Trustees of Keene State College* v. *Sweeney*, 439 US 24 (1978)).[85]

The Civil Rights Act is often used to fight discrimination in compensation, with a differentiation made between disparate treatment and impact. Disparate treatment is concerned with direct or circumstantial discriminatory motives, which lack well-defined criteria (*Spaulding* v. *University of Washington*, 740 F.2d. 686

---

80 Ibid., at Section 706(g).

81 Ibid., at Section 704(a).

82 *Griggs* v. *Duke Power Co.*, 401 US 424 (1971).

83 *American Federation of State, County and Municipal Employees* v. *Washington*, 770 F.2d. 1401 (1985).

84 *McDonnell Douglas Corp.* v. *Green*, 411 US 792 (1973).

85 *Board of Trustees of Keene State College* v. *Sweeney*, 439 US 24 (1978).

(1984)).[86] It involves intent or motive as an essential element of liability concerning the effects of a chosen policy, with awareness alone of adverse consequences on a group being insufficient (*American Federation of State, County and Municipal Employees* v. *Washington*, 770 F.2d. 1401 (1985)).[87] In a disparate treatment approach, the plaintiff in a prima facie case is required to show by a preponderance of the evidence the overt motive. In turn, the defendant must prove that it was non-discriminatory either by the four exceptions, by necessity or by a bona fide occupational qualification. On the other hand, disparate impact is more than an inference of discriminatory impact of outwardly neutral employment practices and adversity (*Spaulding* v. *University of Washington*, 740 F.2d. 686 (1984)).[88] It does not need a profession of intent by the employer to discriminate, only a clearly delineated employment practice (*American Federation of State, County and Municipal Employees* v. *Washington*, 770 F.2d. 1401 (1985)).[89] In a disparate impact approach, the plaintiff need only show the disproportionate impact, the burden then shifting to the defendant to show that it was non-discriminatory.

Fair Labor Standards Act

As American industrialization moved workers from farms and home workshops into urban areas and factory work, children were often preferred, because they were viewed as more manageable, cheaper, and less likely to strike.[90] However, union organizing and child labor reform were often intertwined, which culminated in the Fair Labor Standards Act in 1938, which set federal standards for child labor.[91] Further, in *Tinker* v. *Des Moines Independent School District*, 393 U.S. 503 (1969), the Supreme Court held that children are persons with the full protection of the law: 'Students ... are "persons" under our Constitution. They are possessed of fundamental rights which the State must respect, just as they themselves must respect their obligations to the State.'[92] The United States has ratified the Worst Forms of Child Labour Convention, 1999 (No. 182) (C. 182) in 1999; however, it has not ratified the Minimum Age Convention, 1973 (No.138) (C. 138).

The Fair Labor Standards Act (FLSA) child labor provisions are designed to protect the educational opportunities of minors, and prohibit their employment in

---

86   *Spaulding* v. *University of Washington*, 740 F.2d. 686 (1984).

87   *American Federation of State, County and Municipal Employees* v. *Washington*, 770 F.2d. 1401 (1985).

88   *Spaulding* v. *University of Washington*, 740 F.2d. 686 (1984).

89   *American Federation of State, County and Municipal Employees* v. *Washington*, 770 F.2d. 1401 (1985).

90   Child Labor Public Education Project, Child Labor in U.S. History.

91   Ibid.

92   US Supreme Court, *Tinker* v. *Des Moines Independent School District*, 393 U.S. 503 (1969).

jobs and under conditions detrimental to their health or well-being. Section 3(l) defines oppressive child labor as:

> 3(l) 'Oppressive child labor' means a condition of employment under which (1) any employee under the age of sixteen years is employed by an employer (other than a parent or a person standing in place of a parent employing his own child or a child in his custody under the age of sixteen years in an occupation other than manufacturing or mining or an occupation found by the Secretary of Labor to be particularly hazardous for the employment of children between the ages of sixteen and eighteen years or detrimental to their health or well-being) in any occupation, or
>
> (2) any employee between the ages of sixteen and eighteen years is employed by an employer in any occupation which the Secretary of Labor shall find and by order declare to be particularly hazardous for the employment of children between such ages or detrimental to their health or well-being; but oppressive child labor shall not be deemed to exist by virtue of the employment in any occupation of any person with respect to whom the employer shall have on file an unexpired certificate issued and held pursuant to regulations of the Secretary of Labor certifying that such person is above the oppressive child labor age. The Secretary of Labor shall provide by regulation or by order that the employment of employees between the ages of fourteen and sixteen years in occupations other than manufacturing and mining shall not be deemed to constitute oppressive child labor if and to the extent that the Secretary of Labor determines that such employment is confined to periods which will not interfere with their schooling and to conditions which will not interfere with their health and well-being.[93]

According to Section 12 of the Fair Labor Standards Act 1938 (FLSA), which deals with child labor:

> 12(a) No producer, manufacturer, or dealer shall ship or deliver for shipment in commerce any goods produced in an establishment situated in the United States in or about which within thirty days prior to the removal of such goods therefrom any oppressive child labor has been employed: *Provided*, that any such shipment or delivery for shipment of such goods by a purchaser who acquired them in good faith in reliance on written assurance from the producer, manufacturer, or dealer that the goods were produced in compliance with the requirements of this section, and who acquired such goods for value without notice of any such violation, shall not be deemed prohibited by this subsection: *And provided further*, that a prosecution and conviction of a defendant for the shipment or delivery for shipment of any goods under the conditions herein prohibited shall be a bar to any further prosecution against the same defendant

---

93   Fair Labor Standards Act, at Section 3(l).

for shipments or deliveries for shipment of any such goods before the beginning of said prosecution.

(b) The Secretary of Labor, or any of his authorized representatives, shall make all investigations and inspections under section 11(a) with respect to the employment of minors, and, subject to the direction and control of the Attorney General, shall bring all actions under section 17 to enjoin any act or practice which is unlawful by reason of the existence of oppressive child labor, and shall administer all other provisions of this Act relating to oppressive child labor.

(c) No employer shall employ any oppressive child labor in commerce or in the production of goods for commerce or in any enterprise engaged in commerce or in the production of goods for commerce.

(d) In order to carry out the objectives of this section, the Secretary may by regulation require employers to obtain from any employee proof of age.[94]

Section 13(c) calls for exemptions:

13(c)(1) Except as provided in paragraphs (2) or (4), the provisions of section 12 relating to child labor shall not apply to any employee employed in agriculture outside of school hours for the school district where such employee is living while he is so employed, if such employee

(A) is less than twelve years of age and (i) is employed by his parent, or by a person standing in the place of his parent, on a farm owned or operated by such parent or person, or (ii) is employed, with the consent of his parent or person standing in the place of his parent, on a farm, none of the employees of which are (because of section 13(a)(6)(A)) required to be paid at the wage rate prescribed by section 6(a)(5),

(B) is twelve years or thirteen years of age and (i) such employment is with the consent of his parent or person standing in the place of his parent, or (ii) his parent or such person is employed on the same farm as such employee, or

(C) is fourteen years of age or older.

(2) The provisions of section 12 relating to child labor shall apply to an employee below the age of sixteen employed in agriculture in an occupation that the Secretary of Labor finds and declares to be particularly hazardous for the employment of children below the age of sixteen, except where such employee is employed by his parent or by a person standing in the place of his parent on a farm owned or operated by such parent or person.

(3) The provisions of section 12 relating to child labor shall not apply to any child employed as an actor or performer in motion pictures or theatrical productions, or in radio or television productions.[95]

Finally, penalties are covered under Section 16(e):

---

94   Ibid., at Section 12(a).
95   Ibid., at Section 13(c).

16(e) Any person who violates the provisions ... shall be subject to a civil penalty of not to exceed $10,000 for each employee who was the subject of such a violation. Any person who repeatedly or willfully violates section 6 or 7 shall be subject to a civil penalty of not to exceed $1,000 for each such violation. In determining the amount of any penalty under this subsection, the appropriateness of such penalty to the size of the business of the person charged and the gravity of the violation shall be considered. The amount of any penalty under this subsection, when finally determined, may be

(1) deducted from any sums owing by the United States to the person charged;

(2) recovered in a civil action brought by the Secretary in any court of competent jurisdiction, in which litigation the Secretary shall be represented by the Solicitor of Labor; or

(3) ordered by the court, in an action brought for a violation of section 15(a)(4) or a repeated or willful violation of section 15(a)(2), to be paid to the Secretary.[96]

Conclusion

In order to protect children, the keys to the future of human rights and equality in North America are the implementation and development of the law, the deepening in understanding of specific legal issues relating to children and human rights in the courts, and the raising of the level of awareness of legal rights and obligations in *Little Angels*. Martin Luther King Jr., in his struggle for civil rights, stated:

> I have a dream that one day every valley shall be exalted, every hill and mountain shall be made plain, and the crooked places shall be made straight and the glory of the Lord will be revealed and all flesh shall see it together. This is our hope ... And when we allow freedom to ring, when we let it ring from every village and hamlet, from every state and city, we will be able to join hands and to sing in the words of the old Negro spiritual, 'Free at last, free at last; thank God Almighty, we are free at last.'[97]

---

96   Ibid., at Section 16(e).
97   King Jr., Martin Luther, *March on Washington*, 28 August 1963.

Chapter 7
Little Angels in the North American Free Trade Agreement

Introduction

In the quest for respect for our children and in the fight against child discrimination in *Little Angels*, this chapter will examine efforts against child discrimination in the area of the North American Free Trade Agreement (NAFTA), having an important impact on the labor force generally and on particular classes of workers specifically. It will look at NAFTA from its inception, examining first its benefits and then its drawbacks. It will also look at the North American Agreement on Labor Cooperation (NAALC) and the Free Trade Area of the Americas (FTAA), as well as legislation of the Americas, namely the American Declaration of the Rights and Duties of Man, the American Convention on Human Rights, the Statute of the Inter-American Court on Human Rights, and the Inter-American Democratic Charter.

Toward the North American Free Trade Agreement (NAFTA)

There were several developments in the relationship between the United States and British North America, which was to become Canada. The War of 1812 brought an end to the fear of American annexation of Canada, with a new view of commercial and economic rivalry between the two countries. The Canadian national sentiment favored trade with the United States through transportation via the railways and the waterways.[1] The Elgin–Marcy Reciprocity Treaty 1854 was the first major trade pact between the United States and Canada. Reciprocity was an attempt to create, in North America, a single market area covering several distinct political jurisdictions, where specified types of products were freely exchanged for a partial and limited economic union between British North America and the United States.[2] The American Civil War influenced the economic development of British North America, with new markets in the United States opening for Canadian exports. However, the Treaty was abrogated by the United States on 17 March 1866, due to several antagonizing factors for the United States, namely British support for the Confederacy during the Civil War, new Canadian tariffs, the disastrous effects on

---

1   Hamelin, Jean, *Histoire du Québec*, Edisem, St Hyacinthe, 1976, p. 371.
2   Easterbrook, W.T. and Aitken, Hugh, *Canadian Economic History*, Macmillan, Toronto, 1976, p. 362.

timber- and grain-growing regions of the United States, the resentment by farming and lumber interests toward Canadian competition, the jealousy of shipping and forwarding interests in Buffalo and Philadelphia of the St Lawrence Route and of the Grand Trunk Railway system, with the Victoria Bridge completion in Montreal in 1860 furthering competition, and the manufacturing interests blaming Canadian tariffs for the decline of certain exports.[3] While Canada's policy in economic relations was to favour east–west relations, the natural tendencies were the opposite, north–south.

The 1911 Free Trade Agreement allowed Canada to build up its own manufacturing protection tariff.[4] With the exception of Britain, Canada was the chief trading partner of the United States.[5] American President Taft negotiated for full-scale reciprocity for better trade relations between the United States and Canada, since common interests called for special arrangements, and Canadians and Americans were reminded that there were 3000 miles of joint border between the two countries. Most American tariffs on manufacturing goods were reduced, while most Canadian manufacturing tariffs remained. Canadian Prime Minister Laurier was the first continentalist Prime Minister to appreciate that Canada shares North America with the United States, which shapes the national destiny; however, subsequent Canadian Prime Minister Borden opposed the trade legislation and did not put the reciprocity agreement to a vote, with the United States rescinding its vote eight years later.

The General Agreement on Tariffs and Trade (GATT) 1947 had as its purpose to promote global trade between members through a reduction in tariffs. Canada wished for trade on a liberalized basis, the first Article of GATT, and equal treatment. GATT provided for an impressive reduction of tariffs, with some even impeding economic efficiency, production, competition and growth. It permitted the United States and Canada to enter into free trade, with an agreement to remove customs duties and other restrictions on substantially all bilateral trade.[6] Over the last years of GATT and the advent of the World Trade Organization (WTO), Canadian exports multiplied ten times, the national wealth more than tripled and the number of jobs doubled.[7] Wartime demands required greater cooperation on a

---

3   Fry, Earl, 'Trends in Canada–U.S. Free Trade Discussions', in A.R. Riggs and Tom Welk, *Canadian–American Free Trade: Historical, Political and Economic Dimensions*, The Institute for Research in Public Policy, Montreal, 1987, p. 28.

4   d'Aquino, Thomas, 'Truck and Trade with the Yankees, The Case for a Canada–U.S. Comprehensive Trade Agreement', in A.R. Riggs and Tom Velk, *Canadian–American Free Trade: Historical, Political and Economic Dimensions*, The Institute for Research on Public Policy, Montreal, 1987, p. 74.

5   Velk, Tom, and Riggs, A.R., 'The Ongoing Debate Over Free Trade', in A.R. Riggs and Tom Velk, *Canadian–American Free Trade: (The Sequel) Historical, Political and Economic Dimensions*, The Institute for Research on Public Policy, Montreal, 1988, p. 93.

6   General Agreement on Tariffs and Trade, at Article 24.

7   Laun, Louis, 'U.S.–Canada Free Trade Negotiations: Historical Opportunities', in A.R. Riggs and Tom Velk, *Canadian–American Free Trade: Historical, Political and*

continental basis, with Canada and Mexico being prime sources of raw materials for American factories. Private negotiations on free trade once again took place in 1947 between American President Truman and Canadian Prime Minister King, with the latter approving the agreement at first but later vetoing it, because of fear that the Canadian public would label it continentalist and anti-British.[8]

There is a regional aspect to the overall economic evolution of the North American continent. Canada's industrial development has been North American, with its development based on its natural resources, and its expansion characterized by large-scale monopolistic industries. Over time, Canada's dealings with Britain and the United States changed. Canada once had an autonomous relationship with Britain, producing an anti-American sentiment. Britain use to be the major investor in Canada. However, over the years, the United States has replaced it. Canada went from dependence on Britain to dependence on the United States, thus producing a foreign controlled economy. In addition, the nature of foreign investment had changed, since the British invested indirectly through obligations and finance, while the Americans invested directly, usually as proprietors funding production. The Canadian policy, interestingly, was to increase tariffs and oblige US companies wishing to do business to build factories in Canada. Therefore, the United States penetrated the Canadian economy by installing branch plants for American-made products. Today, Canada sends more than three-quarters of all its exports to the United States, accounting for 25 percent of its annual gross national product.[9] The policy process resulted in the overwhelming trade dependence of Canada on the United States over the years, with Canada's trade pattern from the outset based on the importing of manufactured goods in return for the exporting of staples to more advanced industrialized economies as the engine of growth of the Canadian economy.[10] The commercial rather than industrial bias of the Canadian capitalist class, along with dependent branch plant industrialization, flowed from the unequal alliance with American foreign ownership and capital; Canada was within the tight embrace of the American empire, and occupied whatever room was left open by US capital, becoming the exemplary client State.[11]

National treatment calls for no regulatory distinction between foreign and domestic firms, which is good if there are similar industries for reciprocity and

---

Economic Dimensions, The Institute for Research in Public Policy, Montreal, 1987, p. 205.

   8   Fry, Earl, 'Trends in Canada–U.S. Free Trade Discussions', in A.R., Riggs and Tom Welk, *Canadian–American Free Trade: Historical, Political and Economic Dimensions*, The Institute for Research in Public Policy, Montreal, 1987, p. 9.

   9   Ibid., at p. 27.

   10   Watkins, Mel, 'The Political Economy of Growth', in Wallace Clement and Glen Williams, *The New Canadian Political Economy*, McGill-Queen's University Press, Kingston, 1989, p. 17.

   11   Laun, Louis, 'U.S.–Canada Free Trade Negotiations: Historical Opportunities', in A.R. Riggs and Tom Velk, *Canadian–American Free Trade: Historical, Political and Economic Dimensions*, The Institute for Research in Public Policy, Montreal, 1987, p. 205.

market access.[12] These laws restrict one country's firms transferring staff to the other country. The service industry has subtle impediments, with discrimination being a barrier because of immigration labor laws, which are most evident today with illegal immigration at an all-time high. Further, trade in services encompasses a large number of areas, having different characteristics of trade and efforts for international rule-making.

The 1989 Canada–United States Free Trade Agreement (FTA) had as its goal to remove all or most remaining barriers to cross-border trade in goods and services, and to create an enlarged body of agreed rules to govern trade. President Ronald Reagan called the document, signed on 2 January 1988, the most important bilateral trade negotiation ever undertaken by the United States. It was horizontal not sectoral for market access, and called for mutual restraint on unilateral commercial policies. The United States absorbs 80 percent of Canada's exports, in a southward flow,[13] and has an economy ten times bigger than Canada's, affording the latter greater access to opportunities. This Free Trade Agreement was the biggest trade agreement ever reached between two countries, in excess of $200 billion in trade of goods and services.[14]

North American Free Trade Agreement (NAFTA)

In 1991, Canada, the United States and Mexico began negotiations for the North American Free Trade Agreement (NAFTA). The free trade agenda shifted from a sectoral approach to a comprehensive accord among the three countries, because of a difficulty in matching sectors and in accommodating regional concerns. The 1989 Canada United States Free Trade Agreement laid the foundation for NAFTA, which secured Canada's economic relationship with the United States. Prior to NAFTA coming into effect on 1 January 1994, trade between the United States and Canada had never been larger and was growing faster than the rest of the economy. In addition, the flow of trade and investment among the United States, Canada and Mexico was $500 billion per year.[15] NAFTA was the biggest trade agreement ever

---

12   Neufeld, E.P, 'Financial and Economic Dimensions of Free Trade', in A.R. Riggs and Tom Velk, *Canadian–American Free Trade: Historical, Political and Economic Dimensions*, The Institute for Research on Public Policy, Montreal, 1987, p. 152.

13   d'Aquino, Thomas, 'Truck and Trade with the Yankees, The Case for a Canada–U.S. Comprehensive Trade Agreement', in A.R. Riggs and Tom Velk, *Canadian–American Free Trade: Historical, Political and Economic Dimensions*, The Institute for Research on Public Policy, Montreal, 1987, p. 74.

14   Velk, Tom, and Riggs, A.R., 'The Ongoing Debate Over Free Trade', in A.R. Riggs and Tom Velk, *Canadian–American Free Trade: (The Sequel) Historical, Political and Economic Dimensions*, The Institute for Research on Public Policy, Montreal, 1988, p. 3.

15   A.R. Riggs and Tom Velk, *Canadian–American Free Trade: (The Sequel) Historical, Political and Economic Dimensions*, The Institute for Research on Public Policy, Montreal, 1988.

signed at the time, covering 360 million consumers and far-reaching to remove all tariffs and liberalize non-tariff barriers to trade. It regulates trade in services, liberalizes investment, promotes specialization and implements a mechanism for a binding resolution to disputes, which is unprecedented in free trade. The objectives of NAFTA are the removal of tariff and non-tariff barriers for goods and services, the neutralization of government policies, practices and procedures, and a consistency with the GATT agreement to cover all trade.[16] The long-term goals of free trade are the improvement of real income wages and production, an increase in the number of jobs, a reduction of protectionism, a decrease in competitive pressures from developing and newly industrialized countries, and the mitigation of pressures due to global imbalances.[17] NAFTA provided that tariffs would be removed within ten years in the traditional sectors, accounting for half of the trade, and removed either immediately, in five years or exceptionally in 20 years for the remainder, moving toward a harmonized system of tariff nomenclature.

In terms of employment, cross-border trade in services was first included in the Canada–United States Free Trade Agreement, and NAFTA has extended these codes of binding rules and principles with procedures to encourage the recognition of licenses and certificates through mutually acceptable professional standards and criteria, such as education, experience and professional development. It opens up temporary entry across the border for over 60 professions. Further, there is a provision as to access for temporary personnel in the service and manufacturing sectors, as well as business recognition of professional and sales services in the spirit of freedom of movement. As such, Canada's service industry is the fastest growing sector of the economy, accounting for the employment of roughly ten million Canadians and two-thirds of the workforce, as well as providing 90 percent of all new jobs in Canada in the last several years; Canada's export of services around the world totals an average of $24 billion per year, with business and professional services accounting for 20 percent of these exports. Virtually all services are covered by NAFTA, with key sectors being: accounting, architecture, land transport, publishing, consulting, commercial education, environmental services, enhanced telecommunications, advertising, broadcasting, construction, tourism, engineering, health care, management and legal services. NAFTA does not remove or weaken licensing and certification requirements but, consistent with the principle of non-discrimination, licensing of professionals, such as lawyers, doctors and accountants, is based on objective criteria aimed at ensuring competence, not nationality, so that NAFTA does not permit American, Mexican

16　Laun, Louis, 'U.S.–Canada Free Trade Negotiations: Historical Opportunities', in A.R. Riggs and Tom Velk, *Canadian–American Free Trade: Historical, Political and Economic Dimensions*, The Institute for Research in Public Policy, Montreal, 1987, p. 208.
17　Harris, Richard, 'Some Observations on the Canada–U.S. Free Trade Deal', in A.R. Riggs and Tom Velk, *Canadian–American Free Trade: (The Sequel) Historical, Political and Economic Dimensions*, The Institute for Research on Public Policy, Montreal 1988, p. 52.

or Canadian professionals to practice in the other Member countries, unless they have undergone the same licensing and certification procedures as a national professional. Overall, NAFTA obliges one country's service providers to treat the other country's no less favorably than their own for domestic and cross-border sales, distribution and the right of establishment of facilities, providing for mutually acceptable professional licensing standards. However, the equal employment provision in the Member States must go further to protect against any form of discrimination, including child discrimination and illegal child labor. We will begin by examining the general provisions of NAFTA which are applicable to all, and along the way show how NAFTA is sorely lacking in protection for children.

The Preamble of the North American Free Trade Agreement states:

> The Government of Canada, the Government of the United Mexican States and the Government of the United States of America, resolved to:
> STRENGTHEN the special bonds of friendship and cooperation among their nations;
> CONTRIBUTE to the harmonious development and expansion of world trade and provide a catalyst to broader international cooperation;
> CREATE an expanded and secure market for the goods and services produced in their territories;
> REDUCE distortions to trade;
> ESTABLISH clear and mutually advantageous rules governing their trade;
> ENSURE a predictable commercial framework for business planning and investment;
> BUILD on their respective rights and obligations under the *General Agreement on Tariffs and Trade* and other multilateral and bilateral instruments of cooperation;
> ENHANCE the competitiveness of their firms in global markets;
> FOSTER creativity and innovation, and promote trade in goods and services that are the subject of intellectual property rights;
> CREATE new employment opportunities and improve working conditions and living standards in their respective territories;
> UNDERTAKE each of the preceding in a manner consistent with environmental protection and conservation;
> PRESERVE their flexibility to safeguard the public welfare;
> PROMOTE sustainable development;
> STRENGTHEN the development and enforcement of environmental laws and regulations; and
> PROTECT, enhance and enforce basic workers' rights.[18]

---

18   North American Free Trade Agreement, at the Preamble.

With regard to service providers, NAFTA should have added protection for children who might be employed by service providers, especially in light of the great concern that jobs would head South from Canada and the United States to Mexico where the labor laws are not as strict. In terms of service providers, Article 1201 states:

> 1201.1. This Chapter applies to measures adopted or maintained by a Party relating to cross-border trade in services by service providers of another Party, including measures respecting:
> (a) the production, distribution, marketing, sale and delivery of a service;
> (b) the purchase or use of, or payment for, a service;
> (c) the access to and use of distribution and transportation systems in connection with the provision of a service;
> (d) the presence in its territory of a service provider of another Party; and
> (e) the provision of a bond or other form of financial security as a condition for the provision of a service.[19]

Articles 1202 defines 'National Treatment':

> 1202.1. Each Party shall accord to service providers of another Party treatment no less favorable than that it accords, in like circumstances, to its own service providers.
> 2. The treatment accorded by a Party under paragraph 1 means, with respect to a state or province, treatment no less favorable than the most favorable treatment accorded, in like circumstances, by that state or province to service providers of the Party of which it forms a part.[20]

Further, Article 1203 defines 'Most-Favored-Nation Treatment':

> 1203. Each Party shall accord to service providers of another Party treatment no less favorable than that it accords, in like circumstances, to service providers of any other Party or of a non-Party.[21]

Article 1208 maintains that each Party shall set out in its Schedule to Annex VI its commitments to liberalize quantitative restrictions, licensing requirements, performance requirements or other non-discriminatory measures.

---

19   Ibid., at Article 1201.
20   Ibid., at Article 1202.
21   Ibid., at Article 1203.

1208. Each Party shall set out in its Schedule to Annex VI its commitments to liberalize quantitative restrictions, licensing requirements, performance requirements or other non-discriminatory measures.[22]

With regard to professional services, NAFTA should have added protection in employment and working conditions to underage workers providing professional services. Professional services are defined in Article 1213 as:

1213. ... services, the provision of which requires specialized post-secondary education, or equivalent training or experience, and for which the right to practice is granted or restricted by a Party, but does not include services provided by trades-persons or vessel and aircraft crew members.[23]

Important to all workers, Article 1210 provides for licensing and certification requirements:

1210.1. With a view to ensuring that any measure adopted or maintained by a Party relating to the licensing or certification of nationals of another Party does not constitute an unnecessary barrier to trade, each Party shall endeavor to ensure that any such measure:
(a) is based on objective and transparent criteria, such as competence and the ability to provide a service;
(b) is not more burdensome than necessary to ensure the quality of a service; and
(c) does not constitute a disguised restriction on the cross-border provision of a service.
2. ... a Party shall not be required to extend to a service provider of another Party the benefits of recognition of education, experience, licenses or certifications obtained in another country, whether such recognition was accorded unilaterally or by arrangement or agreement with that other country. The Party according such recognition shall afford any interested Party an adequate opportunity to demonstrate that education, experience, licenses or certifications obtained in that other Party's territory should also be recognized or to negotiate and enter into an agreement or arrangement of comparable effect.
3. ... a Party shall eliminate any citizenship or permanent residency requirement for the licensing and certification of professional service providers in its territory ... [24]

Further, licensing and certification standards for professionals are provided for in Annex 1210.5.A.2.:

---

22   Ibid., at Article 1208.
23   Ibid., at Article 1213.
24   Ibid., at Article 1210.

Annex 1210.5.A.2. The Parties shall encourage the relevant bodies in their respective territories to develop mutually acceptable standards and criteria for licensing and certification of professional service providers and to provide recommendations on mutual recognition to the Commission.[25]

Additionally, Annex 1210.5.A.3. provides for standards and criteria to be developed:

Annex 1210.5.A.3. The standards and criteria referred to in paragraph 2 may be developed with regard to the following matters:
(a) education: accreditation of schools or academic programs;
(b) examinations: qualifying examinations for licensing, including alternative methods of assessment such as oral examinations and interviews;
(c) experience: length and nature of experience required for licensing;
(d) conduct and ethics: standards of professional conduct and the nature of disciplinary action for non-conformity with those standards;
(e) professional development and re-certification: continuing education and ongoing requirements to maintain professional certification;
(f) scope of practice: extent of, or limitations on, permissible activities;
(g) local knowledge: requirements for knowledge of such matters as local laws, regulations, language, geography or climate; and
(h) consumer protection: alternatives to residency requirements, including bonding, professional liability insurance and client restitution funds, to provide for the protection of consumers.[26]

Finally, Annex 1210.5.B.1. provides that each Party shall, in implementing its obligations and commitments regarding foreign legal consultants as set out in its relevant Schedules and subject to any reservations therein, ensure that a national of another Party is permitted to practise or advise on the law of any country in which that national is authorized to practise as a lawyer.[27]

In terms of the temporary entry for people to conduct business, Chapter 16 and specifically Article 1601 specify:

1601. This Chapter reflects the preferential trading relationship between the Parties, the desirability of facilitating temporary entry on a reciprocal basis and of establishing transparent criteria and procedures for temporary entry, and the need to ensure border security and to protect the domestic labor force and permanent employment in their respective territories.[28]

---

25   Ibid., at Annex 1210.5.A.2.
26   Ibid., at Annex 1210.5.A.3.
27   Ibid., at Annex 1210.5.B.1.
28   Ibid., at Article 1601.

Article 1602 outlines the general obligations:

> 1602.1. Each Party shall apply its measures relating to the provisions of this Chapter in accordance with Article 1601 and, in particular, shall apply expeditiously those measures so as to avoid unduly impairing or delaying trade in goods or services or conduct of investment activities under this Agreement.
> 2. The Parties shall endeavor to develop and adopt common criteria, definitions and interpretations for the implementation of this Chapter.[29]

Additional requirements are noted in Annex 1603, in order to gain entry for different classes of individuals in employment situations. Special protection should have been added under Annex 1603 as regards business visitors to better guard against certain business practices which might involve underage employment. Section A provides for business visitors:

> Annex 1603.A.1. Each Party shall grant temporary entry to a business person seeking to engage in a business activity set out in Appendix 1603.A.1, without requiring that person to obtain an employment authorization, provided that the business person otherwise complies with existing immigration measures applicable to temporary entry, on presentation of:
> (a) proof of citizenship of a Party;
> (b) documentation demonstrating that the business person will be so engaged and describing the purpose of entry; and
> (c) evidence demonstrating that the proposed business activity is international in scope and that the business person is not seeking to enter the local labor market.
> 2. Each Party shall provide that a business person may satisfy the requirements of paragraph 1(c) by demonstrating that:
> (a) the primary source of remuneration for the proposed business activity is outside the territory of the Party granting temporary entry; and
> (b) the business person's principal place of business and the actual place of accrual of profits, at least predominantly, remain outside such territory.
> A Party shall normally accept an oral declaration as to the principal place of business and the actual place of accrual of profits. Where the Party requires further proof, it shall normally consider a letter from the employer attesting to these matters as sufficient proof.
> 3. Each Party shall grant temporary entry to a business person seeking to engage in a business activity other than those set out in Appendix 1603.A.1, without requiring that person to obtain an employment authorization, on a basis no less favorable than that provided under the existing provisions of the measures set out in Appendix 1603.A.3, provided that the business person otherwise complies with existing immigration measures applicable to temporary entry.
> 4. No Party may:

---

29   Ibid., at Article 1602.

(a) as a condition for temporary entry under paragraph 1 or 3, require prior approval procedures, petitions, labor certification tests or other procedures of similar effect; or

(b) impose or maintain any numerical restriction relating to temporary entry under paragraph 1 or 3.

5. Notwithstanding paragraph 4, a Party may require a business person seeking temporary entry under this Section to obtain a visa or its equivalent prior to entry. Before imposing a visa requirement, the Party shall consult with a Party whose business persons would be affected with a view to avoiding the imposition of the requirement. With respect to an existing visa requirement, a Party shall consult, on request, with a Party whose business persons are subject to the requirement with a view to its removal.[30]

Section B provides for traders and investors:

Annex 1603.B.1. Each Party shall grant temporary entry and provide confirming documentation to a business person seeking to:

(a) carry on substantial trade in goods or services principally between the territory of the Party of which the business person is a citizen and the territory of the Party into which entry is sought, or

(b) establish, develop, administer or provide advice or key technical services to the operation of an investment to which the business person or the business person's enterprise has committed, or is in the process of committing, a substantial amount of capital, in a capacity that is supervisory, executive or involves essential skills, provided that the business person otherwise complies with existing immigration measures applicable to temporary entry.

2. No Party may:

(a) as a condition for temporary entry under paragraph 1, require labor certification tests or other procedures of similar effect; or

(b) impose or maintain any numerical restriction relating to temporary entry under paragraph 1.

3. Notwithstanding paragraph 2, a Party may require a business person seeking temporary entry under this Section to obtain a visa or its equivalent prior to entry.[31]

Section C provides for intra-company transferees:

Annex 1603.C.1. Each Party shall grant temporary entry and provide confirming documentation to a business person employed by an enterprise who seeks to render services to that enterprise or a subsidiary or affiliate thereof, in a capacity that is managerial, executive or involves specialized knowledge, provided that

---

30   Ibid., at Annex 1603.A.
31   Ibid., at Annex 1603.B.

the business person otherwise complies with existing immigration measures applicable to temporary entry. A Party may require the business person to have been employed continuously by the enterprise for one year within the three-year period immediately preceding the date of the application for admission.

2. No Party may:

(a) as a condition for temporary entry under paragraph 1, require labor certification tests or other procedures of similar effect; or

(b) impose or maintain any numerical restriction relating to temporary entry under paragraph 1.

3. Notwithstanding paragraph 2, a Party may require a business person seeking temporary entry under this Section to obtain a visa or its equivalent prior to entry. Before imposing a visa requirement, the Party shall consult with a Party whose business persons would be affected with a view to avoiding the imposition of the requirement. With respect to an existing visa requirement, a Party shall consult, on request, with a Party whose business persons are subject to the requirement with a view to its removal.[32]

Section D provides for professionals:

Annex 1603.D.1. Each Party shall grant temporary entry and provide confirming documentation to a business person seeking to engage in a business activity at a professional level in a profession set out in Appendix 1603.D.1, if the business person otherwise complies with existing immigration measures applicable to temporary entry, on presentation of:

(a) proof of citizenship of a Party; and

(b) documentation demonstrating that the business person will be so engaged and describing the purpose of entry.

2. No Party may:

(a) as a condition for temporary entry under paragraph 1, require prior approval procedures, petitions, labor certification tests or other procedures of similar effect; or

(b) impose or maintain any numerical restriction relating to temporary entry under paragraph 1.

3. Notwithstanding paragraph 2, a Party may require a business person seeking temporary entry under this Section to obtain a visa or its equivalent prior to entry. Before imposing a visa requirement, the Party shall consult with a Party whose business persons would be affected with a view to avoiding the imposition of the requirement. With respect to an existing visa requirement, a Party shall consult, on request, with a Party whose business persons are subject to the requirement with a view to its removal.

4. Notwithstanding paragraphs 1 and 2, a Party may establish an annual numerical limit, which shall be set out in Appendix 1603.D.4, regarding temporary entry

---

32   Ibid., at Annex 1603.C.

of business persons of another Party seeking to engage in business activities at a professional level in a profession set out in Appendix 1603.D.1, if the Parties concerned have not agreed otherwise prior to the date of entry into force of this Agreement for those Parties. In establishing such a limit, the Party shall consult with the other Party concerned.

5. A Party establishing a numerical limit pursuant to paragraph 4, unless the Parties concerned agree otherwise:

(a) shall, for each year after the first year after the date of entry into force of this Agreement, consider increasing the numerical limit set out in Appendix 1603.D.4 by an amount to be established in consultation with the other Party concerned, taking into account the demand for temporary entry under this Section;

(b) shall not apply its procedures established pursuant to paragraph 1 to the temporary entry of a business person subject to the numerical limit, but may require the business person to comply with its other procedures applicable to the temporary entry of professionals; and

(c) may, in consultation with the other Party concerned, grant temporary entry under paragraph 1 to a business person who practices in a profession where accreditation, licensing, and certification requirements are mutually recognized by those Parties.

6. Nothing in paragraph 4 or 5 shall be construed to limit the ability of a business person to seek temporary entry under a Party's applicable immigration measures relating to the entry of professionals other than those adopted or maintained pursuant to paragraph 1.[33]

Finally, Appendix 1603.D.1 outlines the different professions provided for under NAFTA, along with the minimum educational requirements and alternative credentials.[34]

There are a number of institutions that are part of NAFTA. Article 2001 provides for the Free Trade Commission:

2001.1. The Parties hereby establish the Free Trade Commission, comprising cabinet-level representatives of the Parties or their designees.

2. The Commission shall:

(a) supervise the implementation of this Agreement;

(b) oversee its further elaboration;

(c) resolve disputes that may arise regarding its interpretation or application;

(d) supervise the work of all committees and working groups established under this Agreement ... and

(e) consider any other matter that may affect the operation of this Agreement.

3. The Commission may:

---

33 Ibid., at Annex 1603.D.
34 Ibid., at Appendix 1603.D.1.

(a) establish, and delegate responsibilities to, ad hoc or standing committees, working groups or expert groups;

(b) seek the advice of nongovernmental persons or groups; and

(c) take such other action in the exercise of its functions as the Parties may agree.[35]

Further, Article 2002 provides for the Secretariat:

2002.1. The Commission shall establish and oversee a Secretariat comprising national Sections.

2. Each Party shall:

(a) establish a permanent office of its Section;

(b) be responsible for

(i) the operation and costs of its Section, and

(ii) the remuneration and payment of expenses of panelists and members of committees and scientific review boards established under this Agreement, as set out in Annex 2002.2;

(c) designate an individual to serve as Secretary for its Section, who shall be responsible for its administration and management; and

(d) notify the Commission of the location of its Section's office.

3. The Secretariat shall:

(a) provide assistance to the Commission;

(b) provide administrative assistance to

(i) panels and committees established under Chapter Nineteen (Review and Dispute Settlement in Antidumping and Countervailing Duty Matters), in accordance with the procedures established pursuant to Article 1908, and

(ii) panels established under this Chapter, in accordance with procedures established pursuant to Article 2012; and

(c) as the Commission may direct

(i) support the work of other committees and groups established under this Agreement, and

(ii) otherwise facilitate the operation of this Agreement.[36]

Importantly, in terms of a dispute settlement, cooperation is stressed under Article 2003:

2003. The Parties shall at all times endeavor to agree on the interpretation and application of this Agreement, and shall make every attempt through cooperation and consultations to arrive at a mutually satisfactory resolution of any matter that might affect its operation.[37]

---

35   Ibid., at Article 2001.
36   Ibid., at Article 2002.
37   Ibid., at Article 2003.

In addition to proper legislation and litigation in front of the courts to protect children against underage employment, a dispute settlement mechanism is necessary for best practices and to enforce proper labor laws. Recourse to dispute settlement procedures is enunciated under Articles 1606 and 2004:

> 1606.1. A Party may not initiate proceedings under Article 2007 (Commission – Good Offices, Conciliation and Mediation) regarding a refusal to grant temporary entry under this Chapter or a particular case arising under Article 1602(1) unless:
> (a) the matter involves a pattern of practice; and
> (b) the business person has exhausted the available administrative remedies regarding the particular matter.
> 2. The remedies referred to in paragraph (1)(b) shall be deemed to be exhausted if a final determination in the matter has not been issued by the competent authority within one year of the institution of an administrative proceeding, and the failure to issue a determination is not attributable to delay caused by the business person.[38]

> 2004. Except for the matters covered in Chapter Nineteen (Review and Dispute Settlement in Antidumping and Countervailing Duty Matters) and as otherwise provided in this Agreement, the dispute settlement provisions of this Chapter shall apply with respect to the avoidance or settlement of all disputes between the Parties regarding the interpretation or application of this Agreement or wherever a Party considers that an actual or proposed measure of another Party is or would be inconsistent with the obligations of this Agreement or cause nullification or impairment in the sense of Annex 2004.[39]

Further, in terms of panel proceedings, a request for an arbitral panel is contained in Article 2008:

> 2008.1. If the Commission has convened pursuant to Article 2007(4), and the matter has not been resolved within:
> (a) 30 days thereafter,
> (b) 30 days after the Commission has convened in respect of the matter most recently referred to it, where proceedings have been consolidated pursuant to Article 2007(6), or
> (c) such other period as the consulting Parties may agree,
> any consulting Party may request in writing the establishment of an arbitral panel. The requesting Party shall deliver the request to the other Parties and to its Section of the Secretariat.
> 2. On delivery of the request, the Commission shall establish an arbitral panel.

---

38   Ibid., at Article 1606.
39   Ibid., at Article 2004.

3. A third Party that considers it has a substantial interest in the matter shall be entitled to join as a complaining Party on delivery of written notice of its intention to participate to the disputing Parties and its Section of the Secretariat. The notice shall be delivered at the earliest possible time, and in any event no later than seven days after the date of delivery of a request by a Party for the establishment of a panel.

4. If a third Party does not join as a complaining Party in accordance with paragraph 3, it normally shall refrain thereafter from initiating or continuing:

(a) a dispute settlement procedure under this Agreement, or

(b) a dispute settlement proceeding in the GATT on grounds that are substantially equivalent to those available to that Party under this Agreement,

regarding the same matter in the absence of a significant change in economic or commercial circumstances.

5. Unless otherwise agreed by the disputing Parties, the panel shall be established and perform its functions in a manner consistent with the provisions of this Chapter.[40]

The rules of procedure are outlined in Article 2012:

2012.1. The Commission shall establish by January 1, 1994, Model Rules of Procedure, in accordance with the following principles:

(a) the procedures shall assure a right to at least one hearing before the panel as well as the opportunity to provide initial and rebuttal written submissions; and

(b) the panel's hearings, deliberations and initial report, and all written submissions to and communications with the panel shall be confidential.

2. Unless the disputing Parties otherwise agree, the panel shall conduct its proceedings in accordance with the Model Rules of Procedure.

3. Unless the disputing Parties otherwise agree within 20 days from the date of the delivery of the request for the establishment of the panel, the terms of reference shall be:

'To examine, in the light of the relevant provisions of the Agreement, the matter referred to the Commission (as set out in the request for a Commission meeting) and to make findings, determinations and recommendations as provided in Article 2016(2).'[41]

Third party participation is permitted under Article 2013:

2013. A Party that is not a disputing Party, on delivery of a written notice to the disputing Parties and to its Section of the Secretariat, shall be entitled to attend

---

40 Ibid., at Article 2008.
41 Ibid., at Article 2012.

all hearings, to make written and oral submissions to the panel and to receive written submissions of the disputing Parties.[42]

Importantly, non-implementation and the suspension of benefits are provided for under Article 2019, and this is an especially important tool for businesses who might otherwise be non-compliant in terms of underage labor laws, requiring them to comply or face the loss of benefits:

> 2019.1. If in its final report a panel has determined that a measure is inconsistent with the obligations of this Agreement or causes nullification or impairment in the sense of Annex 2004 and the Party complained against has not reached agreement with any complaining Party on a mutually satisfactory resolution pursuant to Article 2018(1) within 30 days of receiving the final report, such complaining Party may suspend the application to the Party complained against of benefits of equivalent effect until such time as they have reached agreement on a resolution of the dispute.
>
> 2. In considering what benefits to suspend pursuant to paragraph 1:
>
> (a) a complaining Party should first seek to suspend benefits in the same sector or sectors as that affected by the measure or other matter that the panel has found to be inconsistent with the obligations of this Agreement or to have caused nullification or impairment in the sense of Annex 2004; and
>
> (b) a complaining Party that considers it is not practicable or effective to suspend benefits in the same sector or sectors may suspend benefits in other sectors.[43]

In terms of domestic proceedings and a private commercial dispute settlement, Article 2020 provides for referrals of matters in judicial or administrative proceedings:

> 2020.1. If an issue of interpretation or application of this Agreement arises in any domestic judicial or administrative proceeding of a Party that any Party considers would merit its intervention, or if a court or administrative body solicits the views of a Party, that Party shall notify the other Parties and its Section of the Secretariat. The Commission shall endeavor to agree on an appropriate response as expeditiously as possible.
>
> 2. The Party in whose territory the court or administrative body is located shall submit any agreed interpretation of the Commission to the court or administrative body in accordance with the rules of that forum.
>
> 3. If the Commission is unable to agree, any Party may submit its own views to the court or administrative body in accordance with the rules of that forum.[44]

---

42   Ibid., at Article 2013.
43   Ibid., at Article 2019.
44   Ibid., at Article 2020.

Further, private rights are guaranteed under Article 2021:

> 2021. No Party may provide for a right of action under its domestic law against any other Party on the ground that a measure of another Party is inconsistent with this Agreement.[45]

Finally, Article 2022 provides for alternative dispute resolution which is a vital tool to protect children against underage employment, in addition to proper legislation and litigation in front of the courts:

> 2022.1. Each Party shall, to the maximum extent possible, encourage and facilitate the use of arbitration and other means of alternative dispute resolution for the settlement of international commercial disputes between private parties in the free trade area.
> 2. To this end, each Party shall provide appropriate procedures to ensure observance of agreements to arbitrate and for the recognition and enforcement of arbitral awards in such disputes.[46]

North American Agreement on Labor Cooperation (NAALC)

The North American Agreement on Labor Cooperation (NAALC) 1993, a side agreement to NAFTA, promotes the enforcement of national labor laws and transparency in their administration, important for equal rights of workers. Through NAALC, the NAFTA partners seek to improve working conditions and living standards in all three countries, and commit themselves to promoting principles that protect, enhance and enforce basic workers' rights. The Agreement increases cooperation and promotes greater understanding among the Parties in a broad range of labor areas; establishes the obligation of each Party to ensure the enforcement of its domestic labor laws; provides mechanisms to permit problem-solving consultations; enables the Parties to initiate evaluations of patterns of practice by independent committees of experts; and allows for dispute settlement procedures. A trinational Labor Commission is created to facilitate the achievement of the objectives of the Agreement and to deal with labor issues in a cooperative and consultative manner that duly respects the three nations' sovereignty. The Labor Commission consists of a Ministerial Council, an International Coordinating Secretariat (ICS), and three National Administrative Offices (NAOs). The Ministerial Council consists of the Labor Ministers from the three signatory countries, who supervise the implementation of the Agreement, including directing the work of the ICS, and promote cooperative activities. An ICS, under the direction of the Ministerial Council, carries out the day-to-day

---

45   Ibid., at Article 2021.
46   Ibid., at Article 2022.

work of the Commission, and is responsible for assisting the Council in its work, for gathering and periodically publishing information on labor matters in Canada, the United States and Mexico, for planning and coordinating cooperative activities, and for supporting any working groups or evaluation committees established by the Ministerial Council. The NAOs, established by each Party, serve as a point of contact for and facilitate the provision of information to other Parties on domestic law and practice, receive public communications, conduct preliminary reviews and promote the exchange of information relevant to the Agreement.

We will begin by examining the general provisions of NAFTA which are applicable to all, and along the way show how NAALC is sorely lacking in protection for children. The Preamble to the North American Agreement on Labor Cooperation (NAALC) states that the Government of the United States of America, the Government of Canada and the Government of the United Mexican States undertake the agreement:

> RECALLING their resolve in the North American Free Trade Agreement (NAFTA) to:
> create an expanded and secure market for the goods and services produced in their territories,
> enhance the competitiveness of their firms in global markets,
> create new employment opportunities and improve working conditions and living standards in their respective territories, and
> protect, enhance and enforce basic workers' rights;
>
> AFFIRMING their continuing respect for each Party's constitution and law;
>
> DESIRING to build on their respective international commitments and to strengthen their cooperation on labor matters;
>
> RECOGNIZING that their mutual prosperity depends on the promotion of competition based on innovation and rising levels of productivity and quality;
>
> SEEKING to complement the economic opportunities created by the NAFTA with the human resource development, labor-management cooperation and continuous learning that characterize high-productivity economies;
>
> ACKNOWLEDGING that protecting basic workers' rights will encourage firms to adopt high-productivity competitive strategies;
>
> RESOLVED to promote, in accordance with their respective laws, high-skill, high-productivity economic development in North America by:
> investing in continuous human resource development, including for entry into the workforce and during periods of unemployment;

promoting employment security and career opportunities for all workers through referral and other employment services;

strengthening labor-management cooperation to promote greater dialogue between worker organizations and employers and to foster creativity and productivity in the workplace;

promoting higher living standards as productivity increases;

encouraging consultation and dialogue between labor, business and government both in each country and in North America;

fostering investment with due regard for the importance of labor laws and principles;

encouraging employers and employees in each country to comply with labor laws and to work together in maintaining a progressive, fair, safe and healthy working environment;

BUILDING on existing institutions and mechanisms in Canada, Mexico and the United States to achieve the preceding economic and social goals; and

CONVINCED of the benefits to be gained from further cooperation between them on labor matters.[47]

The objectives of the agreement are outlined in Article 1:

1(a) improve working conditions and living standards in each Party's territory;

(b) promote, to the maximum extent possible, the labor principles set out in Annex 1;

(c) encourage cooperation to promote innovation and rising levels of productivity and quality;

(d) encourage publication and exchange of information, data development and coordination, and joint studies to enhance mutually beneficial understanding of the laws and institutions governing labor in each Party's territory;

(e) pursue cooperative labor-related activities on the basis of mutual benefit;

(f) promote compliance with, and effective enforcement by each Party of, its labor law; and

(g) foster transparency in the administration of labor law.[48]

Specifically, in terms of Obligations of the Parties and the Levels of Protection, Article 2 holds:

2. Affirming full respect for each Party's constitution, and recognizing the right of each Party to establish its own domestic labor standards, and to adopt or modify accordingly its labor laws and regulations, each Party shall ensure that

---

47   North American Agreement on Labor Cooperation (NAALC), at the Preamble.
48   Ibid., at Article 1.

its labor laws and regulations provide for high labor standards, consistent with high quality and productivity workplaces, and shall continue to strive to improve those standards in that light.[49]

Importantly, government enforcement action is established under Article 3, which states that each Party shall promote compliance with and effectively enforce its labor law through appropriate government action, such as:

> 3(a) appointing and training inspectors;
> (b) monitoring compliance and investigating suspected violations, including through on-site inspections;
> (c) seeking assurances of voluntary compliance;
> (d) requiring record keeping and reporting;
> (e) encouraging the establishment of worker–management committees to address labor regulation of the workplace;
> (f) providing or encouraging mediation, conciliation and arbitration services; or
> (g) initiating, in a timely manner, proceedings to seek appropriate sanctions or remedies for violations of its labor law.[50]

Critical for discrimination cases, and in protecting children against underage employment through litigation and the strong arm of the courts, the agreement safeguards private action in Article 4:

> 4.1. Each Party shall ensure that persons with a legally recognized interest under its law in a particular matter have appropriate access to administrative, quasijudicial, judicial or labor tribunals for the enforcement of the Party's labor law.
> 2. Each Party's law shall ensure that such persons may have recourse to, as appropriate, procedures by which rights arising under:
> (a) its labor law, including in respect of occupational safety and health, employment standards, industrial relations and migrant workers, and
> (b) collective agreements,
> can be enforced.[51]

Further, under procedural guarantees, Article 5 establishes:

> 5.1. Each Party shall ensure that its administrative, quasijudicial, judicial and labor tribunal proceedings for the enforcement of its labor law are fair, equitable and transparent and, to this end, each Party shall provide that:

---

49 Ibid., at Article 2. However, more should have been done under this article by explicitly outlawing underage employment and stating that it will not be tolerated.

50 Ibid., at Article 3.

51 Ibid., at Article 4.

(a) such proceedings comply with due process of law;

(b) any hearings in such proceedings are open to the public, except where the administration of justice otherwise requires;

(c) the parties to such proceedings are entitled to support or defend their respective positions and to present information or evidence; and

(d) such proceedings are not unnecessarily complicated and do not entail unreasonable charges or time limits or unwarranted delays.

2. Each Party shall provide that final decisions on the merits of the case in such proceedings are:

(a) in writing and preferably state the reasons on which the decisions are based;

(b) made available without undue delay to the parties to the proceedings and, consistent with its law, to the public; and

(c) based on information or evidence in respect of which the parties were offered the opportunity to be heard.

3. Each Party shall provide, as appropriate, that parties to such proceedings have the right, in accordance with its law, to seek review and, where warranted, correction of final decisions issued in such proceedings.

4. Each Party shall ensure that tribunals that conduct or review such proceedings are impartial and independent and do not have any substantial interest in the outcome of the matter.

5. Each Party shall provide that the parties to administrative, quasijudicial, judicial or labor tribunal proceedings may seek remedies to ensure the enforcement of their labor rights. Such remedies may include, as appropriate, orders, compliance agreements, fines, penalties, imprisonment, injunctions or emergency workplace closures.

6. Each Party may, as appropriate, adopt or maintain labor defense offices to represent or advise workers or their organizations.

7. Nothing in this Article shall be construed to require a Party to establish, or to prevent a Party from establishing, a judicial system for the enforcement of its labor law distinct from its system for the enforcement of laws in general.

8. For greater certainty, decisions by each Party's administrative, quasijudicial, judicial or labor tribunals, or pending decisions, as well as related proceedings shall not be subject to revision or reopened under the provisions of this Agreement.[52]

In terms of cooperation for appreciation for child labor issues in the workplace, Article 11 underlines the importance of labor practices and cooperative activities for equality, specifically mentioning child labor under Article 11.1(b):

11.1. The Council shall promote cooperative activities between the Parties, as appropriate, regarding:
a. occupational safety and health;

---

52   Ibid., at Article 5.

b. child labor;

c. migrant workers of the Parties;

d. human resource development;

e. labor statistics;

f. work benefits;

g. social programs for workers and their families;

h. programs, methodologies and experiences regarding productivity improvement;

i. labor–management relations and collective bargaining procedures;

j. employment standards and their implementation;

k. compensation for work-related injury or illness;

l. legislation relating to the formation and operation of unions, collective bargaining and the resolution of labor disputes, and its implementation;

m. the equality of women and men in the workplace;

n. forms of cooperation among workers, management and government;

o. the provision of technical assistance, at the request of a Party, for the development of its labor standards; and

p. such other matters as the Parties may agree.

2. In carrying out the activities referred to in paragraph 1, the Parties may, commensurate with the availability of resources in each Party, cooperate through:

a. seminars, training sessions, working groups and conferences;

b. joint research projects, including sectoral studies;

c. technical assistance; and

d. such other means as the Parties may agree.

3. The Parties shall carry out the cooperative activities referred to in paragraph 1 with due regard for the economic, social, cultural and legislative differences between them.[53]

Importantly, Article 49 defines labor law, which specifically mentions labor protections for children and young persons under Article 49(e):

49.1. For purposes of this Agreement:

'labor law' means laws and regulations, or provisions thereof, that are directly related to:

(a) freedom of association and protection of the right to organize;

(b) the right to bargain collectively;

(c) the right to strike;

(d) prohibition of forced labor;

(e) labor protections for children and young persons;

(f) minimum employment standards, such as minimum wages and overtime pay, covering wage earners, including those not covered by collective agreements;

---

53   Ibid., at Article 11.

(g) elimination of employment discrimination on the basis of grounds such as race, religion, age, sex, or other grounds as determined by each Party's domestic laws;

(h) equal pay for men and women;

(i) prevention of occupational injuries and illnesses;

(j) compensation in cases of occupational injuries and illnesses;

(k) protection of migrant workers.[54]

Further, in Article 7 of Annex 1, labor principles are outlined, which stress the elimination of employment discrimination, and should include children under 'other grounds':

> Annex 1. The following are guiding principles that the Parties are committed to promote, subject to each Party's domestic law, but do not establish common minimum standards for their domestic law. They indicate broad areas of concern where the Parties have developed, each in its own way, laws, regulations, procedures and practices that protect the rights and interests of their respective workforces.
>
> 7. Elimination of employment discrimination on such grounds as race, religion, age, sex or other grounds, subject to certain reasonable exceptions, such as, where applicable, *bona fide* occupational requirements or qualifications and established practices or rules governing retirement ages, and special measures of protection or assistance for particular groups designed to take into account the effects of discrimination.[55]

NAFTA, according to its critics, is not free, since Canada has paid a high price to gain greater access to the American and Mexican markets. Canadian consumers have seen prices rise along with the advent of the Goods and Services Tax, and thousands of jobs have been lost, with unemployment hovering around the 9 percent level.[56] From 1976 until 2010, Canada's Unemployment Rate averaged 8.53 percent, reaching an historical high of 13.10 percent in December of 1982 and a record low of 5.90 percent in September of 2007.[57] The structural adjustment costs, such as a rise in unemployment, tend to be underestimated by free trade advocates. Further, the agreement is also not about trade, and is more about the creation of a new continental model of development for the regulation of capitalism.[58] It serves more as a corporate bill of rights entrenching deregulation and market orientation in an international treaty, while at the same time eroding the national economic, as

---

54 Ibid., at Article 49.

55 Ibid., at Annex 1, Article 7.

56 Merrett, Christopher, *Free Trade, Neither Free Nor About Trade*, Black Rose Books, New York, 1996, p. 270.

57 Statistics Canada, Tradingeconomics.com, 5/11/2012.

58 Merrett (1996), op cit at p. 95.

well as social and political institutions. Neo-conservatives in Canada and the United States wanted a deregulated continental model of development to increase capital mobility in order to restore profitability. Unfortunately, corporate managers have worked in a continent-wide drive to bring down wages and welfare state spending, by playing communities off against one another, doing away with crucial social programs. The hidden goal is to harmonize and integrate Canadian standards and institutions with the United States, and as a result, Canada's economy, political system and labor practices have been significantly altered due to closer ties with the United States' economy. Canada has been forced to acquiesce to the continental model of development by continental market forces and American geopolitical pressures. Free trade is designed to restructure society to suit corporate needs, causing a threat to communities by capital-enhanced geographic mobility, which is not universally beneficial.

Many have benefited, but in the eyes of the critics, many more have been hurt. Sovereignty has been compromised, and the three most important industries for Canada, wood exports, agriculture and automobile manufacturing, have been hurt. 'The burden of Free Trade driven restructuring was shared unequally on a national, regional, class and gender basis.'[59] The critics argue that the new capital labor accord relies on domination instead of negotiation. Canadian workers are suffering from a 'whiplash process', being forced concessions on wage benefits and work rules, and failure to acquiesce has resulted in relocation out of Canada. Mergers, temporary and part-time workers, and cheap labor increase competitiveness at a cost, free-trade-generated jobs not materializing as promised by the advocates. The Continental Model has led to polarization and segmentation of the Canadian labor force, and the discourse of universality has ended, so that there is more social inequality across Canada. The Welfare State is viewed as an impediment to profit in the eyes of business, which has chipped away at it, giving way to a 'policy of stealth'; and with deregulation, budget cuts and privatization, importance is given to corporate profit at the expense of social equality.

'Continental free trade has helped to create a neo-conservative utopia where issues such as social justice and regional equality have become relics' of a bygone era.[60] While opponents of free trade are said to suffer from 'emporiophobia', a fear of free trade, the effects of free trade are something to fear, since hemispheric free trade is now a possibility. It was argued that there would be a 'sucking sound' of jobs going south of the border, ultimately to Mexico.[61] However, no tripartite treaty will disturb the overwhelming dominance that accrues to the United States, because of its geographic position, between Canada and Mexico. A borderland is a region jointly shared by two nations that houses people with common social characteristics in spite of the political boundaries between them, and thus the United States has a strong influence on the other two countries bordering it. The outflow of

---

59   Ibid., at p. 271.

60   Ibid., at p. 279.

61   McPhail, Brenda, *NAFTA Now*, University Press of America, Lanham, 1985, p. 44.

investment and the haemorrhaging of profits and service payments out of Canada is intrinsically intertwined with NAFTA.[62] According to the critics, the human and economic debris will be with us for as long as we can see into the future. The single most important impact of NAFTA is the decline in the overall standard of living of Canadians, which has coincided with the agreements. We must be careful to reform democracy and political institutions so citizens and not just corporate business benefit from change. There is presently more foreign ownership and control in Canada, with fewer and poorer jobs. More imports of goods and services should be sourced in Canada, but there is a failure to develop new competitive products while at the same time having less diversification of exports.

Northrop Frye pointed out long ago about Canada, 'Why go to the trouble of annexing a country that is so easy to exploit without taking any responsibility for it.'[63] Economic penetration has proven simpler than military force. NAFTA, according to its critics, is a neo-conservative Americanization of Canada.[64] The pre-agreement years saw trade on a multilateral level, without abandoning national control of the foreign market. However, the agreement itself is seen as a straitjacket, because it is difficult to introduce new measures to strengthen or expand national control of firms and industries. It can be argued that it is a dangerous and indefensible gamble for Canada to commit to a binding dispute settlement mechanism with a trading partner, the United States, which has such disproportionate power. NAFTA has set up a trading bloc designed to fit Canada and Mexico into the American model of development, keeping Europe and Japan out. Mexico is an attractive site for low-wage production of standardized industrial goods, and with this come Canadian and American job losses, with production shifts to Mexico and a downward pressure on wages. Workers have been displaced from industries and are vulnerable to competition from low-wage countries, with the loss especially to low-income jobs. While the job crisis existed before free trade and was not confined to Canada, NAFTA does nothing for basic labor. There is a conflict between the profitability of individual corporations and the pressures of global capabilities against human needs for high employment levels, decent pay, healthy working conditions and job security. To serve the corporate profit, what has occurred is a decrease in full-time employment and an increase in part-time and temporary employment at the expense of benefits, as well as an increase in unemployment and in welfare levels. As such, this has been 'the longest and deepest unemployment crisis since the Great Depression', with inappropriate monetary policy playing a major role.[65] Further, the global economy today is

---

62   Hurtig, Mel, *The Betrayal of Canada*, Stoddart Publishing, Toronto, 1991, p. 303.

63   Ibid., at p. 89.

64   Watkins, Mel, 'The Political Economy of Growth', in Wallace Clement and Glen Williams, *The New Canadian Political Economy*, McGill-Queen's University Press, Kingston, 1989, p. 3.

65   Campbell, Bruce, *Free Trade, Destroyer of Jobs*, Canadian Centre for Policy Alternatives, Ottawa. 1993, p. 2.

suffering greatly in light of corporate practices, which have been instituted over the last decades and have impacted many unfairly at the expense of corporate profit, including children who are the cheapest labor of all.

There is a gap in the free trade effect between the top corporate executive and the average shop floor worker. Free trade encourages self-reinforcing cycles of destructive competition, exerting great pressure on the Continent. It has eliminated jobs, depressed incomes and standards. The effects of investment diversion and export harassment far outweigh the positive effects of tariff reductions. There is a one-sided advantage for a corporate elite that is globally competitive, increasing profits, surviving and growing unfettered by government controls, and securing the highest rate of return for the interests of financial capital. Decent jobs and decent living standards have become unimportant. However, the employment needs of society must be paramount, and therefore, corporate interests must yield to broader public interests. NAFTA is tilted in the wrong direction. Multilateral trading arrangements with the European Community and Japan would be alternatives to NAFTA and its shortfalls. Canada's social programs are a contrast to those of the United States. Americanization is balkanizing Canada. Regional equality is promised, but individuals, families, communities and regions are being abandoned. Canada was founded on the national principle of building strong communities and regions to serve the needs of residents, not to deplete these areas in order to supply land and factories for economic interests. With layoffs and closures, there is a bitter legacy of unemployment, poverty and inequality, with society becoming distinctly harsher. Those who are able to thrive are doing very well, but the societal gap is growing so that there is a chasm between rich and poor, young and old, black and white, men and women, abled and disabled, with a disappearing middle class. There is a severe strain on the societal fabric, with a sacrificing of the needs of many for the demands of few.[66]

Among those who were opposed to NAFTA, well-known Canadian Mitchell Sharp stated it best:

> From the very beginnings of our country, we have sought to preserve a separate identity, to live in harmony with our next door neighbour but as an independent country. By entering into this … preferential agreement, we would be deciding no longer to resist the continental pull. On the contrary, we would be accelerating the process of the Americanisation of Canada.[67]

Many believe that free trade challenges the fundamentals of Canada's nationhood, with its powers limited by interdependence and domination from foreign multinationals. The benefits of free trade do not fall equally. Free trade serves

---

66   Ibid.

67   Axworthy, Lloyd, 'Free Trade, The Costs for Canada', in A.R. Riggs and Tom Velk, *Canadian–American Free Trade: (The Sequel) Historical, Political and Economic Dimensions*, The Institute for Research on Public Policy, Montreal, 1988, p. 38.

to undermine full employment,[68] but the first essential ingredient for free trade should be a commitment to full employment. Sufficient independence for blueprint choices and for flexible alternatives for long-term planning is needed, looking away from integration. By operating under the deceptive banner of 'free' trade, multinational corporations are working hard to expand their control over the international economy, and to dismantle vital health, safety and environmental protections, which in recent decades have been won by citizens' movements across the globe. According to consumer advocate Ralph Nader, this serves to devalue jobs, depress wage levels, make workplaces less safe, destroy family farms and undermine consumer protections.[69] Because of NAFTA, large global companies have capitalized on poverty in the Developing Economies, including China and India, by lowering safety and wages in employment. As such, workers, consumers and communities will continue to lose, while short-term profits soar and big business wins, in a threat to move South. Thus the centralization of commercial power is unsound, as the allocation of power to lower levels of government bodies tends to increase citizen power. There is a need for community-oriented production in smaller-scale operations, along with more flexibility and adaptability to local needs for sustainable production methods and democratic controls. There is a race 'to the bottom', pitting State against State, for the lowest wage levels, lowest environmental policies and lowest consumer safety standards.[70]

NAFTA has forced Canada to harmonize its social and economic policies to conform to the United States at the expense of its citizens. Free trade calls for privatization and deregulation, but policy intervention is needed to reduce unemployment and raise wage rates. There has been a shift away from service-type jobs, with pressure to decrease wages and provide fewer benefits for the sake of the almighty American dollar. There has been major job loss by sourcing services outside Canada but also outside the United States.[71] It is important to negotiate over the right of establishment and the right to national treatment. Manufacturing is vulnerable to trade liberalization, which will lead to an increase in unemployment and adverse working conditions, and the United States has an advantage over Canada, because of cheap material, capital intensiveness and technological advancement. As well, in the food industry, Canada is again at a disadvantage due to its size and climate. So too in the electrical field where the United States is again favored, because of a rationalization of production for specializations. Overall, there is a 'going South' policy, since Canadian firms want to locate elsewhere, while still having access to the Canadian market, but at the same time, by phasing out import restrictions, the domestic sector is not

---

68   Ibid., at p. 39.
69   Nader, Ralph, *The Case against Free Trade*, Earth Island Press, San Francisco, 1993, p. 1.
70   Ibid., at p. 6.
71   Griffin Cohen, Marjorie, *Free Trade and the Future of Women's Work, Manufacturing and Service Industries*, Garamond Press, Toronto, 1987, p. 16.

protected. American legislation for North American realignment, it is argued, will curtail equal rights legislation, since equal pay is too costly for the industry. Free trade erodes the domestic service economy, with one's own workforce vital to any economy, and should be a means only not an end.[72]

American Declaration of the Rights and Duties of Man

Important for equal rights, including the appreciation for the dignity and rights of the child, the Preamble of the American Declaration of the Rights and Duties of Man 1948 states:

> All men are born free and equal, in dignity and in rights, and, being endowed by nature with reason and conscience, they should conduct themselves as brothers one to another.

> The fulfilment of duty by each individual is a prerequisite to the rights of all. Rights and duties are interrelated in every social and political activity of man. While rights exalt individual liberty, duties express the dignity of that liberty.

> Duties of a juridical nature presuppose others of a moral nature which support them in principle and constitute their basis.

> In as much as spiritual development is the supreme end of human existence and the highest expression thereof, it is the duty of man to serve that end with all his strength and resources.

> Since culture is the highest social and historical expression of that spiritual development, it is the duty of man to preserve, practice and foster culture by every means within his power.

> And, since moral conduct constitutes the noblest flowering of culture, it is the duty of every man always to hold it in high respect.

> Whereas:

> The American peoples have acknowledged the dignity of the individual, and their national constitutions recognize that juridical and political institutions, which regulate life in human society, have as their principal aim the protection of the essential rights of man and the creation of circumstances that will permit him to achieve spiritual and material progress and attain happiness;

---

72   Ibid., at p. 49.

The American States have on repeated occasions recognized that the essential rights of man are not derived from the fact that he is a national of a certain state, but are based upon attributes of his human personality;

The international protection of the rights of man should be the principal guide of an evolving American law;

The affirmation of essential human rights by the American States together with the guarantees given by the internal regimes of the states establish the initial system of protection considered by the American States as being suited to the present social and juridical conditions, not without a recognition on their part that they should increasingly strengthen that system in the international field as conditions become more favourable.[73]

In terms of equal rights and equality, Article II guarantees the right to equality before the law, which should include child discrimination under 'any other factor':

II. All persons are equal before the law and have the rights and duties established in this Declaration, without distinction as to race, sex, language, creed or any other factor.[74]

Further, important for children, the right to education is guaranteed under Article XII:

XII. Every person has the right to an education, which should be based on the principles of liberty, morality and human solidarity.
Likewise every person has the right to an education that will prepare him to attain a decent life, to raise his standard of living, and to be a useful member of society. The right to an education includes the right to equality of opportunity in every case, in accordance with natural talents, merit and the desire to utilize the resources that the state or the community is in a position to provide. Every person has the right to receive, free, at least a primary education.[75]

In addition, important in the fight against child discrimination in employment, the right to work and to fair remuneration are contained in Article XIV, with the important requirement of 'under proper conditions', and unfortunately, so many children who are caught in underage employment are working and suffering under unfair conditions:

---

73   American Declaration of the Rights and Duties of Man, at the Preamble.
74   Ibid., at Article II.
75   Ibid., at Article XII.

XIV. Every person has the right to work, under proper conditions, and to follow his vocation freely, in so far as existing conditions of employment permit. Every person who works has the right to receive such remuneration as will, in proportion to his capacity and skill, assure him a standard of living suitable for himself and for his family.[76]

The scope of the rights of man is outlined in Article XXVIII:

XXVIII. The rights of man are limited by the rights of others, by the security of all, and by the just demands of the general welfare and the advancement of democracy.[77]

In terms of duties, the duty to obey the law is contained in Article XXXIII:

XXXIII. It is the duty of every person to obey the law and other legitimate commands of the authorities of his country and those of the country in which he may be.[78]

Finally, the duty to work is contained in Article XXXVII:

XXXVII. It is the duty of every person to work, as far as his capacity and possibilities permit, in order to obtain the means of livelihood or to benefit his community.[79]

American Convention on Human Rights

The Preamble of the American Convention on Human Rights 1978, which entered into force on 18 July 1978, states:

The American states signatory to the present Convention,
Reaffirming their intention to consolidate in this hemisphere, within the framework of democratic institutions, a system of personal liberty and social justice based on respect for the essential rights of man;
Recognizing that the essential rights of man are not derived from one's being a national of a certain state, but are based upon attributes of the human personality, and that they therefore justify international protection in the form of a convention reinforcing or complementing the protection provided by the domestic law of the American states;

---

76   Ibid., at Article XIV.
77   Ibid., at Article XXVIII.
78   Ibid., at Article XXXIII.
79   Ibid., at Article XXXVII.

Considering that these principles have been set forth in the Charter of the Organization of American States, in the American Declaration of the Rights and Duties of Man, and in the Universal Declaration of Human Rights, and that they have been reaffirmed and refined in other international instruments, worldwide as well as regional in scope;

Reiterating that, in accordance with the Universal Declaration of Human Rights, the ideal of free men enjoying freedom from fear and want can be achieved only if conditions are created whereby everyone may enjoy his economic, social, and cultural rights, as well as his civil and political rights.[80]

Important for equal rights, Article 1 stresses the obligation to respect rights:

1.1. The States Parties to this Convention undertake to respect the rights and freedoms recognized herein and to ensure to all persons subject to their jurisdiction the free and full exercise of those rights and freedoms, without any discrimination for reasons of race, color, sex, language, religion, political or other opinion, national or social origin, economic status, birth, or any other social condition.

2. For the purposes of this Convention, 'person' means every human being.[81]

Important for child discrimination cases, and the protection of the most innocent in society, the right to equal protection is guaranteed under Article 24:

24. All persons are equal before the law. Consequently, they are entitled, without discrimination, to equal protection of the law.[82]

Further, freedom of movement and residence is critical for employment opportunities, and is guaranteed under Article 22, but is especially important in the guarding against the movement of children and other persons for unlawful exploitation for employment purposes:

22. 1. Every person lawfully in the territory of a State Party has the right to move about in it, and to reside in it subject to the provisions of the law.

2. Every person has the right to leave any country freely, including his own.

3. The exercise of the foregoing rights may be restricted only pursuant to a law to the extent necessary in a democratic society to prevent crime or to protect national security, public safety, public order, public morals, public health, or the rights or freedoms of others.

4. The exercise of the rights recognized in paragraph 1 may also be restricted by law in designated zones for reasons of public interest.

---

80   American Convention on Human Rights, at the Preamble.
81   Ibid., at Article 1.
82   Ibid., at Article 24.

5. No one can be expelled from the territory of the state of which he is a national or be deprived of the right to enter it.

6. An alien lawfully in the territory of a State Party to this Convention may be expelled from it only pursuant to a decision reached in accordance with law.

7. Every person has the right to seek and be granted asylum in a foreign territory, in accordance with the legislation of the state and international conventions, in the event he is being pursued for political offenses or related common crimes.

8. In no case may an alien be deported or returned to a country, regardless of whether or not it is his country of origin, if in that country his right to life or personal freedom is in danger of being violated because of his race, nationality, religion, social status, or political opinions.

9. The collective expulsion of aliens is prohibited.[83]

In terms of civil and political rights, the right to juridical personality is contained in Article 3:

3. Every person has the right to recognition as a person before the law.[84]

Further, domestic legal effects are outlined in Article 2:

2. Where the exercise of any of the rights or freedoms referred to in Article 1 is not already ensured by legislative or other provisions, the States Parties undertake to adopt, in accordance with their constitutional processes and the provisions of this Convention, such legislative or other measures as may be necessary to give effect to those rights or freedoms.[85]

Crucially, the right to judicial protection is guaranteed under Article 25:

25.1. Everyone has the right to simple and prompt recourse, or any other effective recourse, to a competent court or tribunal for protection against acts that violate his fundamental rights recognized by the constitution or laws of the state concerned or by this Convention, even though such violation may have been committed by persons acting in the course of their official duties.

2. The States Parties undertake:

a. to ensure that any person claiming such remedy shall have his rights determined by the competent authority provided for by the legal system of the state;

b. to develop the possibilities of judicial remedy; and

c. to ensure that the competent authorities shall enforce such remedies when granted.[86]

---

83   Ibid., at Article 22.
84   Ibid., at Article 3.
85   Ibid., at Article 2.
86   Ibid., at Article 25.

In addition, Article 28 contains a federal clause:

> 28.1. Where a State Party is constituted as a federal state, the national government of such State Party shall implement all the provisions of the Convention over whose subject matter it exercises legislative and judicial jurisdiction.[87]

There are a number of competent organs involved as outlined in Article 33:

> 33. The following organs shall have competence with respect to matters relating to the fulfilment of the commitments made by the States Parties to this Convention:
>
> a. the Inter-American Commission on Human Rights, referred to as 'The Commission'; and
>
> b. the Inter-American Court of Human Rights, referred to as 'The Court'.[88]

In terms of the Inter-American Commission on Human Rights, Article 35 outlines the organization:

> 35. The Commission shall represent all the member countries of the Organization of American States.[89]

The functions of the Inter-American Commission on Human Rights are outlined in Article 41:

> 41. The main function of the Commission shall be to promote respect for and defense of human rights. In the exercise of its mandate, it shall have the following functions and powers:
>
> a. to develop an awareness of human rights among the peoples of America;
>
> b. to make recommendations to the governments of the member states, when it considers such action advisable, for the adoption of progressive measures in favor of human rights within the framework of their domestic law and constitutional provisions as well as appropriate measures to further the observance of those rights;
>
> c. to prepare such studies or reports as it considers advisable in the performance of its duties;
>
> d. to request the governments of the member states to supply it with information on the measures adopted by them in matters of human rights;
>
> e. to respond, through the General Secretariat of the Organization of American States, to inquiries made by the member states on matters related to human rights and, within the limits of its possibilities, to provide those states with the advisory services they request;

---

87 Ibid., at Article 28.
88 Ibid., at Article 33.
89 Ibid., at Article 35.

f. to take action on petitions and other communications pursuant to its authority under the provisions of Articles 44 through 51 of this Convention; and

g. to submit an annual report to the General Assembly of the Organization of American States.[90]

In addition to proper legislation and litigation in front of the courts to protect children against underage employment, the lodging of petitions is necessary for best practices and to enforce proper labor laws, and the competency to lodge petitions with the Inter-American Commission on Human Rights is outlined in Article 44:

44. Any person or group of persons, or any nongovernmental entity legally recognized in one or more member states of the Organization, may lodge petitions with the Commission containing denunciations or complaints of violation of this Convention by a State Party.[91]

Admissibility of petitions is outlined in Article 46:

46.1. Admission by the Commission of a petition or communication ... shall be subject to the following requirements:

a. that the remedies under domestic law have been pursued and exhausted in accordance with generally recognized principles of international law;

b. that the petition or communication is lodged within a period of six months from the date on which the party alleging violation of his rights was notified of the final judgment;

c. that the subject of the petition or communication is not pending in another international proceeding for settlement.

2. The provisions of paragraphs 1.a and 1.b of this article shall not be applicable when:

a. the domestic legislation of the state concerned does not afford due process of law for the protection of the right or rights that have allegedly been violated;

b. the party alleging violation of his rights has been denied access to the remedies under domestic law or has been prevented from exhausting them; or

c. there has been unwarranted delay in rendering a final judgment under the aforementioned remedies.[92]

The procedure is outlined in Article 48:

---

90   Ibid., at Article 41.
91   Ibid., at Article 44.
92   Ibid., at Article 46.

48. 1. When the Commission receives a petition or communication alleging violation of any of the rights protected by this Convention, it shall proceed as follows:

a. If it considers the petition or communication admissible, it shall request information from the government of the state indicated as being responsible for the alleged violations and shall furnish that government a transcript of the pertinent portions of the petition or communication. This information shall be submitted within a reasonable period to be determined by the Commission in accordance with the circumstances of each case.

b. After the information has been received, or after the period established has elapsed and the information has not been received, the Commission shall ascertain whether the grounds for the petition or communication still exist. If they do not, the Commission shall order the record to be closed.

c. The Commission may also declare the petition or communication inadmissible or out of order on the basis of information or evidence subsequently received.

d. If the record has not been closed, the Commission shall, with the knowledge of the parties, examine the matter set forth in the petition or communication in order to verify the facts. If necessary and advisable, the Commission shall carry out an investigation, for the effective conduct of which it shall request, and the states concerned shall furnish to it, all necessary facilities.

e. The Commission may request the states concerned to furnish any pertinent information and, if so requested, shall hear oral statements or receive written statements from the parties concerned.

f. The Commission shall place itself at the disposal of the parties concerned with a view to reaching a friendly settlement of the matter on the basis of respect for the human rights recognized in this Convention.

2. However, in serious and urgent cases, only the presentation of a petition or communication that fulfils all the formal requirements of admissibility shall be necessary in order for the Commission to conduct an investigation with the prior consent of the state in whose territory a violation has allegedly been committed.[93]

In terms of the Inter-American Court of Human Rights, the right of submission is outlined in Article 61:

61.1. Only the States Parties and the Commission shall have the right to submit a case to the Court.[94]

The safeguarding of rights and the provision of measures are contained in Article 63:

---

93   Ibid., at Article 48.
94   Ibid., at Article 61.

63.1. If the Court finds that there has been a violation of a right or freedom protected by this Convention, the Court shall rule that the injured party be ensured the enjoyment of his right or freedom that was violated. It shall also rule, if appropriate, that the consequences of the measure or situation that constituted the breach of such right or freedom be remedied and that fair compensation be paid to the injured party.

2. In cases of extreme gravity and urgency, and when necessary to avoid irreparable damage to persons, the Court shall adopt such provisional measures as it deems pertinent in matters it has under consideration. With respect to a case not yet submitted to the Court, it may act at the request of the Commission.[95]

In terms of procedure, Article 66 calls for reasons for judgments:

66. 1. Reasons shall be given for the judgment of the Court.[96]

Further, finality of judgment is contained in Article 67:

67. The judgment of the Court shall be final and not subject to appeal. In case of disagreement as to the meaning or scope of the judgment, the Court shall interpret it at the request of any of the parties, provided the request is made within ninety days from the date of notification of the judgment.[97]

Finally, compliance with the judgment is underlined in Article 68:

68.1. The States Parties to the Convention undertake to comply with the judgment of the Court in any case to which they are parties.

2. That part of a judgment that stipulates compensatory damages may be executed in the country concerned in accordance with domestic procedure governing the execution of judgments against the state.[98]

Statute of the Inter-American Court on Human Rights

More specifically and carrying on from the American Convention on Human Rights, Article 1 of the Statute of the Inter-American Court on Human Rights 1980, which entered into force on 1 January 1980, outlines the nature of the legal organization:

---

95   Ibid., at Article 63.
96   Ibid., at Article 66.
97   Ibid., at Article 67.
98   Ibid., at Article 68.

1. The Inter-American Court of Human Rights is an autonomous judicial
institution whose purpose is the application and interpretation of the American
Convention on Human Rights. The Court exercises its functions in accordance
with the provisions of the aforementioned Convention and the present Statute.[99]

The jurisdiction of the Court is contained in Article 2:

2. The Court shall exercise adjudicatory and advisory jurisdiction:
1. Its adjudicatory jurisdiction shall be governed by the provisions of Articles
61, 62 and 63 of the Convention, and
2. Its advisory jurisdiction shall be governed by the provisions of Article 64 of
the Convention.[100]

The seat of the Court is contained in Article 3:

3. 1. The seat of the Court shall be San Jose, Costa Rica; however, the Court may
convene in any member state of the Organization of American States (OAS)
when a majority of the Court considers it desirable, and with the prior consent
of the State concerned.[101]

Further, the composition of the Court is contained in Article 4:

4. 1. The Court shall consist of seven judges, nationals of the member states of
the OAS, elected in an individual capacity from among jurists of the highest
moral authority and of recognized competence in the field of human rights,
who possess the qualifications required for the exercise of the highest judicial
functions under the law of the State of which they are nationals or of the State
that proposes them as candidates.
2. No two judges may be nationals of the same State.[102]

The structure of the Court includes the Presidency as outlined in Article 12 and the
Secretariat as outlined in Article 14:

12.1. The Court shall elect from among its members a President and Vice-
President who shall serve for a period of two years; they may be reelected.
2. The President shall direct the work of the Court, represent it, regulate the
disposition of matters brought before the Court, and preside over its sessions.[103]

---

99   Statute of the Inter-American Court on Human Rights, at Article 1.
100 Ibid., at Article 2.
101 Ibid., at Article 3.
102 Ibid., at Article 4.
103 Ibid., at Article 12.

14.1. The Secretariat of the Court shall function under the immediate authority of the Secretary, in accordance with the administrative standards of the OAS General Secretariat, in all matters that are not incompatible with the independence of the Court.

2. The Secretary shall be appointed by the Court. He shall be a full-time employee serving in a position of trust to the Court, shall have his office at the seat of the Court and shall attend any meetings that the Court holds away from its seat.

3. There shall be an Assistant Secretary who shall assist the Secretary in his duties and shall replace him in his temporary absence.

4. The Staff of the Secretariat shall be appointed by the Secretary General of the OAS, in consultation with the Secretary of the Court.[104]

In terms of the workings of the Court, Article 24 outlines the hearings, deliberations and decisions:

24.1. The hearings shall be public, unless the Court, in exceptional circumstances, decides otherwise.

2. The Court shall deliberate in private. Its deliberations shall remain secret, unless the Court decides otherwise.

3. The decisions, judgments and opinions of the Court shall be delivered in public session, and the parties shall be given written notification thereof. In addition, the decisions, judgments and opinions shall be published, along with judges' individual votes and opinions and with such other data or background information that the Court may deem appropriate.[105]

Article 27 stresses the importance of relations with the host country, governments and organizations:

27.1. The relations of the Court with the host country shall be governed through a headquarters agreement. The seat of the Court shall be international in nature.

2. The relations of the Court with governments, with the OAS and its organs, agencies and entities and with other international governmental organizations involved in promoting and defending human rights shall be governed through special agreements.[106]

Finally, Article 28 stresses the importance of the relations with the Inter-American Commission on Human Rights:

---

104 Ibid., at Article 14.
105 Ibid., at Article 24.
106 Ibid., at Article 27.

28. The Inter-American Commission on Human Rights shall appear as a party before the Court in all cases within the adjudicatory jurisdiction of the Court, pursuant to Article 2(1) of the present Statute.[107]

Inter-American Democratic Charter

The Preamble of the Inter-American Democratic Charter 2001, which came into force on 11 September 2001, states:

> THE GENERAL ASSEMBLY,
> CONSIDERING that the Charter of the Organization of American States recognizes that representative democracy is indispensable for the stability, peace, and development of the region, and that one of the purposes of the OAS is to promote and consolidate representative democracy, with due respect for the principle of nonintervention;
> RECOGNIZING the contributions of the OAS and other regional and sub-regional mechanisms to the promotion and consolidation of democracy in the Americas;
> RECALLING that the Heads of State and Government of the Americas, gathered at the Third Summit of the Americas, held from April 20 to 22, 2001 in Quebec City, adopted a democracy clause which establishes that any unconstitutional alteration or interruption of the democratic order in a state of the Hemisphere constitutes an insurmountable obstacle to the participation of that state's government in the Summits of the Americas process;
> BEARING IN MIND that existing democratic provisions in regional and subregional mechanisms express the same objectives as the democracy clause adopted by the Heads of State and Government in Quebec City;
> REAFFIRMING that the participatory nature of democracy in our countries in different aspects of public life contributes to the consolidation of democratic values and to freedom and solidarity in the Hemisphere;
> CONSIDERING that solidarity among and cooperation between American states require the political organization of those states based on the effective exercise of representative democracy, and that economic growth and social development based on justice and equity, and democracy are interdependent and mutually reinforcing;
> REAFFIRMING that the fight against poverty, and especially the elimination of extreme poverty, is essential to the promotion and consolidation of democracy and constitutes a common and shared responsibility of the American states;
> BEARING IN MIND that the American Declaration on the Rights and Duties of Man and the American Convention on Human Rights contain the values and principles of liberty, equality, and social justice that are intrinsic to democracy;

---

107   Ibid., at Article 28.

REAFFIRMING that the promotion and protection of human rights is a basic prerequisite for the existence of a democratic society, and recognizing the importance of the continuous development and strengthening of the inter-American human rights system for the consolidation of democracy;

CONSIDERING that education is an effective way to promote citizens' awareness concerning their own countries and thereby achieve meaningful participation in the decision-making process, and reaffirming the importance of human resource development for a sound democratic system;

RECOGNIZING that a safe environment is essential to the integral development of the human being, which contributes to democracy and political stability;

BEARING IN MIND that the Protocol of San Salvador on Economic, Social, and Cultural Rights emphasizes the great importance of the reaffirmation, development, improvement, and protection of those rights in order to consolidate the system of representative democratic government;

RECOGNIZING that the right of workers to associate themselves freely for the defense and promotion of their interests is fundamental to the fulfillment of democratic ideals;

TAKING INTO ACCOUNT that, in the Santiago Commitment to Democracy and the Renewal of the Inter-American System, the ministers of foreign affairs expressed their determination to adopt a series of effective, timely, and expeditious procedures to ensure the promotion and defense of representative democracy, with due respect for the principle of nonintervention; and that resolution AG/RES. 1080 (XXI-O/91) therefore established a mechanism for collective action in the case of a sudden or irregular interruption of the democratic political institutional process or of the legitimate exercise of power by the democratically-elected government in any of the Organization's member states, thereby fulfilling a long-standing aspiration of the Hemisphere to be able to respond rapidly and collectively in defense of democracy;

RECALLING that, in the Declaration of Nassau [AG/DEC. 1 (XXII-O/92)], it was agreed to develop mechanisms to provide assistance, when requested by a member state, to promote, preserve, and strengthen representative democracy, in order to complement and give effect to the provisions of resolution AG/RES. 1080 (XXI-O/91);

BEARING IN MIND that, in the Declaration of Managua for the Promotion of Democracy and Development [AG/DEC. 4 (XXIII-O/93)], the member states expressed their firm belief that democracy, peace, and development are inseparable and indivisible parts of a renewed and integral vision of solidarity in the Americas; and that the ability of the Organization to help preserve and strengthen democratic structures in the region will depend on the implementation of a strategy based on the interdependence and complementarity of those values;

CONSIDERING that, in the Declaration of Managua for the Promotion of Democracy and Development, the member states expressed their conviction that the Organization's mission is not limited to the defense of democracy wherever its fundamental values and principles have collapsed, but also calls for ongoing and creative work to consolidate democracy as well as a continuing effort to prevent and anticipate the very causes of the problems that affect the democratic system of government;

BEARING IN MIND that the Ministers of Foreign Affairs of the Americas, at the thirty-first regular session of the General Assembly, held in San Jose, Costa Rica, in keeping with express instructions from the Heads of State and Government gathered at the Third Summit of the Americas, in Quebec City, accepted the base document of the Inter-American Democratic Charter and entrusted the Permanent Council of the Organization with strengthening and expanding the document, in accordance with the OAS Charter, for final adoption at a special session of the General Assembly in Lima, Peru;

RECOGNIZING that all the rights and obligations of member states under the OAS Charter represent the foundation on which democratic principles in the Hemisphere are built; and

BEARING IN MIND the progressive development of international law and the advisability of clarifying the provisions set forth in the OAS Charter and related basic instruments on the preservation and defense of democratic institutions, according to established practice.[108]

The anti-discrimination provision is contained in Article 9:

> 9. The elimination of all forms of discrimination, especially gender, ethnic and race discrimination, as well as diverse forms of intolerance, the promotion and protection of human rights of indigenous peoples and migrants, and respect for ethnic, cultural and religious diversity in the Americas contribute to strengthening democracy and citizen participation.[109]

Workers' rights and labor standards, important especially for children who are the weakest in society and are most in need of proper employment laws to protect them against unfair practices, are emphasized in Article 10:

> 10. The promotion and strengthening of democracy requires the full and effective exercise of workers' rights and the application of core labor standards, as recognized in the International Labour Organization (ILO) Declaration on Fundamental Principles and Rights at Work ... adopted in 1998, as well as other related fundamental ILO conventions. Democracy is strengthened by improving standards in the workplace and enhancing the quality of life for workers in the Hemisphere.[110]

The issue of redress for grievances is outlined in Article 8:

---

108   Inter-American Democratic Charter, at the Preamble.
109   Ibid., at Article 9.
110   Ibid., at Article 10.

8. Any person or group of persons who consider that their human rights have been violated may present claims or petitions to the inter-American system for the promotion and protection of human rights in accordance with its established procedures.

Member states reaffirm their intention to strengthen the inter-American system for the protection of human rights for the consolidation of democracy in the Hemisphere.[111]

Further, in terms of democracy and the inter-American system, Article 4 espouses the requirement of transparency:

4. Transparency in government activities, probity, responsible public administration on the part of governments, respect for social rights, and freedom of expression and of the press are essential components of the exercise of democracy.

The constitutional subordination of all state institutions to the legally constituted civilian authority and respect for the rule of law on the part of all institutions and sectors of society are equally essential to democracy.[112]

Finally, in terms of human rights, Article 7 stresses the need for democracy:

7. Democracy is indispensable for the effective exercise of fundamental freedoms and human rights in their universality, indivisibility and interdependence, embodied in the respective constitutions of states and in inter-American and international human rights instruments.[113]

Conclusion

By recognizing that we share a hemisphere, NAFTA sets an important precedent for north–south continental trade, and looks toward the future by allowing for participation by other countries. Latin American countries have expressed an interest in becoming signatory members of the Free Trade Agreement. In addition, the Canadian Province of Quebec has already given thought to joining as a separate member in the event it becomes a separate nation., but wishes to maintain the current division of legislative powers, respect fully its unique social policy, language and culture, maintain a leeway to modernize and develop its economy, provide for transitional periods for businesses in less competitive sectors, adopt a dispute settlement mechanism, maintain its special status for agriculture and fisheries, and protect its right to decide on the Agreement in light of its

---

111   Ibid., at Article 8.
112   Ibid., at Article 4.
113   Ibid., at Article 7.

interests. The Parties to the North American Free Trade Agreement (NAFTA) are cooperating to advance trade liberalization not only within North America with the NAFTA Superhighway, but also in the negotiations for the Free Trade Area of the Americas (FTAA), encompassing 34 countries. The FTAA would eliminate trade and investment barriers on virtually all goods and services traded by member countries, reduce prices for consumers and create new markets for producers throughout the hemisphere. However, more needs to be done to legislate for the protection of children in the labor force. President John F. Kennedy stated with regard to the relationship between Canada and the United States: 'Geography has made us neighbors, history has made us friends, the economy has made us partners and necessity has made us allies.'[114] NAFTA has been one of the most important agreements affecting labor and employment laws, due to its large scale impact involving so many people in 3 countries, and is expected to expand further into the Americas; but as we have seen in this chapter, NAFTA along with the other agreements mentioned need to go further in explicitly outlawing unfair child labor practices. In this spirit, important in the fight against child discrimination and child labor, we need to work together to bring about full equality and protection in the Americas, in the pursuit of `Little Angel'.

114   President John F. Kennedy.

Chapter 8
Little Angels in the United Kingdom and Ireland

Introduction

In the quest for respect for our children and in the fight against child discrimination in *Little Angels*, this chapter will examine child issues in the United Kingdom and Ireland. It will initially look at the United Kingdom, which encompasses England, Scotland, Wales and Northern Ireland, examining such legislation as the Race Relations Act and Race Relations Act (Amendment) Regulations, the Sex Discrimination Act, the Equal Pay Act, Equal Opportunities Commission (EOC) and the *Code of Practice on Equal Pay*, the Human Rights Act, the Equality Acts, the Children and Young Persons Acts, the Children Acts, and in Northern Ireland, the Children (Northern Ireland) Order; and then in the Republic of Ireland, the Constitution, the Employment Equality Act, the Equal Status Act, and the Protection of Young Persons (Employment) Act.

United Kingdom

Child labor laws are designed to protect children from exploitation and to regulate various working conditions affecting underage employment. The United Kingdom has ratified the Worst Forms of Child Labour Convention, 1999 (No. 182) (C. 182) in 2000, and has ratified the Minimum Age Convention, 1973 (No. 138) (C. 138) in 2000.

Although children from poor families in England had worked for centuries, it was not until the Industrial Revolution that child labor came to be seen as a social problem.[1] The United Kingdom has ratified the Worst Forms of Child Labour Convention, 1999 (No. 182) (C. 182) in 2000, and has ratified the Minimum Age Convention, 1973 (No. 138) (C. 138) in 2000.

Race Relations Act and Race Relations Act (Amendment) Regulations

For minority children who suffer age and race/ethnic discrimination, the Race Relations Act 1976 defines direct and indirect discrimination, and victimization. The Act outlaws racial and ethnic discrimination in employment, training,

---

1   Ibid.

Table 8.1 Employment statistics for the United Kingdom by age, showing underage employment.

Age group	Total			Men			Women		
	Total population	Active population	Activity rate	Total population	Active population	Activity rate	Total population	Active population	Activity rate
Total	60540	31118	51.4	29755	16872	56.7	30786	14246	46.3
0–9	7071	–	–	3617	–	–	3454	–	–
10–15	3687	–	–	1896	–	–	1790	–	–
16–19	3898	1698	43.6	1997	873	43.7	1901	824	43.3
20–24	4137	3097	74.9	2100	1679	80.0	2037	1418	69.6
25–29	4044	3429	84.8	2021	1864	92.2	2023	1565	77.4
30–34	3805	3228	84.8	1886	1775	94.1	1919	1453	75.7
35–39	4425	3743	84.6	2184	2025	92.7	2241	1718	76.7
40–44	4691	4029	85.9	2323	2145	92.3	2369	1884	79.5
45–49	4318	3731	86.4	2127	1940	91.2	2191	1791	81.7
50–54	3782	3126	82.7	1867	1629	87.3	1915	1498	78.2
55–59	3627	2635	72.6	1784	1428	80.0	1843	1207	65.5
60–64	3604	1694	47.0	1759	1056	60.0	1845	637	34.5
65–69	2733	471	17.2	1315	295	22.4	1418	176	12.4
70–74	2365	167	7.1	1107	112	10.1	1258	55	4.4
75+	4355	70	1.6	1772	51	2.9	2583	20	0.8

Source: International Labour Organization, Laborsta, 2008.

education, housing, public appointments, and the provision of goods, facilities and services. The Commission for Racial Equality (CRE) has the power to enforce the duties specified in the Act. Under the Race Relations Act 1976 and the Race Relations Act (Amendment) Regulations 2006, racial discrimination is defined under Section 1:

> 1(1) A person discriminates against another in any circumstances relevant for the purposes of any provision of this Act if
>
> (a) on racial grounds he treats that other less favourably than he treats or would treat other persons; or
>
> (b) he applies to that other a requirement or condition which he applies or would apply equally to persons not of the same racial group as that other but
>
> (i) which is such that the proportion of persons of the same racial group as that other who can comply with it is considerably smaller than the proportion of persons not of that racial group who can comply with it; and
>
> (ii) which he cannot show to be justifiable irrespective of the colour, race, nationality or ethnic or national origins of the person to whom it is applied; and
>
> (iii) which is to the detriment of that other because he cannot comply with it.
>
> (1A) A person also discriminates against another if, in any circumstances relevant for the purposes of any provision referred to in subsection (1B), he applies to that other a provision, criterion or practice which he applies or would apply equally to persons not of the same race or ethnic or national origins as that other, but
>
> (a) which puts or would put persons of the same race or ethnic or national origins as that other at a particular disadvantage when compared with other persons,
>
> (b) which puts that other at that disadvantage, and
>
> (c) which he cannot show to be a proportionate means of achieving a legitimate aim.[2]

Further, Section 2 covers discrimination by way of victimization:

> 2(1) A person ('the discriminator') discriminates against another person ('the person victimised') in any circumstances relevant for the purposes of any provision of this Act if he treats the person victimised less favourably than in those circumstances he treats or would treat other persons, and does so by reason that the person victimised has
>
> (a) brought proceedings against the discriminator or any other person under this Act; or
>
> (b) given evidence or information in connection with proceedings brought by any person against the discriminator or any other person under this Act; or

---

2   Race Relations Act 1976 and the Race Relations Act (Amendment) Regulations 2006, UK, at Section 1.

(c) otherwise done anything under or by reference to this Act in relation to the discriminator or any other person; or

(d) alleged that the discriminator or any other person has committed an act which (whether or not the allegation so states) would amount to a contravention of this Act,

or by reason that the discriminator knows that the person victimised intends to do any of those things, or suspects that the person victimised has done, or intends to do, any of them.

(2) Subsection (1) does not apply to treatment of a person by reason of any allegation made by him if the allegation was false and not made in good faith.[3]

Importantly, the meaning of racial grounds and racial group is outlined in Section 3:

3(1) In this Act, unless the context otherwise requires
'racial grounds' means any of the following grounds, namely colour, race, nationality or ethnic or national origins;
'racial group' means a group of persons defined by reference to colour, race, nationality or ethnic or national origins, and references to a person's racial group refer to any racial group into which he falls.

(2) The fact that a racial group comprises two or more distinct racial groups does not prevent it from constituting a particular racial group for the purposes of this Act.

(3) In this Act
(a) references to discrimination refer to any discrimination falling within section 1 or 2; and
(b) references to racial discrimination refer to any discrimination falling within section 1,
and related expressions shall be construed accordingly.

(4) A comparison of the case of a person of a particular racial group with that of a person not of that group under section 1(1) must be such that the relevant circumstances in the one case are the same, or not materially different, in the other.[4]

Further, harassment is covered:

3A(1) A person subjects another to harassment in any circumstances relevant for the purposes of any provision referred to in section 1(1B) where, on grounds of race or ethnic or national origins, he engages in unwanted conduct which has the purpose or effect of
(a) violating that other person's dignity, or

---

3   Ibid., at Section 2.
4   Ibid., at Section 3.

(b) creating an intimidating, hostile, degrading, humiliating or offensive environment for him.

(2) Conduct shall be regarded as having the effect specified in paragraph (a) or (b) of subsection (1) only if, having regard to all the circumstances, including in particular the perception of that other person, it should reasonably be considered *as having that effect.*[5]

Section 4 outlaws discrimination by employers:

4(1) It is unlawful for a person, in relation to employment by him at an establishment in Great Britain, to discriminate against another

(a) in the arrangements he makes for the purpose of determining who should be offered that employment; or

(b) in the terms on which he offers him that employment; or

(c) by refusing or deliberately omitting to offer him that employment.

(2) It is unlawful for a person, in the case of a person employed by him at an establishment in Great Britain, to discriminate against that employee

(a) in the terms of employment which he affords him; or

(b) in the way he affords him access to opportunities for promotion, transfer or training, or to any other benefits, facilities or services, or by refusing or deliberately omitting to afford him access to them; or

(c) by dismissing him, or subjecting him to any other detriment.

(2A) It is unlawful for an employer, in relation to employment by him at an establishment in Great Britain, to subject to harassment a person whom he employs or who has applied to him for employment.

(3) Except in relation to discrimination falling within section 2 [or discrimination on grounds of race or ethnic or national origins], subsections (1) and (2) do not apply to employment for the purposes of a private household.

(4) Subsection (2) does not apply to benefits, facilities or services of any description if the employer is concerned with the provision (for payment or not) of benefits, facilities or services of that description to the public, or to a section of the public comprising the employee in question, unless

(a) that provision differs in a material respect from the provision of the benefits, facilities or services by the employer to his employees; or

(b) the provision of the benefits, facilities or services to the employee in question is regulated by his contract of employment; or

(c) the benefits, facilities or services relate to training.

(4A) In subsection (2)(c) reference to the dismissal of a person from employment includes, where the discrimination is on grounds of race or ethnic or national origins, reference

(a) to the termination of that person's employment by the expiration of any period (including a period expiring by reference to an event or circumstance),

---

5   Ibid., at Section 3A.

not being a termination immediately after which the employment is renewed on the same terms; and

(b) to the termination of that person's employment by any act of his (including the giving of notice) in circumstances such that he is entitled to terminate it without notice by reason of the conduct of the employer.[6]

However, there is an exception for genuine occupational requirement:

4A(2) This subsection applies where, having regard to the nature of the employment or the context in which it is carried out

(a) being of a particular race or of particular ethnic or national origins is a genuine and determining occupational requirement;

(b) it is proportionate to apply that requirement in the particular case; and

(c) either

(i) the person to whom that requirement is applied does not meet it, or

(ii) the employer is not satisfied, and in all the circumstances it is reasonable for him not to be satisfied, that that person meets it.[7]

Further, Section 5 states:

5(1) In relation to racial discrimination in cases where section 4A does not apply

(a) section 4(1)(a) or (c) does not apply to any employment where being of a particular racial group is a genuine occupational qualification for the job; and

(b) section 4(2)(b) does not apply to opportunities for promotion or transfer to, or training for, such employment.

(2) Being of a particular racial group is a genuine occupational qualification for a job only where

(a) the job involves participation in a dramatic performance or other entertainment in a capacity for which a person of that racial group is required for reasons of authenticity; or

(b) the job involves participation as an artist's or photographic model in the production of a work of art, visual image or sequence of visual images for which a person of that racial group is required for reasons of authenticity; or

(c) the job involves working in a place where food or drink is (for payment or not) provided to and consumed by members of the public or a section of the public in a particular setting for which, in that job, a person of that racial group is required for reasons of authenticity; or

(d) the holder of the job provides persons of that racial group with personal services promoting their welfare, and those services can most effectively be provided by a person of that racial group.

---

6   Ibid., at Section 4.
7   Ibid., at Section 4A(2).

(3) Subsection (2) applies where some only of the duties of the job fall within paragraph (a), (b), (c) or (d) as well as where all of them do.

(4) Paragraph (a), (b), (c) or (d) of subsection (2) does not apply in relation to the filling of a vacancy at a time when the employer already has employees of the racial group in question

(a) who are capable of carrying out the duties falling within that paragraph; and

(b) whom it would be reasonable to employ on those duties; and

(c) whose numbers are sufficient to meet the employer's likely requirements in respect of those duties without undue inconvenience.[8]

Finally, the burden of proof for employment tribunals is established under Section 54A:

54A(1) This section applies where a complaint is presented under section 54 and the complaint is that the respondent

(a) has committed an act of discrimination, on grounds of race or ethnic or national origins, which is unlawful by virtue of any provision referred to in section 1(1B)(a), (e) or (f), or Part IV in its application to those provisions, or

(b) has committed an act of harassment.

(2) Where, on the hearing of the complaint, the complainant proves facts from which the tribunal could, apart from this section, conclude in the absence of an adequate explanation that the respondent

(a) has committed such an act of discrimination or harassment against the complainant, or

(b) is by virtue of section 32 or 33 to be treated as having committed such an act of discrimination or harassment against the complainant,

the tribunal shall uphold the complaint unless the respondent proves that he did not commit or, as the case may be, is not to be treated as having committed, that act.[9]

Sex Discrimination Act

For female children who suffer age and gender discrimination, the Sex Discrimination Act 1975 defines direct and indirect discrimination in Section 1:

1(1) In any circumstances relevant for the purposes of any provision of this Act ... a person discriminates against a woman if:

(a) on the ground of her sex he treats her less favourably than he treats or would treat a man, or

(b) he applies to her a requirement or condition which he applies or would apply equally to a man but:

---

8   Ibid., at Section 5.
9   Ibid., at Section 54A.

(i) which is such that the proportion of women who can comply with it is considerably smaller than the proportion of men who can comply with it, and
(ii) which he cannot show to be justifiable irrespective of the sex of the person to whom it is applied, and
1(1)(b)(iii) which is to her detriment because she cannot comply with it.[10]

In terms of sex discrimination against men and boys, Section 2 holds that Section 1 is to be read as applying equally to the treatment of males, and for that purpose shall have effect with such modifications as are required.[11]

In looking at discrimination in the employment stage, Section 6(2) states:

6(2) It is unlawful for a person, in the case of a woman employed by him at an establishment in Great Britain, to discriminate against her:
(a) in the way he affords her access to opportunities for promotion, transfer or training, or to any other benefits, facilities or services, or by refusing or deliberately omitting to afford her access to them, or
(b) by dismissing her, or subjecting her to any other detriment.[12]

There is an exception to the rule where sex is a genuine occupational qualification, which is contained in Section 7:

7(1) In relation to sex discrimination:
(a) section 6(1)(a) or (c) does not apply to any employment where being a man is a genuine occupational qualification for the job.
7(2) Being a man is a genuine occupational qualification for a job only where:
(a) the essential nature of the job calls for a man for reasons of physiology (excluding physical strength or stamina) or, in dramatic performances or other entertainment, for reasons of authenticity, so that the essential nature of the job would be materially different if carried out by a woman; or
(b) the job needs to be held by a man to preserve decency or privacy … or
(c) the nature or location of the establishment makes it impracticable for the holder of the job to live elsewhere than in premises provided by the employer …
(d) the nature of the establishment, or of the part of it within which the work is done, requires it to be held by a man … or
(e) the job needs to be held by a man because of restrictions imposed by the laws regulating the employment of women, or
(f) the holder of the job provides individuals with personal services promoting their welfare or education, or similar personal services, and those services can most effectively be provided by a man, or

---

10   Sex Discrimination Act, UK, at Section 1.
11   Ibid., at Section 2.
12   Ibid., at Section 6(2).

(g) the job needs to be held by a man because it is likely to involve the performance of duties outside the United Kingdom in a country whose laws or customs are such that the duties could not, or could not effectively, be performed by a woman, or

(h) the job is one of two to be held by a married couple.[13]

The SDA prohibits direct and indirect sex discrimination. Direct sex discrimination is where a woman or man is treated less favorably than a person of the opposite sex in comparable circumstances is, or would be, because of their gender. The test is: was the treatment less favorable than the treatment which was or would be accorded to a person of the opposite sex?; and was the treatment less favorable because of the gender of the person involved? Indirect sex discrimination is where a condition or practice is applied to both sexes but it adversely affects a considerably larger proportion of one sex than the other, and it is not justifiable, irrespective of sex, to apply that condition or practice. In a claim of sex discrimination presented to an employment tribunal, it is first up to the applicant to establish facts, which constitute a 'prima facie' case of discrimination. The burden of proof is initially on the employee to show on the balance of probabilities that her male comparator is doing the same or broadly similar work, or that her work has been rated as equivalent to his, or that her work is of equal value, and that his contract contains a more favorable term. The burden of proof then shifts from the applicant to the employer to show that there is a non-discriminatory reason for their actions, that is the difference between the contracts is genuinely due to a material factor which is not the difference of gender. The material factor defense is the reason put forward by the employer to explain why the comparator, although doing equal work, is paid more than the applicant. To be successful, this factor must be significant and relevant; that is, it must be an important cause of the difference and apply to the jobs in question. The difference in pay must be genuinely due to the material factor which must not be tainted by gender discrimination. If the reason given for paying the comparator more is that he has certain skills which the applicant does not have, then the employer would have to demonstrate that these skills are necessary for the job, and genuinely applied during the performance of the job, and are not simply rewarded because past pay agreements recognized and rewarded skills which are no longer applicable. To succeed in a defense, the employer needs to show that the material factor accounts for the whole of the difference in pay.

Equal Pay Act, Equal Opportunities Commission (EOC) and the Code of Practice on Equal Pay

Under the Equal Pay Act 1970 (EPA), genuine occupational qualification is recognized in Section 1(3):

13　Ibid., at Section 7.

1(3) An equality clause shall not operate in relation to a variation between the woman's contract and the man's contract if the employer proves that the variation is genuinely due to a material factor which is not the difference of sex ...[14]

Section 2(1) guarantees the important right of tribunal recourse for redress:

2(1) Any claim in respect of the contravention of a term modified or included by virtue of an equality clause, including a claim for arrears of remuneration or damages in respect of the contravention, may be presented by way of a complaint to an employment tribunal.[15]

The Equal Pay Act covers all contractual terms and not simply those relating to pay, with claims taken initially to an Industrial Tribunal.

The Equal Opportunities Commission recommends that a pay systems review should involve the following stages: stage one, undertake a thorough analysis of the pay system to produce a breakdown of all employees, which covers job title, grade, whether part-time or full-time, with basic pay, performance ratings and all other elements of remuneration; stage two, examine each element of the pay system against the data obtained in stage one; stage three, identify any elements of the pay system that the review indicates may be the source of any discrimination; stage four, change any rules or practices, including those in collective agreements, which stages one to three have identified as likely to give rise to discrimination in pay, in consultation with employees, trade unions or staff representatives where appropriate.[16] Stages one to three may reveal that practices and procedures in relation to recruitment, selection and access to training have contributed to discrimination in pay, and these should be addressed. There follow stage five, analyze the likely effects of any proposed changes in practice to the pay system before implementation, to identify and rectify any discrimination that could be caused; stage six, give equal pay to current employees. Where the review shows that some employees are not receiving equal pay for equal work and the reasons cannot be shown to be free of bias, then a plan must be developed for dealing with this; stage seven is to set up a system of regular monitoring to allow checks to be made to pay practices; and stage eight, draw up and publish an equal pay policy with provision for assessing the new pay system or modification to a system in terms of discrimination.[17]

---

14   Equal Pay Act, UK, at Section 1(3).
15   Ibid., at Section 2(1).
16   Equal Opportunities Commission, *Code of Practice on Equal Pay*, UK.
17   Ibid.

Human Rights Act

The Human Rights Act (HRA), entitled 'An Act to give further effect to rights and freedoms guaranteed under the European Convention on Human Rights', came into force mostly on 2 October 2000. Regarding the interpretation of legislation, Section 3 states:

> 3(1) So far as it is possible to do so, primary legislation and subordinate legislation must be read and given effect in a way which is compatible with the Convention rights.
> (2) This section
> (a) applies to primary legislation and subordinate legislation whenever enacted;
> (b) does not affect the validity, continuing operation or enforcement of any incompatible primary legislation; and
> (c) does not affect the validity, continuing operation or enforcement of any incompatible subordinate legislation if (disregarding any possibility of revocation) primary legislation prevents removal of the incompatibility.[18]

Further, the concept of declaration of incompatibility is covered under Section 4:

> 4(1) Subsection (2) applies in any proceedings in which a court determines whether a provision of primary legislation is compatible with a Convention right.
> (2) If the court is satisfied that the provision is incompatible with a Convention right, it may make a declaration of that incompatibility.
> (3) Subsection (4) applies in any proceedings in which a court determines whether a provision of subordinate legislation, made in the exercise of a power conferred by primary legislation, is compatible with a Convention right.
> (4) If the court is satisfied
> (a) that the provision is incompatible with a Convention right, and
> (b) that (disregarding any possibility of revocation) the primary legislation concerned prevents removal of the incompatibility,
> it may make a declaration of that incompatibility.[19]

Finally, in terms of Acts of Public Authorities, Section 6 states:

> 6(1) It is unlawful for a public authority to act in a way which is incompatible with a Convention right.
> (2) Subsection (1) does not apply to an act if
> (a) as the result of one or more provisions of primary legislation, the authority could not have acted differently; or

---

18   Human Rights Act, UK, at Section 3.
19   Ibid., at Section 4.

(b) in the case of one or more provisions of, or made under, primary legislation which cannot be read or given effect in a way which is compatible with the Convention rights, the authority was acting so as to give effect to or enforce those provisions.

(3) In this section 'public authority' includes

(a) a court or tribunal, and

(b) any person certain of whose functions are functions of a public nature,

but does not include either House of Parliament or a person exercising functions in connection with proceedings in Parliament.

...

(5) In relation to a particular act, a person is not a public authority by virtue only of subsection (3)(b) if the nature of the act is private.

(6) 'An act' includes a failure to act but does not include a failure to

(a) introduce in, or lay before, Parliament a proposal for legislation; or

(b) make any primary legislation or remedial order.[20]

Equality Acts

In terms of the Equality Act 2006, entitled 'An Act to make provision for the establishment of the Commission for Equality and Human Rights; to dissolve the Equal Opportunities Commission, the Commission for Racial Equality and the Disability Rights Commission; to make provision about discrimination on grounds of religion or belief; to enable provision to be made about discrimination on grounds of sexual orientation; to impose duties relating to sex discrimination on persons performing public functions; to amend the Disability Discrimination Act 1995; and for connected purposes', the general duty of the Commission is outlined in Section 3:

3. The Commission shall exercise its functions under this Part with a view to encouraging and supporting the development of a society in which

(a) people's ability to achieve their potential is not limited by prejudice or discrimination,

(b) there is respect for and protection of each individual's human rights,

(c) there is respect for the dignity and worth of each individual,

(d) each individual has an equal opportunity to participate in society, and

(e) there is mutual respect between groups based on understanding and valuing of diversity and on shared respect for equality and human rights.[21]

Equality and diversity are to be promoted under Section 8:

8(1) The Commission shall, by exercising the powers conferred by this Part

---

20   Ibid., at Section 6.

21   Equality Act 2006, UK, at Section 3.

(a) promote understanding of the importance of equality and diversity,

(b) encourage good practice in relation to equality and diversity,

(c) promote equality of opportunity,

(d) promote awareness and understanding of rights under the equality enactments,

(e) enforce the equality enactments,

(f) work towards the elimination of unlawful discrimination, and

(g) work towards the elimination of unlawful harassment.[22]

Importantly, human rights are to be promoted under Section 9:

9(1) The Commission shall, by exercising the powers conferred by this Part

(a) promote understanding of the importance of human rights,

(b) encourage good practice in relation to human rights,

(c) promote awareness, understanding and protection of human rights, and

(d) encourage public authorities to comply with section 6 of the Human Rights Act (compliance with Convention rights).[23]

As to groups, Section 10 states:

10(1) The Commission shall, by exercising the powers conferred by this Part

(a) promote understanding of the importance of good relations

(i) between members of different groups, and

(ii) between members of groups and others,

(b) encourage good practice in relation to relations

(i) between members of different groups, and

(ii) between members of groups and others,

(c) work towards the elimination of prejudice against, hatred of and hostility towards members of groups, and

(d) work towards enabling members of groups to participate in society.

(2) In this Part 'group' means a group or class of persons who share a common attribute in respect of any of the following matters

(a) age,

(b) disability,

(c) gender,

(d) proposed, commenced or completed reassignment of gender (within the meaning given by section 82(1) of the Sex Discrimination Act 1975 (c. 65)),

(e) race,

(f) religion or belief, and

(g) sexual orientation.

(3) For the purposes of this Part a reference to a group (as defined in subsection (2)) includes a reference to a smaller group or smaller class, within a group, of

---

22   Ibid., at Section 8.

23   Ibid., at Section 9.

persons who share a common attribute (in addition to the attribute by reference to which the group is defined) in respect of any of the matters specified in subsection (2)(a) to (g).[24]

Finally, in terms of monitoring of the law, Section 11 states:

11(1) The Commission shall monitor the effectiveness of the equality and human rights enactments.

(2) The Commission may

(a) advise central government about the effectiveness of any of the equality and human rights enactments;

(b) recommend to central government the amendment, repeal, consolidation (with or without amendments) or replication (with or without amendments) of any of the equality and human rights enactments;

(c) advise central or devolved government about the effect of an enactment (including an enactment in or under an Act of the Scottish Parliament);

(d) advise central or devolved government about the likely effect of a proposed change of law.[25]

Overall, the domestic law has been mainly contained in the Equal Pay Act 1970; the Sex Discrimination Act 1975; the Race Relations Act 1976; the Disability Discrimination Act 1995; the Employment Equality (Religion or Belief) Regulations 2003; the Employment Equality (Sexual Orientation) Regulations 2003; the Employment Equality (Age) Regulations 2006; the Equality Act 2006, Part 2; and the Equality Act (Sexual Orientation) Regulations 2007. However, the Equality Act 2010 has two main purposes: to harmonize discrimination law, and to strengthen the law to support progress on equality. It, therefore, brings together and restates all the enactments in the above Acts as amended, and harmonizes existing provisions to give a single approach. While most of the existing legislation will be repealed, according to Schedule 27, the Equality Act 2006 will remain in force (as amended by the Act) so far as it relates to the constitution and operation of the Equality and Human Rights Commission, as will the Disability Discrimination Act 1995, so far as it relates to Northern Ireland.[26]

In terms of the Equality Act 2010, entitled 'An Act to make provision to require Ministers of the Crown and others when making strategic decisions about the exercise of their functions to have regard to the desirability of reducing socio-economic inequalities; to reform and harmonise equality law and restate the greater part of the enactments relating to discrimination and harassment related to certain personal characteristics; to enable certain employers to be required to publish information about the differences in pay between male and female employees; to

---

24   Ibid., at Section 10.
25   Ibid., at Section 11.
26   Equality Act 2010, Explanatory Notes.

prohibit victimisation in certain circumstances; to require the exercise of certain functions to be with regard to the need to eliminate discrimination and other prohibited conduct; to enable duties to be imposed in relation to the exercise of public procurement functions; to increase equality of opportunity; to amend the law relating to rights and responsibilities in family relationships; and for connected purposes', Section 4 outlines the protected characteristics:

> 4. The following characteristics are protected characteristics
> age;
> disability;
> gender reassignment;
> marriage and civil partnership;
> pregnancy and maternity;
> race;
> religion or belief;
> sex;
> sexual orientation.[27]

Section 13 defines direct discrimination:

> 13(1) A person (A) discriminates against another (B) if, because of a protected characteristic, A treats B less favourably than A treats or would treat others.
> (2) If the protected characteristic is age, A does not discriminate against B if A can show A's treatment of B to be a proportionate means of achieving a legitimate aim.
> (3) If the protected characteristic is disability, and B is not a disabled person, A does not discriminate against B only because A treats or would treat disabled persons more favourably than A treats B.
> (4) If the protected characteristic is marriage and civil partnership, this section applies to a contravention of Part 5 (work) only if the treatment is because it is B who is married or a civil partner.
> (5) If the protected characteristic is race, less favourable treatment includes segregating B from others.
> (6) If the protected characteristic is sex
> (a) less favourable treatment of a woman includes less favourable treatment of her because she is breast-feeding;
> (b) in a case where B is a man, no account is to be taken of special treatment afforded to a woman in connection with pregnancy or childbirth.[28]

Further, Section 14 defines combined discrimination and its dual characteristics:

---

27   Ibid., at Section 4.
28   Ibid., at Section 13.

14(1) A person (A) discriminates against another (B) if, because of a combination of two relevant protected characteristics, A treats B less favourably than A treats or would treat a person who does not share either of those characteristics.

(2) The relevant protected characteristics are

(a) age;

(b) disability;

(c) gender reassignment;

(d) race;

(e) religion or belief;

(f) sex;

(g) sexual orientation.

(3) For the purposes of establishing a contravention of this Act by virtue of subsection (1), B need not show that A's treatment of B is direct discrimination because of each of the characteristics in the combination (taken separately).

(4) But B cannot establish a contravention of this Act by virtue of subsection (1) if, in reliance on another provision of this Act or any other enactment, A shows that A's treatment of B is not direct discrimination because of either or both of the characteristics in the combination.

(5) Subsection (1) does not apply to a combination of characteristics that includes disability in circumstances where, if a claim of direct discrimination because of disability were to be brought, it would come within section 116 (special educational needs).[29]

Finally, Section 19 defines indirect discrimination:

19(1) A person (A) discriminates against another (B) if A applies to B a provision, criterion or practice which is discriminatory in relation to a relevant protected characteristic of B's.

(2) For the purposes of subsection (1), a provision, criterion or practice is discriminatory in relation to a relevant protected characteristic of B's if

(a) A applies, or would apply, it to persons with whom B does not share the characteristic,

(b) it puts, or would put, persons with whom B shares the characteristic at a particular disadvantage when compared with persons with whom B does not share it,

(c) it puts, or would put, B at that disadvantage, and

(d) A cannot show it to be a proportionate means of achieving a legitimate aim.

(3) The relevant protected characteristics are

age;

disability;

gender reassignment;

marriage and civil partnership;

---

29   Ibid., at Section 14.

race;

religion or belief;

sex;

sexual orientation.[30]

Section 26 outlaws harassment:

26(1) A person (A) harasses another (B) if

(a) A engages in unwanted conduct related to a relevant protected characteristic, and

(b) the conduct has the purpose or effect of

(i) violating B's dignity, or

(ii) creating an intimidating, hostile, degrading, humiliating or offensive environment for B.

(2) A also harasses B if

(a) A engages in unwanted conduct of a sexual nature, and

(b) the conduct has the purpose or effect referred to in subsection (1)(b).

(3) A also harasses B if

(a) A or another person engages in unwanted conduct of a sexual nature or that is related to gender reassignment or sex,

(b) the conduct has the purpose or effect referred to in subsection (1)(b), and

(c) because of B's rejection of or submission to the conduct, A treats B less favourably than A would treat B if B had not rejected or submitted to the conduct.

(4) In deciding whether conduct has the effect referred to in subsection (1)(b), each of the following must be taken into account

(a) the perception of B;

(b) the other circumstances of the case;

(c) whether it is reasonable for the conduct to have that effect.

(5) The relevant protected characteristics are

age;

disability;

gender reassignment;

race;

religion or belief;

sex;

sexual orientation.[31]

Further, Section 27 outlaws victimization:

27(1) A person (A) victimises another person (B) if A subjects B to a detriment because

---

30   Ibid., at Section 19.

31   Ibid., at Section 26.

(a) B does a protected act, or

(b) A believes that B has done, or may do, a protected act.

(2) Each of the following is a protected act

(a) bringing proceedings under this Act;

(b) giving evidence or information in connection with proceedings under this Act;

(c) doing any other thing for the purposes of or in connection with this Act;

(d) making an allegation (whether or not express) that A or another person has contravened this Act.

(3) Giving false evidence or information, or making a false allegation, is not a protected act if the evidence or information is given, or the allegation is made, in bad faith.

(4) This section applies only where the person subjected to a detriment is an individual.

(5) The reference to contravening this Act includes a reference to committing a breach of an equality clause or rule.[32]

Finally, Section 39 deals with discrimination involving employees and applicants:

39(1) An employer (A) must not discriminate against a person (B)

(a) in the arrangements A makes for deciding to whom to offer employment;

(b) as to the terms on which A offers B employment;

(c) by not offering B employment.

(2) An employer (A) must not discriminate against an employee of A's (B)

(a) as to B's terms of employment;

(b) in the way A affords B access, or by not affording B access, to opportunities for promotion, transfer or training or for receiving any other benefit, facility or service;

(c) by dismissing B;

(d) by subjecting B to any other detriment.

(3) An employer (A) must not victimise a person (B)

(a) in the arrangements A makes for deciding to whom to offer employment;

(b) as to the terms on which A offers B employment;

(c) by not offering B employment.

(4) An employer (A) must not victimise an employee of A's (B)

(a) as to B's terms of employment;

(b) in the way A affords B access, or by not affording B access, to opportunities for promotion, transfer or training or for any other benefit, facility or service;

(c) by dismissing B;

(d) by subjecting B to any other detriment.

(5) A duty to make reasonable adjustments applies to an employer.

---

32   Ibid., at Section 27.

(6) Subsection (1)(b), so far as relating to sex or pregnancy and maternity, does not apply to a term that relates to pay

(a) unless, were B to accept the offer, an equality clause or rule would have effect in relation to the term, or

(b) if paragraph (a) does not apply, except in so far as making an offer on terms including that term amounts to a contravention of subsection (1)(b) by virtue of section 13, 14 or 18.

(7) In subsections (2)(c) and (4)(c), the reference to dismissing B includes a reference to the termination of B's employment

(a) by the expiry of a period (including a period expiring by reference to an event or circumstance);

(b) by an act of B's (including giving notice) in circumstances such that B is entitled, because of A's conduct, to terminate the employment without notice.

(8) Subsection (7)(a) does not apply if, immediately after the termination, the employment is renewed on the same terms.[33]

Children and Young Persons Acts

In terms of the Children and Young Persons Act 1933, Section 18 deals with restrictions on employment of children:

18(1) Subject to the provisions of this section and of any byelaws made thereunder no child shall be employed

[(a)so long as he is under the age of [fourteen years]]; or

[(aa) to do any work other than light work or;]

(b) before the close of school hours on any day on which he is required to attend school; or

[(c) before seven o'clock in the morning or after seven o'clock in the evening or any day; or]

(d) for more than two hours on any day on which he is required to attend school; or

[(da) for more than twelve hours in any week in which he is required to attend school; or]

(e) for more than two hours on any Sunday; or

(f) …

(g) for more than eight hours or, if he is under the age of fifteen years, for more than five hours in any day

(i) on which he is not required to attend school, and

(ii) which is not a Sunday; or

(h) for more than thirty-five hours or, if he is under the age of fifteen years, for more than twenty-five hours in any week in which he is not required to attend school; or

---

33   Ibid., at Section 39.

(i) for more than four hours in any day without a rest break of one hour; or

(j) at any time in a year unless at that time he has had, or could still have, during a period in the year in which he is not required to attend school, at least two consecutive weeks without employment.]

(2) A local authority may make byelaws with respect to the employment of children, and any such byelaws may distinguish between children of different ages and sexes and between different localities, trades, occupations and circumstances, and may contain provisions

(a) authorising

[(i) the employment [on an occasional basis] of children [aged thirteen years] (notwithstanding anything in paragraph (a) of the last foregoing subsection) by their parents or guardians in light agricultural or horticultural work.]

[(ia) the employment of children aged thirteen years (notwithstanding anything in paragraph (a) of the last foregoing subsection) in categories of light work specified in the byelaw.]

(ii) the employment of children (notwithstanding anything in paragraph (b) of the last foregoing subsection) for not more than one hour before the commencement of school hours on any day on which they are required to attend school;

(b) prohibiting absolutely the employment of children in any specified occupation;

(c) prescribing

(i) the age below which children are not to be employed;

(ii) the number of hours in each day, or in each week, for which, and the times of day at which, they may be employed;

(iii) the intervals to be allowed to them for meals and rest;

(iv) the holidays or half-holidays to be allowed to them;

(v) any other conditions to be observed in relation to their employment;

so, however, that no such byelaws shall modify the restrictions contained in the last foregoing subsection save in so far as is expressly permitted by paragraph (a) of this subsection, and any restriction contained in any such byelaws shall have effect in addition to the said restrictions.

[(2A) In this section

'light work' means work which, on account of the inherent nature of the tasks which it involves and the particular conditions under which they are performed

(a) is not likely to be harmful to the safety, health or development of children; and

(b) is not such as to be harmful to their attendance at school or to their participation in work experience in accordance with section 560 of the Education Act 1996 , or their capacity to benefit from the instruction received or, as the case may be, the experience gained;

'week' means any period of seven consecutive days; and

'year', except in expressions of age, means a period of twelve months beginning with 1st January.]

[(3) Nothing in this section, or in any bylaw made under this section, shall prevent a child from [doing anything]

(a) under the authority of a licence granted under this Part of this Act; or

(b) in a case where by virtue of section 37(3) of the Children and Young Persons Act 1963 no licence under that section is required for him to [do it].][34]

Section 30 defines the meaning of child:

30. [(1)] For the purposes of this Part of this Act and of any byelaws [or regulations] made thereunder

[The expression 'child' means

(a) in relation to England and Wales, a person who is not [over compulsory school age (construed in accordance with section 8 of the Education Act 1996)]

(b) in relation to Scotland, a person who is not for the purposes of the Education (Scotland) Act 1980 over school age; and

(c) in relation to Northern Ireland, a person who is not for the purposes of the Education and Libraries (Northern Ireland) Order 1986 over compulsory school age;] ...[35]

In terms of the Children and Young Persons Act 1963, entitled 'An Act to amend the law relating to children and young persons; and for purposes connected therewith', Section 34 amends the hours of employment:

34. For paragraph (c) of section 18(1) of the principal Act (which prohibits the employment of children before six o'clock in the morning or after eight o'clock in the evening) and for paragraph (c) of section 28(1) of the principal Scottish Act (which prohibits such employment before six o'clock in the morning or after seven o'clock in the evening or at certain times of the year eight o'clock in the evening) there shall be substituted the following paragraph:

'(c)before seven o'clock in the morning or after seven o'clock in the evening on any day ; or'.[36]

Section 37 deals with restriction on persons under 16 taking part in public performances:

37[(1) Subject to the provisions of this section, a child shall not

(a) take part in a performance to which subsection (2) of this section applies, or

(b) otherwise take part in a sport, or work as a model, where payment in respect of his doing so, other than for defraying expenses, is made to him or to another person,]

---

34   Children and Young Persons Act 1933, at Section 18.

35   Ibid., at Section 30.

36   Children and Young Persons Act 1963, at Section 34.

except under the authority of a licence granted by the local authority in whose area he resides or, if he does not reside in Great Britain, by the local authority in whose area the applicant or one of the applicants for the licence resides or has his place of business.

(2) This [subsection] applies to

(a) any performance in connection with which a charge is made (whether for admission or otherwise);

(b) any performance in licensed premises within the meaning of [the Licensing Act 1964] or [the Licensing (Scotland) Act 1976] or in premises in respect of which a club is registered under [the said Act of 1964 or the said Act of 1976];

(c) any broadcast performance;

[[(d) any performance not falling within paragraph (c) above but included in a programme service (within the meaning of the Broadcasting Act 1990);]

(e) any performance recorded (by whatever means) with a view to its use in a broadcast or such a service or in a film intended for public exhibition;]

and a child shall be treated for the purposes of this section as taking part in a performance if he takes the place of a performer in any rehearsal or in any preparation for the recording of the performance.

(3) A licence under this section shall not be required for any child to take part in a performance to which [subsection (2) of] this section applies if [no payment in respect of his taking part in the performance, other than for defraying expenses, is made to him or to another person, and]

(a) in the six months preceding the performance he has not taken part in other performances to which [subsection (2) of] this section applies on more than three days; or

(b) the performance is given under arrangements made by a school (within the meaning of [the Education Act 1996] or the Education (Scotland) Act 1962) or made by a body of persons approved for the purposes of this section by the Secretary of State or by the local authority in whose area the performance takes place …

but the Secretary of State may by regulations made by statutory instrument prescribe conditions to be observed with respect to the hours of work, rest or meals of children taking part in performances as mentioned in paragraph (a) of this subsection.

(4) The power to grant licences under this section shall be exercisable subject to such restrictions and conditions as the Secretary of State may by regulations made by statutory instrument prescribe and a local authority shall not grant a licence for a child to [do anything] unless they are satisfied that he is fit to [do it], that proper provision has been made to secure his health and kind treatment and that, having regard to such provision (if any) as has been or will be made therefor, his education will not suffer; but if they are so satisfied, in the case of an application duly made for a licence under this section which they have power to grant, they shall not refuse to grant the licence.

(5) Regulations under this section may make different provision for different circumstances and may prescribe, among the conditions subject to which a licence is to be granted, conditions requiring the approval of a local authority and may provide for that approval to be given subject to conditions imposed by the authority.

(6) Without prejudice to the generality of the preceding subsection, regulations under this section may prescribe, among the conditions subject to which a licence may be granted, a condition requiring sums earned by the child in respect of whom the licence is granted in [any activity] to which the licence relates to be paid into the county court (or, in Scotland, consigned in the sheriff court) or dealt with in a manner approved by the local authority.

(7) A licence under this section shall specify the times, if any, during which the child in respect of whom it is granted may be absent from school for the purposes authorised by the licence; and for the purposes of the enactments relating to education a child who is so absent during any times so specified shall be deemed to be absent with leave granted by a person authorised in that behalf by the managers, governors or proprietor of the school or, in Scotland, with reasonable excuse.

(8) Any statutory instrument made under this section shall be subject to annulment in pursuance of a resolution of either House of Parliament.[37]

Children Acts

In terms of the Children Act 1972, entitled 'An Act to secure that the minimum age at which children may be employed is not affected by any further change in the school-leaving age', Section 1 defines the minimum age of employment:

1.(2) Accordingly in each of those sections for subsection (1)(a) there shall be substituted the paragraph
'(a) so long as he is under the age of thirteen years';
and in subsection (2) (which allows the general rules in subsection (1) to be modified by local authority bye-laws) for paragraph (a)(i) there shall be substituted the sub-paragraph
'(i) the employment of children under the age of thirteen years (notwithstanding anything in paragraph (a) of the last foregoing subsection) by their parents or guardians in light agricultural or horticultural work'.[38]

In terms of the Children Act 1989, entitled 'An Act to reform the law relating to children; to provide for local authority services for children in need and others; to amend the law with respect to children's homes, community homes, voluntary homes and voluntary organisations; to make provision with respect to fostering,

---

37   Ibid., at Section 37.
38   Children Act 1972, at Section 1.

child minding and day care for young children and adoption; and for connected purposes', Section 1 deals with the welfare of the child:

> 1(1) When a court determines any question with respect to
> (a) the upbringing of a child; or
> (b) the administration of a child's property or the application of any income arising from it,
> the child's welfare shall be the court's paramount consideration.
> (2) In any proceedings in which any question with respect to the upbringing of a child arises, the court shall have regard to the general principle that any delay in determining the question is likely to prejudice the welfare of the child.
> (3) In the circumstances mentioned in subsection (4), a court shall have regard in particular to
> (a) the ascertainable wishes and feelings of the child concerned (considered in the light of his age and understanding);
> (b) his physical, emotional and educational needs;
> (c) the likely effect on him of any change in his circumstances;
> (d) his age, sex, background and any characteristics of his which the court considers relevant;
> (e) any harm which he has suffered or is at risk of suffering;
> (f) how capable each of his parents, and any other person in relation to whom the court considers the question to be relevant, is of meeting his needs;
> (g) the range of powers available to the court under this Act in the proceedings in question.
> (4) The circumstances are that
> (a) the court is considering whether to make, vary or discharge a section 8 order, and the making, variation or discharge of the order is opposed by any party to the proceedings; or
> (b) the court is considering whether to make, vary or discharge [a special guardianship order or] an order under Part IV.
> (5) Where a court is considering whether or not to make one or more orders under this Act with respect to a child, it shall not make the order or any of the orders unless it considers that doing so would be better for the child than making no order at all.[39]

Section 2 deals with parental responsibility for children:

> 2(1) Where a child's father and mother were married to each other at the time of his birth, they shall each have parental responsibility for the child.
> (2) Where a child's father and mother were not married to each other at the time of his birth
> (a) the mother shall have parental responsibility for the child;

---

39   Children Act 1989, at Section 1.

(b) the father [shall have parental responsibility for the child if he has acquired it (and has not ceased to have it)] in accordance with the provisions of this Act.

(3) References in this Act to a child whose father and mother were, or (as the case may be) were not, married to each other at the time of his birth must be read with section 1 of the Family Law Reform Act 1987 (which extends their meaning).

(4) The rule of law that a father is the natural guardian of his legitimate child is abolished.

(5) More than one person may have parental responsibility for the same child at the same time.

(6) A person who has parental responsibility for a child at any time shall not cease to have that responsibility solely because some other person subsequently acquires parental responsibility for the child.

(7) Where more than one person has parental responsibility for a child, each of them may act alone and without the other (or others) in meeting that responsibility; but nothing in this Part shall be taken to affect the operation of any enactment which requires the consent of more than one person in a matter affecting the child.

(8) The fact that a person has parental responsibility for a child shall not entitle him to act in any way which would be incompatible with any order made with respect to the child under this Act.

(9) A person who has parental responsibility for a child may not surrender or transfer any part of that responsibility to another but may arrange for some or all of it to be met by one or more persons acting on his behalf.

(10) The person with whom any such arrangement is made may himself be a person who already has parental responsibility for the child concerned.

(11) The making of any such arrangement shall not affect any liability of the person making it which may arise from any failure to meet any part of his parental responsibility for the child concerned.[40]

In terms of the Children Act 2004, entitled 'An Act to make provision for the establishment of a Children's Commissioner; to make provision about services provided to and for children and young people by local authorities and other persons; to make provision in relation to Wales about advisory and support services relating to family proceedings; to make provision about private fostering, child minding and day care, adoption review panels, the defence of reasonable punishment, the making of grants as respects children and families, child safety orders, the Children's Commissioner for Wales, the publication of material relating to children involved in certain legal proceedings and the disclosure by the Inland Revenue of information relating to children', Section 1 deals with the establishment of the Commissioner:

---

40   Ibid., at Section 2.

1(1) There is to be an office of Children's Commissioner.[41]

Section 2 deals with its functions:

2(1) The Children's Commissioner has the function of promoting awareness of the views and interests of children in England.

(2) The Children's Commissioner may in particular under this section

(a) encourage persons exercising functions or engaged in activities affecting children to take account of their views and interests;

(b) advise the Secretary of State on the views and interests of children;

(c) consider or research the operation of complaints procedures so far as relating to children;

(d) consider or research any other matter relating to the interests of children;

(e) publish a report on any matter considered or researched by him under this section.

(3) The Children's Commissioner is to be concerned in particular under this section with the views and interests of children so far as relating to the following aspects of their well-being

(a) physical and mental health and emotional well-being;

(b) protection from harm and neglect;

(c) education, training and recreation;

(d) the contribution made by them to society;

(e) social and economic well-being.

(4) The Children's Commissioner must take reasonable steps to involve children in the discharge of his function under this section, and in particular to

(a) ensure that children are made aware of his function and how they may communicate with him; and

(b) consult children, and organisations working with children, on the matters he proposes to consider or research under subsection (2)(c) or (d).

(5) Where the Children's Commissioner publishes a report under this section he must, if and to the extent that he considers it appropriate, also publish the report in a version which is suitable for children (or, if the report relates to a particular group of children, for those children).

(6) The Children's Commissioner must for the purposes of subsection (4) have particular regard to groups of children who do not have other adequate means by which they can make their views known.

(7) The Children's Commissioner is not under this section to conduct an investigation of the case of an individual child.

(8) The Children's Commissioner or a person authorised by him may for the purposes of his function under this section at any reasonable time

(a) enter any premises, other than a private dwelling, for the purposes of interviewing any child accommodated or cared for there; and

---

41   Children Act 2004, at Section 1.

(b) if the child consents, interview the child in private.

(9) Any person exercising functions under any enactment must supply the Children's Commissioner with such information in that person's possession relating to those functions as the Children's Commissioner may reasonably request for the purposes of his function under this section (provided that the information is information which that person may, apart from this subsection, lawfully disclose to him).

(10) Where the Children's Commissioner has published a report under this section containing recommendations in respect of any person exercising functions under any enactment, he may require that person to state in writing, within such period as the Children's Commissioner may reasonably require, what action the person has taken or proposes to take in response to the recommendations.

(11) In considering for the purpose of his function under this section what constitutes the interests of children (generally or so far as relating to a particular matter) the Children's Commissioner must have regard to the United Nations Convention on the Rights of the Child.

(12) In subsection (11) the reference to the United Nations Convention on the Rights of the Child is to the Convention on the Rights of the Child adopted by the General Assembly of the United Nations on 20th November 1989, subject to any reservations, objections or interpretative declarations by the United Kingdom for the time being in force.[42]

Inquiries initiated by the Commissioner are covered under Section 3:

3(1) Where the Children's Commissioner considers that the case of an individual child in England raises issues of public policy of relevance to other children, he may hold an inquiry into that case for the purpose of investigating and making recommendations about those issues.

(2) The Children's Commissioner may only conduct an inquiry under this section if he is satisfied that the inquiry would not duplicate work that is the function of another person (having consulted such persons as he considers appropriate).

(3) Before holding an inquiry under this section the Children's Commissioner must consult the Secretary of State.

(4) The Children's Commissioner may, if he thinks fit, hold an inquiry under this section, or any part of it, in private.

(5) As soon as possible after completing an inquiry under this section the Children's Commissioner must

(a) publish a report containing his recommendations; and

(b) send a copy to the Secretary of State.

(6) The report need not identify any individual child if the Children's Commissioner considers that it would be undesirable for the identity of the child to be made public.

42   Ibid., at Section 2.

(7) Where the Children's Commissioner has published a report under this section containing recommendations in respect of any person exercising functions under any enactment, he may require that person to state in writing, within such period as the Children's Commissioner may reasonably require, what action the person has taken or proposes to take in response to the recommendations.

(8) Subsections (2) and (3) of section 250 of the Local Government Act 1972 (c. 70) apply for the purposes of an inquiry held under this section with the substitution for references to the person appointed to hold the inquiry of references to the Children's Commissioner.[43]

Finally, Section 5 deals with the functions of the Children's Commissioner in Wales:

5(1) The Children's Commissioner has the function of promoting awareness of the views and interests of children in Wales, except in so far as relating to any matter falling within the remit of the Children's Commissioner for Wales under section 72B, 73 or 74 of the Care Standards Act 2000 (c. 14).

...

(4) Where the Children's Commissioner considers that the case of an individual child in Wales raises issues of public policy of relevance to other children, other than issues relating to a matter referred to in subsection (1) above, he may hold an inquiry into that case for the purpose of investigating and making recommendations about those issues.[44]

Section 6 deals with the functions of Children's Commissioner in Scotland:

6(1) The Children's Commissioner has the function of promoting awareness of the views and interests of children in Scotland in relation to reserved matters.

...

(4) Where the Children's Commissioner considers that the case of an individual child in Scotland raises issues of public policy of relevance to other children in relation to a reserved matter, he may hold an inquiry into that case for the purpose of investigating and making recommendations about those issues.[45]

Section 7 deals with the functions of the Children's Commissioner in Northern Ireland:

7(1) The Children's Commissioner has the function of promoting awareness of the views and interests of children in Northern Ireland in relation to excepted matters.

---

43 Ibid., at Section 3.
44 Ibid., at Section 5.
45 Ibid., at Section 6.

...

(4) Where the Children's Commissioner considers that the case of an individual child in Northern Ireland raises issues of public policy which are of relevance to other children in relation to an excepted matter, he may hold an inquiry into that case for the purpose of investigating and making recommendations about those issues.[46]

Children (Northern Ireland) Order

Further, in terms of Northern Ireland, the Children (Northern Ireland) Order 1995 specifies general restrictions on the employment of children under Section 135, which states:

135(1) No child shall be employed

(a) so long as he is under the age of 13 years; or

(b) before the close of school hours on any day on which he is required to attend school; or

(c) before seven o'clock in the morning or after seven o'clock in the evening on any day; or

(d) for more than two hours on any day on which he is required to attend school, except in accordance with any statutory provision (including this Part and regulations made under it).

(2) No child shall be employed in any occupation likely to be injurious to his life, limb, health or education, regard being had to his physical condition.

(3) If any education and library board serves on the employer of any child a copy of a certificate signed by a medical practitioner that any specified occupation is likely to be injurious to the life, limb, health or education of the child, the certificate shall be admissible as evidence in any subsequent proceedings against the employer in respect of the employment of the child.

(4) No child shall engage in or be employed in street trading.[47]

Section 136 covers regulations with respect to the employment of children:

136(1) The Department may, with the approval of the Department of Education, make regulations with respect to the employment of children and any such regulations may contain provisions

(a) authorising the employment of children (notwithstanding anything in paragraph (1)(b) of Article 135) for not more than one hour before the commencement of school hours on any day on which they are required to attend school;

(b) specifying the occupations in which children may or may not be employed;

---

46 Ibid., at Section 7.

47 Children (Northern Ireland) Order, at Section 135.

(c) prescribing

(i) the age below which children are not to be employed;

(ii) the number of hours in each day, or in each week, for which, and the times of day at which, they may be employed;

(iii) the intervals to be allowed to them for meals and rest;

(iv) the holidays or half-holidays to be allowed to them;

(v) any other conditions to be observed in relation to their employment.

(2) Except in so far as is expressly permitted by paragraph (1)(a) and (c)(i), regulations under this Article shall not modify the restrictions contained in Article 135, and any restrictions contained in regulations under this Article shall have effect in addition to the restrictions contained in that Article.

(3) Nothing in Article 135 or in regulations under this Article shall prevent a child from taking part in a performance

(a) under the authority of a licence granted under this Part; or

(b) in a case where by virtue of paragraph (3) of Article 137 no licence under that Article is required for him to take part in the performance.[48]

Ireland

Constitution of Ireland

The Constitution of Ireland (Bunreacht Na hEireann) was enacted by the People on 1 July 1937 and came into operation on 29 December 1937. The Preamble of the Constitution of Ireland states:

> In the Name of the Most Holy Trinity, from Whom is all authority and to Whom, as our final end, all actions both of men and States must be referred,
> We, the people of Éire,
> Humbly acknowledging all our obligations to our Divine Lord, Jesus Christ, Who sustained our fathers through centuries of trial,
> Gratefully remembering their heroic and unremitting struggle to regain the rightful independence of our Nation,
> And seeking to promote the common good, with due observance of Prudence, Justice and Charity, so that the dignity and freedom of the individual may be assured, true social order attained, the unity of our country restored, and concord established with other nations,
> Do hereby adopt, enact, and give to ourselves this Constitution.[49]

Fundamental freedoms are guaranteed as personal rights under Article 40:

---

48 Ibid., at Section 136.

49 Constitution of Ireland, Ireland, at the Preamble.

Table 8.2   Employment statistics for Ireland by age, showing underage employment.

Age group	Total			Men			Women		
	Total population	Active population	Activity rate	Total population	Active population	Activity rate	Total population	Active population	Activity rate
Total	4422.1	2236.0	50.6	2206.4	1271.0	57.6	2215.6	965.0	43.6
Total (15+)	3510.2	2224.0	63.4	1739.2	1264.9	72.7	1770.7	959.1	54.2
0–9	631.1	–	–	323.1	–	–	308.0	–	–
10–14	280.9	–	–	144.1	–	–	136.8	–	–
15–19	283.9	69.2	24.4	144.6	37.1	25.7	139.3	32.1	23.0
20–24	334.3	249.6	74.7	165.9	131.1	79.0	168.4	118.5	70.4
25–29	416.7	358.8	86.1	209.4	191.9	91.6	207.2	167.0	80.6
30–34	367.0	307.0	83.7	185.3	172.2	92.9	181.7	134.8	74.2
35–39	342.0	280.5	82.0	173.9	162.6	93.5	168.1	117.9	70.1
40–44	310.2	248.1	80.0	155.8	143.4	92.0	154.4	104.8	67.9
45–49	286.1	230.2	80.5	143.3	130.8	91.3	142.7	99.4	69.7
50–54	257.2	194.0	75.4	129.1	112.1	86.8	128.0	81.9	64.0
55–59	232.0	145.7	62.8	117.0	88.2	75.4	115.0	57.4	49.9
60–64	199.2	94.0	47.2	100.4	60.5	60.3	98.8	33.4	33.8
65–69	148.8	27.0	18.1	73.6	18.7	25.4	75.2	8.3	11.0
70–74	120.8	11.6	9.6	57.5	9.2	16.0	63.3	2.4	3.8
75+	212.0	8.3	3.9	83.4	7.1	8.5	128.6	1.2	0.9

Source: International Labour Organization, Laborsta, 2008.

40.1. All citizens shall, as human persons, be held equal before the law.

This shall not be held to mean that the State shall not in its enactments have due regard to differences of capacity, physical and moral, and of social function.

2(1) Titles of nobility shall not be conferred by the State.

(2) No title of nobility or of honour may be accepted by any citizen except with the prior approval of the Government.

3(1) The State guarantees in its laws to respect, and, as far as practicable, by its laws to defend and vindicate the personal rights of the citizen.

(2) The State shall, in particular, by its laws protect as best it may from unjust attack and, in the case of injustice done, vindicate the life, person, good name, and property rights of every citizen.

(3) The State acknowledges the right to life of the unborn and, with due regard to the equal right to life of the mother, guarantees in its laws to respect, and, as far as practicable, by its laws to defend and vindicate that right.

This subsection shall not limit freedom to travel between the State and another state.

This subsection shall not limit freedom to obtain or make available, in the State, subject to such conditions as may be laid down by law, information relating to services lawfully available in another state.

4(1) No citizen shall be deprived of his personal liberty save in accordance with law.

(2) Upon complaint being made by or on behalf of any person to the High Court or any judge thereof alleging that such person is being unlawfully detained, the High Court and any and every judge thereof to whom such complaint is made shall forthwith enquire into the said complaint and may order the person in whose custody such person is detained to produce the body of such person before the High Court on a named day and to certify in writing the grounds of his detention, and the High Court shall, upon the body of such person being produced before that Court and after giving the person in whose custody he is detained an opportunity of justifying the detention, order the release of such person from such detention unless satisfied that he is being detained in accordance with the law.

(3) Where the body of a person alleged to be unlawfully detained is produced before the High Court in pursuance of an order in that behalf made under this section and that Court is satisfied that such person is being detained in accordance with a law but that such law is invalid having regard to the provisions of this Constitution, the High Court shall refer the question of the validity of such law to the Supreme Court by way of case stated and may, at the time of such reference or at any time thereafter, allow the said person to be at liberty on such bail and subject to such conditions as the High Court shall fix until the Supreme Court has determined the question so referred to it.

(4) The High Court before which the body of a person alleged to be unlawfully detained is to be produced in pursuance of an order in that behalf made under this section shall, if the President of the High Court or, if he is not available, the

senior judge of that Court who is available so directs in respect of any particular case, consist of three judges and shall, in every other case, consist of one judge only.

(5) Nothing in this section, however, shall be invoked to prohibit, control, or interfere with any act of the Defence Forces during the existence of a state of war or armed rebellion.

(6) Provision may be made by law for the refusal of bail by a court to a person charged with a serious offence where it is reasonably considered necessary to prevent the commission of a serious offence by that person.

5. The dwelling of every citizen is inviolable and shall not be forcibly entered save in accordance with law.

6(1) The State guarantees liberty for the exercise of the following rights, subject to public order and morality:

i. The right of the citizens to express freely their convictions and opinions.

The education of public opinion being, however, a matter of suchgrave import to the common good, the State shall endeavour to ensure that organs of public opinion, such as the radio, the press, the cinema, while preserving their rightful liberty of expression, including criticism of Government policy, shall not be used to undermine public order or morality or the authority of the State.

The publication or utterance of blasphemous, seditious, or indecent matter is an offence which shall be punishable in accordance with law.

ii. The right of the citizens to assemble peaceably and without arms.

Provision may be made by law to prevent or control meetings which are determined in accordance with law to be calculated to cause a breach of the peace or to be a danger or nuisance to the general public and to prevent or control meetings in the vicinity of either House of the Oireachtas.

iii. The right of the citizens to form associations and unions.

Laws, however, may be enacted for the regulation and control in the public interest of the exercise of the foregoing right.

(2) Laws regulating the manner in which the right of forming associations and unions and the right of free assembly may be exercised shall contain no political, religious or class discrimination.[50]

Further, the family is protected under Article 41:

41.1(1) The State recognises the Family as the natural primary and fundamental unit group of Society, and as a moral institution possessing inalienable and imprescriptible rights, antecedent and superior to all positive law.

(2) The State, therefore, guarantees to protect the Family in its constitution and authority, as the necessary basis of social order and as indispensable to the welfare of the Nation and the State.

---

50   Ibid., at Article 40.

2(1) In particular, the State recognises that by her life within the home, woman gives to the State a support without which the common good cannot be achieved. (2) The State shall, therefore, endeavour to ensure that mothers shall not be obliged by economic necessity to engage in labour to the neglect of their duties in the home.

3(1) The State pledges itself to guard with special care the institution of Marriage, on which the Family is founded, and to protect it against attack.

(2) A Court designated by law may grant a dissolution of marriage where, but only where, it is satisfied that

i. at the date of the institution of the proceedings, the spouses have lived apart from one another for a period of, or periods amounting to, at least four years during the five years,

ii. there is no reasonable prospect of a reconciliation between the spouses,

iii. such provision as the Court considers proper having regard to the circumstances exists or will be made for the spouses, any children of either or both of them and any other person prescribed by law, and

iv. any further conditions prescribed by law are complied with.

(3) No person whose marriage has been dissolved under the civil law of any other State but is a subsisting valid marriage under the law for the time being in force within the jurisdiction of the Government and Parliament established by this Constitution shall be capable of contracting a valid marriage within that jurisdiction during the lifetime of the other party to the marriage so dissolved.[51]

Finally, the right to education is paramount under Article 42:

42.1. The State acknowledges that the primary and natural educator of the child is the Family and guarantees to respect the inalienable right and duty of parents to provide, according to their means, for the religious and moral, intellectual, physical and social education of their children.

2. Parents shall be free to provide this education in their homes or in private schools or in schools recognised or established by the State.

3(1) The State shall not oblige parents in violation of their conscience and lawful preference to send their children to schools established by the State, or to any particular type of school designated by the State.

(2) The State shall, however, as guardian of the common good, require in view of actual conditions that the children receive a certain minimum education, moral, intellectual and social.

4. The State shall provide for free primary education and shall endeavour to supplement and give reasonable aid to private and corporate educational initiative, and, when the public good requires it, provide other educational facilities or institutions with due regard, however, for the rights of parents, especially in the matter of religious and moral formation.

---

51   Ibid., at Article 41.

5. In exceptional cases, where the parents for physical or moral reasons fail in their duty towards their children, the State as guardian of the common good, by appropriate means shall endeavour to supply the place of the parents, but always with due regard for the natural and imprescriptible rights of the child.[52]

Employment Equality Act

In the fight against discrimination, the Employment Equality Act 1998 outlines the concept of discrimination in Section 6:

6.(1) For the purposes of this Act, discrimination shall be taken to occur where, on any of the grounds in *subsection (2)* (in this Act referred to as 'the discriminatory grounds'), one person is treated less favourably than another is, has been or would be treated.

(2) As between any 2 persons, the discriminatory grounds (and the descriptions of those grounds for the purposes of this Act) are:

(*a*) that one is a woman and the other is a man (in this Act referred to as 'the gender ground'),

(*b*) that they are of different marital status (in this Act referred to as 'the marital status ground'),

(*c*) that one has family status and the other does not (in this Act referred to as 'the family status ground'),

(*d*) that they are of different sexual orientation (in this Act referred to as 'the sexual orientation ground'),

(*e*) that one has a different religious belief from the other, or that one has a religious belief and the other has not (in this Act referred to as 'the religion ground'),

(*f*) that they are of different ages, but subject to *subsection (3)* (in this Act referred to as 'the age ground'),

(*g*) that one is a person with a disability and the other either is not or is a person with a different disability (in this Act referred to as 'the disability ground'),

(*h*) that they are of different race, colour, nationality or ethnic or national origins (in this Act referred to as 'the ground of race'),

(*i*) that one is a member of the traveller community and the other is not (in this Act referred to as 'the traveller community ground').

(3) Where:

(*a*) a person has attained the age of 65 years, or

(*b*) a person has not attained the age of 18 years,

Then … treating that person more favourably or less favourably than another (whatever that other person's age) shall not be regarded as discrimination on the age ground.

---

52   Ibid., at Article 42.

(4) The Minister shall review the operation of this Act, within 2 years of the date of the coming into operation of this section, with a view to assessing whether there is a need to add to the discriminatory grounds set out in this section.[53]

Section 7(1) establishes like work:

7.(1) Subject to *subsection (2)*, for the purposes of this Act, in relation to the work which one person is employed to do, another person shall be regarded as employed to do like work if:

(*a*) both perform the same work under the same or similar conditions, or each is interchangeable with the other in relation to the work,

(*b*) the work performed by one is of a similar nature to that performed by the other and any differences between the workperformed or the conditions under which it is performed by each either are of small importance in relation to the work as a whole or occur with such irregularity as not to be significant to the work as a whole, or

(*c*) the work performed by one is equal in value to the work performed by the other, having regard to such matters as skill, physical or mental requirements, responsibility and working conditions.

...

(3) In any case where:

(*a*) the remuneration received by one person ('the primary worker') is less than the remuneration received by another ('the comparator'), and

(*b*) the work performed by the primary worker is greater in value than the work performed by the comparator, having regard to the matters mentioned in *subsection (1)(c)*,

then, for the purposes of *subsection (1)(c)*, the work performed by the primary worker shall be regarded as equal in value to the work performed by the comparator.[54]

Discrimination by employers is covered under Section 8:

8.(1) In relation to:

(*a*) access to employment,

(*b*) conditions of employment,

(*c*) training or experience for or in relation to employment,

(*d*) promotion or re-grading, or

(*e*) classification of posts,

an employer shall not discriminate against an employee or prospective employee and a provider of agency work shall not discriminate against an agency worker.

...

---

53   Employment Equality Act, Ireland, at Section 6.
54   Ibid., at Section 7.

(5) Without prejudice to the generality of *subsection (1)*, an employer shall be taken to discriminate against an employee or prospective employee in relation to access to employment if the employer discriminates against the employee or prospective employee:

(*a*) in any arrangements the employer makes for the purpose of deciding to whom employment should be offered, or

(*b*) by specifying, in respect of one person or class of persons, entry requirements for employment which are not specified in respect of other persons or classes of persons, where the circumstances in which both such persons or classes would be employed are not materially different.

(6) Without prejudice to the generality of *subsection (1)*, an employer shall be taken to discriminate against an employee or prospective employee in relation to conditions of employment if, on any of the discriminatory grounds, the employer does not offer or afford to that employee or prospective employee or to a class of persons of whom he or she is one:

(*a*) the same terms of employment (other than remuneration and pension rights),

(*b*) the same working conditions, and

(*c*) the same treatment in relation to overtime, shift work, short time, transfers, lay-offs, redundancies, dismissals and disciplinary measures,

as the employer offers or affords to another person or class of persons, where the circumstances in which both such persons or classes are or would be employed are not materially different.

(7) Without prejudice to the generality of subsection (1), an employer shall be taken to discriminate against an employee in relation to training or experience for, or in relation to, employment if, on any of the discriminatory grounds, the employer refuses to offer or afford to that employee the same opportunities or facilities for employment counseling, training (whether on or off the job) and work experience as the employer offers or affords to other employees, where the circumstances in which that employee and those other employees are employed are not materially different.

(8) Without prejudice to the generality of subsection (1), an employer shall be taken to discriminate against an employee in relation to promotion if, on any of the discriminatory grounds:

(a) the employer refuses or deliberately omits to offer or afford the employee access to opportunities for promotion in circumstances in which another eligible and qualified person is offered or afforded such access, or

(b) the employer does not in those circumstances offer or afford the employee access in the same way to those opportunities.[55]

In guarding against discrimination, comparators are necessary as outlined in Section 28:

---

55   Ibid., at Section 8.

28.(1) For the purpose of this Part, 'C' and 'D' represent 2 persons who differ as follows:

(*a*) in relation to the marital status ground, C and D have different marital status;

(*b*) in relation to the family status ground, C has family status and D does not, or *vice versa*;

(*c*) in relation to the sexual orientation ground, C and D are of different sexual orientations;

(*d*) in relation to the religion ground, C and D have different religious beliefs or C has a religious belief and D does not, or *vice versa*;

(*e*) in relation to the age ground, C and D are of different ages;

(*f*) in relation to the disability ground, C is a person with a disability and D is not, or *vice versa*, or C and D are persons with different disabilities;

(g) in relation to the ground of race, C and D differ as to race, colour, nationality or ethnic or national origins or any combination of those factors;

(*h*) in relation to the traveller community ground, C is a member of the traveller community and D is not, or *vice versa*.

(2) In the following provisions of this Part, any reference to C and D which does not apply to a specific discriminatory ground shall be treated as a reference to C and D in the context of each of the discriminatory grounds (other than the gender ground) considered separately.

(3) Any reference in this Act to persons having the same relevant characteristic as C (or as D) shall be construed by reference to the discriminatory ground in relation to which the reference applies or, as the case may be, in relation to each of the discriminatory grounds (other than the gender ground) separately, so that

(*a*) in relation to the marital status ground, the relevant characteristic is having the same marital status as C (or, as the case may be, as D), and

(*b*) in relation to the family status ground, the relevant characteristic is having the same, or the same lack of, family status as C (or, as the case may be, as D),

and so on for each of the other discriminatory grounds.[56]

Entitlement to equal remuneration is covered under Section 29:

29.(1) It shall be a term of the contract under which C is employed that, subject to this Act, C shall at any time be entitled to the same rate of remuneration for the work which C is employed to do as D who, at that or any other relevant time, is employed to do like work by the same or an associated employer.

...

(3) For the purposes of this Part, where D's employer is an associated employer of C's employer, C and D shall not be regarded as employed to do like work

---

56   Ibid., at Section 28.

unless they both have the same or reasonably comparable terms and conditions of employment.

(4) Where a term of a contract of employment or a criterion applied to employees (including C and D):

   (*a*) applies to all employees of a particular employer or to a particular class of such employees (including C and D),

   (*b*) is such that the remuneration of those who fulfil the term or criterion is different from that of those who do not,

   (*c*) is such that the proportion of employees who can fulfil the term or criterion is substantially smaller in the case of the employees having the same relevant characteristic as C when compared with the employees having the same relevant characteristic as D, and

   (*d*) cannot be justified as being reasonable in all the circumstances of the case,

then, for the purposes of *subsection (1)*, C and D shall each be treated as fulfilling or, as the case may be, as not fulfilling the term or criterion, whichever results in the higher remuneration.

(5) Subject to *subsection (4)*, nothing in this Part shall prevent an employer from paying, on grounds other than the discriminatory grounds, different rates of remuneration to different employees.[57]

An equality clause is outlined under Section 30:

30.(1) If and so far as the terms of a contract of employment do not include (expressly or by reference to a collective agreement or otherwise) a non-discriminatory equality clause, they shall be taken to include one.

(2) A non-discriminatory equality clause is a provision relating to the terms of a contract of employment, other than a term relating to remuneration or pension rights, which has the effect that if:

   (*a*) C is employed in circumstances where the work done by C is not materially different from that done by D in the same employment, and

   (*b*) at any time C's contract of employment would (but for the non-discriminatory equality clause):

      (i) contain a term which is or becomes less favourable to C than a term of a similar kind in D's contract of employment, or

      (ii) not include a term corresponding to a term in D's contract of employment which benefits D,

then the terms of C's contract of employment shall be treated as modified so that the term in question is not less favourable to C or, as the case may be, so that they include a similar term benefiting C.

(3) A non-discriminatory equality clause shall not operate in relation to a difference between C's contract of employment and D's contract of employment

---

57   Ibid., at Section 29.

if the employer proves that the difference is genuinely based on grounds which are not among those specified in *paragraphs (a) to (h) of section 28(1)*.[58]

Indirect discrimination is covered in Section 31:

31.(1) Where a provision (whether in the nature of a requirement, practice or otherwise) relating to employment:

(*a*) applies to all the employees or prospective employees of a particular employer who include C and D or, as the case may be, to a particular class of those employees or prospective employees which includes C and D,

(*b*) operates to the disadvantage of C, as compared with D, in relation to any of the matters specified in *paragraphs (a) to (e) of section 8(1)*,

(*c*) in practice can be complied with by a substantially smaller proportion of the employees or prospective employees having the same relevant characteristic as C when compared with the employees or prospective employees having the same relevant characteristic as D, and

(*d*) cannot be justified as being reasonable in all the circumstances of the case,

then … for the purposes of this Act the employer shall be regarded as discriminating against C, contrary to *section 8*, on whichever of the discriminatory grounds gives rise to the relevant characteristics referred to in *paragraph (c)*.[59]

Harassment in the workplace is covered under Section 32:

32.(1) If, at a place where C is employed (in this section referred to as 'the workplace'), or otherwise in the course of C's employment, another individual ('E') harasses C by reference to the relevant characteristic of C and:

(*a*) C and E are both employed at that place or by the same employer,

(*b*) E is C's employer, or

(*c*) E is a client, customer or other business contact of C's employer and the circumstances of the harassment are such that C's employer ought reasonably to have taken steps to prevent it,

then, for the purposes of this Act, the harassment constitutes discrimination by C's employer, in relation to C's conditions of employment, on whichever discriminatory ground is relevant to persons having the same relevant characteristic as C.

(6) If, as a result of any act or conduct of E another person ('F') who is C's employer would, apart from this subsection, be regarded … as discriminating against C, it shall be a defence for F to prove that F took such steps as are reasonably practicable:

---

58   Ibid., at Section 30.
59   Ibid., at Section 31.

(*a*) ... to prevent C being treated differently in the workplace or otherwise in the course of C's employment and, if and so far as any such treatment has occurred, to reverse the effects of it, and

(*b*) ... to prevent E from harassing C (or any class of persons of whom C is one).[60]

Positive action is permitted as contained in Section 33:

33.(1) Nothing in this Part or *Part II* shall prevent the taking of such measures as are specified in *subsection (2)* in order to facilitate the integration into employment, either generally or in particular areas or a particular workplace, of:

(*a*) persons who have attained the age of 50 years,

(*b*) persons with a disability or any class or description of such persons, or

(*c*) members of the traveller community.

(2) The measures mentioned in *subsection (1)* are those intended to reduce or eliminate the effects of discrimination against any of the persons referred to in *paragraphs (a)* to *(c)* of that subsection.

(3) Nothing in this Part or *Part II* shall render unlawful the provision, by or on behalf of the State, of training or work experience for a disadvantaged group of persons if the Minister certifies that, in the absence of the provision in question, it is unlikely that that disadvantaged group would receive similar training or work experience.[61]

The functions of the Equality Authority are outlined in Section 39:

39. The Authority shall have, in addition to the functions assigned to it by any other provision of this Act or of any other Act, the following general functions:

(*a*) to work towards the elimination of discrimination in relation to employment;

(*b*) to promote equality of opportunity in relation to the matters to which this Act applies.[62]

The forum for seeking redress is covered under Section 77:

77.(1) A person who claims:

(*a*) to have been discriminated against by another in contravention of this Act,

---

60   Ibid., at Section 32.
61   Ibid., at Section 33.
62   Ibid., at Section 39.

(*b*) not to be receiving remuneration in accordance with an equal remuneration term,

(*c*) not to be receiving a benefit under an equality clause, or

(*d*) to have been penalized in circumstances amounting to victimization,

may, subject to *subsections (2)* to *(8)*, seek redress by referring the case to the Director.

(2) If a person claims to have been dismissed:

(*a*) in circumstances amounting to discrimination by another in contravention of this Act, or

(*b*) in circumstances amounting to victimization,

then, subject to *subsection (3)*, a claim for redress for the dismissal may be brought to the Labour Court and shall not be brought to the Director.

(3) If the grounds for such a claim as is referred to in *subsection (1)* or *(2)* arise:

(*a*) under *Part III*, or

(*b*) in any other circumstances (including circumstances amounting to victimization) to which the Equal Pay Directive or the Equal Treatment Directive is relevant,

then ... the person making the claim may seek redress by referring the case to the Circuit Court, instead of referring it to the Director under *subsection (1)* or, as the case may be, to the Labour Court under *subsection (2)*.

(4) In this Part, in relation to a case referred under any provision of this section:

(*a*) 'the complainant' means the person by whom it is referred, and

(*b*) 'the respondent' means the person who is alleged to have discriminated against the complainant or, as the case may be, who is responsible for providing the remuneration to which the equal remuneration term relates or who is responsible for providing the benefit under the equality clause or who is alleged to be responsible for the victimization.[63]

Enforcement of determinations, decisions and mediated settlements is outlined under Section 91:

91.(1) If an employer or any other person who is bound by the terms of:

(*a*) a final determination of the Labour Court under this Part, or

(*b*) a final decision of the Director under this Part,

fails to comply with the terms of the determination or decision then, on an application under this section, the Circuit Court shall make, subject to *section 93*, an order directing the person affected (that is to say, the employer or other person concerned) to carry out the determination or decision in accordance with its terms.

(2) If an employer or the person who is a party to a settlement ... fails to give effect, in whole or in part, to the terms of the settlement, then, on an application under this section, the Circuit Court may make an order directing the person

---

63   Ibid., at Section 77.

affected (that is to say, the employer or the person who is a party to the settlement) to carry out those terms or, as the case may be, the part of those terms to which the application relates; but the Circuit Court shall not, by virtue of this subsection, direct any person to pay any sum or do any other thing which (had the matter been dealt with otherwise than by mediation) could not have been provided for by way of redress …

(3) An application under this section may not be made before the expiry of:

(*a*) in the case of a determination or decision, the period within which an appeal might be brought against the determination or decision, and

(*b*) in the case of a settlement reached as a result of mediation, 42 days from the date of the written record of the settlement.

(4) An application under this section may be made:

(*a*) by the complainant, or

(*b*) in a case where the Authority is not the complainant, then, by the Authority with the consent of the complainant if the Authority considers that the determination, decision or settlement is unlikely to be implemented without its intervention.

(5) On an application under this section, the Circuit Court shall exercise its functions under *subsection (1)* or *(2)* on being satisfied:

(*a*) of the existence and terms of the determination, decision or settlement, and

(*b*) of the failure by the person affected to comply with those terms.

(6) For the purposes of this section, a determination or decision is final if no appeal lies from it under this Part or if the time for bringing an appeal has expired and either:

(*a*) no appeal has been brought, or

(*b*) any appeal which was brought has been abandoned.

(7) Without prejudice to the power of the Circuit Court to make an order for costs in favour of the complainant or the person affected, where an application is made by the Authority by virtue of *subsection (4)(b)*, the costs of the Authority may be awarded by the Circuit Court.

(8) The jurisdiction conferred on the Circuit Court by this section shall be exercised by the judge for the time being assigned to the circuit where the respondent ordinarily resides or carries on any profession, business or occupation.[64]

Finally, compensation in lieu of reinstatement or reengagement is outlined under Section 93:

93.(1) On an application under *section 91* which relates to a determination requiring an employer to re-instate or re-engage an employee, the Circuit Court may, if in all the circumstances it considers it appropriate to do so, instead of

---

64   Ibid., at Section 91.

making an order under *subsection (1)* of that section, make a compensation order under this section.

(2) A compensation order under this section is an order directing the employer (*in lieu* of re-instatement or re-engagement) to pay compensation to the employee.

(3) The maximum amount of compensation which may be ordered under this section is an amount equal to 104 times the amount of the employee's weekly remuneration at the rate which the employee was receiving at the date of the reference of the case under *section 77* or would have received at that date but for the discrimination in question.[65]

Equal Status Act

In the fight against discrimination, the Equal Status Act 2000 outlines discrimination in Section 3:

3.(1) For the purposes of this Act, discrimination shall be taken to occur where:

(a) on any of the grounds specified in subsection (2) (in this Act referred to as 'the discriminatory grounds') which exists at present or previously existed but no longer exists or may exist in the future, or which is imputed to the person concerned, a person is treated less favourably than another person is, has been or would be treated,

(b)(i) a person who is associated with another person is treated, by virtue of that association, less favourably than a person who is not so associated is, has been or would be treated, and

(ii) similar treatment of that person on any of the discriminatory grounds would, by virtue of paragraph (a), constitute discrimination,

or

(c)(i) a person is in a category of persons who share a common characteristic by reason of which discrimination may, by virtue of paragraph (a), occur in respect of those persons,

(ii) the person is obliged by the provider of a service … to comply with a condition (whether in the nature of a requirement, practice or otherwise) but is unable to do so,

(iii) substantially more people outside the category than within it are able to comply with the condition, and

(iv) the obligation to comply with the condition cannot be justified as being reasonable in all the circumstances of the case.

(2) As between any two persons, the discriminatory grounds (and the descriptions of those grounds for the purposes of this Act) are:

(*a*) that one is male and the other is female (the 'gender ground'),

(*b*) that they are of different marital status (the 'marital status ground'),

---

65   Ibid., at Section 93.

(*c*) that one has family status and the other does not or that one has a different family status from the other (the 'family status ground'),

(*d*) that they are of different sexual orientation (the 'sexual orientation ground'),

(*e*) that one has a different religious belief from the other, or that one has a religious belief and the other has not (the 'religion ground'),

(*f*) that they are of different ages (the 'age ground'),

(*g*) that one is a person with a disability and the other either is not or is a person with a different disability (the 'disability ground'),

(*h*) that they are of different race, colour, nationality or ethnic or national origins (the 'ground of race'),

(*i*) that one is a member of the traveller community and the other is not (the 'traveller community ground'),

(*j*) that one:

(i) has in good faith applied for any determination or redress provided for in *Part II* or *III*,

(ii) has attended as a witness before the Authority, the Director or a court in connection with any inquiry or proceedings under this Act,

(iii) has given evidence in any criminal proceedings under this Act,

(iv) has opposed by lawful means an act which is unlawful under this Act, or

(v) has given notice of an intention to take any of the actions specified in *subparagraphs (i)* to *(iv)*,

and the other has not (the 'victimization ground').[66]

Certain measures or activities are not prohibited under Section 14:

14. Nothing in this Act shall be construed as prohibiting:

(*a*) the taking of any action that is required by or under:

(i) any enactment or order of a court,

(ii) any act done or measure adopted by the European Union, by the European Communities or institutions thereof or by bodies competent under the Treaties establishing the European Communities, or

(iii) any convention or other instrument imposing an international obligation on the State,

or

(*b*) preferential treatment or the taking of positive measures which are *bona fide* intended to:

(i) promote equality of opportunity for persons who are, in relation to other persons, disadvantaged or who have been or are likely to be unable to avail themselves of the same opportunities as those other persons, or

---

66   Equal Status Act, Ireland, at Section 3.

(ii) cater for the special needs of persons, or a category of persons, who, because of their circumstances, may require facilities, arrangements, services or assistance not required by persons who do not have those special needs.[67]

Further, certain activities are not considered discrimination under Section 15:

15.(1) For greater certainty, nothing in this Act prohibiting discrimination shall be construed as requiring a person to dispose of goods or premises, or to provide services or accommodation or services and amenities related to accommodation, to another person ('the customer') in circumstances which would lead a reasonable individual having the responsibility, knowledge and experience of the person to the belief, on grounds other than discriminatory grounds, that the disposal of the goods or premises or the provision of the services or accommodation or the services and amenities related to accommodation, as the case may be, to the customer would produce a substantial risk of criminal or disorderly conduct or behaviour or damage to property at or in the vicinity of the place in which the goods or services are sought or the premises or accommodation are located.[68]

Redress in respect of prohibited grounds is covered under Section 21:

21.(1) A person who claims that prohibited conduct has been directed against him or her may, subject to this section, seek redress by referring the case to the Director.
(2) Before seeking redress under this section the complainant:
(*a*) shall, within 2 months after the prohibited conducted is alleged to have occurred, or, where more than one incident of prohibited conduct is alleged to have occurred, within 2 months after the last such occurrence, notify the respondent in writing of:
(i) the nature of the allegation,
(ii) the complainant's intention, if not satisfied with the respondent's response to the allegation, to seek redress by referring the case to the Director, and
(*b*) may in that notification, with a view to assisting the complainant in deciding whether to refer the case to the Director, question the respondent in writing so as to obtain material information and the respondent may, if the respondent so wishes, reply to any such questions.
(3) If, on application by the complainant, the Director is satisfied:
(*a*) that exceptional circumstances prevented the complainant from notifying the respondent in accordance with *subsection (2)*, and
(*b*) that it is just and equitable, having regard to the nature of the alleged conduct and to any other relevant circumstances, that the period for doing

---

67   Ibid., at Section 14.
68   Ibid., at Section 15.

so should be extended beyond the period of 2 months provided for in that subsection,

the Director may direct that, in relation to that case, *subsection (2)* shall have effect as if for the reference to 2 months there were substituted a reference to such period not exceeding 4 months as is specified in the direction; and where such a direction is given, this Part shall have effect accordingly.

(4) The Director shall not investigate a case unless he or she is satisfied either that the respondent has replied to the notification or that at least one month has elapsed after it was sent to the respondent.

(5) The Minister may by regulations prescribe the form to be used by a complainant and respondent for the purposes of *subsection (2)*.

(6) Subject to subsection (7), a claim for redress in respect of prohibited conduct may not be referred under this section after the end of the period of 6 months from the date of the occurrence of the prohibited conduct to which the case relates or, as the case may be, the date of its most recent occurrence.

(7) If, on application by the complainant, the Director is satisfied that exceptional circumstances prevented the complainant's case from being referred within the time limit specified in subsection (6):

(a) the Director may direct that, in relation to that case, subsection (6) shall have effect as if for the reference to a period of 6 months there were substituted a reference to such period not exceeding 12 months as is specified in the direction, and

(b) where such a direction is given, this Part shall have effect accordingly.

(8) Information is material information for the purposes of this section if it is:

(a) information as to the respondent's reasons for doing or omitting to do any relevant act and as to any practices or procedures material to any such act,

(b) information, other than confidential information, about the treatment of other persons who stand in relation to the respondent in the same or a similar position as the complainant, or

(c) other information which is not confidential information and which, in the circumstances of the case in question, it is reasonable for the complainant to require.

(9) In subsection (8) 'confidential information' means any information which relates to a particular individual, which can be identified as so relating and to the disclosure of which that individual does not agree.[69]

Protection of Young Persons (Employment) Act

The Protection of Young Persons (Employment) Act, entitled 'An Act to revise and extend the law relating to the Protection of Young Persons in Employment and to enable effect to be given to Council Directive No. 94/33/EC of 22 June 1994 on the Protection of Young People at Work (other than Articles 6 and 7) and for those

---

69   Ibid., at Section 21.

purposes to repeal the Protection of Young Persons (Employment) Act, 1977, and certain provisions of the Conditions of Employment Act, 1936, and to provide for related matters', was enacted on 26 June 1996. Section 1 provides definitions, particularly that of child, employee and young persons:

> 1(1) In this Act
>
> ...
>
> '**child**' means a person who is under 16 years of age or the school-leaving age, whichever is the higher;
>
> ...
>
> '**employee**' means a child or a young person who has entered into or works under (or, where the employment has ceased, entered into or worked under) a contract of employment and references, in relation to an employer, to an employee shall be construed as references to an employee employed by that employer; and for the purposes of this Act, a person holding office under, or in the service of, the State (including a member of the Garda Síochána or the Defence Forces) or otherwise as a civil servant, within the meaning of the Civil Service Regulation Act, 1956, shall be deemed to be an employee employed by the State or Government, as the case may be, and an officer or servant of a local authority for the purposes of the Local Government Act, 1941, a harbour authority, a health board or a vocational education committee shall be deemed to be an employee employed by the authority, board or committee, as the case may be;
>
> ...
>
> '**young person**' means a person who has reached 16 years of age or the school-leaving age (whichever is higher) but is less than 18 years of age.[70]

Section 3 constrains child employment:

> 3(1)Subject to this section and *section 9*, an employer shall not employ a child to do work.
> (2) The Minister may, by licence, authorise in individual cases, the employment of a child in cultural, artistic, sports or advertising activities which are not likely to be harmful to the safety, health or development of the child and which are not likely to interfere with the child's attendance at school, vocational guidance or training programmes or capacity to benefit from the instruction received.
> (3) The Minister may, by regulations, authorise the employment of children over the age of 13 years in cultural, artistic, sports or advertising activities which are not harmful to the safety, health or development of children and which are not likely to interfere with their attendance at school, vocational guidance or training programmes or capacity to benefit from the instruction received.

---

70   Protection of Young Persons (Employment) Act, at Section 1.

(4) An employer may employ a child who is over the age of 14 years to do light work during any period outside the school term:
Provided that

(*a*) the hours of work do not exceed 7 hours in any day or 35 hours in any week,

(*b*) the work is not harmful to the safety, health and development of the child, and

(*c*) during the period of the summer holidays, the child does not do any work for a period of at least 21 days.

(5) An employer may employ a child who is over the age of 15 years to do light work during school term time, provided that the hours of work do not exceed 8 hours in any week.

(6) Subject to *subsection (7)*, an employer may employ a child who is over the age of 14 years and who is a full-time student at an institute of secondary education pursuant to any arrangements made or approved of by the Minister for Education as part of a programme of work experience or educational programme:

Provided that the hours of work do not exceed 8 hours in any day or 40 hours in any week.

(7) The Minister may, after consultation with the Minister for Education and such other interested parties as the Minister sees fit, by regulations, make exemptions from *subsection (6)* in relation to the hours of work of children participating in a work experience or training programme approved by the Minister for Education under *subsection (6)*.

(8) An employer may employ a child over the age of 15 years to participate in a training or work experience programme pursuant to arrangements made or approved of by the Minister or FÁS – the Employment and Training Authority, provided that the hours of work do not exceed 8 hours in any day or 40 hours in any week.

(9) Whenever the Minister grants a licence under *subsection (2)* or makes regulations under *subsection (3)* or *(7)*, the Minister may attach to such licence or provide in such regulations such conditions as the Minister sees fit.

(10) An employer may retain in his or her employment any child of 15 years of age who was in his or her employment immediately before the commencement of this section:

Provided that the hours of work do not exceed 7 hours in any day or 35 hours in any week.

(11) An employer who contravenes *subsection (1)* shall be guilty of an offence.[71]

Further, Section 4 limits employment of children:

4(1) An employer shall not employ any child on any work between 8 p.m. on any one day and 8 a.m. on the following day.

---

71   Ibid., at Section 3.

(2) Subject to *subsection (3)*, an employer shall ensure that an employee who is a child receives a minimum rest period of 14 consecutive hours in each period of 24 hours.

(3) The minimum consecutive hours of rest in each period of 24 hours specified in *subsection (2)* may be interrupted by an employer in the case of a child employed on activities that do not extend beyond 2 hours in each day or are separated, exclusive of breaks, over the day, provided that, in each period of 24 hours, the child receives a minimum rest period of 14 hours.

(4) An employer shall ensure that an employee who is a child receives, in any period of 7 days, a minimum rest period of 2 days which shall as far as is practicable be consecutive.

(5) The minimum period of rest during each period of 7 days specified in *subsection (4)* may be interrupted by an employer in the case of a child employed on activities that do not extend beyond 2 hours in each day or are separated, exclusive of breaks, over the day, provided that, in each period of 7 days, the cumulative rest period is 2 days.

(6) The Minister may, by regulations, reduce the minimum period of rest specified in *subsection (4)* to 36 consecutive hours in respect of any class of employees or class of work where in the opinion of the Minister this is justified for technical or organisational reasons.

(7) Whenever the Minister makes regulations under *subsection (6)*, the Minister may provide in such regulations such conditions as the Minister sees fit.

(8) An employer shall not permit a child employed by him or her to do for him or her any work for any period exceeding 4 hours without a break of at least 30 consecutive minutes.

(9) A child shall not be entitled to be paid in respect of the break specified in *subsection (8)*.

(10) An employer who contravenes *subsection (1)*, *(2)*, *(4)* or *(8)* shall be guilty of an offence.[72]

In addition, Section 6 sets limits on the employment of young persons:

6(1) An employer shall not employ a young person on any work except where, subject to this section and *sections 7, 8* and *9*, the employer

(*a*) does not require or permit the young person to work for more than 8 hours in any day or 40 hours in any week,

(*b*) does not require or permit the young person to work

(i) between 10 p.m. on any one day and 6 a.m. on the following day, or

(ii) between 11 p.m. on any one day (provided the day is not before a school day during a school term where such young person is attending school) and 7 a.m. on the following day, where the Minister is satisfied, following consultation with such representatives of employers and representatives of

---

72   Ibid., at Section 4.

employees as the Minister considers appropriate, that there are exceptional circumstances affecting a particular branch of activity or a particular area of work as may be prescribed,

(*c*) ensures that the young person receives a minimum rest period of 12 consecutive hours in each period of 24 hours,

(*d*) ensures that the young person receives in any period of 7 days a minimum rest period of 2 days which shall, as far as is practicable, be consecutive, and

(*e*) does not require or permit the young person to do for him or her any work for any period exceeding 4½ hours without a break of at least 30 consecutive minutes.

(2) The minimum consecutive hours of rest in each period of 24 hours specified in *subsection (1)(c)* may be interrupted by an employer in the case of a young person employed on activities that do not extend beyond 2 hours in each day or are separated, exclusive of breaks, over the day provided that, in each period of 24 hours, the young person receives a minimum rest period of 12 hours.

(3) The minimum periods of rest during each period of 7 days specified in *subsection (1)(d)* may be interrupted by an employer in the case of a young person employed on activities that do not extend beyond 2 hours in each day or are separated, exclusive of breaks, over the day provided that, in each period of 7 days, the cumulative rest period is 2 days.

(4) The minimum periods of rest in each period of 24 hours and each period of 7 days specified in *subsection (1)(c)* and *(d)* shall not apply to a young person who is employed in the shipping or fishing sectors:

Provided that

(*a*) there are objective grounds justifying the non-application of the provisions;

(*b*) such young persons receive appropriate compensatory rest times at some time during each period of 24 hours and each period of 7 days, and

(*c*) the trade union or representative of the young person isconsulted.

(5) The limitations on hours of work and on night work specified in *subsection (1)(a)* and *(b)*, and the minimum periods of rest specified in *subsection (1)(c)* and *(d)* shall not apply to young persons who are members of the Defence Forces when they are

(*a*) on active service within the meaning of section 5 of the Defence Act, 1954, or deemed to be on active service, within the meaning of section 4 (1) of the Defence (Amendment) (No. 2) Act, 1960;

(*b*) engaged in action in the course of operational duties at sea;

(*c*) engaged in operations in aid of the civil power; or

(*d*) engaged in training directly associated with any of the aforesaid activities:

Provided that such young persons are allowed equivalent compensatory rest times within 3 weeks of having ceased to engage in the aforesaid activities.

(6) A young person shall not be entitled to be paid in respect of the break specified in *subsection (1)(e)*.

(7) An employer who contravenes *subsection (1)* shall be guilty of an offence.[73]

Duties of employers are outlined in Section 5:

5(1) Subject to *section 9*, any employer who employs a young person or child to work for him or her shall

(*a*) before employing the young person or child, require the production of a copy of the birth certificate of, or other satisfactory evidence of the age of, the young person or child, as the case may be,

(*b*) before employing a child, obtain the written permission of the parent or guardian of the child, and

(*c*) maintain a register, or other satisfactory record, containing, in relation to every young person or child employed by him or her, the following particulars

(i) the full name of the young person or child,

(ii) the date of birth of the young person or child,

(iii) the time the young person or child commences work each day,

(iv) the time the young person or child finishes work each day,

(v) the rate of wages or salary paid to the young person or child for his or her normal working hours each day, week, month or year, as the case may be, and

(vi) the total amount paid to each young person or child by way of wages or salary.

(2) An employer who fails to comply with the provisions of this section and the parent or guardian of a young person or child who aids or abets an employer in the contravention of this section shall be guilty of an offence.[74]

Section 10 prohibits double work:

10(1) Subject to *section 9*, an employer shall not permit an employee to do for him or her any form of work on any day on which the employee has done any form of work for any other employer, except where the aggregate of the periods for which the employee does work for such employers on that day does not exceed the period for which such employee could lawfully be employed to do work for one employer on that day.

(2) Whenever an employer employs an employee in contravention of this section, the employer shall be guilty of an offence and the employee, if he or she is a young person, shall also be guilty of an offence.

(3) The parent or guardian of an employee who aids or abets an employer in the contravention of this section shall be guilty of an offence.

(4) Whenever an employer is prosecuted for an offence under this section it shall be a defence for him or her to prove either that he or she did not know, or could

73 Ibid., at Section 6.
74 Ibid., at Section 5.

not by reasonable enquiry have known, that the employee had done work for any other employer on the day in respect of which the prosecution is brought or that he or she did not know, or could not by reasonable enquiry have known, that the aggregate of the periods for which the employee did work on that day exceeded the period for which he or she could lawfully be employed to do work for one employer on that day.[75]

There is protection under Section 17 for children refusing to breach the Act:

17. An employer shall not penalise an employee for having in good faith opposed by lawful means an act which is unlawful under this Act.[76]

Further, Section 18 ensures that parents may bring a complaint:

18(1) The parent or guardian of a child or young person may present a complaint to a rights commissioner that the employer of the child or young person has contravened section 13 or 17 in relation to the child or young person.

(2) Where a complaint under *subsection (1)* is made, the rights commissioner shall give the parties an opportunity to be heard by the commissioner and to present to the commissioner any evidence relevant to the complaint, shall give a recommendation in writing in relation to it and shall communicate the recommendation to the parties.

(3) A recommendation of a rights commissioner under *subsection (2)* shall do one or more of the following

(*a*) declare that the complaint was or, as the case may be, was not well founded,

(*b*) order the employer to take a specific course of action,

(*c*) order the employer to pay to the employee compensation of such amount (if any) as is just and equitable having regard to all the circumstances, and the references in the foregoing paragraphs to an employer shall be construed, in a case where ownership of the business of the employer changes after a contravention to which the complaint relates, as references to the person who, by virtue of the change, becomes entitled to such ownership.

(4) A rights commissioner shall not entertain a complaint under this section unless it is presented to him within the period of 6 months beginning on the date of the contravention to which the complaint relates or (in a case where the rights commissioner is satisfied that exceptional circumstances prevented the presentation of the complaint within the period aforesaid) such further period not exceeding 6 months as the rights commissioner considers reasonable.

---

75   Ibid., at Section 10.
76   Ibid., at Section 17.

(5)(*a*) A complaint shall be presented by giving notice thereof in writing to a rights commissioner and the notice shall contain such particulars and be in such form as may be specified from time to time by the Minister.

(*b*) A copy of a notice under *paragraph (a)* shall be given to the other party concerned by the rights commissioner concerned.

(6) Proceedings under this section before a rights commissioner shall be conducted otherwise than in public.

(7) A rights commissioner shall furnish the Tribunal with a copy of any recommendation given by the commissioner under *subsection (2)*.

(8) The Minister may by regulations

(*a*) provide for any matters relating to proceedings under this section that the Minister considers appropriate, and

(*b*) amend *paragraph (c)* of *subsection (3)* so as to vary the maximum amount of the compensation provided for in that paragraph, and this section shall have effect in accordance with the provisions of any regulations under this paragraph for the time being in force.[77]

Finally, penalties are provided for under Section 25:

25(1) A person guilty of an offence under this Act shall be liable on summary conviction to a fine not exceeding £1,500.

(2) Where a person after conviction for an offence under this Act continues to contravene the provision concerned, the person shall be guilty of an offence on every day on which the contravention continues and for each such offence shall be liable to a fine on summary conviction not exceeding £250.[78]

Ireland has ratified the Worst Forms of Child Labour Convention, 1999 (No. 182) (C. 182) in 1999, and has ratified the Minimum Age Convention, 1973 (No. 138) (C. 138) in 1978.

Conclusion

Children are vulnerable members of society and therefore require the utmost protection; their inexperience and immaturity require the prevention of their exploitation. The protection of child rights and redressing child inequality are a responsibility shared by all aspects of government stakeholders in discrimination analysis, planning and training. The increased participation of all groups, for the sake of our children, at decision-making levels in conflict prevention, mediation and resolution, is vital, as shown in *Little Angels*.

---

77   Ibid., at Section 18.
78   Ibid., at Section 25.

Chapter 9
Little Angels in the European Union

Introduction

In the quest for respect for our children and in the fight against child discrimination in *Little Angels*, this chapter will examine efforts against child discrimination in the European Union (EU). As well as examining the European Court of Justice, it will review the European Union treaties from their inception, as well as other important legislation, namely the Treaty of Paris, the Treaty of Rome, the Maastricht Treaty, the Treaty of Amsterdam, the Treaty Establishing a Constitution for Europe and the Charter of Fundamental Rights of the European Union, the Treaty of Lisbon, the European Convention for the Protection of Human Rights and Fundamental Freedoms (ECHR), and the European Social Charter. Finally, important European Council legislation affecting child discrimination will be analyzed, namely Council Decision 2000/750/EC establishing a Community action programme to combat discrimination (2001 to 2006); Council Directive 2000/78/EC establishing a general framework for equal treatment in employment and occupation; and especially important for children, Council Directive 1994/33/EC of 22 June 1994 on the protection of young people at work.

Legislation

Initially, many centuries ago, Europe was united within the Roman Empire. Throughout its history, the European continent has naturally been divided by ethnicity, language and religion, and national ambitions and self-interest have been the predominant political forces throughout the twentieth century. However, with the two World Wars and the threat of the Cold War, European integration by peaceful methods was seriously reconsidered as an alternative to the independent aggressive nation state; with democratic governments reinstated in liberated Europe in the post-war era, the restructuring of the region began. A Congress of Europe was held in the Hague in 1948, bringing together leading figures from France, Britain, the Netherlands, Belgium, Germany, Italy and elsewhere. Britain's Prime Minister Churchill referred to the idea of a setting up of 'a kind of United States of Europe', which made a powerful impact.[1] Political integration is the peaceful creation of a larger political unit out of several separate ones, which voluntarily

---

1   Nicoll, William and Salmon, Trevor, *Understanding the New European Community*, Prentice Hall, Exeter, 1994, p. 11.

give up some powers to a central authority and renounce the use of force toward the other units.[2]

Treaty of Paris

To escape national rivalries and move toward integration, the European Community was first established under the Coal and Steel Community, also known as the Treaty of Paris, signed on 18 April 1951, which entered into force on 23 July 1952. It removed the coal and steel industries from full national control to a supranational stewardship; the High Authority, which it created, was presided over by Jean Monnet and comprised delegates from the Member States, making decisions in consultation with the Assembly. The Preamble of the Treaty of Paris states:

> Considering that world peace can be safeguarded only by creative efforts commensurate with the dangers that threaten it,
> Convinced that the contribution which an organised and vital Europe can make to civilisation is indispensable to the maintenance of peaceful relations,
> Recognising that Europe can be built only through practical achievements which will first of all create real solidarity, and through the establishment of common bases for economic development,
> Anxious to help, by expanding their basic production, to raise the standard of living and further the works of peace,
> Resolved to substitute for age-old rivalries the merging of their essential interests; to create by establishing an economic community, the basis for a broader and deeper community among peoples long divided by bloody conflicts; and to lay the foundations for institutions which will give direction to a destiny henceforward shared
> Have decided to create a European Coal and Steel Community ...[3]

Treaty of Rome

The Treaty of Rome was signed by France, Italy, West Germany, Luxembourg, the Netherlands and Belgium on 25 March 1957, and entered into force on 1 January 1958, creating the European Economic Community (EEC). With the Treaty of Rome, the European Economic Community States transferred to the Community the power to conclude treaties with international organizations and with non-member countries.[4] Lord Denning, a leading constitutional expert, stated 'the Treaty of Rome is like an incoming tide. It flows into the estuaries and up

---

2   Daltrop, Anne (1982), *Political Realities, Politics and the European Community*, Longman, London, 1982, p. 2.

3   Treaty of Paris, at the Preamble.

4   Ibid., at p. 20.

the rivers. It cannot be held back.'[5] The Member States agreed to work together for an integrated multinational economy for the free movement of labor and capital in the Community, while having joint institutions and common policies toward underdeveloped regions of the Community and toward those outside the Community. The Treaty gave the community institutions power to take the necessary steps to adjust national legal rules through harmonization procedures; this was required in order to remove national legal arrangements inhibiting the free movement of products, people and resources. By 1 July 1968, all internal tariffs had been abolished among the Member States for a Community-wide production and distribution of products and services,[6] and with the abolition of tariffs encouraging mutual trade, intra-Community trade in manufactured products was about 50 percent higher than previously. The long-term implications of the Treaty of Rome were a system of majority voting among the representatives of the national governments in the Council, a supranational bureaucracy over which national governments would have little control, a directly elected European Parliament and a commitment by the Member States to work for a closer union. The Preamble of the Treaty of Rome states:

> Determined to lay the foundations of an ever closer union among the peoples of Europe,
>
> Resolved to ensure the economic and social progress of their countries by common action to eliminate the barriers which divide Europe,
>
> Affirming as the essential objective of their efforts the constant improvement of the living and working conditions of their peoples,
>
> Recognising that the removal of existing obstacles calls for concerted action in order to guarantee steady expansion, balanced trade and fair competition,
>
> Anxious to strengthen the unity of their economies and to ensure their harmonious development by reducing the differences existing between the various regions and the backwardness of the less favoured regions,
>
> Desiring to contribute, by means of a common commercial policy, to the progressive abolition of restrictions on international trade,
>
> Intending to confirm the solidarity which binds Europe and the overseas countries and desiring to ensure the development of their prosperity, in accordance with the principles of the Charter of the United Nations,
>
> Resolved by thus pooling their resources to preserve and strengthen peace and liberty, and calling upon the other peoples of Europe who share their ideal to join in their efforts,
>
> Have decided to create a European Economic Community ...[7]

---

5   Ibid., at p. 99.

6   Daltrop, Anne (1982), *Political Realities, Politics and the European Community*, Longman, London, 1982, p. 18.

7   Treaty of Rome, at the Preamble.

In accordance with Article 3 of the Treaty of Rome, the activities of the Community include:

> 3(a) the elimination as between Member States, of customs duties and quantitative restrictions on the import and export of goods, and of all other measures having equivalent effect;
> (b) a common commercial policy;
> (c) an internal market characterised by the abolition, as between Member States, of obstacles to the free movement of goods, persons, services and capital;
> (d) measures concerning the entry and movement of persons in the internal market ...
> (e) a common policy in the sphere of agriculture and fisheries;
> (f) a common policy in the sphere of transport;
> (g) a system ensuring that competition in the common market is not distorted;
> (h) the approximation of the laws of the Member States to the extent required for the functioning of the common market;
> (i) a policy in the social sphere comprising a European Social Fund;
> (j) the strengthening of economic and social cohesion;
> (k) a policy in the sphere of the environment;
> (l) the strengthening of the competitiveness of Community industry;
> (m) the promotion of research and technological development;
> (n) encouragement for the establishment and development of trans-European networks;
> (o) a contribution to the attainment of a high level of health protection;
> (p) a contribution to education and training of quality and to the flowering of the cultures of the Member States;
> (q) a policy in the sphere of development cooperation;
> (r) the association of the overseas countries and territories in order to increase trade and promote jointly economic and social development;
> (s) a contribution to the strengthening of consumer protection;
> (t) measures in the spheres of energy, civil protection and tourism.[8]

Important for equal rights and the fight against discrimination, Article 6(a) prohibits discrimination:

> 6(a) Within the scope of application of this Treaty, and without prejudice to any special provisions contained therein, any discrimination on grounds of nationality shall be prohibited.[9]

Further, in terms of the free movement of persons, services and capital, in particular workers, Article 48 provides:

---

8   Ibid., at Article 3.
9   Ibid., at Article 6(a).

48.1. Freedom of movement for workers shall be secured within the Community by the end of the transitional period at the latest.

2. Such freedom of movement shall entail the abolition of any discrimination based on nationality between workers of the Member States as regards employment, remuneration and other conditions of work and employment.

3. It shall entail the right, subject to limitations justified on grounds of public policy, public security or public health:

    a. to accept offers of employment actually made;

    b. to move freely within the territory of Member States for this purpose;

    c. to stay in a Member State for the purpose of employment in accordance with the provisions governing the employment of nationals of that State laid down by law, regulation or administrative action;

    d. to remain in the territory of a Member State after having been employed in that State, subject to conditions which shall be embodied in implementing regulations to be drawn up by the Commission.

4. The provisions of this Article shall not apply to employment in the public service.[10]

Article 117 deals with workers' rights:

117. Member States agree upon the need to promote improved working conditions and an improved standard of living for workers, so as to make possible their harmonisation while the improvement is being maintained.

They believe that such a development will ensue not only from the functioning of the common market, which will favour the harmonisation of social systems, but also from the procedures provided for in this Treaty and from the approximation of provisions laid down by law, regulation or administrative action.[11]

Finally, important for females, in terms of equal pay, Article 119 states:

119. Each Member State shall during the first stage ensure and subsequently maintain the application of the principle that men and women should receive equal pay for equal work.

For the purpose of this Article, 'pay' means the ordinary basic or minimum wage or salary and any other consideration, whether in cash or in kind, which the worker receives, directly or indirectly, in respect of his employment from his employer.

Equal pay without discrimination based on sex means:

(a) that pay for the same work at piece rates shall be calculated on the basis of the same unit of measurement;

---

10   Ibid., at Article 48.
11   Ibid., at Article 117.

(b) that pay for work at time rates shall be the same for the same job.[12]

Maastricht Treaty

The Maastricht Treaty was signed on 7 February 1992 and entered into force on 1 November 1993, creating the European Union (EU). The EU became an internal market of over 340 million people providing for the free movement of goods, capital, services and citizens of Member States. The Preamble of the Maastricht Treaty states:

> Resolved to mark a new stage in the process of European integration undertaken with the establishment of the European Communities,
> Recalling the historic importance of the ending of the division of the European continent and the need to create firm bases for the construction of the future Europe,
> Confirming their attachment to the principles of liberty, democracy and respect for human rights and fundamental freedoms and of the rule of law,
> Desiring to deepen the solidarity between their peoples while respecting their history, their culture and their traditions,
> Desiring to enhance further the democratic and efficient functioning of the institutions so as to enable them better to carry out, within a single institutional framework, the tasks entrusted to them,
> Resolved to achieve the strengthening and the convergence of their economies and to establish an economic and monetary union including, in accordance with the provisions of this Treaty, a single and stable currency,
> Determined to promote economic and social progress for their peoples, within the context of the accomplishment of the internal market and of reinforced cohesion and environmental protection, and to implement policies ensuring that advances in economic integration are accompanied by parallel progress in other fields,
> Resolved to establish a citizenship common to nationals of their countries,
> Resolved to implement a common foreign and security policy including the eventual framing of a common defence policy, which might in time lead to a common defence, thereby reinforcing the European identity and its independence in order to promote peace, security and progress in Europe and in the world,
> Reaffirming their objective to facilitate the free movement of persons, while ensuring the safety and security of their peoples, by including provisions on justice and home affairs in this Treaty,
> Resolved to continue the process of creating an ever closer union among the peoples of Europe, in which decisions are taken as closely as possible to the citizen in accordance with the principle of subsidiarity,

---

12   Ibid., at Article 119.

In view of further steps to be taken in order to advance European integration,
Have decided to establish a European Union.[13]

Article A of the Maastricht Treaty states:

> By this Treaty, the High Contracting Parties establish among themselves a
> European Union, hereinafter called 'the Union'.
> This Treaty marks a new stage in the process of creating an ever closer union
> among the peoples of Europe, in which decisions are taken as closely as possible
> to the citizen.
> The Union shall be founded on the European Communities, supplemented by
> the policies and forms of cooperation established by this Treaty. Its task shall
> be to organise, in a manner demonstrating consistency and solidarity, relations
> between the Member States and between their peoples.[14]

Further, Article B states:

> B. The Union shall set itself the following objectives:
> to promote economic and social progress which is balanced and sustainable, in
> particular through the creation of an area without internal frontiers, through the
> strengthening of economic and social cohesion and through the establishment
> of economic and monetary union, ultimately including a single currency in
> accordance with the provisions of this Treaty;
> to assert its identity on the international scene, in particular through the
> implementation of a common foreign and security policy including the eventual
> framing of a common defence policy, which might in time lead to a common
> defence;
> to strengthen the protection of the rights and interests of the nationals of its
> Member States through the introduction of a citizenship of the Union;
> to develop close cooperation on justice and home affairs;
> to maintain in full the 'acquis communautaire' and build on it with ... the aim
> of ensuring the effectiveness of the mechanisms and the institutions of the
> Community.[15]

Treaty of Amsterdam

The Treaty of Amsterdam, the treaty establishing the European Community,
amending previous Treaties, was signed on 2 October 1997 and entered into
force on 1 May 1999. The following was added to the Preamble of the Treaty
establishing the European Community:

---

13 Maastrict Treaty, at the Preamble.
14 Ibid., at Article A.
15 Ibid., at Article B.

Determined to promote the development of the highest possible level of
knowledge for their peoples through a wide access to education and through its
continuous updating.[16]

Article 2 enumerates some of the principles of the Treaty:

2. The Community shall have as its task, by establishing a common market
and an economic and monetary union and by implementing common policies
or activities ... to promote throughout the Community a harmonious, balanced
and sustainable development of economic activities, a high level of employment
and of social protection, equality between men and women, sustainable and
non-inflationary growth, a high degree of competitiveness and convergence
of economic performance, a high level of protection and improvement of the
quality of the environment, the raising of the standard of living and quality of
life, and economic and social cohesion and solidarity among Member States.[17]

Important for all people, in order to combat discrimination, Article 13 amends
Article 6(a) of the Treaty of Rome:

13. Without prejudice to the other provisions of this Treaty and within the
limits of the powers conferred by it upon the Community, the Council, acting
unanimously on a proposal from the Commission and after consulting the
European Parliament, may take appropriate action to combat discrimination
based on sex, racial or ethnic origin, religion or belief, disability, age or sexual
orientation.[18]

Further, in terms of the free movement of persons, services and capital, in particular
workers, Article 39, amending Article 48 of the Treaty of Rome, states:

39(1) Freedom of movement for workers shall be secured within the Community.
(2) Such freedom of movement shall entail the abolition of any discrimination
based on nationality between workers of the Member States as regards
employment, remuneration and other conditions of work and employment.
(3) It shall entail the right, subject to limitations justified on grounds of public
policy, public security or public health:
(a) to accept offers of employment actually made;
(b) to move freely within the territory of Member States for this purpose;
(c) to stay in a Member State for the purpose of employment in accordance with
the provisions governing the employment of nationals of that State laid down by
law, regulation or administrative action;

---

16 Treaty of Amsterdam, at the Preamble.
17 Ibid., at Article 2.
18 Ibid., at Article 13.

(d) to remain in the territory of a Member State after having been employed in that State, subject to conditions which shall be embodied in implementing regulations to be drawn up by the Commission.

(4) The provisions of this Article shall not apply to employment in the public service.[19]

Finally, important for females, in terms of equal pay, Article 141, amending Article 119 of the Treaty of Rome, states:

141(1) Each Member State shall ensure that the principle of equal pay for male and female workers for equal work or work of equal value is applied.

(2) For the purpose of this Article, 'pay' means the ordinary basic or minimum wage or salary and any other consideration, whether in cash or in kind, which the worker receives directly or indirectly, in respect of his employment, from his employer.

Equal pay without discrimination based on sex means:

(a) that pay for the same work at piece rates shall be calculated on the basis of the same unit of measurement;

(b) that pay for work at time rates shall be the same for the same job.

(3) The Council, ... after consulting the Economic and Social Committee, shall adopt measures to ensure the application of the principle of equal opportunities and equal treatment of men and women in matters of employment and occupation, including the principle of equal pay for equal work or work of equal value.

(4) With a view to ensuring full equality in practice between men and women in working life, the principle of equal treatment shall not prevent any Member State from maintaining or adopting measures providing for specific advantages in order to make it easier for the under-represented sex to pursue a vocational activity or to prevent or compensate for disadvantages in professional careers.[20]

Treaty Establishing a Constitution for Europe and Charter of Fundamental Rights of the European Union

The Heads of State or Government of the then 25 Member States and the candidate countries signed the Treaty establishing a Constitution for Europe on 29 October 2004, but it was not ratified by all Member States of the enlarged Union. The Preamble of the Treaty 2004/C 310/01 establishing a Constitution for Europe states:

Drawing inspiration from the cultural, religious and humanist inheritance of Europe, from which have developed the universal values of the inviolable and

---

19   Ibid., at Article 39.
20   Ibid., at Article 141.

inalienable rights of the human person, freedom, democracy, equality and the
rule of law,
Believing that Europe, reunited after bitter experiences, intends to continue
along the path of civilisation, progress and prosperity, for the good of all its
inhabitants, including the weakest and most deprived; that it wishes to remain
a continent open to culture, learning and social progress; and that it wishes to
deepen the democratic and transparent nature of its public life, and to strive for
peace, justice and solidarity throughout the world,
Convinced that, while remaining proud of their own national identities and
history, the peoples of Europe are determined to transcend their former divisions
and, united ever more closely, to forge a common destiny,
Convinced that, thus 'United in diversity', Europe offers them the best chance of
pursuing, with due regard for the rights of each individual and in awareness of
their responsibilities towards future generations and the Earth, the great venture
which makes of it a special area of human hope,
Determined to continue the work accomplished within the framework of the
Treaties establishing the European Communities and the Treaty on European
Union, by ensuring the continuity of the Community *acquis*,
Who having exchanged their full powers, found in good and due form.[21]

Article I-1 on the establishment of the Union states:

I-1.1. Reflecting the will of the citizens and States of Europe to build a common
future, this Constitution establishes the European Union, on which the Member
States confer competences to attain objectives they have in common. The Union
shall coordinate the policies by which the Member States aim to achieve these
objectives, and shall exercise in the Community way the competences they
confer on it.
2. The Union shall be open to all European States which respect its values and
are committed to promoting them together.[22]

The Union's values are outlined in Article I-2:

I-2. The Union is founded on the values of respect for human dignity, liberty,
democracy, equality, the rule of law and respect for human rights, including
the rights of persons belonging to minorities. These values are common to the
Member States in a society in which pluralism, non-discrimination, tolerance,
justice, solidarity and equality between women and men prevail.[23]

---

21 Treaty establishing a Constitution for Europe, at the Preamble.
22 Ibid., at Article I-1.
23 Ibid., at Article I-2.

Further, the Union's objectives are outlined in Article I-3, which include combating discrimination and protecting the rights of the child:

> I-3.1. The Union's aim is to promote peace, its values and the well-being of its peoples.
> 2. The Union shall offer its citizens an area of freedom, security and justice without internal frontiers, and an internal market where competition is free and undistorted.
> 3. The Union shall work for the sustainable development of Europe based on balanced economic growth and price stability, a highly competitive social market economy, aiming at full employment and social progress, and a high level of protection and improvement of the quality of the environment. It shall promote scientific and technological advance.
> It shall combat social exclusion and discrimination, and shall promote social justice and protection, equality between women and men, solidarity between generations and protection of the rights of the child.
> It shall promote economic, social and territorial cohesion, and solidarity among Member States.
> It shall respect its rich cultural and linguistic diversity, and shall ensure that Europe's cultural heritage is safeguarded and enhanced.
> 4. In its relations with the wider world, the Union shall uphold and promote its values and interests. It shall contribute to peace, security, the sustainable development of the Earth, solidarity and mutual respect among peoples, free and fair trade, eradication of poverty and the protection of human rights, in particular the rights of the child, as well as to the strict observance and the development of international law, including respect for the principles of the United Nations Charter.
> 5. The Union shall pursue its objectives by appropriate means commensurate with the competences which are conferred upon it in the Constitution.[24]

Important for equal rights, fundamental freedoms and non-discrimination are upheld in Article I-4:

> I-4.1. The free movement of persons, services, goods and capital, and freedom of establishment shall be guaranteed within and by the Union, in accordance with the Constitution.
> 2. Within the scope of the Constitution, and without prejudice to any of its specific provisions, any discrimination on grounds of nationality shall be prohibited.[25]

The primacy of Union law is emphasized in Article I-6:

---

24   Ibid., at Article I-3.
25   Ibid., at Article I-4.

I-6. The Constitution and law adopted by the institutions of the Union in exercising competences conferred on it shall have primacy over the law of the Member States.[26]

Further, relations between the Union and Member States are contained in Article I-5:

I-5.1. The Union shall respect the equality of Member States before the Constitution as well as their national identities, inherent in their fundamental structures, political and constitutional, inclusive of regional and local self-government. It shall respect their essential State functions, including ensuring the territorial integrity of the State, maintaining law and order and safeguarding national security.

2. Pursuant to the principle of sincere cooperation, the Union and the Member States shall, in full mutual respect, assist each other in carrying out tasks which flow from the Constitution.

The Member States shall take any appropriate measure, general or particular, to ensure fulfillment of the obligations arising out of the Constitution or resulting from the acts of the institutions of the Union.

The Member States shall facilitate the achievement of the Union's tasks and refrain from any measure which could jeopardise the attainment of the Union's objectives.[27]

The Preamble of the Charter of Fundamental Rights of the European Union, part of the Constitution of Europe, states:

The peoples of Europe, in creating an ever closer union among them, are resolved to share a peaceful future based on common values.

Conscious of its spiritual and moral heritage, the Union is founded on the indivisible, universal values of human dignity, freedom, equality and solidarity; it is based on the principles of democracy and the rule of law. It places the individual at the heart of its activities, by establishing the citizenship of the Union and by creating an area of freedom, security and justice.

The Union contributes to the preservation and to the development of these common values while respecting the diversity of the cultures and traditions of the peoples of Europe as well as the national identities of the Member States and the organisation of their public authorities at national, regional and local levels; it seeks to promote balanced and sustainable development and ensures

---

26   Ibid., at Article I-6.
27   Ibid., at Article I-5.

free movement of persons, goods, services and capital, and the freedom of establishment.

To this end, it is necessary to strengthen the protection of fundamental rights in the light of changes in society, social progress and scientific and technological developments by making those rights more visible in a Charter.

This Charter reaffirms, with due regard for the powers and tasks of the Community and the Union and the principle of subsidiarity, the rights as they result, in particular, from the constitutional traditions and international obligations common to the Member States, the Treaty on European Union, the Community Treaties, the European Convention for the Protection of Human Rights and Fundamental Freedoms, the Social Charters adopted by the Community and by the Council of Europe and the case law of the Court of Justice of the European Communities and of the European Court of Human Rights.

Enjoyment of these rights entails responsibilities and duties with regard to other persons, to the human community and to future generations.

The Union therefore recognises the rights, freedoms and principles set out hereafter.[28]

Importantly, equality before the law is contained in Article II-80:

II-80. Everyone is equal before the law.[29]

Further, Article II-81 and Article III-118 prohibit discrimination:

II-81.1. Any discrimination based on any ground such as sex, race, colour, ethnic or social origin, genetic features, language, religion or belief, political or any other opinion, membership of a national minority, property, birth, disability, age or sexual orientation shall be prohibited.
2. Within the scope of application of the Treaty establishing the European Community and of the Treaty on European Union, and without prejudice to the special provisions of those Treaties, any discrimination on grounds of nationality shall be prohibited.[30]

---

28   Treaty establishing a Constitution for Europe, the Charter of Fundamental Rights, at the Preamble.
29   Ibid., at Article II-80.
30   Ibid., at Article II-81.

III-118. In defining and implementing the policies and activities referred to in this Part, the Union shall aim to combat discrimination based on sex, racial or ethnic origin, religion or belief, disability, age or sexual orientation.[31]

Finally, Article III-124 provides for measures for combating discrimination:

III-124.1. Without prejudice to the other provisions of the Constitution and within the limits of the powers assigned by it to the Union, a European law or framework law of the Council may establish the measures needed to combat discrimination based on sex, racial or ethnic origin, religion or belief, disability, age or sexual orientation. The Council shall act unanimously after obtaining the consent of the European Parliament.

2. By way of derogation from paragraph 1, European laws or framework laws may establish basic principles for Union incentive measures and define such measures, to support action taken by Member States in order to contribute to the achievement of the objectives referred to in paragraph 1, excluding any harmonisation of their laws and regulations.[32]

Treaty of Lisbon

Finally, the Treaty of Lisbon amending the Treaty on European Union and the Treaty establishing the European Community was signed at Lisbon on 13 December 2007, after the rejection of the Constitution for Europe. The Preamble of the Treaty of Lisbon, which came into effect on 1 December 2009, states:

Drawing inspiration from the cultural, religious and humanist inheritance of Europe, from which have developed the universal values of the inviolable and inalienable rights of the human person, freedom, democracy, equality and the rule of law.[33]

Specifically, Article 5(b) stresses the need to combat discrimination:

5(b) In defining and implementing its policies and activities, the Union shall aim to combat discrimination based on sex, racial or ethnic origin, religion or belief, disability, age or sexual orientation.[34]

---

31   Ibid., at Article III-118.
32   Ibid., at Article III-124.
33   Treaty of Lisbon, at the Preamble.
34   Ibid., at Article 5(b).

European Law and the European Court of Justice

The extension of civil rights marks another step toward European integration. The concept of citizenship is based on the principle that nationals of Member States have certain rights to move freely across national borders in the common market. There are five European Union (EU) institutions, each playing a specific role, namely the European Parliament, which is elected by the citizens of the Member States; the Council of the European Union, which represents the governments of the Member States; the European Commission, which is the executive body; the European Court of Justice, which ensures compliance with the law; and the Court of Auditors, which controls sound and lawful management of the European Union budget. There are five other important bodies, namely the European Economic and Social Committee, which expresses the opinions of organized civil society on economic and social issues; the Committee of the Regions, which expresses the opinions of regional and local authorities; the European Central Bank, which is responsible for monetary policy and managing the Euro; the European Ombudsman, who deals with citizens' complaints about maladministration by any European Union institution or body; and the European Investment Bank, which helps achieve European Union objectives by financing investment projects. A number of agencies and other bodies complete the system.[35]

Specifically, the Commission is responsible for making legislative proposals, executing policies and monitoring the compliance of Member States with their obligations. It is the driving force behind European integration by its right of initiative. It is also the guardian of the Treaties by its right to intervene with Member States and to demand compliance with their obligations. If Member States breach their Treaty obligations, they will face Commission action and possible legal proceedings in the European Court of Justice. As assistance to the European Court of Justice, the Commission is the European Union watchdog for the observance of the Treaties, as it originates and administers European Union law. The Council of Ministers is composed of representatives of Member State governments, and decides on Commission proposals. It is the Union's legislator, with all decisions involving new policies requiring unanimity. The Assembly is charged with proposing, to the Council, arrangements for universal direct elections. In addition, the Council, in turn, commends them to the Member States for adoption under constitutional procedures. The Assembly is consultative and can, if it has a sufficient majority, express its non-confidence in the Commission by dismissing it.

The European Court of Justice (ECJ) is the European Union's supreme constitutional authority. It renders judgments on the obligations of the institutions, Member States and citizens. The very existence of the European Union is conditional on the recognition of the binding nature of its rules, by the Member States, by the

---

35 Nicoll, William and Salmon, Trevor, *Understanding the New European Community*, Prentice Hall, Exeter, 1994, p. 97.

institutions, and by individuals. European Union law has successfully embedded itself thoroughly in the legal life of the Member States through the supervision of the European Court of Justice. The founding European Treaties are the primary source of European Union law, and therein is found the central jurisdiction of the European Court of Justice. European Union law involves primary law, namely Treaties, and secondary law, namely legislative Acts, both of which are binding on national governments and take precedence over national law. The nature of the European Union, its existence and its functions, demand a consistent application of European Union law between Member States.

The ECJ was to provide the legal sanctions for the carrying out of the Treaties. The supremacy of European Union law is implicit in the nature of the European Union. European Union law is directly applicable to Member States, and there is no requirement that it be passed into national law for its validity, since the rights and obligations accrue directly to European Union citizens. This surrender of sovereignty cannot be reversed by measures taken by national authorities in conflict with European Union law, relinquishing far-reaching powers to an independent legal order, which binds Member States. Under national law, the national court of the Member State is within its limits of discretion, when interpreting domestic law. However, domestic law must be in accord with the requirements of European Union law, and if this is not possible, then domestic law is inapplicable. This is a strong incentive for national courts to rule against child discrimination. The European Union can legislate directly through regulations, which are binding in law and are automatically incorporated into the national legal systems of Member States, without the need for specific individual ratification; it can also work through the legal systems of the Member States, by the use of the Commission, which implements directives with broad objectives. Although directives require some legal action, such as legislation, by the Member States before they become national law, they are laws transposed into Member States' legislation to enforce Treaty principles. Decisions by the European Court of Justice are binding as force of law, whereas recommendations and opinions by the Council of Ministers or the Commission are not.

European Union legislation establishes that a citizen of the European Union should not be discriminated against in the workplace. In employment, discrimination can occur in two ways: direct discrimination when people are treated differently solely on the basis of a discriminatory ground; and indirect discrimination when people are treated differently because of an apparently neutral provision, criterion or practice determining recruitment, pay, working conditions, dismissal, and social security, in practice disadvantaging a substantially higher proportion of the members of one group. Such provisions, criteria or practices are prohibited under European Union law, unless it is proven that they are justified by objective reasons in no way related to child discrimination. In examining positive action, European Union law allows European Union countries and companies to undertake several initiatives to counter child discrimination. Historically, there have been discriminatory policies directly on their face or indirectly, applied to different groups. Positive action is needed not only to help guarantee equality, but also to combat the perpetuation of traditional discriminatory attitudes so as to ensure access to equal opportunities for all. The European Court of Justice is at the heart of the legal system, and ensures that European Union law is observed in the interpretation and application of the Treaties; its judgments are binding on Member States.[36]

Fundamental rights are part of the bedrock of the European Union's legal order. The European Court of Justice held that the protection of such rights, while inspired by the constitutional traditions common to Member States, must be ensured within the framework of the structure and objectives of the European Union (*Internationale Handelsgesellschaft* [1970] ECR 1125, [1972] CMLR 255).[37] Importantly, in a seminal case, the European Court of Justice stated:

> The integration into the laws of each Member State of provisions which derive from the Community, and more generally the terms and the spirit of the Treaty, make it impossible for the States, as a corollary, to accord precedence to a unilateral and subsequent measure over a legal system accepted by them on a basis of reciprocity ... The executive force of Community law cannot vary from one State to another ... without jeopardising the attainment of the object of the Treaty ... It follows from all these observations that the law stemming from the treaty, an independent source of law, could not, because of its special and original nature, be overridden by domestic legal provisions, however framed, without being deprived of its character as Community law and without the legal basis of the Community itself being called into question (*Costa* v. *ENEL* [1964] CMLR 425).[38]

In terms of the burden of proof, in the European Court of Justice, the plaintiff has the burden of showing, in indirect cases, that a neutral policy has a disproportionate impact (*Teuling* v. *Bredrijfsvereniging*, [1987] ECR 2497).[39] The burden is then shifted to the defendant who must justify this by objective reasons other than discrimination. The plaintiff must then show that the explanation is not effective for the purpose, or that there is an alternative provision to accomplish it in a manner that has a less discriminatory impact. Otherwise, if there is a difference in treatment, it must be justified by objective factors other than discrimination. If a provision is neutral on its terms, but factually disadvantages a particular group, an employer bears the burden of justification. The European Court of Justice requires a showing of objective justification as a defense to discrimination.

---

36 Ibid.
37 *Internationale Handelsgesellschaft* [1970] ECR 1125, [1972] CMLR 255.
38 *Costa* v. *ENEL* [1964] CMLR 425.
39 *Teuling* v. *Bredrijfsvereniging* [1987] ECR 2497.

European Convention for the Protection of Human Rights and Fundamental Freedoms (ECHR)

Crucially for human rights, the European Convention for the Protection of Human Rights and Fundamental Freedoms came into being on 4 November 1950, which affords protection against discrimination. In the Preamble of the European Convention for the Protection of Human Rights and Fundamental Freedoms, the governments signatory thereto, being Members of the Council of Europe, undertake the agreement:

> Considering the Universal Declaration of Human Rights proclaimed by the General Assembly of the United Nations on 10th December 1948;
> Considering that this Declaration aims at securing the universal and effective recognition and observance of the Rights therein declared;
> Considering that the aim of the Council of Europe is the achievement of greater unity between its Members and that one of the methods by which the aim is to be pursued is the maintenance and further realisation of Human Rights and Fundamental Freedoms;
> Reaffirming their profound belief in those Fundamental Freedoms which are the foundation of justice and peace in the world and are best maintained on the one hand by an effective political democracy and on the other by a common understanding and observance of the Human Rights upon which they depend;
> Being resolved, as the Governments of European countries which are like-minded and have a common heritage of political traditions, ideals, freedom and the rule of law to take the first steps for the collective enforcement of certain of the Rights stated in the Universal Declaration.[40]

Article 1 guarantees:

> 1. The High Contracting Parties shall secure to everyone within their jurisdiction the rights and freedoms defined.[41]

The prohibition of discrimination is espoused under Article 14:

> 14. The enjoyment of the rights and freedoms set forth in this Convention shall be secured without discrimination on any ground such as sex, race, colour, language, religion, political or other opinion, national or social origin, association with a national minority, property, birth or other status.[42]

---

40 European Convention for the Protection of Human Rights and Fundamental Freedoms (ECHR), at the Preamble.
41 Ibid., at Article 1.
42 European Convention for the Protection of Human Rights and Fundamental Freedoms (ECHR), at Article 14.

Further, Section 4 prohibits slavery and forced labor:

> 4.1. No one shall be held in slavery or servitude.
>
> 2. No one shall be required to perform forced or compulsory labour.
>
> 3. ... the term 'forced or compulsory labour' shall not include:
>
> (a) any work required to be done in the ordinary course of detention imposed according to the provisions of Article 5 of the Convention or during conditional release from such detention;
>
> (b) any service of a military character or, in case of conscientious objectors in countries where they are recognised, service exacted instead of compulsory military service;
>
> (c) any service exacted in case of an emergency or calamity threatening the life or well-being of the community;
>
> (d) any work or service which forms part of normal civic obligations.[43]

The right to an effective remedy is secured by Article 13:

> 13. Everyone whose rights and freedoms as set forth in this Convention are violated shall have an effective remedy before a national authority notwithstanding that the violation has been committed by persons acting in an official capacity.[44]

Further, Article 17 provides for the prohibition of abuse of rights:

> 17. Nothing in this Convention may be interpreted as implying for any State, group or person any right to engage in any activity or perform any act aimed at the destruction of any of the rights and freedoms set forth herein or at their limitation to a greater extent than is provided for in the Convention.[45]

Importantly, the European Court of Human Rights is established under Article 19:

> 19. To ensure the observance of the engagements undertaken by the High Contracting Parties in the Convention and the Protocols thereto, there shall be set up a European Court of Human Rights, hereinafter referred to as 'the Court'. It shall function on a permanent basis.[46]

Article 32 outlines the jurisdiction of the Court:

---

43   Ibid., at Section 4.
44   Ibid., at Article 13.
45   Ibid., at Article 17.
46   Ibid., at Article 19.

32.1. The jurisdiction of the Court shall extend to all matters concerning the interpretation and application of the Convention and the protocols thereto which are referred to it as provided in Articles 33, 34 and 47.
2. In the event of dispute as to whether the Court has jurisdiction, the Court shall decide.[47]

Article 27 outlines the structure of the Committees, the Chambers and the Grand Chamber:

27.1. To consider cases brought before it, the Court shall sit in committees of three judges, in Chambers of seven judges and in a Grand Chamber of seventeen judges. The Court's Chambers shall set up committees for a fixed period of time.
2. There shall sit as an ex officio member of the Chamber and the Grand Chamber the judge elected in respect of the State Party concerned or, if there is none or if he is unable to sit, a person of its choice who shall sit in the capacity of judge.
3. The Grand Chamber shall also include the President of the Court, the Vice-Presidents, the Presidents of the Chambers and other judges chosen in accordance with the rules of the Court. When a case is referred to the Grand Chamber under Article 43, no judge from the Chamber which rendered the judgment shall sit in the Grand Chamber, with the exception of the President of the Chamber and the judge who sat in respect of the State Party concerned.[48]

Inter-State cases are provided for under Article 33:

33. Any High Contracting Party may refer to the Court any alleged breach of the provisions of the Convention and the protocols thereto by another High Contracting Party.[49]

Individual applications are provided for under Article 34:

34. The Court may receive applications from any person, non-governmental organisation or group of individuals claiming to be the victim of a violation by one of the High Contracting Parties of the rights set forth in the Convention or the protocols thereto. The High Contracting Parties undertake not to hinder in any way the effective exercise of this right.[50]

Further, third party intervention is provided for under Article 36:

---

47   Ibid., at Article 32.
48   Ibid., at Article 27.
49   Ibid., at Article 33.
50   Ibid., at Article 34.

36.1. In all cases before a Chamber or the Grand Chamber, a High Contracting Party one of whose nationals is an applicant shall have the right to submit written comments and to take part in hearings.

2. The President of the Court may, in the interest of the proper administration of justice, invite any High Contracting Party which is not a party to the proceedings or any person concerned who is not the applicant to submit written comments or take part in hearings.[51]

Article 35 contains the admissibility of evidence criteria:

35.1. The Court may only deal with the matter after all domestic remedies have been exhausted, according to the generally recognised rules of international law, and within a period of six months from the date on which the final decision was taken.

2. The Court shall not deal with any application submitted under Article 34 that:

(a) is anonymous; or

(b) is substantially the same as a matter that has already been examined by the Court or has already been submitted to another procedure of international investigation or settlement and contains no relevant new information.

3. The Court shall declare inadmissible any individual application submitted under Article 34 which it considers incompatible with the provisions of the Convention or the protocols thereto, manifestly ill-founded, or an abuse of the right of application.

4. The Court shall reject any application which it considers inadmissible under this Article. It may do so at any stage of the proceedings.[52]

Further, Article 37 contains the striking out of applications:

37.1. The Court may at any stage of the proceedings decide to strike an application out of its list of cases where the circumstances lead to the conclusion that:

(a) the applicant does not intend to pursue his application; or

(b) the matter has been resolved; or

(c) for any other reason established by the Court, it is no longer justified to continue the examination of the application.

However, the Court shall continue the examination of the application if respect for human rights as defined in the Convention and the protocols thereto so requires.

2. The Court may decide to restore an application to its list of cases if it considers that the circumstances justify such a course.[53]

---

51   Ibid., at Article 36.
52   Ibid., at Article 35.
53   Ibid., at Article 37.

Article 38 outlines the examination of the case and friendly settlement proceedings:

> 38.1. If the Court declares the application admissible, it shall:
> (a) pursue the examination of the case, together with the representatives of the parties, and if need be, undertake an investigation, for the effective conduct of which the States concerned shall furnish all necessary facilities;
> (b) place itself at the disposal of the parties concerned with a view to securing a friendly settlement of the matter on the basis of respect for human rights as defined in the Convention and the protocols thereto.
> 2. Proceedings conducted under paragraph 1.b shall be confidential.[54]

Further, Article 39 outlines the finding of a friendly settlement:

> 39. If a friendly settlement is effected, the Court shall strike the case out of its list by means of a decision which shall be confined to a brief statement of the facts and of the solution reached.[55]

Public hearings and access to documents are provided for under Article 40:

> 40.1. Hearings shall be in public unless the Court in exceptional circumstances decides otherwise.
> 2. Documents deposited with the Registrar shall be accessible to the public unless the President of the Court decides otherwise.[56]

Further, Article 41 provides for just satisfaction:

> 41. If the Court finds that there has been a violation of the Convention or the protocols thereto, and if the internal law of the High Contracting Party concerned allows only partial reparation to be made, the Court shall, if necessary, afford just satisfaction to the injured party.[57]

Importantly, final judgments are contained in Article 44:

> 44.1. The judgment of the Grand Chamber shall be final.
> 2. The judgment of a Chamber shall become final:
> (a) when the parties declare that they will not request that the case be referred to the Grand Chamber; or
> (b) three months after the date of the judgment, if reference of the case to the Grand Chamber has not been requested; or

---

54   Ibid., at Article 38.
55   Ibid., at Article 39.
56   Ibid., at Article 40.
57   Ibid., at Article 41.

(c) when the panel of the Grand Chamber rejects the request to refer under Article 43.

3. The final judgment shall be published.[58]

Further, reasons for judgments and decisions are contained in Article 45:

45.1. Reasons shall be given for judgments as well as for decisions declaring applications admissible or inadmissible.

2. If a judgment does not represent, in whole or in part, the unanimous opinion of the judges, any judge shall be entitled to deliver a separate opinion.[59]

In addition, binding force and execution of judgments are contained in Article 46:

46.1. The High Contracting Parties undertake to abide by the final judgment of the Court in any case to which they are parties.

2. The final judgment of the Court shall be transmitted to the Committee of Ministers, which shall supervise its execution.[60]

Finally, Article 47 provides for advisory opinions:

47.1. The Court may, at the request of the Committee of Ministers, give advisory opinions on legal questions concerning the interpretation of the Convention and the protocols thereto.

2. Such opinions shall not deal with any question relating to the content or scope of the rights or freedoms defined in Section I of the Convention and the protocols thereto, or with any other question which the Court or the Committee of Ministers might have to consider in consequence of any such proceedings as could be instituted in accordance with the Convention.

3. Decisions of the Committee of Ministers to request an advisory opinion of the Court shall require a majority vote of the representatives entitled to sit on the Committee.[61]

In addition, the Preamble of Protocol No. 1, entitled Enforcement of Certain Rights and Freedoms not included in Section I of the Convention, states that:

The Governments signatory hereto, being Members of the Council of Europe,

Being resolved to take steps to ensure the collective enforcement of certain rights and freedoms other than those already included in Section I of the Convention

---

58   Ibid., at Article 44.
59   Ibid., at Article 45.
60   Ibid., at Article 46.
61   Ibid., at Article 47.

for the Protection of Human Rights and Fundamental Freedoms signed at Rome
on 4th November, 1950 (hereinafter referred to as 'the Convention') ...[62]

Further, important for equal rights, in the Preamble of Protocol No. 12 to the
European Convention for the Protection of Human Rights and Fundamental
Freedoms, the Member States of the Council of Europe signatory thereto,
undertake the agreement:

> Having regard to the fundamental principle according to which all persons are
> equal before the law and are entitled to the equal protection of the law;
> Being resolved to take further steps to promote the equality of all persons
> through the collective enforcement of a general prohibition of discrimination by
> means of the Convention for the Protection of Human Rights and Fundamental
> Freedoms signed at Rome on 4 November 1950 (hereinafter referred to as 'the
> Convention');
> Reaffirming that the principle of non-discrimination does not prevent States
> Parties from taking measures in order to promote full and effective equality,
> provided that there is an objective and reasonable justification for those
> measures.[63]

Article 1 outlines the general prohibition against discrimination:

> 1(1) The enjoyment of any right set forth by law shall be secured without
> discrimination on any ground such as sex, race, colour, language, religion,
> political or other opinion, national or social origin, association with a national
> minority, property, birth or other status.
> (2) No one shall be discriminated against by any public authority on any ground
> such as those mentioned in paragraph 1.[64]

It is noteworthy that the words 'other status' in Article 14 of the ECHR should
include child discrimination, and such a specific inclusion was considered
unnecessary from a legal point of view, since the list of non-discrimination grounds
is not exhaustive, and since inclusion of any particular additional ground might
give rise to unwarranted *a contrario* interpretations as regards discrimination
based on grounds not so included. According to the Explanatory Memorandum
prepared by the Council of Europe, the expression 'any right set forth by law' in
Article 1 of Protocol 12 is meant to cover (i) the enjoyment of any right specifically
granted to an individual by national law; (ii) the enjoyment of a right which may

---

62   European Convention for the Protection of Human Rights and Fundamental
Freedoms as amended by Protocol No. 1, at the Preamble.
63   European Convention for the Protection of Human Rights and Fundamental
Freedoms as amended by Protocol No. 12, at the Preamble.
64   Ibid., at Article 1.

be inferred from a clear obligation of a public authority under national law, such as where a public authority is obliged under national law to behave in a particular manner; (iii) the exercise of a discretionary power by a public authority; and (iv) any other act or omission by a public authority.[65] The prime objective of Article 1 is to embody a negative obligation on public authorities not to discriminate; it does not impose a general positive obligation to take measures to prevent or prohibit all instances of discrimination between private persons. The duty to 'secure' might entail a positive obligation where there is a clear gap in protection from discrimination under domestic law, and would oblige a ratifying State to secure protection against discrimination on all the proscribed grounds, including discrimination against children.[66]

European Social Charter

In the Preamble to the European Social Charter of 18 October 1961, the governments signatory thereto, being members of the Council of Europe, undertake the agreement:

> Considering that the aim of the Council of Europe is the achievement of greater unity between its members for the purpose of safeguarding and realising the ideals and principles which are their common heritage and of facilitating their economic and social progress, in particular by the maintenance and further realisation of human rights and fundamental freedoms;
> Considering that in the Convention for the Protection of Human Rights and Fundamental Freedoms signed at Rome on 4th November 1950, and the Protocol thereto signed at Paris on 20th March 1952, the member States of the Council of Europe agreed to secure to their populations the civil and political rights and freedoms therein specified;
> Considering that the enjoyment of social rights should be secured without discrimination on grounds of race, colour, sex, religion, political opinion, national extraction or social origin;
> Being resolved to make every effort in common to improve the standard of living and to promote the social well-being of both their urban and rural populations by means of appropriate institutions and action.[67]

In the Preamble to the European Social Charter (revised) of 3 May 1996, the governments signatory thereto, being members of the Council of Europe, undertake the agreement:

---

65 Council of Europe, Explanatory Memorandum.
66 Ibid.
67 European Social Charter, at the Preamble.

Considering that the aim of the Council of Europe is the achievement of greater unity between its members for the purpose of safeguarding and realising the ideals and principles which are their common heritage and of facilitating their economic and social progress, in particular by the maintenance and further realisation of human rights and fundamental freedoms;

Considering that in the Convention for the Protection of Human Rights and Fundamental Freedoms signed at Rome on 4 November 1950, and the Protocols thereto, the member States of the Council of Europe agreed to secure to their populations the civil and political rights and freedoms therein specified;

Considering that in the European Social Charter opened for signature in Turin on 18 October 1961 and the Protocols thereto, the member States of the Council of Europe agreed to secure to their populations the social rights specified therein in order to improve their standard of living and their social well-being;

Recalling that the Ministerial Conference on Human Rights held in Rome on 5 November 1990 stressed the need, on the one hand, to preserve the indivisible nature of all human rights, be they civil, political, economic, social or cultural and, on the other hand, to give the European Social Charter fresh impetus;

Resolved, as was decided during the Ministerial Conference held in Turin on 21 and 22 October 1991, to update and adapt the substantive contents of the Charter in order to take account in particular of the fundamental social changes which have occurred since the text was adopted;

Recognising the advantage of embodying in a Revised Charter, designed progressively to take the place of the European Social Charter, the rights guaranteed by the Charter as amended, the rights guaranteed by the Additional Protocol of 1988 and to add new rights.[68]

Important for all workers, under Part I, several rights and principles are espoused, including under point 7, the special protection afforded to children, and more specifically, under point 17, social, legal and economic protection afforded to children:

The Parties accept as the aim of their policy, to be pursued by all appropriate means both national and international in character, the attainment of conditions in which the following rights and principles may be effectively realised:

1. Everyone shall have the opportunity to earn his living in an occupation freely entered upon.
2. All workers have the right to just conditions of work.
3. All workers have the right to safe and healthy working conditions.
4. All workers have the right to a fair remuneration sufficient for a decent standard of living for themselves and their families.

---

68   European Social Charter (revised), at the Preamble.

5. All workers and employers have the right to freedom of association in national or international organisations for the protection of their economic and social interests.

6. All workers and employers have the right to bargain collectively.

7. Children and young persons have the right to a special protection against the physical and moral hazards to which they are exposed.

8. Employed women, in case of maternity, have the right to a special protection.

9. Everyone has the right to appropriate facilities for vocational guidance with a view to helping him choose an occupation suited to his personal aptitude and interests.

10. Everyone has the right to appropriate facilities for vocational training.

11. Everyone has the right to benefit from any measures enabling him to enjoy the highest possible standard of health attainable.

12. All workers and their dependents [*sic*] have the right to social security.

13. Anyone without adequate resources has the right to social and medical assistance.

14. Everyone has the right to benefit from social welfare services.

15. Disabled persons have the right to independence, social integration and participation in the life of the community.

16. The family as a fundamental unit of society has the right to appropriate social, legal and economic protection to ensure its full development.

17. Children and young persons have the right to appropriate social, legal and economic protection.

18. The nationals of any one of the Parties have the right to engage in any gainful occupation in the territory of any one of the others on a footing of equality with the nationals of the latter, subject to restrictions based on cogent economic or social reasons.

19. Migrant workers who are nationals of a Party and their families have the right to protection and assistance in the territory of any other Party.

20. All workers have the right to equal opportunities and equal treatment in matters of employment and occupation without discrimination on the grounds of sex.

21. Workers have the right to be informed and to be consulted within the undertaking.

22. Workers have the right to take part in the determination and improvement of the working conditions and working environment in the undertaking.

23. Every elderly person has the right to social protection.

24. All workers have the right to protection in cases of termination of employment.

25. All workers have the right to protection of their claims in the event of the insolvency of their employer.

26. All workers have the right to dignity at work.

27. All persons with family responsibilities and who are engaged or wish to engage in employment have a right to do so without being subject to

discrimination and as far as possible without conflict between their employment and family responsibilities.

28. Workers' representatives in undertakings have the right to protection against acts prejudicial to them and should be afforded appropriate facilities to carry out their functions.

29. All workers have the right to be informed and consulted in collective redundancy procedures.

30. Everyone has the right to protection against poverty and social exclusion.

31. Everyone has the right to housing.[69]

Under Part II, the right to work is provided for in Article 1:

1. With a view to ensuring the effective exercise of the right to work, the Parties undertake:

1. to accept as one of their primary aims and responsibilities the achievement and maintenance of as high and stable a level of employment as possible, with a view to the attainment of full employment;

2. to protect effectively the right of the worker to earn his living in an occupation freely entered upon;

3. to establish or maintain free employment services for all workers;

4. to provide or promote appropriate vocational guidance, training and rehabilitation.[70]

Further, Article 4 guarantees the right to a fair remuneration and equal pay:

4. With a view to ensuring the effective exercise of the right to a fair remuneration, the Parties undertake:

1. to recognise the right of workers to a remuneration such as will give them and their families a decent standard of living;

2. to recognise the right of workers to an increased rate of remuneration for overtime work, subject to exceptions in particular cases;

3. to recognise the right of men and women workers to equal pay for work of equal value;

4. to recognise the right of all workers to a reasonable period of notice for termination of employment;

5. to permit deductions from wages only under conditions and to the extent prescribed by national laws or regulations or fixed by collective agreements or arbitration awards. The exercise of these rights shall be achieved by freely concluded collective agreements, by statutory wage-fixing machinery, or by other means appropriate to national conditions.[71]

---

69   Ibid., at Part I.
70   Ibid., at Part II, Article 1.
71   Ibid., at Article 4.

In addition, Article 24 provides for termination of employment under appropriate means:

> 24.1 It is understood that for the purposes of this article the terms 'termination of employment' and 'terminated' mean termination of employment at the initiative of the employer.
>
> 2. It is understood that this article covers all workers but that a Party may exclude from some or all of its protection the following categories of employed persons:
>
> a. workers engaged under a contract of employment for a specified period of time or a specified task;
>
> b. workers undergoing a period of probation or a qualifying period of employment, provided that this is determined in advance and is of a reasonable duration;
>
> c. workers engaged on a casual basis for a short period.
>
> 3. For the purpose of this article the following, in particular, shall not constitute valid reasons for termination of employment:
>
> a. trade union membership or participation in union activities outside working hours, or, with the consent of the employer, within working hours;
>
> b. seeking office as, acting or having acted in the capacity of a workers' representative;
>
> c. the filing of a complaint or the participation in proceedings against an employer involving alleged violation of laws or regulations or recourse to competent administrative authorities;
>
> d. race, colour, sex, marital status, family responsibilities, pregnancy, religion, political opinion, national extractionor social origin;
>
> e. maternity or parental leave;
>
> f. temporary absence from work due to illness or injury.
>
> 4. It is understood that compensation or other appropriate relief in case of termination of employment without valid reasons shall be determined by national laws or regulations, collective agreements or other means appropriate to national conditions.[72]

Pursuant to Article 22, the Parties undertake to adopt or encourage measures enabling all workers, in accordance with national legislation and practice, to contribute to the determination and the improvement of the working conditions, work organization and working environment; to the protection of health and safety within the undertaking; to the organization of social and sociocultural services

---

72 Ibid., at Article 24.

and facilities within the undertaking; and to the supervision of the observance of regulations on these matters.[73]

Finally, importantly, under Part V, Article E is a provision on non-discrimination:

> E. The enjoyment of the rights set forth in this Charter shall be secured without discrimination on any ground such as race, colour, sex, language, religion, political or other opinion, national extraction or social origin, health, association with a national minority, birth or other status.[74]

Council Decision 2000/750/EC Establishing a Community Action Programme to Combat Discrimination (2001 to 2006)

Important for equal rights and in the fight against child discrimination, the Preamble of Council Decision 2000/750/EC of 27 November 2000 establishing a Community action programme to combat discrimination states:

> (1) The European Union is founded on the principles of liberty, democracy, respect for human rights and fundamental freedoms, and the rule of law, principles which are common to all Member States. In accordance with Article 6(2) of the Treaty on European Union, the Union should respect fundamental rights as guaranteed by the European Convention for the Protection of Human Rights and Fundamental Freedoms and as derived from the shared constitutional traditions common to the Member States, as general principles of Community law.
>
> (2) The European Parliament has strongly and repeatedly urged the European Union to develop and strengthen its policy in the field of equal treatment and equal opportunities across all grounds of discrimination.
>
> (3) The European Union rejects theories which attempt to determine the existence of separate human races. The use of the term 'racial origin' in this Decision does not imply an acceptance of such theories.
>
> (4) In the implementation of the programme, the Community will seek, in accordance with the Treaty, to eliminate inequalities and promote equality between men and women, particularly because women are often the victims of multiple discrimination.
>
> (5) The different forms of discrimination cannot be ranked: all are equally intolerable. The programme is intended both to exchange existing good practice in the Member States and to develop new practice and policy for combating

---

73   Ibid., at Article 22.
74   Ibid., at Part V, Article E.

discrimination, including multiple discrimination. This Decision may help to put in place a comprehensive strategy for combating all forms of discrimination on different grounds, a strategy which should henceforward be developed in parallel.

(6) Experience of action at Community level, in particular in the field of gender, has shown that combating discrimination in practice calls for a combination of measures and in particular of legislation and of practical action designed to be mutually reinforcing. Similar lessons can be drawn from experience dealing with racial and ethnic origin and disability.

(7) The programme should deal with all grounds of discrimination with the exception of sex, which is dealt with by specific Community action. Discrimination on different grounds can have similar features and can be combated in similar ways. Experience built up over many years in combating discrimination on some grounds, including sex, can be used to the benefit of other grounds. However, the specific features of the diverse forms of discrimination should be accommodated. Therefore, the particular needs of people with disabilities should be taken into account in terms of the accessibility of activities and results.

(8) Access to the programme should be open to all public and/or private bodies and institutions involved in the fight against discrimination. In this connection account must be taken of the experience and abilities of both local and national non-governmental organisations.

(9) Many non-governmental organisations at European level have experience and expertise in fighting discrimination, as well as acting at European level as the advocates of people who are exposed to discrimination. They can therefore make an important contribution towards a better understanding of the diverse forms and effects of discrimination and to ensuring that the design, implementation and follow-up of the programme take account of the experience of people exposed to discrimination. The Community has in the past provided core funding for various organisations working in the area of discrimination. The core funding of effective non-governmental organisations may be a valuable asset in combating discrimination.

(10) The measures necessary for the implementation of this Decision should be adopted in accordance with Council Decision 1999/468/EC of 28 June 1999 laying down the procedures for the exercise of implementing powers conferred on the Commission (4).

(11) It is necessary, in order to reinforce the added value of Community action, that the Commission, in cooperation with the Member States, should ensure,

at all levels, the coherence and complementarity of actions implemented in the framework of this Decision and other relevant Community policies, instruments and actions, in particular those in the fields of education and training and equal opportunities between men and women under the European Social Fund and those to promote social inclusion. Consistency and complementarity with the relevant activities of the European Monitoring Centre on Racism and Xenophobia should also be ensured.

(12) The Agreement on the European Economic Area (EEA Agreement) provides for greater cooperation in the social field between the European Community and its Member States, on the one hand, and the countries of the European Free Trade Association participating in the European Economic Area (EFTA/EEA), on the other. Provision should be made to open up this programme to participation by the candidate countries of Central and Eastern Europe, in accordance with the conditions established in the Europe Agreements, in their additional protocols and in the decisions of the respective Association Councils, to Cyprus, Malta and Turkey, funded by additional appropriations in accordance with the procedures to be agreed with those countries.

(13) A financial reference amount, within the meaning of point 34 of the Interinstitutional Agreement of 6 May 1999 between the European Parliament, the Council and the Commission (5) is included in this Decision for the entire duration of the programme, without thereby affecting the powers of the budgetary authority as they are defined by the Treaty.

(14) The Commission and the Member States should make efforts to ensure that all the texts, guidelines and calls for proposals published under this programme are written in clear, simple and accessible language.

(15) It is appropriate that account should be taken of the need to provide special assistance, where appropriate, to enable people to overcome the obstacles to their participation in the programme.

(16) It is necessary for the success of any Community action to monitor and evaluate the results set against the objectives.

(17) In accordance with the principle of subsidiarity as defined in Article 5 of the Treaty, the objectives of the proposed action concerning the contribution of the Community to combating discrimination cannot be sufficiently achieved by the Member States because, inter alia, of the need for multilateral partnerships, the transnational exchange of information and the Community-wide dissemination of good practice. In accordance with the principle of proportionality as defined

in the said Article, this Decision does not go beyond what is necessary to achieve those objectives.[75]

Article 1 announces the establishment of the program:

1. This Decision establishes a Community action programme, hereinafter referred to as 'the programme', to promote measures to combat direct or indirect discrimination based on racial or ethnic origin, religion or belief, disability, age or sexual orientation ...[76]

Objectives of the program are outlined in Article 2:

2. Within the limits of the Community's powers, the programme shall support and supplement the efforts at Community level and in the Member States to promote measures to prevent and combat discrimination whether based on one or on multiple factors, taking account, where appropriate, of future legislative developments. It shall have the following objectives:
(a) to improve the understanding of issues related to discrimination through improved knowledge of this phenomenon and through evaluation of the effectiveness of policies and practice;
(b) to develop the capacity to prevent and address discrimination effectively, in particular by strengthening organisations' means of action and through support for the exchange of information and good practice and networking at European level, while taking into account the specific characteristics of the different forms of discrimination;
(c) to promote and disseminate the values and practices underlying the fight against discrimination, including through the use of awareness-raising campaigns.[77]

Further, Article 3 stipulates the Community actions to be undertaken:

3.1. With a view to achieving the objectives set out in Article 2, the following actions may be implemented within a transnational framework:
(a) analysis of factors related to discrimination, including through studies and the development of qualitative and quantitative indicators and benchmarks, in accordance with national law and practices, and the evaluation of anti-discrimination legislation and practice, with a view to assessing its effectiveness and impact, with effective dissemination of the results;

---

75   Council Decision 2000/750/EC of 27 November 2000 establishing a Community Action Programme to Combat Discrimination (2001 to 2006), at the Preamble.

76   Ibid., at Article 1.

77   Ibid., at Article 2.

(b) transnational cooperation and the promotion of networking at European level between partners active in the prevention of, and the fight against, discrimination, including non-governmental organisations;

(c) awareness-raising, in particular to emphasise the European dimension of the fight against discrimination and to publicise the results of the programme, in particular through communications, publications, campaigns and events.[78]

Finally, Article 8 deals with the consistency and complementarity within the Union:

8.1. The Commission shall, in cooperation with the Member States, ensure overall consistency with other Union and Community policies, instruments and actions, in particular by establishing appropriate mechanisms to coordinate the activities of the programme with relevant activities relating to research, employment, equality between women and men, social inclusion, culture, education, training and youth policy and in the field of the Community's external relations.

2. The Commission and the Member States shall ensure consistency and complementarity between action undertaken under the programme and other relevant Union and Community action, in particular under the Structural Funds and the Community initiative Equal.

3. Member States shall make all possible efforts to ensure consistency and complementarity between activities under the programme and those carried out at national, regional and local levels.[79]

Council Directive 2000/78/EC Establishing a General Framework for Equal Treatment in Employment and Occupation

Important for equal rights in employment, the Preamble of Council Directive 2000/78/EC of 27 November 2000 establishing a general framework for equal treatment in employment and occupation states:

(1) In accordance with Article 6 of the Treaty on European Union, the European Union is founded on the principles of liberty, democracy, respect for human rights and fundamental freedoms, and the rule of law, principles which are common to all Member States and it respects fundamental rights, as guaranteed by the European Convention for the Protection of Human Rights and Fundamental Freedoms and as they result from the constitutional traditions common to the Member States, as general principles of Community law.

---

78   Ibid., at Article 3.
79   Ibid., at Article 8.

(2) The principle of equal treatment between women and men is well established by an important body of Community law, in particular in Council Directive 76/207/EEC of 9 February 1976 on the implementation of the principle of equal treatment for men and women as regards access to employment, vocational training and promotion, and working conditions (5).

(3) In implementing the principle of equal treatment, the Community should, in accordance with Article 3(2) of the EC Treaty, aim to eliminate inequalities, and to promote equality between men and women, especially since women are often the victims of multiple discrimination.

(4) The right of all persons to equality before the law and protection against discrimination constitutes a universal right recognised by the Universal Declaration of Human Rights, the United Nations Convention on the Elimination of All Forms of Discrimination against Women, United Nations Covenants on Civil and Political Rights and on Economic, Social and Cultural Rights and by the European Convention for the Protection of Human Rights and Fundamental Freedoms, to which all Member States are signatories. Convention No 111 of the International Labour Organization (ILO) prohibits discrimination in the field of employment and occupation.

(5) It is important to respect such fundamental rights and freedoms. This Directive does not prejudice freedom of association, including the right to establish unions with others and to join unions to defend one's interests.

(6) The Community Charter of the Fundamental Social Rights of Workers recognises the importance of combating every form of discrimination, including the need to take appropriate action for the social and economic integration of elderly and disabled people.

(7) The EC Treaty includes among its objectives the promotion of coordination between employment policies of the Member States. To this end, a new employment chapter was incorporated in the EC Treaty as a means of developing a coordinated European strategy for employment to promote a skilled, trained and adaptable workforce.

(8) The Employment Guidelines for 2000 agreed by the European Council at Helsinki on 10 and 11 December 1999 stress the need to foster a labour market favourable to social integration by formulating a coherent set of policies aimed at combating discrimination against groups such as persons with disability. They also emphasise the need to pay particular attention to supporting older workers, in order to increase their participation in the labour force.

(9) Employment and occupation are key elements in guaranteeing equal opportunities for all and contribute strongly to the full participation of citizens in economic, cultural and social life and to realising their potential.

(10) On 29 June 2000 the Council adopted Directive 2000/43/EC (6) implementing the principle of equal treatment between persons irrespective of racial or ethnic origin. That Directive already provides protection against such discrimination in the field of employment and occupation.

(11) Discrimination based on religion or belief, disability, age or sexual orientation may undermine the achievement of the objectives of the EC Treaty, in particular the attainment of a high level of employment and social protection, raising the standard of living and the quality of life, economic and social cohesion and solidarity, and the free movement of persons.

(12) To this end, any direct or indirect discrimination based on religion or belief, disability, age or sexual orientation as regards the areas covered by this Directive should be prohibited throughout the Community. This prohibition of discrimination should also apply to nationals of third countries but does not cover differences of treatment based on nationality and is without prejudice to provisions governing the entry and residence of third-country nationals and their access to employment and occupation.

(13) This Directive does not apply to social security and social protection schemes whose benefits are not treated as income within the meaning given to that term for the purpose of applying Article 141 of the EC Treaty, nor to any kind of payment by the State aimed at providing access to employment or maintaining employment.

(14) This Directive shall be without prejudice to national provisions laying down retirement ages.

(15) The appreciation of the facts from which it may be inferred that there has been direct or indirect discrimination is a matter for national judicial or other competent bodies, in accordance with rules of national law or practice. Such rules may provide, in particular, for indirect discrimination to be established by any means including on the basis of statistical evidence.

(16) The provision of measures to accommodate the needs of disabled people at the workplace plays an important role in combating discrimination on grounds of disability.

(17) This Directive does not require the recruitment, promotion, maintenance in employment or training of an individual who is not competent, capable and

available to perform the essential functions of the post concerned or to undergo the relevant training, without prejudice to the obligation to provide reasonable accommodation for people with disabilities.

(18) This Directive does not require, in particular, the armed forces and the police, prison or emergency services to recruit or maintain in employment persons who do not have the required capacity to carry out the range of functions that they may be called upon to perform with regard to the legitimate objective of preserving the operational capacity of those services.

(19) Moreover, in order that the Member States may continue to safeguard the combat effectiveness of their armed forces, they may choose not to apply the provisions of this Directive concerning disability and age to all or part of their armed forces. The Member States which make that choice must define the scope of that derogation.

(20) Appropriate measures should be provided, i.e. effective and practical measures to adapt the workplace to the disability, for example adapting premises and equipment, patterns of working time, the distribution of tasks or the provision of training or integration resources.

(21) To determine whether the measures in question give rise to a disproportionate burden, account should be taken in particular of the financial and other costs entailed, the scale and financial resources of the organisation or undertaking and the possibility of obtaining public funding or any other assistance.

(22) This Directive is without prejudice to national laws on marital status and the benefits dependent thereon.

(23) In very limited circumstances, a difference of treatment may be justified where a characteristic related to religion or belief, disability, age or sexual orientation constitutes a genuine and determining occupational requirement, when the objective is legitimate and the requirement is proportionate. Such circumstances should be included in the information provided by the Member States to the Commission.

(24) The European Union in its Declaration No 11 on the status of churches and non-confessional organisations, annexed to the Final Act of the Amsterdam Treaty, has explicitly recognised that it respects and does not prejudice the status under national law of churches and religious associations or communities in the Member States and that it equally respects the status of philosophical and non-confessional organisations. With this in view, Member States may maintain or lay down specific provisions on genuine, legitimate and justified occupational requirements which might be required for carrying out an occupational activity.

(25) The prohibition of age discrimination is an essential part of meeting the aims set out in the Employment Guidelines and encouraging diversity in the workforce. However, differences in treatment in connection with age may be justified under certain circumstances and therefore require specific provisions which may vary in accordance with the situation in Member States. It is therefore essential to distinguish between differences in treatment which are justified, in particular by legitimate employment policy, labour market and vocational training objectives, and discrimination which must be prohibited.

(26) The prohibition of discrimination should be without prejudice to the maintenance or adoption of measures intended to prevent or compensate for disadvantages suffered by a group of persons of a particular religion or belief, disability, age or sexual orientation, and such measures may permit organisations of persons of a particular religion or belief, disability, age or sexual orientation where their main object is the promotion of the special needs of those persons.

(27) In its Recommendation 86/379/EEC of 24 July 1986 on the employment of disabled people in the Community (7), the Council established a guideline framework setting out examples of positive action to promote the employment and training of disabled people, and in its Resolution of 17 June 1999 on equal employment opportunities for people with disabilities (8), affirmed the importance of giving specific attention inter alia to recruitment, retention, training and lifelong learning with regard to disabled persons.

(28) This Directive lays down minimum requirements, thus giving the Member States the option of introducing or maintaining more favourable provisions. The implementation of this Directive should not serve to justify any regression in relation to the situation which already prevails in each Member State.

(29) Persons who have been subject to discrimination based on religion or belief, disability, age or sexual orientation should have adequate means of legal protection. To provide a more effective level of protection, associations or legal entities should also be empowered to engage in proceedings, as the Member States so determine, either on behalf or in support of any victim, without prejudice to national rules of procedure concerning representation and defence before the courts.

(30) The effective implementation of the principle of equality requires adequate judicial protection against victimisation.

(31) The rules on the burden of proof must be adapted when there is a prima facie case of discrimination and, for the principle of equal treatment to be applied effectively, the burden of proof must shift back to the respondent when evidence of such discrimination is brought. However, it is not for the respondent

to prove that the plaintiff adheres to a particular religion or belief, has a particular disability, is of a particular age or has a particular sexual orientation.

(32) Member States need not apply the rules on the burden of proof to proceedings in which it is for the court or other competent body to investigate the facts of the case. The procedures thus referred to are those in which the plaintiff is not required to prove the facts, which it is for the court or competent body to investigate.

(33) Member States should promote dialogue between the social partners and, within the framework of national practice, with non-governmental organisations to address different forms of discrimination at the workplace and to combat them.

(34) The need to promote peace and reconciliation between the major communities in Northern Ireland necessitates the incorporation of particular provisions into this Directive.

(35) Member States should provide for effective, proportionate and dissuasive sanctions in case of breaches of the obligations under this Directive.

(36) Member States may entrust the social partners, at their joint request, with the implementation of this Directive, as regards the provisions concerning collective agreements, provided they take any necessary steps to ensure that they are at all times able to guarantee the results required by this Directive.

(37) In accordance with the principle of subsidiarity set out in Article 5 of the EC Treaty, the objective of this Directive, namely the creation within the Community of a level playing-field as regards equality in employment and occupation, cannot be sufficiently achieved by the Member States and can therefore, by reason of the scale and impact of the action, be better achieved at Community level. In accordance with the principle of proportionality, as set out in that Article, this Directive does not go beyond what is necessary in order to achieve that objective.[80]

The scope of the Directive is outlined in Article 3:

3(1) Within the limits of the areas of competence conferred on the Community, this Directive shall apply to all persons, as regards both the public and private sectors, including public bodies, in relation to:

---

80 Council Directive 2000/78/EC 27 November 2000 Establishing a General Framework for Equal Treatment in Employment and Occupation, at the Preamble.

a. conditions for access to employment, to self-employment or to occupation, including selection criteria and recruitment conditions, whatever the branch of activity and at all levels of the professional hierarchy, including promotion;

b. access to all types and to all levels of vocational guidance, vocational training, advanced vocational training and retraining, including practical work experience;

c. employment and working conditions, including dismissals and pay;

d. membership of, and involvement in, an organisation of workers or employers, or any organisation whose members carry on a particular profession, including the benefits provided for by such organisations.[81]

Importantly, the concept of discrimination is defined under Article 2:

2(1) For the purposes of this Directive, the 'principle of equal treatment' shall mean that there shall be no direct or indirect discrimination whatsoever on any of the grounds referred to in Article 1.

(2) For the purposes of paragraph 1:

a. direct discrimination shall be taken to occur where one person is treated less favourably than another is, has been or would be treated in a comparable situation, on any of the grounds referred to in Article 1;

(3) Harassment shall be deemed to be a form of discrimination within the meaning of paragraph 1, when unwanted conduct related to any of the grounds referred to in Article 1 takes place with the purpose or effect of violating the dignity of a person and of creating an intimidating, hostile, degrading, humiliating or offensive environment. In this context, the concept of harassment may be defined in accordance with the national laws and practice of the Member States.

(4) An instruction to discriminate against persons on any of the grounds referred to in Article 1 shall be deemed to be discrimination within the meaning of paragraph 1.[82]

Further, Article 11 guards against victimization:

11. Member States shall introduce into their national legal systems such measures as are necessary to protect employees against dismissal or other adverse treatment by the employer as a reaction to a complaint within the undertaking or to any legal proceedings aimed at enforcing compliance with the principle of equal treatment.[83]

However, Article 4 contains genuine occupational requirements:

---

81 Ibid., at Article 3.
82 Ibid., at Article 2.
83 Ibid., at Article 11.

4(1) Notwithstanding Article 2(1) and (2), Member States may provide that a difference of treatment which is based on a characteristic related to any of the grounds referred to in Article 1 shall not constitute discrimination where, by reason of the nature of the particular occupational activities concerned or of the context in which they are carried out, such a characteristic constitutes a genuine and determining occupational requirement, provided that the objective is legitimate and the requirement is proportionate.[84]

Further, Article 8 provides for minimum requirements:

8(1) Member States may introduce or maintain provisions which are more favourable to the protection of the principle of equal treatment than those laid down in this Directive.
(2) The implementation of this Directive shall under no circumstances constitute grounds for a reduction in the level of protection against discrimination already afforded by Member States in the fields covered by this Directive.[85]

Positive action is provided for under Article 7:

7(1) With a view to ensuring full equality in practice, the principle of equal treatment shall not prevent any Member State from maintaining or adopting specific measures to prevent or compensate for disadvantages linked to any of the grounds referred to in Article 1.[86]

Importantly, in terms of remedies and enforcement, Article 9 provides for defence of rights:

9(1) Member States shall ensure that judicial and/or administrative procedures, including where they deem it appropriate conciliation procedures, for the enforcement of obligations under this Directive are available to all persons who consider themselves wronged by failure to apply the principle of equal treatment to them, even after the relationship in which the discrimination is alleged to have occurred has ended.
(2) Member States shall ensure that associations, organisations or other legal entities which have, in accordance with the criteria laid down by their national law, a legitimate interest in ensuring that the provisions of this Directive are complied with, may engage, either on behalf or in support of the complainant, with his or her approval, in any judicial and/or administrative procedure provided for the enforcement of obligations under this Directive.[87]

---

84   Ibid., at Article 4.
85   Ibid., at Article 8.
86   Ibid., at Article 7.
87   Ibid., at Article 9.

The burden of proof is detailed in Article 10:

> 10(1) Member States shall take such measures as are necessary, in accordance
> with their national judicial systems, to ensure that, when persons who consider
> themselves wronged because the principle of equal treatment has not been
> applied to them establish, before a court or other competent authority, facts from
> which it may be presumed that there has been direct or indirect discrimination, it
> shall be for the respondent to prove that there has been no breach of the principle
> of equal treatment.[88]

Article 16 provides for compliance:

> 16. Member States shall take the necessary measures to ensure that:
> a. any laws, regulations and administrative provisions contrary to the principle
> of equal treatment are abolished;
> b. any provisions contrary to the principle of equal treatment which are included
> in contracts or collective agreements, internal rules of undertakings or rules
> governing the independent occupations and professions and workers' and
> employers' organisations are, or may be, declared null and void or are amended.[89]

Finally, Article 17 deals with sanctions:

> 17. Member States shall lay down the rules on sanctions applicable to
> infringements of the national provisions adopted pursuant to this Directive and
> shall take all measures necessary to ensure that they are applied. The sanctions,
> which may comprise the payment of compensation to the victim, must be
> effective, proportionate and dissuasive. Member States shall notify those
> provisions to the Commission by 2 December 2003 at the latest and shall notify
> it without delay of any subsequent amendment affecting them.[90]

Council Directive 1994/33/EC on the Protection of Young People at Work

The Preamble of Council Directive 1994/33/EC of 22 June 1994 on the protection
of young people at work states:

> The Council of the European Union,
>
> Having regard to the Treaty establishing the European Community, and in
> particular Article 118a thereof,

---

88   Ibid., at Article 10.
89   Ibid., at Article 16.
90   Ibid., at Article 17.

Having regard to the proposal from the Commission (1),

Having regard to the opinion of the Economic and Social Committee (2),

Acting in accordance with the procedure referred to in Article 189c of the Treaty (3),

Whereas Article 118a of the Treaty provides that the Council shall adopt, by means of directives, minimum requirements to encourage improvements, especially in the working environment, as regards the health and safety of workers;

Whereas, under that Article, such directives must avoid imposing administrative, financial and legal constraints in a way which would hold back the creation and development of small and medium-sized undertakings;

Whereas points 20 and 22 of the Community Charter of the Fundamental Social Rights of Workers, adopted by the European Council in Strasbourg on 9 December 1989, state that:

'20. Without prejudice to such rules as may be more favourable to young people, in particular those ensuring their preparation for work through vocational training, and subject to derogations limited to certain light work, the minimum employment age must not be lower than the minimum school-leaving age and, in any case, not lower than 15 years;

22. Appropriate measures must be taken to adjust labour regulations applicable to young workers so that their specific development and vocational training and access to employment needs are met.

The duration of work must, in particular, be limited – without it being possible to circumvent this limitation through recourse to overtime – and night work prohibited in the case of workers of under eighteen years of age, save in the case of certain jobs laid down in national legislation or regulations.';

Whereas account should be taken of the principles of the International Labour Organization regarding the protection of young people at work, including those relating to the minimum age for access to employment or work;

Whereas, in this Resolution on child labour (4), the European Parliament summarized the various aspects of work by young people and stressed its effects on their health, safety and physical and intellectual development, and pointed to the need to adopt a Directive harmonizing national legislation in the field;

Whereas Article 15 of Council Directive 89/391/EEC of 12 June 1989 on the introduction of measures to encourage improvements in the safety and health of workers at work (5) provides that particularly sensitive risk groups must be protected against the dangers which specifically affect them;

Whereas children and adolescents must be considered specific risk groups, and measures must be taken with regard to their safety and health;

Whereas the vulnerability of children calls for Member States to prohibit their employment and ensure that the minimum working or employment age is not lower than the minimum age at which compulsory schooling as imposed by national law ends or 15 years in any event; whereas derogations from the prohibition on child labour may be admitted only in special cases and under the conditions stipulated in this Directive; whereas, under no circumstances, may such derogations be detrimental to regular school attendance or prevent children benefiting fully from their education;

Whereas, in view of the nature of the transition from childhood to adult life, work by adolescents should be strictly regulated and protected;

Whereas every employer should guarantee young people working conditions appropriate to their age;

Whereas employers should implement the measures necessary to protect the safety and health of young people on the basis of an assessment of work-related hazards to the young;

Whereas Member States should protect young people against any specific risks arising from their lack of experience, absence of awareness of existing or potential risks, or from their immaturity;

Whereas Member States should therefore prohibit the employment of young people for the work specified by this Directive;

Whereas the adoption of specific minimal requirements in respect of the organization of working time is likely to improve working conditions for young people;

Whereas the maximum working time of young people should be strictly limited and night work by young people should be prohibited, with the exception of certain jobs specified by national legislation or rules;

Whereas Member States should take the appropriate measures to ensure that the working time of adolescents receiving school education does not adversely affect their ability to benefit from that education;

Whereas time spent on training by young persons working under a theoretical and/or practical combined work/training scheme or an in-plant work-experience should be counted as working time;

Whereas, in order to ensure the safety and health of young people, the latter should be granted minimum daily, weekly and annual periods of rest and adequate breaks;

Whereas, with respect to the weekly rest period, due account should be taken of the diversity of cultural, ethnic, religious and other factors prevailing in the Member States; whereas in particular, it is ultimately for each Member State to decide whether Sunday should be included in the weekly rest period, and if so to what extent;

Whereas appropriate work experience may contribute to the aim of preparing young people for adult working and social life, provided it is ensured that any harm to their safety, health and development is avoided;

Whereas, although derogations from the bans and limitations imposed by this Directive would appear indispensable for certain activities or particular situations, applications thereof must not prejudice the principles underlying the established protection system;

Whereas this Directive constitutes a tangible step towards developing the social dimension of the internal market;

Whereas the application in practice of the system of protection laid down by this Directive will require that Member States implement a system of effective and proportionate measures;

Whereas the implementation of some provisions of this Directive poses particular problems for one Member State with regard to its system of protection for young people at work; whereas that Member State should therefore be allowed to refrain from implementing the relevant provisions for a suitable period,

Has adopted this Directive.[91]

---

91   Council Directive 1994/33/EC on the protection of young people at work, at the Preamble.

Article 1 defines the purpose of the Directive, including the prohibition of work by children:

> 1.1. Member States shall take the necessary measures to prohibit work by children.
> They shall ensure, under the conditions laid down by this Directive, that the minimum working or employment age is not lower than the minimum age at which compulsory full-time schooling as imposed by national law ends or 15 years in any event.
> 2. Member States ensure that work by adolescents is strictly regulated and protected under the conditions laid down in this Directive.
> 3. Member States shall ensure in general that employers guarantee that young people have working conditions which suit their age.
> They shall ensure that young people are protected against economic exploitation and against any work likely to harm their safety, health or physical, mental, moral or social development or to jeopardize their education.[92]

Further, Article 2 defines the scope of the Directive:

> 2.1. This Directive shall apply to any person under 18 years of age having an employment contract or an employment relationship defined by the law in force in a Member State and/or governed by the law in force in a Member State.
> 2. Member States may make legislative or regulatory provision for this Directive not to apply, within the limits and under the conditions which they set by legislative or regulatory provision, to occasional work or short-term work involving:
> (a) domestic service in a private household, or
> (b) work regarded as not being harmful, damaging or dangerous to young people in a family undertaking.[93]

Importantly, definitions, including young person, child and adolescent, are included in Article 3:

> 3. For the purposes of this Directive:
> (a) 'young person' shall mean any person under 18 years of age referred to in Article 2 (1);
> (b) 'child' shall mean any young person of less than 15 years of age or who is still subject to compulsory full-time schooling under national law;
> (c) 'adolescent' shall mean any young person of at least 15 years of age but less than 18 years of age who is no longer subject to compulsory full-time schooling under national law;

92　Ibid., at Article 1.
93　Ibid., at Article 2.

(d) 'light work' shall mean all work which, on account of the inherent nature of the tasks which it involves and the particular conditions under which they are performed:

(i) is not likely to be harmful to the safety, health or development of children, and

(ii) is not such as to be harmful to their attendance at school, their participation in vocational guidance or training programmes approved by the competent authority or their capacity to benefit from the instruction received;

(e) 'working time' shall mean any period during which the young person is at work, at the employer's disposal and carrying out his activity or duties in accordance with national legislation and/or practice;

(f) 'rest period' shall mean any period which is not working time.[94]

Article 4 prohibits work by children:

4.1. Member States shall adopt the measures necessary to prohibit work by children.

2. Taking into account the objectives set out in Article 1, Member States may make legislative or regulatory provision for the prohibition of work by children not to apply to:

(a) children pursuing the activities set out in Article 5;

(b) children of at least 14 years of age working under a combined work/training scheme or an in-plant work-experience scheme, provided that such work is done in accordance with the conditions laid down by the competent authority;

(c) children of at least 14 years of age performing light work other than that covered by Article 5; light work other than that covered by Article 5 may, however, be performed by children of 13 years of age for a limited number of hours per week in the case of categories of work determined by national legislation.

3. Member States that make use of the opinion referred to in paragraph 2(c) shall determine, subject to the provisions of this Directive, the working conditions relating to the light work in question.[95]

However, an exception exists for cultural or similar activities under Article 5:

5.1. The employment of children for the purposes of performance in cultural, artistic, sports or advertising activities shall be subject to prior authorization to be given by the competent authority in individual cases.

2. Member States shall by legislative or regulatory provision lay down the working conditions for children in the cases referred to in paragraph 1 and the details of the prior authorization procedure, on condition that the activities:

---

94   Ibid., at Article 3.
95   Ibid., at Article 4.

(i) are not likely to be harmful to the safety, health or development of children, and

(ii) are not such as to be harmful to their attendance at school, their participation in vocational guidance or training programmes approved by the competent authority or their capacity to benefit from the instruction received.

3. By way of derogation from the procedure laid down in paragraph 1, in the case of children of at least 13 years of age, Member States may authorize, by legislative or regulatory provision, in accordance with conditions which they shall determine, the employment of children for the purposes of performance in cultural, artistic, sports or advertising activities.

4. The Member States which have a specific authorization system for modelling agencies with regard to the activities of children may retain that system.[96]

General obligations of employers are contained under Article 6:

6.1. Without prejudice to Article 4 (1), the employer shall adopt the measures necessary to protect the safety and health of young people, taking particular account of the specific risks referred to in Article 7 (1).

2. The employer shall implement the measures provided for in paragraph 1 on the basis of an assessment of the hazards to young people in connection with their work.

The assessment must be made before young people begin work and when there is any major change in working conditions and must pay particular attention to the following points:

(a) the fitting-out and layout of the workplace and the workstation;

(b) the nature, degree and duration of exposure to physical, biological and chemical agents;

(c) the form, range and use of work equipment, in particular agents, machines, apparatus and devices, and the way in which they are handled;

(d) the arrangement of work processes and operations and the way in which these are combined (organization of work);

(e) the level of training and instruction given to young people.

Where this assessment shows that there is a risk to the safety, the physical or mental health or development of young people, an appropriate free assessment and monitoring of their health shall be provided at regular intervals without prejudice to Directive 89/391/EEC.

The free health assessment and monitoring may form part of a national health system.

3. The employer shall inform young people of possible risks and of all measures adopted concerning their safety and health.

Furthermore, he shall inform the legal representatives of children of possible risks and of all measures adopted concerning children's safety and health.

---

96   Ibid., at Article 5.

4. The employer shall involve the protective and preventive services referred to in Article 7 of Directive 89/391/EEC in the planning, implementation and monitoring of the safety and health conditions applicable to young people.[97]

The vulnerability of young people and the prohibition of work are underlined in Article 7:

7.1. Member States shall ensure that young people are protected from any specific risks to their safety, health and development which are a consequence of their lack of experience, of absence of awareness of existing or potential risks or of the fact that young people have not yet fully matured.

2. Without prejudice to Article 4 (1), Member States shall to this end prohibit the employment of young people for:

(a) work which is objectively beyond their physical or psychological capacity;

(b) work involving harmful exposure to agents which are toxic, carcinogenic, cause heritable genetic damage, or harm to the unborn child or which in any other way chronically affect human health;

(c) work involving harmful exposure to radiation;

(d) work involving the risk of accidents which it may be assumed cannot be recognized or avoided by young persons owing to their insufficient attention to safety or lack of experience or training; or

(e) work in which there is a risk to health from extreme cold or heat, or from noise or vibration.

Work which is likely to entail specific risks for young people within the meaning of paragraph 1 includes:

– work involving harmful exposure to the physical, biological and chemical agents referred to in point I of the Annex, and

– processes and work referred to in point II of the Annex.

3. Member States may, by legislative or regulatory provision, authorize derogations from paragraph 2 in the case of adolescents where such derogations are indispensable for their vocational training, provided that protection of their safety and health is ensured by the fact that the work is performed under the supervision of a competent person within the meaning of Article 7 of Directive 89/391/EEC and provided that the protection afforded by that Directive is guaranteed.[98]

Further, the Annex to the Directive includes a list of agents, processes and work to protect children at work:

ANNEX. Non-exhaustive list of agents, processes and work (Article 7(2), second subparagraph)

---

97 Ibid., at Article 6.
98 Ibid., at Article 7.

I. Agents

1. Physical agents

(a) Ionizing radiation;

(b) Work in a high-pressure atmosphere, e.g. in pressurized containers, diving.

2. Biological agents

(a) Biological agents belonging to groups 3 and 4 within the meaning of Article 2 (d) of Council Directive 90/679/EEC of 26 November 1990 on the protection of workers from risks related to exposure to biological agents at work (Seventh individual Directive within the meaning of Article 16(1) of Directive 89/391/ EEC) (1).

3. Chemical agents

(a) Substances and preparations classified according to Council Directive 67/548/EEC of 27 June 1967 on the approximation of laws, regulations and administrative provisions relating to the classification, packaging and labelling of dangerous substances (2) with amendments and Council Directive 88/379/EEC of 7 June 1988 on the approximation of the laws, regulations and administrative provisions of the Member States relating to the classification, packaging and labelling of dangerous preparations (3) as toxic (T), very toxic (Tx), corrosive (C) or explosive (E);

(b) Substances and preparations classified according to Directives 67/548/EEC and 88/379/EEC as harmful (Xn) and with one or more of the following risk phrases:

– danger of very serious irreversible effects (R39),

– possible risk of irreversible effects (R40),

– may cause sensitization by inhalation (R42),

– may cause sensitization by skin contact (R43),

– may cause cancer (R45),

– may cause heritable genetic damage (R46),

– danger of serious damage to health by prolonged exposure (R48),

– may impair fertility (R60),

– may cause harm to the unborn child (R61);

(c) Substances and preparations classified according to Directives 67/548/EEC and 88/379/EEC as irritant (Xi) and with one or more of the following risk phrases:

– highly flammable (R12);

– may cause sensitization by inhalation (R42),

– may cause sensitization by skin contact (R43),

(d) Substances and preparations referred to Article 2 (c) of Council Directive 90/394/EEC of 28 June 1990 on the protection of workers from the risks related to exposure to carcinogens at work (Sixth individual Directive within the meaning of Article 16(1) of Directive 89/391/EEC; (4)

(e) Lead and compounds thereof, inasmuch as the agents in question are absorbable by the human organism;

(f) Asbestos.

II. Processes and work

1. Processes at work referred to in Annex I to Directive 90/394/EEC.

2. Manufacture and handling of devices, fireworks or other objects containing explosives.

3. Work with fierce or poisonous animals.

4. Animal slaughtering on an industrial scale.

5. Work involving the handling of equipment for the production, storage or application of compressed, liquified or dissolved gases.

6. Work with vats, tanks, reservoirs or carboys containing chemical agents referred to in 1.3.

7. Work involving a risk of structural collapse.

8. Work involving high-voltage electrical hazards.

9. Work the pace of which is determined by machinery and involving payment by results.[99]

Working time is outlined under Article 8:

8.1. Member States which make use of the option in Article 4 (2) (b) or (c) shall adopt the measures necessary to limit the working time of children to:

(a) eight hours a day and 40 hours a week for work performed under a combined work/training scheme or an in-plant work-experience scheme;

(b) two hours on a school day and 12 hours a week for work performed in term-time outside the hours fixed for school attendance, provided that this is not prohibited by national legislation and/or practice;

in no circumstances may the daily working time exceed seven hours; this limit may be raised to eight hours in the case of children who have reached the age of 15;

(c) seven hours a day and 35 hours a week for work performed during a period of at least a week when school is not operating; these limits may be raised to eight hours a day and 40 hours a week in the case of children who have reached the age of 15;

(d) seven hours a day and 35 hours a week for light work performed by children no longer subject to compulsory full-time schooling under national law.

2. Member States shall adopt the measures necessary to limit the working time of adolescents to eight hours a day and 40 hours a week.

3. The time spent on training by a young person working under a theoretical and/or practical combined work/training scheme or an in-plant work-experience scheme shall be counted as working time.

4. Where a young person is employed by more than one employer, working days and working time shall be cumulative.

---

99   Ibid., at Annex.

5. Member States may, by legislative or regulatory provision, authorize derogations from paragraph 1 (a) and paragraph 2 either by way of exception or where there are objective grounds for so doing.

Member States shall, by legislative or regulatory provision, determine the conditions, limits and procedure for implementing such derogations.[100]

Further, 'night work' is outlined under Article 9:

9.1.(a) Member States which make use of the option in Article 4 (2) (b) or (c) shall adopt the measures necessary to prohibit work by children between 8 p.m. and 6 a.m.

(b) Member States shall adopt the measures necessary to prohibit work by adolescents either between 10 p.m. and 6 a.m. or between 11 p.m. and 7 a.m.

2.(a) Member States may, by legislative or regulatory provision, authorize work by adolescents in specific areas of activity during the period in which night work is prohibited as referred to in paragraph 1 (b).

In that event, Member States shall take appropriate measures to ensure that the adolescent is supervised by an adult where such supervision is necessary for the adolescent's protection.

(b) If point (a) is applied, work shall continue to be prohibited between midnight and 4 a.m.

However, Member States may, by legislative or regulatory provision, authorize work by adolescents during the period in which night work is prohibited in the following cases, where there are objective grounds for so doing and provided that adolescents are allowed suitable compensatory rest time and that the objectives set out in Article 1 are not called into question:

– work performed in the shipping or fisheries sectors;

– work performed in the context of the armed forces or the police;

– work performed in hospitals or similar establishments;

– cultural, artistic, sports or advertising activities.

3. Prior to any assignment to night work and at regular intervals thereafter, adolescents shall be entitled to a free assessment of their health and capacities, unless the work they do during the period during which work is prohibited is of an exceptional nature.[101]

Additionally, 'rest period' is outlined under Article 10:

10.1.(a) Member States which make use of the option in Article 4 (2) (b) or (c) shall adopt the measures necessary to ensure that, for each 24-hour period, children are entitled to a minimum rest period of 14 consecutive hours.

---

100   Ibid., at Article8.
101   Ibid., at Article 9.

(b) Member States shall adopt the measures necessary to ensure that, for each 24-hour period, adolescents are entitled to a minimum rest period of 12 consecutive hours.

2. Member States shall adopt the measures necessary to ensure that, for each seven-day period:

– children in respect of whom they have made use of the option in Article 4 (2) (b) or (c), and

– adolescents

are entitled to a minimum rest period of two days, which shall be consecutive if possible.

Where justified by technical or organization reasons, the minimum rest period may be reduced, but may in no circumstances be less than 36 consecutive hours. The minimum rest period referred to in the first and second subparagraphs shall in principle include Sunday.

3. Member States may, by legislative or regulatory provision, provide for the minimum rest periods referred to in paragraphs 1 and 2 to be interrupted in the case of activities involving periods of work that are split up over the day or are of short duration.

4. Member States may make legislative or regulatory provision for derogations from paragraph 1 (b) and paragraph 2 in respect of adolescents in the following cases, where there are objective grounds for so doing and provided that they are granted appropriate compensatory rest time and that the objectives set out in Article 1 are not called into question:

(a) work performed in the shipping or fisheries sectors;

(b) work performed in the context of the armed forces or the police;

(c) work performed in hospitals or similar establishments;

(d) work performed in agriculture;

(e) work performed in the tourism industry or in the hotel, restaurant and café sector;

(f) activities involving periods of work split up over the day.[102]

Annual rest is contained in Article 11:

11. Member States which make use of the option referred to in Article 4 (2) (b) or (c) shall see to it that a period free of any work is included, as far as possible, in the school holidays of children subject to compulsory full-time schooling under national law.[103]

Further, breaks are contained in Article 12:

---

102   Ibid., at Article 10.
103   Ibid., at Article 11.

12. Member States shall adopt the measures necessary to ensure that, where daily working time is more than four and a half hours, young people are entitled to a break of at least 30 minutes, which shall be consecutive if possible.[104]

Work by adolescents in the event of force majeure is contained in Article 13:

13. Member States may, by legislative or regulatory provision, authorize derogations from Article 8 (2), Article 9 (1) (b), Article 10 (1) (b) and, in the case of adolescents, Article 12, for work in the circumstances referred to in Article 5 (4) of Directive 89/391/EEC, provided that such work is of a temporary nature and must be performed immediately, that adult workers are not available and that the adolescents are allowed equivalent compensatory rest time within the following three weeks.[105]

Necessary measures by Member States to combat child labor are stressed under Article 14:

14. Each Member State shall lay down any necessary measures to be applied in the event of failure to comply with the provisions adopted in order to implement this Directive; such measures must be effective and proportionate.[106]

Finally, Article 16 is a non-reducing clause affording the ultimate protection to children:

16. Without prejudice to the right of Member States to develop, in the light of changing circumstances, different provisions on the protection of young people, as long as the minimum requirements provided for by this Directive are complied with, the implementation of this Directive shall not constitute valid grounds for reducing the general level of protection afforded to young people.[107]

The European Union is at a crossroads, challenged to adapt the vision of the 'founding fathers' that was first designed for six Member States to a future union of over twenty States. In essence, Europe is now the biggest frontier-free market in the world. The single market removed three types of barriers to free movement, namely physical, technical and fiscal. The four freedoms of the Union, for goods, services, people and capital, have become a reality. Further, the new single currency, the euro, was introduced as legal tender on 1 January 1999, and replaced the currencies of those Member States in agreement on 1 January 2002. Currently, the Member States of the European Union are: Austria, Belgium, Denmark, Finland,

---

104 Ibid., at Article 12.
105 Ibid., at Article 13.
106 Ibid., at Article 14.
107 Ibid., at Article 16.

France, Germany, Greece, Ireland, Italy, Luxembourg, the Netherlands, Portugal, Spain, Sweden and the United Kingdom, and since 1 May 2004, Cyprus (Greek part), the Czech Republic, Estonia, Hungary, Latvia, Lithuania, Malta, Poland, Slovakia and Slovenia expanded it from 15 to 25 Member States, and since 1 January 2007, Bulgaria and Romania, bringing the number to 27 Member States. Candidate countries are Croatia, the Former Yugoslav Republic of Macedonia, and Turkey. The remaining European Countries which are not Member States of the European Union are Albania, Andorra, Belarus, Bosnia-Herzegovina, Iceland, Liechtenstein, Moldova, Monaco, Montenegro, Norway, Russia, San Marino, Serbia, Switzerland, Ukraine and Vatican City. The criteria used for a nation to secure membership in the ever-growing European Union are: (1) democratic institutions and the rule of law, with respect for human rights and minorities within the borders; (2) a functioning market economy capable of competing within the Union's single market; and (3) the acceptance of obligations of membership, signing onto the Union's body of rules. The latter is perhaps the most important criterion for equal rights and their enforcement. European enlargement has increased the population of the European Union to roughly 500 million inhabitants, the third most populated political entity in the world after China and India.[108]

According to the 57th Eurobarometer survey on discrimination, few respondents reported personally experiencing discrimination on any of the six grounds explored, but the most often cited ground for discrimination was age (5 percent), followed by race or ethnicity (3 percent), religion or beliefs (2 percent), physical disability, learning difficulties or mental illness (2 percent), and sexual orientation (less than 1 percent).[109] Young people, the better educated and those on the left of the political spectrum were more likely to report having experienced discrimination. Further, those who personally experienced discrimination, young people and respondents with leftist political views were significantly more likely to report witnessing discrimination. The most often-cited ground for witnessed discrimination was race or ethnicity (22 percent), followed by learning difficulties or mental illness (12 percent), physical disability (11 percent), religion or beliefs (9 percent), age (6 percent) and sexual orientation (6 percent). The young, better-educated and non-manually-employed women are more likely to oppose discrimination, older male manual workers with little education less so, but there is no clear evidence that the tendency to believe discrimination right or wrong, or to attribute such views to others, is socially determined to any great degree.[110] 2007 was designated as the European Year of Equal Opportunities for All, with the aim to inform people of their rights, to celebrate diversity and to promote equal

---

108   Commission Report on the Social Situation in the European Union, Report on social protection in Europe.

109   Marsh, Alan and Sahin-Dikmen, Melahat, *Discrimination in Europe*, Policy Studies Institute, London, 2002.

110   Ibid.

opportunities for everyone in the European Union. A large proportion of Europeans are still of the opinion that discrimination is widespread in their country.[111]

Thus, it will be necessary to develop incentives to change people's behavior with regard to child issues and to combat discrimination. The European Union has provided important contributions to the ending of child discrimination in the coming together of people of different nations, and equality in employment is a real commitment for the Member States. The right of all individuals to equality before the law and to protection from discrimination is a fundamental principle of all democratic societies.[112] Establishing an effective set of laws against discrimination is an essential part of stamping out unfair treatment, but laws themselves are not enough; if discrimination is to be eliminated, attitudes and behavior must also change.

Conclusion

Although European laws have gone a long way to improving the plight of many in the European Union, in reality, some have yet to enjoy the equality they are entitled to in theory. The European Union is a political structure, which emerged out of a general act of will of heterogeneous States. Therefore, European Union law is the motor to enable the European Union to move toward its ultimate aim, the 'ever closer union'. The European Union is based on partnership, cooperation and mutual dependence; the concern is to enhance the social, economic and cultural welfare of all citizens in an atmosphere of peace. This, thereby, advances the cause for child rights in stamping out child discrimination, through the effective use of laws and the courts, as shown in *Little Angels*.

---

111   Special Eurobarometer 263, *Discrimination in the European Union*, 2007.
112   Eurobarometer 57, *Discrimination in Europe, for Diversity against Discrimination*, Alan Marsh and Melahat Sahin-Dikmen, The European Opinion Research Group (EEIG) for the European Commission Directorate General Employment and Social Affairs.

Chapter 10

Conclusion to *Little Angels*

In the quest for respect for our children and in the fight against child discrimination in *Little Angels*, a deep embedded patriarchal authority is still keeping society on the designated track, as de jure discrimination has given way to de facto discrimination, and in essence, inequality, once obvious and accepted, is now hidden and protected in a most dangerous way. Since within society there is an a priori assumption of freedom and impartiality, the burden is high on the attackers of this universal opinion. Discrimination which is so blatant and open as to focus on children is most persistent and threatening to society. Therefore, seeking out child inequality and bringing it to the forefront of microscopic debate can only serve to advance all quests for equality.

Both legislation and the court system have made inroads into child rights. It is important to have adequate legislation to influence conduct and outcomes, as well as an appropriate legal system to achieve favorable and enforceable results. By cooperating and learning from other similarly disadvantaged groups in the fight for equality of opportunity, more advances can be made in the fight for child equality. We will never totally correct the injustices of the past or of the present. However, with a greater appreciation of child issues, as well as a better understanding of the importance of adequate legislation, future endeavors in the field will help to improve the situation, but for all people. Child rights' legislation and court challenges are required, in order to better improve the situation of all in the workplace. The desire is for equal social rights for all. Therefore, the law needs to be enforced by way of the courts to achieve greater equality in an effort to modify historical attitudes, so that nations conform to certain standards.

The central importance of equality legislation in order to bring about change is evident and indeed critical. Our very rights as human beings emanate from the word of the law and the interpretation given by the highest courts in the land. Therefore, it is imperative that the struggle for child equality encompass the legal system. The concept of total equality has never truly existed, nor was it ever meant to be anything more than empty promises of change. Absolute equality is not sought in this book, nor is it realistic. However, in a feeling of mutual respect for our children, a better equality among all groups is possible and desirable through society's laws and legal institutions. The keys to the future are the implementation and development of the law, the deepening in understanding of specific legal issues relating to employment discrimination, and the raising of the level of awareness of legal rights and obligations. We must all strive to promote and improve the situation of our children through networks of awareness, in the raising of initiatives, the dissemination of information and the provision of support for equality.[1]

It is realistic to say that inequality in general exists, but especially inequality of opportunity within the labor force. Laws have been enacted and courts have enforced them in a traditionally white male-dominant way. However, our children too need to be a rallying symbol of political and economic force, so that equality can become a reality. The impact of equality legislation will depend on the legislative provisions as well as the effectiveness of the legislation's enforcement. The full and equal enjoyment of all human rights and fundamental freedoms should be a priority for all and is essential for the advancement of all. Unless the human rights of all, as defined by international human rights instruments, are fully recognized and effectively protected, applied, implemented and enforced in national law as well as in national practice in family, civil, penal, labor and commercial codes and administrative rules and regulations, they will exist in name only.[2]

In the fight against discrimination, the late Robert F. Kennedy stated:

> Every time a man stands up for an ideal, or acts to improve the lot of others, or strikes out against injustice, he sends forth a tiny ripple of hope, and crossing each other from a million different centers of energy and daring those ripples build a current which can sweep down the mightiest walls of oppression and resistance.[3]

It is evident that we are moving in the right direction, since some change has taken place. However, further change is necessary and plausible. By working on the very thing that controls and defines all of our lives, the law, can further progress be made. Once again, the memorable words of the Rev. Martin Luther King Jr. in his struggle for civil rights are most relevant today in the struggle for child rights in *Little Angels*:

> I have a dream that one day every valley shall be exalted, every hill and mountain shall be made low, the rough places shall be made plain, and the crooked places shall be made straight and the glory of the Lord will be revealed and all flesh shall see it together. This is our hope ... And when we allow freedom to ring, when we let it ring from every village and hamlet, from every state and city, we will be able to speed up that day when all of God's children ... will be able to join hands and to sing in the words of the old Negro spiritual, 'Free at last, free at last; thank God Almighty, we are free at last.'[4]

---

1 Commission of the European Communities, *Promotion of Positive Action*, Brussels, p. 4.

2 United Nations, Beijing Declaration and Platform for Action.

3 Robert F. Kennedy.

4 King Jr., Martin Luther, *March on Washington*, 1963.

Bibliography

African Charter on Human and Peoples' Rights, 1981.

American Convention on Human Rights, 1978.

American Declaration of the Rights and Duties of Man, 1948.

American Federation of State, County and Municipal Employees v. *Washington*, 770 F.2d. 1401 (1985).

American Nurses Association v. *State of Illinois*, 783 F.2d. 716 (1985).

Anti-Discrimination Act 1991, Australia.

Australia's Beijing Plus Five Action Plan 2001–2005.

Axworthy, Lloyd (1988), 'Free Trade, the Costs for Canada', in A.R. Riggs and Tom Velk (eds), *Canadian–American Free Trade (The Sequel): Historical, Political and Economic Dimensions*, The Institute for Research on Public Policy, Montreal.

Basi v. *Canadian National Railway* (1984), 9 CHRR 4. D/5029 (CHR Tribunal).

Bill of Rights Act 1990, New Zealand.

Black, Sandra, Devereux, Paul, and Salvanes, Kjell, 'Why the Apple Doesn't Fall Far: Understanding Intergenerational Transmission of Human Capital', in *The American Economic Review*, vol. 95, No. 1 (March 2005), pp. 437–49.

Blake v. *Ministry of Correctional Services and Mimico Correctional Institute* (1984), 5 CHRR D/2417 (Ontario).

Board of Trustees of Keene State College v. *Sweeney*, 439 US 24 (1978).

Brecher, Irving (1987), 'The Free Trade Initiative, On Course or Off', in A.R. Riggs and Tom Velk (eds), *Canadian–American Free Trade: Historical, Political and Economic Dimensions*, The Institute for Research in Public Policy, Montreal.

Brennan v. *City Stores*, 479 F.2d. 235 (1973).

British North America Act 1867, Canada.

Campbell, Bruce (1993), *Free Trade, Destroyer of Jobs*, Canadian Centre for Policy Alternatives, Ottawa.

Canada Employment Equity Act 1995, Canada.

Canada Labour Code, 1985.

Canada–United States Free Trade Agreement, 1989.

Canadian Advisory Council on the Status of Women (1992), *Feminist Guide to the Canadian Constitution*, Ottawa.

Canadian Bill of Rights 1960, Canada.

Canadian Human Rights Act 1978, Canada.

Cassin, René (1969), *From the Ten Commandments to the Rights of Man*, France.

Charter of the Organization of African Unity, 1963.

Child Employment Act 2003, Victoria, Australia.

Child Employment Act 2006, Queensland, Australia.

Child Labor Public Education Project, Child Labor in U.S. History.

Children and Community Services Act 2004, Western Australia, Australia.

Children Act 1972, UK.

Children Act 1989, UK.

Children Act 2004, UK.

Children and Young Persons Act 1933, UK.

Children and Young Persons Act 1963, UK.

Children and Young Persons (Care and Protection – Child Employment) Regulation 2010, NSW, Australia.

Children (Northern Ireland) Order, 1995.

Children's Act 2005, South Africa.

Civil Rights Act 1964, United States.

Coleman, Frank (1977), *Hobbes and America*, University of Toronto, Toronto.

Commission for Labour Cooperation, Guide to Child Labour Laws in Canada.

Commission for Racial Equality (2002), *Code of Practice on the Duty to Promote Race Equality*, UK.

Commission of the European Communities, *Promotion of Positive Action*, Brussels.

Commission Report on the social situation in the European Union, Report on social protection in Europe 2004 (not published in the Official Journal).

Constitución Política de los Estados Unidos Mexicanos 1917, Mexico.

Constitution Act 1867, Canada.

Constitution Act 1982, Canada.

Constitution of Ireland 1937, Ireland.

Constitution of South Africa, 1996.

Corning Glass Works v. *Brennan*, 417 US 188 (1974).

Costa v. *ENEL* [1964] CMLR 425.

Council Decision 2000/750/EC of 27 November 2000 establishing a Community action programme to combat discrimination (2001 to 2006).

Council Directive 1994/33/EC of 22 June 1994 on the protection of young people at work.

Council Directive 2000/78/EC of 27 November 2000 establishing a general framework for equal treatment in employment and occupation.

County of Allegheny v. *American Civil Liberties Union Greater Pittsburgh Chapter*, 492 U.S. 573 (1989).

Cox, Archibald (1967), *Civil Rights, the Constitution and the Court*, Harvard University Press, Cambridge, MA.

Cox, Archibald (1976), *The Role of the Supreme Court in American Government*, Oxford University Press, New York.

Daltrop, Anne (1982), *Political Realities, Politics and the European Community*, Longman, London.

d'Aquino, Thomas (1987), 'Truck and Trade with the Yankees, the Case for a Canada–U.S. Comprehensive Trade Agreement', in A.R. Riggs and Tom Velk (eds), *Canadian–American Free Trade: Historical, Political and Economic Dimensions*, The Institute for Research on Public Policy, Montreal.

Davis v. *Passman*, 442 U.S. 228 (1979).

Declaration of Independence 1776, United States.

DeJong, Peter, Brawer, Milton, and Robin, Stanley, 'Patterns of Female Intergenerational Occupational Mobility: A Comparison with Male Patterns of Intergenerational Occupational Mobility', in *American Sociological Review*, vol. 36, No. 6 (December 1971), pp. 1033–42.

Discrimination Act 1991, Australia.

Easterbrook, W.T. and Aitken, Hugh (1976), *Canadian Economic History*, Macmillan, Toronto.

Economic Commission for Africa (2002), *Economic Report on Africa*.

Education Act 1989, New Zealand.

Ely, J. (1980), *Democracy and Distrust*, Harvard University Press, Cambridge, MA.

Employment Contracts Act 1991, New Zealand.

Employment Equality Act 1998, Ireland.

Employment Equity Act 1998, South Africa.

Employment Relations Act 2000, New Zealand.

Employment Rights Act 1996, UK.

Equal Opportunities Commission, *Code of Practice on Equal Pay*, UK.

Equal Pay Act 1963, United States.

Equal Pay Act 1970, UK.

Equal Status Act 2000, Ireland.

Equality Act 2006, UK.

Equality Act 2010, UK.

Eurobarometer 57, Discrimination in Europe, For Diversity Against Discrimination, 2003, Alan Marsh and Melahat Sahin-Dikmen, The European Opinion Research Group (EEIG) for the European Commission Directorate General Employment and Social Affairs.

European Convention for the Protection of Human Rights and Fundamental Freedoms, 1950.

European Convention for the Protection of Human Rights and Fundamental Freedoms as amended by Protocol No. 12, 2000.

European Social Charter, 1961.

European Social Charter (revised), 1996.

Fair Labor Standards Act 1938, United States.

Fair Work Act 2009, Australia.

Federal Task Force on Disability Issues, *Equal Citizenship for Canadians with Disabilities: The Will to Act*, 1996.

Federalist Papers, United States, 1787–88.

Folch v. *Canadian Airlines*, 1992 CHRT.

Fried, Morton (1967), *The Evolution of Political Society*, Random House, New York.

Fry, Earl (1987), 'Trends in Canada–U.S. Free Trade Discussions', in A.R. Riggs and Tom Velk, *Canadian–American Free Trade: Historical, Political and Economic Dimensions*, The Institute for Research in Public Policy, Montreal.

General Agreement on Tariffs and Trade, 1947.

Gillette v. *United States*, 401 U.S. 437 (1971).

Government of Canada, Minimum Age for Employment in Canada.

Government of Canada (1993), *The North American Free Trade Agreement at a Glance*, Ottawa.

Government of Canada (2002), *NAFTA at Eight*, Ottawa.

Government of South Africa, Code of Good Practice: Preparation, Implementation and Monitoring of Employment Equity Plans.

Griffin Cohen, Marjorie (1987), *Free Trade and the Future of Women's Work, Manufacturing and Service Industries*, Garamond Press, Toronto.

Griggs v. *Duke Power Co.*, 401 U.S. 424 (1971).

Grismer: Terry Grismer (Estate) v. *The British Columbia Superintendent of Motor Vehicles et al.*, [1999] 3 S.C.R. 868.

Habermas, Jurgen (1998), *Between Facts and Norms*, MIT Press, Cambridge, MA.

Hague Global Child Labour Conference 2010, Towards a World without Child Labour.

Hallman, K., and Grant, M. (2004) 'Poverty, Educational Attainment, and Livelihoods: How Well Do Young People Fare in KwaZulu Natal, South Africa?', Horizons Research Summary, Population Council, Washington DC.

Hamelin, Jean (1976), *Histoire du Québec*, Edisem, St Hyacinthe.

Harris, Diana K. (2005), 'Age Norms', in Erdman B. Palmore, Laurence Branch and Diana K. Harris (eds), *Encyclopedia of Ageism*, The Haworth Press, Inc., New York.

Harris, Richard (1988), 'Some Observations on the Canada–U.S. Free Trade Deal', in A.R. Riggs and Tom Velk (eds), *Canadian–American Free Trade (The Sequel): Historical, Political and Economic Dimensions*, The Institute for Research on Public Policy, Montreal.

Hatfield, Robert, 'Duty to Accommodate', *Just Labour*, vol. 5 (Winter 2005).

Hayes, Bernadette, 'Female Intergenerational Occupational Mobility Within Northern Ireland and the Republic of Ireland', *British Journal of Sociology*, vol. 38, May 1987, p. 66.

Health and Safety in Employment Act 1992, New Zealand.

Health and Safety in Employment Regulations 1995, New Zealand.

Helsinki Final Act, 1975.

Human Resources and Social Development Canada.

Human Rights Act 1993, New Zealand.

Human Rights Act 1998, UK.

Human Rights Act 2004, Australia.

Human Rights and Equal Opportunity Commission Act 1986, Australia.

Hurtig, Mel (1991), *The Betrayal of Canada*, Stoddart Publishing, Toronto.

Inter-American Democratic Charter, 2001.

Interim Constitution of South Africa, Schedule 4.

International Labour Office, Accelerating Action against Child Labour, Global Report under the follow-up to the ILO Declaration on Fundamental Principles and Rights at Work 2010.

International Labour Organization, Abolition of Forced Labour Convention (No. 105).

International Labour Organization, Forced Labour Convention (No. 29).

International Labour Organization, Laborsta, 2008.

International Labour Organization, Minimum Age Convention (No. 138).

International Labour Organization, Minimum Age (Industry) Convention (No. 5).

International Labour Organization, Night Work of Young Persons (Industry) Convention

(No. 6).

International Labour Organization, Worst Forms of Child Labour Convention (No. 182).

International Organisation of Employers, The Effective Abolition of Child Labour Report, 2011.

Internationale Handelsgesellschaft, [1970] ECR 1125, [1972] CMLR 255.

Kimel v. *Florida Board of Regents*, 528 U.S. 62 (2000).

King, Martin Luther, Jr. (1963), speech at March on Washington.

Labor Canada (1986), *Equal Pay for Work of Equal Value*, Ottawa.

Laun, Louis (1987), 'U.S.–Canada Free Trade Negotiations: Historical Opportunities', in A.R. Riggs and Tom Velk (eds), *Canadian–American Free Trade: Historical, Political and Economic Dimensions*, The Institute for Research in Public Policy, Montreal.

Layton, Robert (1987), 'Why Canada Needs Free Trade', in A.R. Riggs and Tom Velk (eds), *Canadian–American Free Trade: Historical, Political and Economic Dimensions*, The Institute for Research in Public Policy, Montreal.

Ley del Seguro Social, Mexico.

Ley Federal de Trabajo, Mexico.

Lipsey, Richard (1987), 'Canada's Trade Options', in A.R. Riggs and Tom Velk (eds), *Canadian–American Free Trade: Historical, Political and Economic Dimensions*, The Institute for Research in Public Policy, Montreal.

Maastricht Treaty, 1992.

Magna Carta, Great Britain, 1215.

Mandel, Michael (1989), *The Charter of Rights and the Legalization of Politics in Canada*, Wall & Thompson, Toronto.

Marbury v. *Madison*, 1 Cranch 137 (1803).

Marsh Alan, Sahin-Dikmen, Melahat (2002), *Discrimination in Europe*, Policy Studies Institute, London.

McCullough v. *Maryland*, 4 Wheaton 415 (1819).

McDonnell Douglas Corp. v. *Green*, 411 US 792 (1973).

McGowan v. *Maryland*, 366 U.S. 420 (1961).

McPhail, Brenda (1985), *NAFTA Now*, University Press of America, Lanham, MD.

Merrett, Christopher (1996), *Free Trade, Neither Free Nor About Trade*, Black Rose Books, New York.

Mexican Investment Board (1994), *Mexico, Your Partner for Growth, Regulatory Reform and Competition Policy, Setting the Incentives for an Efficient Economy*, Mexico.

Ministry in the Office of the President (1995), Reconstruction and Development Programme, Key Indicators of Poverty in South Africa.

Murphy v. *Miller Brewer Co.*, 307 F.Supp. 829 (1969).

Nader, Ralph (1993), *The Case Against Free Trade*, Earth Island Press, San Francisco.

Neufeld, E.P. (1987), 'Financial and Economic Dimensions of Free Trade', in A.R. Riggs and Tom Velk (eds), *Canadian–American Free Trade: Historical, Political and Economic Dimensions*, The Institute for Research on Public Policy, Montreal.

New Zealand Government, Speech on the Global Report, A Future without Child Labour, John Chetwin, Secretary of Labour, 2002.

Nicoll, William, and Salmon, Trevor (1994), *Understanding the New European Community*, Prentice Hall, Exeter.

North, Arthur (1964), *The Supreme Court, Judicial Process and Judicial Politics*, Appleton Century Crofts, New York.

North American Agreement on Labor Cooperation, 1993.

North American Free Trade Agreement, 1994.

Northern Ireland Act, 1998.

Ontario Human Rights Commission v. *Simpsons-Sears Ltd*, [1985] SCR 536.

Osborn, Alan (2008), 'Europe: Raising Education Standards', *University World News*, vol. 37.

OSCE Parliamentary Assembly Declaration 1995.

Parkinson, Patrick (2001), 'The Child Labour Problem in Australia', *Australian Children's Rights News*, No. 30.

Pope John XXIII (1963), *Pacem in Terris*, Rome.

Pope John Paul II (1981), *Laborem Exercens*, Rome.

President John F. Kennedy, address before the Canadian Parliament, Ottawa, May 17, 1961.

Promotion of Equality and Prevention of Unfair Discrimination Act 2000, South Africa.

Protection of Young Persons (Employment) Act 1996, Ireland.

Protocol on the Rights of Women in Africa, 2003.

Protocol to the African Charter on Human and Peoples' Rights on the Establishment of an African Court on Human and Peoples' Rights, 2003.

Quebec Charter of Rights and Freedoms.

Race Relations Act 1971, New Zealand.

Race Relations Act 1976, UK.

Race Relations Act (Amendment) Regulations 2006, UK.

Race Relations Act (Statutory Duties) Order 2001, 2003, 2004, UK.

Racial Discrimination Act 1975, Australia.

Racial Hatred Act 1995, Australia.

Raynauld, Andre (1987), 'Looking Outward Again', in A.R. Riggs and Tom Velk (eds), *Canadian–American Free Trade: Historical, Political and Economic Dimensions*, The Institute for Research on Public Policy, Montreal.

Regina v. *Oakes*, [1986] 1 S.C.R. 103.

Rosenfeld, Rachel (1978), 'Women's Intergenerational Occupational Mobility', in *American Sociological Review*, vol. 43, No. 1, pp. 36–46.

Sex Discrimination Act 1984, Australia.

Sex Discrimination Act 1975, UK.

Shakes v. *Rex Pak Ltd*, (1982) 3 CHRR D/1001.

Soldatos, P. (1988), 'Canada's Foreign Policy in Search of a Fourth Option: Continuity and Change in Orientation Towards the U.S.', in A.R. Riggs and Tom Velk (eds), *Canadian–American Free Trade (The Sequel): Historical, Political and Economic Dimensions*, The Institute for Research on Public Policy, Montreal.

Spaulding v. *University of Washington*, 740 F.2d. 686 (1984).

Special Eurobarometer 263, Discrimination in the European Union, 2007.

Statistics Canada, Tradingeconomics.com, (5/11/2012).

Statute of the Inter-American Court on Human Rights, 1980.

Stone, Frank (1987), 'Removing Barriers to Canada', in A.R. Riggs and Tom Velk (eds), *Canadian–American Free Trade: Historical, Political and Economic Dimensions*, The Institute for Research on Public Policy, Montreal.

Teuling v. *Bredrijfsvereniging*, [1987] ECR 2497.

Tinker v. *Des Moines Independent School District*, 393 U.S. 503 (1969).

Treaty establishing a Constitution for Europe, 2004.

Treaty of Amsterdam, 1997.

Treaty of Lisbon, 2007.

Treaty of Paris, 1951.

Treaty of Rome, 1957.

Treaty of Waitangi, New Zealand, 1840.

United Nations (1945), Charter of the United Nations.

United Nations (1945), Statute of the International Court of Justice.

United Nations (1948), Universal Declaration of Human Rights.

United Nations (1951), Equal Remuneration Convention (ILO No. 100).

United Nations (1958), Discrimination (Employment and Occupation) Convention (ILO No. 111).

United Nations (1960), Convention against Discrimination in Education.

United Nations (1964), Employment Policy Convention (ILO No. 122).

United Nations (1965), International Convention on the Elimination of All Forms of Racial Discrimination.

United Nations (1966), International Covenant on Civil and Political Rights.

United Nations (1966), International Covenant on Economic, Social and Cultural Rights.

United Nations (1966), Optional Protocol to the International Covenant on Civil and Political Rights.

United Nations (1979), Convention on the Elimination of all Forms of Discrimination against Women.

United Nations (1989), Convention on the Rights of the Child.

United Nations(1995), Beijing Declaration and Platform for Action.

United Nations (1999), Optional Protocol to the Convention on the Elimination of All Forms of Discrimination against Women.

United Nations (2002), Optional Protocol to the Convention on the Rights of the Child on the involvement of children in armed conflict.

United Nations (2002), Optional Protocol to the Convention on the Rights of the Child on the sale of children, child prostitution and child pornography.

United Nations (2003), Protocol to prevent, suppress and punish trafficking in persons, especially women and children, supplementing the United Nations Convention against Transnational Organized Crime.

United Nations Development Programme (1994), *Human Development Report*, Oxford University Press, Oxford.

United States Constitution, United States, 1776.

US Department of Labor, Bureau of International Labor Affairs (2004), *Laws Governing Exploitative Child Labor Report: Australia*.

Velk, Tom and Riggs, A.R. (1987), 'The Ongoing Debate Over Free Trade', in A.R. Riggs and Tom Velk (eds), *Canadian–American Free Trade: Historical, Political and Economic Dimensions*, The Institute for Research on Public Policy, Montreal.

Watkins, Mel (1989), 'The Political Economy of Growth', in Wallace Clement and Glen Williams (eds), *The New Canadian Political Economy*, McGill-Queen's University Press, Kingston.

Wigle, Randall (1987), 'The Received Wisdom of the Canada–U.S. Free Trade Qualifications', in A.R. Riggs and Tom Velk (eds), *Canadian–American Free Trade: Historical, Political and Economic Dimensions*, The Institute for Research in Public Policy, Montreal.

Wirth, L. (1945), 'The Problem of Minority Groups', in R. Linton (ed.), *The Science of Man in the World Crisis*, Columbia University Press, New York, pp. 347–72.

Workplace Relations Act 1996, Australia.

World Declaration on Education for All: Meeting Basic Learning Needs, The Framework for Action to Meet Basic Learning Needs, 1990.

World Summit for Social Development, 1995.

Index